Global Entrepreneurship

MARICOPA COUNTY COMMUNITY COLLEGES
SOUTH MOUNTAIN COMMUNITY LIBRARY
SOUTH MOUNTAIN COMMUNITY COLLEGE
7050 SOUTH 24TH STREET
PHOENIX, AZ 85042

Nir Kshetri's *Global Entrepreneurship: Environment and Strategy* provides a window into the economic, political, cultural, geographical, and technological environments that affect entrepreneurs as they exploit opportunities and create value in economies across the world. The book begins with a discussion of the theories, concepts, indicators, and measurements that impact entrepreneurship differently in different regions; from there, it offers helpful insights into global variations in entrepreneurial ecosystems and finance. Kshetri methodically examines entrepreneurship patterns in diverse economies through the lenses of economic system, political system, culture and religion, and geography (both by country and continent). Offering case studies at the end of each chapter illustrating concepts learned, as well as three detailed cases in an appendix for broader reflection, the book also includes online data resources, and international business planning support, making it a valuable resource for students in entrepreneurship, and international business classes.

Nir Kshetri is a professor at the University of North Carolina-Greensboro, USA, and a research fellow at Kobe University, Japan. He has authored four books and about seventy journal articles. Nir participated as lead discussant at the peer review meeting of the United Nations' *Information Economy Report 2013*. He has given lectures or presented research papers in more than forty countries.

Global Entrepreneurship

Environment and Strategy

Nir Kshetri, PhD

NEW YORK AND LONDON

First published 2014
by Routledge
711 Third Avenue, New York, NY 10017

and by Routledge
2 Park Square, Milton Park, Abingdon, Oxon OX14 4RN

Routledge is an imprint of the Taylor & Francis Group, an informa business

© 2014 Taylor & Francis

The right of Nir Kshetri to be identified as author of this work has been
asserted by him in accordance with sections 77 and 78 of the Copyright,
Designs and Patents Act 1988.

All rights reserved. No part of this book may be reprinted or reproduced or
utilized in any form or by any electronic, mechanical, or other means, now
known or hereafter invented, including photocopying and recording, or in
any information storage or retrieval system, without permission in writing
from the publishers.

Trademark notice: Product or corporate names may be trademarks or
registered trademarks, and are used only for identification and explanation
without intent to infringe.

Library of Congress Cataloging-in-Publication Data

Kshetri, Nir.
  Global entrepreneurship : environment and strategy / Nir Kshetri, Ph.D.
    pages cm
  Includes bibliographical references and index.
  1. Entrepreneurship. 2. Entrepreneurship—Developing
countries. I. Title.
  HB615.K76 2013
  658.4'21—dc23
  2013039461

ISBN: 978-0-415-88799-1 (hbk)
ISBN: 978-0-415-88800-4 (pbk)
ISBN: 978-1-315-79560-7 (ebk)

Typeset in Adobe Caslon Pro
by Apex CoVantage, LLC

Printed and bound in the United States of America
by Edwards Brothers Malloy

Brief Contents

Contents

Illustrations

Figures

Tables

Preface and Acknowledgements

The appetite for entrepreneurial ventures has increased significantly worldwide. While the global financial crisis has disrupted key ingredients of the entrepreneurial ecosystem and led to a decline in entrepreneurial activities in major industrialized economies, there are reasons to believe that this may represent the downslope of a cycle rather than a long-term trend. In general, the global entrepreneurial trend has been powerfully upward, which is apparent in the rise of the entrepreneurial spirit across the world and the increased overall trends of various forms of entrepreneurial financing.

Global entrepreneurship is a comparatively young area of inquiry. A close observation of entrepreneurship patterns across the world raises many interesting questions such as: How are entrepreneurs regarded in various societies across the world? How is the societal orientation of entrepreneurship changing? What are the real and perceived barriers in pursuing an entrepreneurial career in various societies? What are the major catalysts in breaking these barriers? What factors breed entrepreneurial success? How do societies differ in terms of the set of entrepreneurial challenges they face? How do societies differ in the degree to which they are willing to take risks? How is entrepreneurial success measured? How do other key elements of the entrepreneurial ecosystem interact with, interpret, evaluate and respond to various actions of an entrepreneur? How are entrepreneurial success and failure viewed by the entrepreneurs and society? What factors determine the profiles of entrepreneurs that are favored by a society's entrepreneurial ecosystem? Does the degree of favor vary across the lifecycle of a firm? How is the structure of an entrepreneurial ecosystem associated with its performance in attracting potential entrepreneurs? Once they are attracted, would it provide opportunity to grow?

By exploring the above questions and examining key ingredients of the entrepreneurial ecosystem, this book attempts to accomplish many goals. From an academic perspective, this book would provide researchers with a clearer understanding of key elements of entrepreneurial ecosystems, interrelationships among them and their variation across the world. By doing so, I hope to foster more interest in the study of global entrepreneurship itself and of entrepreneurs and entrepreneurial firms worldwide more generally. From a managerial perspective, a clearer understanding of entrepreneurship patterns and potential in economies across the world would help practitioners and professionals make better decisions related to starting, joining, or holding stakes in ventures in economies across the world. Finally, from a public policy perspective, a deeper understanding of factors that facilitate or hinder entrepreneurship would help take measures that can stimulate entrepreneurship, economic growth and job creation and reduce poverty.

This book is inter-disciplinary in focus, orientation and scope. It crosses disciplines such as development economics, law, business and management, international affairs, sociology, anthropology, cultural studies and criminology to develop theory and provide information that could move theory and practice forward in the study of global entrepreneurship. This book is also theory-based but practical and accessible to the wider audience.

This book is primarily targeted at upper-level undergraduate and graduate students. The book will also be of interest to academic specialists and policy makers. In addition, practitioners and professionals interested in starting, joining or holding stakes in international ventures are also the target audience. I have attempted to write the book in an easy-to-understand format so that anyone with a basic knowledge of business and economic concepts should be able to read it.

I acknowledge course development grants for international entrepreneurship from Building Entrepreneurial Learning for Life (BELL) and Bryan School of Business and Economics at the University of North Carolina at Greensboro which greatly facilitated the research and writing of this book. I am also very grateful to Kauffman Foundation for its generous research grant to study entrepreneurial firms in OECD economies.

A book project involves many people. First, I am grateful to John Szilagyi, and Sharon Golan at Routledge, who enthusiastically supported the idea of this book and carefully shepherded its progress from proposal submission to publication. Also, Manjula Raman and Sara Werden have been very supportive, helpful, and encouraging in guiding and managing this project. I received invaluable help and support from my very talented graduate assistants Aroop Menon and Jun (Johnny) Situ at UNCG.

As for the ideas, concepts, content and theories presented in this book, I am indebted and grateful to several people for comments, suggestions, support, encouragement and feedback. Papers related to this book were presented at scholarly meetings such as the Cornell-McGill Conference on Institutions & Entrepreneurship, Cornell University, 2007; the fifth annual AIB/JIBS frontiers conference, Miami, 2007; the Annual International Business Research Forum, Philadelphia, 2008, 2009 and 2011; the Conference on Offshoring and Outsourcing, Mila, Italy, 2008; the twelfth Annual Conference of the International Society for New Institutional Economics (ISNIE), Toronto, 2008; the fifth Annual Mason Entrepreneurship Research Conference, Fairfax, VA, 2009; the Southern Management Association (SMA) Conference, 2009; the Base of the Pyramid (BOP) Conference, Johannesburg, 2009; the AIB-India Conference, International Conference on Global Economic Crisis, Delhi, 2009; the Pacific Telecommunications Council Annual Conference, Hawaii, 2010 and 2012; the sixth Annual Mason Entrepreneurship Research Conference 2010; the "Entrepreneurship in Africa" Conference, Syracuse University, 2010; the eleventh Annual International Business Research Forum, Philadelphia, 2010; the ninth International Business Week Congress, University of Minho, Portugal, 2010; Congreso Internacional Integración Regional,

Quito, Ecuador, 2011; the Conference on Small and Medium Sized Enterprises, Cluj, Napoca, Romania, 2011 and 2013; and the fifth Dialogue on Social Market Economy, Tartu, Estonia, 2013. I thank the many professionals involved in these meetings, who provided comments and suggestions and helped me refine my thinking. Thanks go as well to anonymous Routledge peer reviewers who had helpful and encouraging comments on my book proposal and draft chapters. In addition, feedbacks and suggestions from the students in my International Entrepreneurship classes at UNCG greatly helped to refine, simplify and improve the ideas and concepts presented in the book.

Finally, a supportive family is what keeps one motivated to create the foundation for a demanding project such as this book. My mother, to whom this book is dedicated, and my wife Maya were constant sources of inspiration and motivation. I express my love and sincere gratitude to them. Without their patience, support and encouragement this book would not have existed at all.

Abbreviations

ADB	Asia Development Bank
ADM	African Diaspora Marketplace
ALR	annual lending rate
AP	Andhra Pradesh
APIIDC	AP Industrial Infrastructure Development Corporation
BIAC	Business and Industry Advisory Committee
BP	business process
BPO	business process outsourcing
BRIC	Brazil, Russia, India, China
BRVM	Bourse Régionale des Valeurs Mobilières
BSE	Bombay Stock Exchange
BWA	Business Women Association
CBN	Central Bank of Nigeria
CCP	Chinese Communist Party
CFP	crowdfunding platform
CGAP	Consultative Group to Assist the Poor
COO	country of origin
CT	clean technology
CVCRI	China Venture Capital Research Institute
EBAN	European Business Angels Network
EC	European Commission

EU	European Union
FDI	foreign direct investment
FSU&CEE	Former Soviet Union and Central and Eastern Europe
GB	Grameen Bank
GCC	Gulf Cooperation Council
GEM	Global Entrepreneurship Monitor
GFC	global financial crisis
GP	GrameenPhone
GVCA	Gulf Venture Capital Association
HDI	human development index
HDR	Human Development Report
HR	human resources
IBP	international business plan
ICRG	International Country Risk Guide
ICT	information and communication technology
IDC	Indian Development Center
IFAD	International Fund for Agricultural Development
IFC	International Finance Corporation
IIIT	Indian Institute of Information Technology
IMF	International Monetary Fund
IOM	International Organization for Migration
IP	intellectual property
IPO	initial public offering
IPR	intellectual property right
ISP	Internet service provider
ITO	information technology outsourcing
ITU	International Telcommunications Union
JFTC	Japan Fair Trade Commission
JOBS	Jumpstart Our Business Startups
JPO	Japan Patent Office
M&A	mergers and acquisitions
MABS	Microenterprise Access to Banking Services
MFI	microfinance institution
MOJ	Ministry of Justice
MOP	Ministry of Public Works
MoU	memorandum of understanding

MSST	Microsoft School for Software Technology
NATO	North Atlantic Treaty Organization
NGO	non-governmental organization
OCS	Office of the Chief Scientist
ODA	official development assistance
ODCA	Open Data Center Alliance
OECD	Organization for Economic Co-operation and Development
OEM	original equipment manufacturer
P2PT	person-to-person transfer
PCT	Patent Cooperation Treaty
PDA	personal digital assistant
PDP	Productive Development Policy
PRS	Political Risk Services
PS	post-socialist
REE	rare earth element
RGDN	Rwanda Global Diaspora Network
SAB	South African Breweries
SBI	State Bank of India
SOE	state-owned enterprise
SSA	Sub-Saharan Africa
STP	software technology park
SWOT	strengths, weaknesses, opportunities and threats
TI	Transparency International
UAE	United Arab Emirates
UNDP	United Nations Development Program
USPTO	US Patent and Trademark Office
USTR	US Trade Representative
VC	venture capital
VSO	Voluntary Service Overseas
WDI	World Development Indicators
WHI	WaterHealth International
WIPO	World Intellectual Property Organization
WTO	World Trade Organization

1

GLOBAL ENTREPRENEURSHIP

The Current Status, Definitions, Types and Measures

Abstract

Entrepreneurship has become a truly global phenomenon as indicated by an increased appetite for entrepreneurial ventures worldwide. Economies across the world, however, differ in terms of the natures of entrepreneurial activities, environments to support these activities and other key ingredients of entrepreneurship such as regulations, policy, culture, access to market, and availability and types of finances and technology. This chapter provides an overview of the context, mechanisms and processes associated with the current Global Entrepreneurial Revolution. We introduce and define a number of key concepts related to global entrepreneurship. Also discussed are key indicators related to determinants, performance and impacts of entrepreneurship.

This chapter's objectives include:

1. To demonstrate an understanding of the current Global Entrepreneurial Revolution.
2. To identify the major trends and forces shaping the Global Entrepreneurial Revolution.
3. To analyze various metrics in order to measure the determinants, performance and impacts of entrepreneurship in an economy.
4. To apply the tools and concepts learnt in the chapter to assess an economy's entrepreneurial performance and success.
5. To demonstrate an understanding of the international heterogeneity in the development of entrepreneurship and entrepreneurial capability.

1.1. A Global Entrepreneurial Revolution

A number of trends and indicators point towards the fact that entrepreneurship has become a truly global phenomenon. One such indicator concerns the appetite for entrepreneurial ventures. Highly successful entrepreneurial firms are found across the world. In the 2013 Forbes' global list of the 2000 biggest public companies, 63 countries were represented.[1] Moreover, companies from emerging markets such as Brazil, Chile, China, Mexico and India were represented in the 130 Global High Performers in the Forbes' global list, which were described as "fast growing, nimble and well-managed companies" and grew 28 percent annually in the average. Various forces and events have shaped this global entrepreneurial revolution.

1.1.1. Favorable Attitudes Toward Capitalism and Social Acceptance of Entrepreneurship

One important trend facilitating a global entrepreneurial revolution and growing entrepreneurial spirit concerns a favorable attitude toward free-market capitalism. Note that capitalism is the foundation of entrepreneurship. Among the most encouraging developments in the global entrepreneurial arena has been the acceptance of the ideas of free-market capitalism in countries with a history of socialism. For instance, in a 2009 Global Attitudes Survey conducted by the Pew Research Center, the proportions of respondents agreeing to the question: "Most people are better off in a free-market economy, even though some people are rich and some are poor", were: 79 percent in China, 65 percent in Poland and 51 percent in Russia. As a point of comparison, the corresponding proportion was 41 percent for Japan, which is historically a capitalist country. Likewise, according to a survey conducted by the Yury Levada Analytical Center, about 80 percent of young Russians said that they had successfully adapted to capitalism.[2] This does not mean that these young Russians have a favorable attitude toward the country's wealthy business tycoons, also known as the "oligarchs". Nonetheless, they have readily and enthusiastically accepted the idea that free-market economy is good for society.

The development of a successful entrepreneurial society rests upon social acceptance of entrepreneurship and entrepreneurial activities.

Positive developments on this front are worth noting in emerging economies. For instance, a survey conducted by YouGov, which was released in August 2010, found that about 50 percent of respondents in China and India believed that their societies were more welcoming of entrepreneurial activities compared to a decade ago.[3]

1.1.2. Responses of Policy Makers and Non-governmental Organizations

In response to the demands of various forces and as their own priority, policy makers in most countries are directing efforts to encourage entrepreneurship among local communities and promoting the creation of entrepreneurial societies. They have realized the potential contributions of entrepreneurship to economic growth and development. According to the World Bank's Doing Business 2011 report (www. doingbusiness.org/reports/global-reports/doingbusiness-2011/), during 2006–2010, about 85 percent of the world's economies made over 1,500 improvements in business regulations, which made it easier for entrepreneurs to start and operate businesses. Likewise, in 2011/2012, 108 economies had implemented 201 regulatory reforms. Governments in many countries have made entrepreneurship an explicit policy priority.

There are also a number of international initiatives at the non-governmental levels for inspiring, motivating and mentoring young people to create innovative businesses. In this regard, Global Entrepreneurship Week (GEW), which was started in 2008, deserves mention. In the inaugural year (November 17–23, 2008), three million people from 77 countries participated in more than 25,000 events and activities.[4] As of 2012, GEW expanded to 130 countries, in which twenty million people participated in 125,000 activities, which were supported by a network of 24,000 organizations.[5]

1.1.3. Young People's Engagement in Entrepreneurial Activities

One of the most encouraging trends in global entrepreneurship in recent years has been young people's engagement in high-impact entrepreneurial activities in emerging economies. For instance, while only 1.6 percent of Chinese college graduates started businesses in

2011, some young entrepreneurs have been highly successful. They have started many successful entrepreneurial ventures including the introduction of Disney movies to the country, efficient health care delivery, cutting-edge online games and web applications.[6] Likewise, at the time of starting their companies, the average ages of founders in Saudi Arabia's fastest growing one hundred companies were aged 30–33 years in 2009 and 2010.[7] In other Arab countries, young people have demonstrated high levels of entrepreneurial inclination. For instance, according to a 2009 Gallup poll conducted among Arab youth who did not own businesses, the proportion that were planning to start their own businesses "in the next 12 months" were 38 percent in Tunisia, Comoros and Iraq, 39 percent in Djibouti, and 46 percent in Sudan.[8] These are big achievements for these countries, where entrepreneurship is a relatively new phenomenon.

1.1.4. The Global Financial Crisis and Entrepreneurship

Despite the above evidence regarding the surge of entrepreneurship, a global financial crisis (GFC) led decline in entrepreneurial activities is reported in major industrialized economies. A report of the Global Entrepreneurship Monitor (GEM) found that overall entrepreneurial activity has decreased in industrialized nations in recent years. In 2009, there were 10 percent fewer entrepreneurs in innovation-driven economies such as Belgium, Japan and Israel and a 24 percent drop in the US. Likewise, the GFC led to a reduction in the resources devoted to R&D and innovation. For instance, international patent filings under the World Intellectual Property Organization's (WIPO) Patent Cooperation Treaty (PCT) fell by 4.5 percent in 2009.[9]

On the plus side, despite the GFC, there is a robust and persistent preference for free market and capitalism. For instance, most people in the US prefer capitalism and the free enterprise system over socialism. According to a Gallup poll conducted in January 2010, 61 percent of Americans had a positive view of capitalism and about the same proportion had a negative view of socialism. Another survey conducted in March 2009 by the Pew Research Centre found that 70 percent of Americans thought they would be better off in a free-market economy.[10] Thus, overall, there are reasons to believe that the decreasing entrepreneurial activities observed in the GFC represent the downslope of a cycle rather than a long-term trend.

1.2. Various Types of Capitalism and their Influences on Entrepreneurial Activities

Capitalism is the foundation of entrepreneurial opportunities. In capitalistic economies, the means of production are mostly privately owned, and a market economy operates. That is, economic decisions are influenced by competition, supply and demand. However, it would be erroneous to conclude that only one form of capitalism exists. There are a number of variations in the way capitalism functions across the world.

At least four prevalent forms of capitalism have been identified: (1) entrepreneurial, (2) big firm, (3) state directed, and (4) oligarchic.[11] Entrepreneurial capitalism is characterized by the presence of high-impact entrepreneurs with radical ideas in which small, innovative firms play a major role. Note that high-impact entrepreneurs are people involved in the launching and growing of companies with an above average impact on the creation of jobs and wealth.[12] Some examples include the founders of companies such as Twitter, Apple, Facebook, Yahoo, Microsoft and Google. These entrepreneurs have the capability to introduce innovative products, services and business models that meet marketplace needs. The US is viewed as a fertile place for high-impact entrepreneurs due to its pro-private-sector culture and a smaller state sector compared to Western European countries.

In big firm capitalism, radical entrepreneurship tends to be absent and the economic growth is mainly driven by the government through collaboration with big businesses. This form of capitalism is prevalent in Japan and some European countries. Japan has many innovative large firms but the country has among the lowest per capita rate of entrepreneurial activities.

Some developing countries such as China have found state-guided capitalism to be a way to achieve economic growth (Chapter 8). In this model, the government tends to guide the market, typically by supporting few industries that are expected to perform well. For one thing, its deep entrenchment in the economy allows the Chinese government to intervene quickly and to produce desired outputs. The cash-rich Chinese government has also been pressuring as well as providing a wide range of incentives for its firms to expand overseas.

In oligarchic capitalism, small groups of individuals and families control the majority of national wealth and power, in some cases with the support of corrupt politicians. This form of capitalism is thus associated with and facilitated by "politically-embedded cronyism".[13] In this form of capitalism, entrepreneurs use political power, capital and social networks to maximize economic rewards. That is, a small group of wealthy people tend to maintain a grip over the country's economy, polity, and society.[14] In some cases, oligarchic capitalism is characterized by a symbiosis of political and economic elites. That is, political elites such as rulers, elected officials, party leaders and bureaucrats are also economic elites or successful entrepreneurs. In such a system, state incumbents may generate and maintain the uneven distribution of property rights, which favor a few private actors. The role of societal groups tends to be limited.

This system may serve as a tactic of survival for a ruling regime. In some economies, such as the Ukraine, powerful oligarchs tend to provide financial resources to the ruling elites and, in return, they exert a strong influence on government policies. For instance, three top oligarchs[15] in the Ukraine reportedly played key roles in supporting the former President Kuchma's regime. Some developing economies in Asia (e.g., India), Africa, Latin America (e.g., Colombia) and the Middle East have also exhibited characteristics of this form of capitalism. Despite the existence of certain elements of a market economy and political democracy, this form of capitalism lacks a true market system.

1.3. Variation in Entrepreneurial Activities across the World

While the general trend discussed above suggests a growth in entrepreneurial ventures worldwide, significant cross-country variation exists in entrepreneurial success and a number of features of entrepreneurship. This section sheds light on some of the important international differences in various aspects of entrepreneurial opportunities, behaviors and performance.

First, economies worldwide differ drastically in terms of their populations' willingness to engage, and actual engagement in entrepreneurial ventures as well as the nature of entrepreneurial activities pursued. For instance, only 0.18 percent of the population in Indonesia is engaged in entrepreneurial activities[16] compared to about 7.5 percent in the US.[17] According to a Global Entrepreneurship Monitor study, less than 1 percent of Indonesians wanted to start a business compared to 14.5 percent in the US. Dominance of the economy by natural resource-based industries such as mining and agriculture, lack of access to capital for small businesses, and poor education for would-be entrepreneurs appear to be important factors contributing to Indonesia's weak entrepreneurial performance.[18]

1.3.1. Qualitative Differences

In addition to the quantitative variations, qualitative differences also exist in entrepreneurial activities worldwide. While an increasing number of people in developing countries have started businesses, high-impact entrepreneurship is severely lacking. Many developing countries do not provide the environment to produce highly successful entrepreneurs such as Microsoft founder Bill Gates and Wal-Mart founder Sam Walton. These countries' entrepreneurship landscapes mainly consist of small-scale entrepreneurs such as peasant farmers, street hawkers, market vendors, owners of small restaurants and florists. For instance, while India has some high performing global firms such as Wipro, TCS and Infosys, the country lags behind developed and some developing countries in terms of high-expectation business launchers per capita.

1.3.2. Motivation and Intended Goals of Entrepreneurial Activities

People across the world also differ in terms of motivation and intended goals of entrepreneurial activities. While most people in industrialized countries engage in entrepreneurial activity to take advantage of business opportunities, necessity or the lack of other opportunities is an important driver in most developing economies. Moreover, entrepreneurial success may mean different things to entrepreneurs from different political, social and cultural environments. For instance, according to the 2009 GEM report, proportionately more entrepreneurs in China than in the US are motivated by the desire to make money. The GEM study found that fewer than 40 percent of Chinese entrepreneurs started businesses to have more independence, and more than 60 percent of them did so to increase their income. On the contrary, in the US, only about 40 percent of entrepreneurs start businesses to increase income, while almost 60 percent do so to gain more independence.[19] This means that compared to US entrepreneurs, Chinese entrepreneurs are more likely to measure their "success" in terms of the wealth they generate than in terms of personal autonomy.

1.3.3. Gender Bias and Other Types of Disparity in Entrepreneurship

A large gender bias in access to resources and the participation rate of entrepreneurial activities is probably the most serious concern. Studies have found that women's low rate of participation in entrepreneurship is due to the lack of support such as access to advice, money, and training rather than the lack of basic traits. For instance, an analysis of data from cross-country Business Environment and Enterprise Performance Survey (BEEPS) suggested that female-managed firms were less likely to obtain a bank loan than male-managed ones. Moreover, for the approved loan applications, female entrepreneurs were charged higher interest rates than their male counterparts.[20] A study of the UAE's Dubai School of Governance showed that many aspiring female entrepreneurs in the Gulf Cooperation Council (GCC) region lack confidence in business skills, which discourages them from seeking access to money. Moreover, lenders' low confidence in women's business skills leads to women's inadequate access to money in GCC countries. Likewise, according to a Gallup poll conducted in GCC countries, women in these countries are less likely than men to have access to a mentor who can give them advice on managing a business.[21]

Other types of disparities—affecting people disadvantaged because of their social and economic backgrounds—are important too. Institutions in some economies have built-in biases that systematically favor the participation of certain segments of the population in entrepreneurial activities. For instance, in Indonesia, only influential people are often granted a business license in the country's lucrative business sectors such as mines, palm oil plantations and oilfields.[22] Likewise, observers have noted that potential entrepreneurs in India who have graduated from a less well-known university or those who belong to a poor family face difficulties in getting funding.[23]

1.3.4. Effects of Political, Cultural and Other Broad Environmental Factors

In order to understand the sources of the above-mentioned international heterogeneity in entrepreneurial outcomes, we first provide a brief review of political, cultural and other broad environmental factors. The Centre for Global Competitiveness and Performance of the Geneva-based World Economic Forum publishes the Global Competitiveness Report (GCR) and other reports which examine the business competitiveness of over 130 economies. The GCR ranks world economies in terms of twelve indicators: institutions, infrastructure, macroeconomic environment, health and primary education, higher education and training, goods market efficiency, labor market efficiency, financial market development, technological readiness, market size, business sophistication, and innovation.[24] According to the Global Competitiveness Report 2011–2012 (www3.weforum.org/docs/WEF_GCR_Report_2011–12.pdf), Switzerland had the world's best political and economic foundations for long-term growth among the 139 economies considered. Singapore, Sweden, and Finland ranked second, third and fourth respectively. The three least competitive economies were Chad (No. 139), Haiti (No. 138) and Burundi (No. 137). The World Economic Forum introduced the competitiveness index in 2004.

The World Bank's annual "Doing Business" report is probably the most well-known and most frequently referenced source in a comparison of the entrepreneurial climate in economies worldwide. As indicated in Fig. 1.1, various geographical regions, and economic groups differ widely in the number of procedures, time and cost required to start a business. OECD economies are among the best performers. For instance, according to the World Bank's "Doing Business 2013" report, out of 185 economies, New Zealand's overall rank was third, the highest ranked OECD country. In New Zealand, starting a new business requires only one procedure, which can be completed in one day and costs only 0.4 percent of the country's per capita GDP.

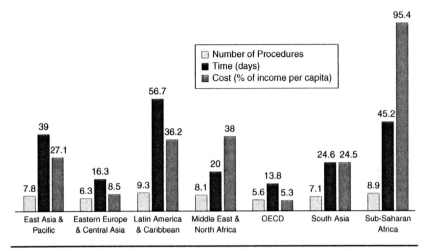

Figure 1.1 A comparison of the number of procedures, time and cost required in starting a business
Source: The World Bank's Doing Business 2011 report, www.doingbusiness.org/reports/global-reports/doing-business-2011/

The top two economies in 2012 were Singapore and Hong Kong, which have driven the overall performance of East Asia and Pacific. Singapore has topped the global ranking on the ease of doing business for seven consecutive years. In Singapore, starting a new business requires three procedures, which can be completed in three days and cost 0.6 percent of the country's per capita GDP.

The worst performers, especially in terms of the cost required to start a business are Sub-Saharan African economies. In Central African Republic, which ranked 185, a potential entrepreneur needs to complete eight procedures to start a business which takes an average of twenty-two days and costs 173 percent of the country's per capita GDP. Likewise, enforcing a contract in the country requires completing forty-three procedures, which take an average of 660 days.

Since small to medium enterprises (SMEs) play a significant role in job creation, the exports and economic growth of most economies, SME-friendly regulations need attention. In 2007, *Fortune Small Business* magazine ranked the world's fifty-three countries' friendliness to small businesses. The list was based on data from the World Bank Doing Business survey and the GEM ratings of high-expectation entrepreneurial firms. The ranking considered factors such as number of steps required to start a new business, marginal tax rates, and legal systems to protect intellectual property, enforce contracts and adjudicate disputes. The friendliest countries were New Zealand, the US, Canada, and Australia. The least friendly countries to small businesses were Brazil, the Philippines, Greece and Indonesia.[25]

As to the cultural context, desire for business ownership varies across countries. According to the 1997/1998 ISSP Module on Work Orientations/General Social Survey, the proportion of people who say they would prefer to be self-employed varied from 26.9 percent in Norway to 79.9 percent in Poland.[26] The same survey found that the proportion of self-employment varied from 6.1 percent in the then East Germany to 30.2 percent in Poland. According to the 2009 Eurobarometer Survey on Entrepreneurship, among the surveyed countries, the strongest preference for self-employment was in China and the weakest was in Japan: 71 percent of Chinese and 39 percent of Japanese preferred to be self-employed.[27]

People across the world also differ in the way they view entrepreneurs and entrepreneurship. In some societies, a negative societal perception of entrepreneurs leads to a lower propensity to engage in entrepreneurial activities. According to the 2009 Eurobarometer Survey, 49 percent of Europeans had a good opinion about entrepreneurs (Fig. 1.2). The

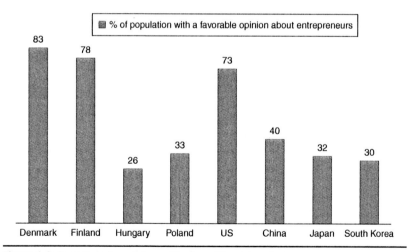

Figure 1.2 Proportion of populations with a favorable opinion of entrepreneurs

Source: 2009 Eurobarometer Survey, http://ec.europa.eu/enterprise/policies/sme/facts-figures-analysis/euro-barometer/ese_2009_en.htm

corresponding proportions for other professions were: liberal professions (lawyers, doctors, architects etc.), 58 percent; civil servants,
35 percent; top-managers, 28 percent; bankers, 25 percent; politicians,
12 percent. As shown in Fig. 1.2, while Western capitalist societies
have a good opinion of entrepreneurs, some collectivist and post-
socialist societies express a less favorable one.

1.4. Definitions and Types of Entrepreneurial Activity and their Variations Worldwide

We follow the OECD's definition of entrepreneurship, entrepreneurial
activity and entrepreneurs. Entrepreneurship is defined as—the phenomenon associated with entrepreneurial activity.[28] Entrepreneurial
activity is the enterprising human action in pursuit of the generation of
value, through the creation or expansion of economic activity, by identifying and exploiting new products, processes or markets. Entrepreneurs are those persons (business owners) who seek to generate value,
through the creation or expansion of economic activity, by identifying
and exploiting new products, processes or markets. Global entrepreneurship, on the other hand, can be defined as a discipline of study and
practice focused on comparative analysis of entrepreneurship across
economies with diverse environmental settings.

1.4.1. Productive, Unproductive and Destructive Entrepreneurship

Entrepreneurs tend to maximize their own wealth, power and prestige
by means of entrepreneurial activities, which can have positive as well
as negative effects on society.

To consider the societal effects of entrepreneurial ventures, the
concepts of productive, unproductive and destructive entrepreneurship are employed.[29] Pivotal to this view is the idea that a society's
rules of the game determine the distribution of these various forms of
entrepreneurship.

Free-market entrepreneurs rely on competition, supply and demand,
and engage in socially and economically useful activities that help generate jobs and wealth and hence are productive. The most obvious

examples are entrepreneurial activities that take place in high-growth industries, which create jobs and lead to technological innovations.

Unproductive entrepreneurial activities are those that contribute little or nothing to economic growth. Activities involving wealth distribution through political and legal channels such as lobbying are considered to be unproductive entrepreneurial activities.[30] Some analysts consider entrepreneurial activities related to activities such as trades on crude oil as unproductive. One estimate suggested that the world's daily crude oil consumption amounted to eighty-five million barrels in mid-2010. However, 1.1 billion barrels of crude oil is traded daily.[31] Some observe that the entrepreneurial activities of a large proportion of the world's billionaires are unproductive. A *Canberra Times* article commenting on the Forbes' list of 1,011 billionaires published in March 2010 put it best:

> Too few of the world's billionaires can claim to be honest-to-God productive entrepreneurs who have enlarged the economic pie by dint of hard work, imagination, risk taking and innovation although thankfully a useful proportion do populate the list. But a depressingly large number constitute a ragbag of monopolists, oligarchs gifted assets and profits by the state, megafinancial engineers or just family plutocrats. And once on the list you tend to stay there; there is little churn. The arteries of capitalism are hardening.[32]

In destructive entrepreneurship, entrepreneurs are engaged in detrimental activities such as those related to criminal and quasi-criminal behaviors, which lead to net social loss. The idea here is that if the perceived benefits of engaging in illegal entrepreneurial activity exceed their costs, some entrepreneurs are likely to engage in destructive entrepreneurship. Some examples include activities involving illegal drug production, and organized crime extortion and corruption. While lobbying is described above as an unproductive entrepreneurial activity, it can also be viewed as destructive entrepreneurship since significant amounts of resources are typically wasted by companies in lobbying efforts.[33] In many cases, the lobbying efforts are mostly directed towards acquiring a monopoly right. This type of entrepreneurship may be destructive since monopoly rights often lead to a welfare loss, which means that the losses to society would outweigh the gains.[34]

1.5. Entrepreneurship Indicators

To explore the heterogeneity discussed above in more detail, in this section, we introduce several entrepreneurship indicators. There have been international efforts to develop and measure various entrepreneurship indicators. The OECD/EUROSTAT framework stands out as the most developed effort to conceptualize, measure and compare entrepreneurial activities in OECD countries. This framework for entrepreneurship indicators consists of three main building blocks: Determinants, Performance and Impacts. Ahmad and Hoffmann provide a useful analogy to understand interrelationships among them: Assume that passengers would like to go from point A to point B by time t (policy objective, Impact). There may be various means of transport available. Factors such as a car's engine size, fuel consumption rate, etc. are the Determinants. During their journey, passengers are informed about their current status regarding direction and time by technologies such as speedometers and GPS readings (the Performance indicators). Note too that different passengers (policy makers) would like to go to different places and get there at different times (different Impacts), using different modes of transport (Determinant).[35]

Determinants of entrepreneurship are the factors that affect entrepreneurial performance. We discuss various determinants of entrepreneurship in terms of three categories: (1) regulatory framework, (2) values, culture and skills, (3) access to finance, market, R&D and technology.

Entrepreneurial performance measures are the entrepreneurial actions that are instrumental in delivering the impacts of entrepreneurs and entrepreneurship. Put differently, target indicators used in measuring entrepreneurial performance demonstrate progress towards achieving the ultimate objectives. Indicators related to creation, survival and mortality rates of various types of firm are used to measure entrepreneurial performance. Birth and concentration rates of high-growth enterprises and gazelle enterprises could provide even better measures of entrepreneurial performance. The OECD defines high-growth enterprises as those with an average annual growth rates (in employees or turnover) greater than 20 percent over a three-year period, and with ten employees at the beginning of the observation period.[36] High-growth enterprises up to five years old are referred to as gazelles. Note that these performance indicators are only a means of achieving various entrepreneurial goals rather than an end in themselves.

Entrepreneurial impacts reflect the value created by entrepreneurs and entrepreneurship and are the ultimate objectives that policy makers want to achieve. Various objectives such as job creation, economic growth, poverty reduction and the formalization of the informal sector have been identified.

In this section, we mainly focus on the determinants and impacts of entrepreneurship.

1.5.1. Entrepreneurial Impacts Indicators

Job Creation

Regional- and national-level studies have found that entrepreneurship is positively related to job creation. A high proportion of net job creation in the US is attributable to startup ventures that are less than five years old. Likewise, a comparison of different regions across Germany indicated that in the 1990s, regions with higher startup rates experienced higher employment growth.[37]

Job creation has been a critical policy challenge faced by many governments, especially in emerging economies. In fact, unavailability of job opportunities for young citizens is an important factor that contributed to the toppling of governments in many Arab countries. For instance, the proportion of youth that neither work nor study range from 21 percent in Jordan to 49 percent in Yemen.[38] For citizens in the Arab world, especially for those under 30, addressing the lack of quality jobs is arguably no less important than human rights, the rule of law and political freedoms. An estimated 100 million jobs need to be created in the region by 2020.[39]

Economic Growth

The high economic growth rates of economies such as Ireland, Taiwan and Singapore can be attributed to entrepreneurial activity.[40] Various measures of entrepreneurship are found to have positive effects on economic growth. The GEM has found that national entrepreneurial activity—as measured by the share of people actively involved in starting a new venture and/or managing a business less than forty-two months old—has significant positive correlation with subsequent economic growth rate. GEM data also suggest that there are no countries with high levels of entrepreneurship and low levels of economic growth.[41] A possible indicator of entrepreneurship is the number of competitors since the introduction of a new product or the startup of a new firm. In this regard, a study of manufacturing firms in the UK indicated that an increase in the number of competitors positively affected economic growth as measured by total factor productivity growth.[42]

Using the share of SMEs as a measure of entrepreneurship, researchers have found similar results. A study of manufacturing industries conducted in thirteen European countries indicated that a higher share of small businesses led to higher output growth in subsequent years. The results indicate that industries with a high share of small enterprises relative to the same industries in other countries performed better in terms of output growth during the subsequent three to four years.[43]

Formalization of the Informal Sector
Significant entrepreneurial activities take place in the informal economy (also referred to as the undeclared, shadow, black or underground economy). Informal economic sectors encompass direct subsistence workers (self-employed, unpaid family workers, and domestic servants who are usually the lowest paid workers), informal salaried workers, and informal entrepreneurs. In some economies, such as Georgia, the informal economy also includes those with double employment. That is, most workers in the informal sector receive formal wages and also engage in non-reported income-generating activities, in most cases at formal employment workplaces.[44]

Although precise estimates regarding the size of the informal economy are hard to come by, various attempts have been made to estimate the size of informal sectors as a proportion of the GDP and total employment. One estimate published in 2000 suggested that the size of the informal economy ranged from over 75 percent of the official gross domestic product (GDP) in Nigeria to about 10 percent in the US.[45] In general, the proportion of informal economy tends to be higher if a country is economically less developed. The Peruvian Economist Hernando De Soto estimated that the world's poor have about US$9 trillion in savings in the forms of unregistered assets, such as homes and businesses.[46] Among the industrialized economies, the informal economy as a proportion of the total official economy is the highest in Greece, with 31 percent of GDP in 2007.[47] In terms of employment, a report of the International Labor Organization in 2002 indicated that the informal economy as a proportion of total nonagricultural employment was 65 percent in Asia, 48 percent in North Africa, 51 percent in Latin America and 72 percent in Sub-Saharan Africa (78 percent if South Africa is excluded).[48] Likewise, in Papua New Guinea, the formal sector accounts for only about one-sixth of jobs.[49] A large informal sector significantly reduces a country's development potential and acts as a constraining factor in fighting against poverty (watch the video "With the Weight of Life on their Shoulders—Bolivia": www. youtube.com/watch?feature = player_detailpage&v=-oDwx2YObqw). Various potential advantages to formal-sector participation include police and judicial protection (and less vulnerability to corruption and the demand for bribes), access to formal credit institutions, and the ability to use formal labor contracts.[50] Formal-sector participation also leads to greater access to a wider marketplace including foreign markets, which would allow these businesses to specialize and make them more productive and competitive.

Formalization can encourage and stimulate entrepreneurial activities. Studies have also shown that people who have a formal title to their property are likely to invest up to 47 percent more in businesses.[51] Most informal businesses pay lower wages and have lower growth rates than formal ones. They also have poorer safety records, are less likely to pay taxes and are the targets of corrupt government officials.[52]

One reason behind informality concerns burdensome regulations, defective policies and procedures. Corruption, bureaucracy, red tape and a lack of simple legal rules tend to discourage entrepreneurs from registering their businesses. Factors such as high tax rates and the absence of monitoring and compliance of both registration and tax regulations also decrease the attractiveness of formal registration.[53] A high proportion of entrepreneurial firms in developing countries thus remain informal, because formalization entails significant costs.

Poverty Reduction

Entrepreneurial activities contribute to poverty reduction through a number of mechanisms. One of the most important ways in which entrepreneurship could help poor people get out of the poverty trap is through job creation.[54] In this regard, it is worth noting that in developing countries, the private sector accounts for about 90 percent of jobs, and poor people consider self-employment and availability of jobs as the two most important ways to improve their lives. There is more. Entrepreneurial activities lead to a higher degree of availability and low prices of goods and services consumed by poor people. A further mechanism whereby entrepreneurship can contribute to poverty reduction is through increased taxes. Taxes to corporations and commercial transactions are the main sources of government revenues, which can be invested in health, education and other public goods targeted to the poor.[55] In addition, increased taxes would also allow direct income transfers to poor households through government aids.

While some developing economies have experienced significant economic growth, the lack of mechanisms to trickle down the benefits to the poor represents a fundamental challenge facing them. The benefits of economic growth in most developing economies are highly concentrated and disproportionately distributed to the well-connected and wealthiest individuals. For instance, while Indonesia's GDP growth rate has been substantial (6–7 percent), there has been relatively little job growth and only wealthy elites have benefited from the economic growth. Likewise, about ten families control more than 80 percent of the stock in India's largest corporations.[56] According to Human Development Report 2011 (http://hdr.undp.org/en/media/HDR_2011_EN_Tables.pdf), 42 percent of India's population survived on less than US$1.25 a day and 28 percent of the population was below the national poverty line during 2000–2009.

THE CURRENT STATUS, DEFINITIONS

1.5.2. Determinants of Entrepreneurship

A study conducted in European countries found that very little of the difference in a worker's propensity to engage in self-employment is explained by observable characteristics of the worker.[57] This means that various aspects of the business environment such as government regulations, societal perception of entrepreneurship, and access to finance and other resources affect individuals' ability and willingness to engage in entrepreneurial activities. As noted earlier, key determinants of entrepreneurship include: (1) regulatory framework, (2) values, culture and skills, (3) access to finance, market, R&D and technology.

In Chapter 2, we discuss these factors as key elements of an entrepreneurial ecosystem with special emphasis on the roles of policy and regulation, and illustrate them with a number of success stories. Since the lack of finance is arguably often the biggest roadblock to potential entrepreneurs to materialize the goal of starting their own business, in Chapter 3, we undertake an in-depth treatment of the various sources of entrepreneurial finances and their variation across the world.

In Chapters 4 to 9, we examine the above key determinants of entrepreneurship in the contexts of a range of economies such as the OECD countries (Chapter 4), economies in the Former Soviet Union and Central and Eastern Europe (FSU&CEE) (Chapter 5), Gulf Cooperation Council (GCC) economies (Chapter 6), Africa (Chapter 7), China (Chapter 8) and India (Chapter 9). In Appendix 1, these factors are analyzed in the narrower context of entrepreneurship in the Brazilian offshoring and outsourcing industry.

Regulatory Framework
Government policies and actions affect the costs, risks and barriers to competition faced by entrepreneurial firms and hence the range of opportunities that are potentially profitable. While there have been a lot of complaints about high tax rates in some economies, studies have shown that there are other bigger obstacles. In some countries, poor infrastructure, burdensome regulation, contract enforcement difficulties, crime and corruption can amount to over 25 percent of revenues or over three times of what firms pay as taxes.[58] While there are a variety of mechanisms by which laws, regulations and policy could

affect a country's entrepreneurial performance, this section focuses on three major aspects: corporate bankruptcy laws, labor regulations and property rights.

Corporate Bankruptcy Laws Corporate bankruptcy laws are among the most discussed issues. This issue is important as the average time taken by bankruptcy proceedings is less than two years in industrialized countries compared to 4.5 years in South Asia. US corporate bankruptcy law has been a role model for many countries. In an attempt to provide reorganization opportunities for corporations experiencing financial difficulties, dozens of countries are upgrading their regulative institutions. For instance, since 2002, the UK has passed a series of Enterprise Acts, which aim to make it easier for failed entrepreneurs to enjoy a fresh start. China's new bankruptcy law adopted in 2007 has made restructuring of insolvent firms easier. Some Islamic countries, which still have a negative view of bankruptcy, are also adopting more lenient bankruptcy laws. The US Department of Commerce's Commercial Law Development Program (CLDP) reported that it advised GCC economies such as Oman, Bahrain and the United Arab Emirates on new draft insolvency laws.[59]

According to the World Bank, during 2004–2009, 59 percent of industrialized economies improved corporate bankruptcy laws. The proportions for developing countries were 33 percent in East Asia, 22 percent in Latin America, 16 percent in the Middle East and 13 percent in South Asia.[60] Inefficiency in legal systems and retributive attitudes towards the debtor have made the adoption of American corporate bankruptcy law difficult in developing countries.

Labor Regulations Some labor regulations limit businesses' capacity to grow and compete in the global economy. In India, for instance, companies with more than a hundred employees require government permission to dismiss workers. In order to fire a worker in Burkina Faso, an employer is required to retrain a worker, find another job and pay a severance package equivalent to eighteen months' wages.[61] Similarly, firing workers is almost impossible in Venezuela. Furthermore, many employees in the country want nationalization of their companies so they can become government employees, which have better perks and a higher level of job security than most private firms.[62]

Property Rights Clear property rights would allow entrepreneurs to use the assets as collateral and thus increase their access to capital. Especially for entrepreneurial firms that rely heavily on intellectual property (IP), they face a unique challenge in economies with weak IP protection laws and enforcement mechanisms. In most industrialized countries, duties and obligations to one's former employer, confidentiality clauses and non-compete agreements would prohibit a departing worker from taking valuable information with them. Observers have noted that such agreements are ineffective in some economies such as Russia. For instance, an employee in the Russian Internet advertiser, System. ru reportedly took the firm's entire client database to a newly formed rival.[63] In this regard, strong property rights allow an existing company to prevent other entrepreneurs from starting their own ventures using the IP developed by the former. Conversely, young startups that own strong property rights can be in a position to compete against established companies.

Values, Culture and Skills

Values and Culture The underlying values and culture of a society affect the entrepreneurial patterns. First, societies across the world vary in their propensity to take risks. In the Arab world, for instance, large corporate bureaucracies are found to be risk averse. The lack of a tradition of private entrepreneurship in many of the economies in Former Soviet Union and Central and Eastern European countries is arguably related to an underdeveloped risk-taking culture in the absence of local norms and social networks providing support for such a culture.[64] Managers with experience in state-owned enterprises in these economies tend to be risk averse. Likewise, some suggest that the Chinese tend to have a low risk-taking propensity.

In some societies, family and social obligations act as barriers to productive entrepreneurship. Entrepreneurs are expected to provide jobs and even redistribute their wealth and income to the members of their extended family and to the society. For instance, accumulating a huge amount of wealth is still a delicate subject in China and some people in that society expect entrepreneurs to provide socialist benefits. Some Chinese entrepreneurs are thus still sensitive to society and the communist party resistance to ideas related to the ownership of private property.

Hall's framework of high-context and low-context cultures would help us understand the international differences in entrepreneurial orientation.[65] In high-context cultures such as those of Asia and the Middle East, which are characterized by relational and collectivist values, people prefer to enter well-established institutions and organizations. For instance, in Japan, employment in large corporations is viewed as more prestigious and respected than in the US. Thus, in Japan more educated and qualified people tend to gravitate towards careers in large corporations. Likewise, a survey conducted in 2010 indicated that 52 percent of the Arab population in the 15–29 age group preferred government employment over a private-sector job. Moreover, 45 percent of aspiring entrepreneurs in the region preferred a public-sector job.[66]

Cultural differences are also linked to difference in personal characteristics between entrepreneurs and people with other occupations. For instance, a comparative study of Japan and the US showed that entrepreneurs in Japan had significantly different personal characteristics than the managers of large corporations. Silicon Valley entrepreneurs, on the other hand, showed less personality differences from managers from large corporations.[67]

Entrepreneurial Skills   Economies worldwide exhibit a high degree of heterogeneity in terms of how well their education systems prepare students for entrepreneurship. This is important, as a study conducted with self-employed individuals enrolled in a Peruvian micro-finance program indicated that even a little entrepreneurship training can significantly enhance business performance.[68]

For instance, researchers have found that one reason for Chinese graduates' lack of preparedness for entrepreneurship concerns the Chinese education system, which is traditionally based on rote learning. A number of surveys have indicated that while critical thinking is encouraged in the West, this aspect is not emphasized in China. The

lack of skills and experience to manage various types of entrepreneurial venture has hindered Chinese companies' international expansion
activities. For instance, China is reported to have a large number of
venture capitalists interested in funding US startups, but they lack the
skills and experience to manage venture investments.[69]

The lack of entrepreneurial education and training has also been
a matter of concern in EU economies. According to a Flash Eurobarometer study conducted in 2009, 39 percent of EU respondents
agreed with the statement "My school education gave me the skills
and know-how that enabled me to run a business" compared to 67
percent in the US. Similarly, with respect to another statement—"My
school education helped me to develop my sense of initiatives—a sort
of entrepreneurial attitude," 49 percent of EU respondents agreed
compared to 73 percent in the US.[70]

Access to Finance, Market, R&D and Technology
Access to Market   Access to and the demands of an entrepreneurial
firm's products in the domestic and foreign markets are a critical
factor determining the attractiveness of entrepreneurial activities. In
addition to private demand, procurement regulations and policies that
give priority to new companies in government contracts for goods and
services would create better opportunities for potential entrepreneurs.
In the same vein, governments' export-promotion strategies in various
countries have expanded entrepreneurial firms' opportunities in foreign
countries.

On the other hand, the lack of antitrust laws in some economies leaves
anticompetitive conducts entirely unregulated. In such economies, one or
a few dominant firms misuse their market power, in some cases by forming anticompetitive collusion or anticompetitive mergers, which create
entry barriers to new firms and deter entrepreneurship. For instance, in
Mexico, markets that lack competition account for 30 percent of consumer spending, which has forced Mexicans to spend 40 percent more
than they would in the presence of better antitrust laws and enforcement.[71] A *Canberra Times* article commented on Mexican billionaire
Carlos Slim, who overtook Bill Gates as the world's richest man in the
Forbes' list published in March 2010: "[Carlos Slim] made his fortune

from being the monopolist who controls 90 per cent of Mexico's telephone landlines and 80 per cent of its mobile phone subscribers. The OECD notes that he charges among the highest usage fees in the world."[72] As of 2011, in half of Mexico's 400 local areas, only Slim's company had the infrastructure to make calls to landlines. It is estimated that the average costs of home and business landlines in Mexico are 45 percent and 63 percent more respectively than the OECD averages.[73]

Access to Finance   Entrepreneurs need capital in all phases of business life. A critical practical challenge that most potential entrepreneurs face is the ability to acquire the capital, from access to early seed funds to access to the stock markets. In general, initial wealth is positively related to an individual's entry into entrepreneurship.[74] When there is limited credit availability and the entrepreneurs' initial capital requirements are substantial, low wealth households face higher barriers to starting an entrepreneurial venture.

Unavailability of bank loans in many developing economies is partly due to improper management of assets rather than unavailability of funds. Banks in many developing countries have adopted lending policies that are too conservative, as reflected in the liquidity ratio of liquid assets to total deposits. They tend to maintain high proportions of their assets in liquid forms such as cash, deposits with other banks, central bank debt, and short-term government securities. In a study of a sample of thirty-five developing countries, the mean of liquidity ratio was 45 percent and the ratio was 126 percent in Argentina compared to 2 percent in the UK and 6.5 percent in the US.[75]

Access to finance is thus a more serious obstacle in less developed economies than developed ones. For instance, according to the World Bank's Enterprise Surveys, access to finance was identified as a key obstacle to their businesses for 45 percent of firms in Sub-Saharan Africa (SSA) compared to 13 percent in OECD countries. In many developing economies, access to financial services is a broader economic and social problem. For instance, in Bogotá and São Paulo, fewer than 40 percent of families have access to the financial system.[76] Likewise, according to an adviser to the Central Bank of Nigeria (CBN), 60 percent of Nigerians are under-banked.

Entrepreneurs rely on a variety of funding sources to support their entrepreneurial activities. There are important differences across economies in terms of the availability and sources of finance. SMEs account for less than 4 percent of the total loans of three of China's four largest banks. Consequently, most of the entrepreneurial funding in China is reported to come from unofficial, informal and even illegal channels. According to China's central bank, Wenzhou city's 89 percent of people and 57 percent of enterprises have borrowed money from such channels, and reportedly pay interest rates as high as 10 percent for thirty days, which translates to 214 percent for a year.[77] Quoting a Wenzhou businessman, an *Economist* article explained that there were 100,000 people in Wenzhou city, who could raise as much as 1 billion yuan (US$150 million) each, within forty-eight hours.[78]

R&D and Technology   Access to technology greatly facilitates entrepreneurial activities. According to a 2012 report of the Internet Innovation and the Small Business and Entrepreneurship Council, a small business startup can save over US$16,000 by using high-speed broadband. For instance, high-speed broadband allows working from home rather than in the office, reducing costs associated with travel and office space. Similarly, due to lower startup costs for an online shop-front, Internet-based technologies can provide small firms with the opportunity to overcome the limitations of size and compete more effectively and/or in larger markets with bigger-sized establishments. According to an EU-commissioned study on internationalization of SMEs released in 2010, a firm's e-commerce adoption is positively correlated with its chance of being active in export or import markets.

Unaffordability and unavailability of Internet and broadband would thus hamper entrepreneurial activities. According to the ITU's World Telecommunication/ICT Indicators Database (www.itu.int/ ITU-D/ict/statistics/), wired broadband subscription rates per 100 inhabitants in 2011 were less than 0.1 percent in some developing economies such as Benin, Congo, Mali, Sudan, Tajikistan, Tanzania, Turkmenistan and Zambia.

Finally, R&D can provide opportunities for high-quality entrepreneurship and enhance an entrepreneurial business's competitiveness. R&D can help create new inventions and innovations, which
can be used to develop new products, services or processes. Firm- and
country-level studies have linked R&D activities with high entrepreneurial performance. A comparison of East Asian economies indicated
that successful entrepreneurial economies were related to a higher
R&D performance.[79] At the firm level, the probability of successfully
launching a new product increases with an increase in R&D investment. R&D activities affect performances of new and existing firms
via different mechanisms, and perhaps in different contexts. Since most
startups are less likely to have direct access to large R&D facilities, they
often rely on employees who have gained R&D-related knowledge
and experience with previous employers. In this way, while existing
firms engage in R&D activities to improve existing products, startups
benefit from knowledge spillovers and the existing stock of knowledge
by combining in new and innovative ways to launch new products.[80]
In China, for instance, a number of trained researchers working in
multinationals have become new entrepreneurs, which has become an
important mechanism of knowledge spillovers. To take one example,
China Techfaith Wireless was formed by a fourteen-person team that
left Motorola China in 2002. The company filed for a US$150-million
initial public offering in the US in May 2005 and was listed on the
NASDAQ. Photonic Bridge, another R&D firm in China, was also
founded by a team of engineers and researchers from Lucent.[81]

1.6. Becoming a Successful Entrepreneur in Different Countries

While entrepreneurial traits such as a high need for achievement,
innovative thinking, creativity, breakthrough ideas, high-risk-taking
propensity, perseverance and flexibility are more or less universal for
becoming a successful entrepreneur, the ability to fit to the environment is no less important. The success of an entrepreneur interested
in starting an entrepreneurial venture in multiple countries may hinge
on the ability to learn and adapt to the unique environmental contexts,
overcome the challenges and take advantage of the various international differences. For instance, an entrepreneur needs to have a good

understanding of the market and market dynamics, knowledge of customers' needs, and wants, and the ability to acquire financial resources and recruit people with appropriate knowledge, skills and experience and manage them. An entrepreneur who successfully manages these factors in one institutional setting may not necessarily be able to do so in other settings.

In some cases, the fact that important ingredients are missing in the economy means that entrepreneurial firms need to take extra efforts and measures. For instance, due to the lack of entrepreneurial education in India, the country's successful companies invest heavily in employees through extensive training and development in firm-specific skills. One study found that firms in the country's IT industry provide sixty days of formal training to newly hired employees and they are paid during this period. Some firms go even further. For instance, Tata Consultancy Services is reported to have a seven-month training program for science graduates to convert them into business consultants, and every employee in the company gets fourteen days of formal training annually.[82]

In some countries, entrepreneurial successes have to be achieved within a culture that is hostile to capitalism and entrepreneurship. While small-scale entrepreneurs may not be in a position to change such perception, large organizations, either singly or in cooperation with other organizations or the government agencies, can take measures to change the negative social image associated with entrepreneurs and entrepreneurship. In many emerging economies, a market economy does not function well. In these economies, institutional rules related to entrepreneurship tend to be incomplete, ambiguous and sometimes conflict with one another. In countries with an underdeveloped market economy, some entrepreneurs also take initiatives to create new market institutions. Such entrepreneurs are known as institutional entrepreneurs.

Financing sources that are common in industrialized countries, such as bank loans or personal and business credit cards, are not readily available in most developing countries. In such cases, alternative sources such as informal financing may be more appropriate. Entrepreneurs can also take advantage of special sources such as subsidized government financing in some countries.

Relevant cultural, religious and spiritual networks also help increase market access for some entrepreneurs. Some examples include entrepreneurs utilizing the Mouride Brotherhood in Senegal and the Gambia, and Indian Sikhs.[83] Many followers of the Mouride Brotherhood, with roots in Senegal's Touba, for instance, work as street vendors selling sunglasses, bags and souvenirs, and other small-scale entrepreneurial activities in Western countries such as Italy, France, Spain and the US. Mouridism preaches the responsibility to look after others within the Brotherhood. The followers of the Brotherhood, abroad and at home, donate to the Brotherhood, which in turn provides business loans and assistance to other followers. Likewise, studies conducted among immigrants living in Europe, the Americas and Australia have indicated that diaspora-based networks from China, India, Pakistan, South Korea, Sri Lanka, Vietnam and other parts of the world help immigrants from their countries of origin to access resources and develop business ideas as well as facilitate market access.[84]

Finally, the true success of an entrepreneurial activity, irrespective of wherever it has been carried out, can only be assessed by the impact it has upon society, the economy and the environment. Entrepreneurial activities need to be performed in such a way that they minimize negative impacts and maximize positive impacts on society, the economy and the environment.

1.7. Creating an Entrepreneurial Economy and Society

Policymakers keen to improve entrepreneurial outcomes can take various measures. Policy interventions can be oriented to create rewards for productive entrepreneurial activity and reduce rewards for unproductive or destructive ones. An improvement in the legal system in areas such as contract and property rights and favorable tax policy is a promising way to stimulate productive entrepreneurial activity. There is also a need to infuse and nurture a value system and culture in which creating jobs is encouraged more than getting a job.

Various entrepreneurial outcome indicators discussed above can be improved by encouraging foreign multinationals to engage in local procurement and sourcing, and to collaborate with local suppliers, distributors and retailers to create value and increase efficiency in the supply chain. For instance, Nestle sources milk locally from nearly 150,000 Pakistani farmers. A study on Unilever in Indonesia shows that by supporting such linkages the company created approximately ninety additional jobs for each direct job created in the company.[85] Evidence from economies such as China and Taiwan indicates that linkages to multinational corporations could provide an efficient channel to gain access to technical know-how.[86]

The most promising entrepreneurial activities are those that encourage the participation of the most underrepresented population segment and produce positive impacts on the economy, society and the environment. To take an example, female entrepreneurs in Mali use solar energy to dry mango products and market them.[87] Government support for such activities could significantly contribute to creating a successful entrepreneurial society. In particular, reducing gender disparity in access to resources can lead to better entrepreneurial outcomes. One study found that agricultural productivity can be increased by as much as 20 percent in SSA, if women's access to land, seed and fertilizer and other resources is increased to the same level as men's.[88]

Research has also indicated that individuals who have gained access to training and education are likely to have an improved entrepreneurial orientation. For instance, it was found that over 70 percent of students that participated in the Young Enterprise entrepreneurship program developed positive attitudes towards starting their own businesses. Likewise, half of the trainees that graduate from the International Labor Organization's (ILO) training program start a new business.[89]

In light of the various benefits that can arise from the formal sector, policy makers should formulate strategies to formalize the informal sector. Formalization of the informal sector is likely to contribute in a significant way to poverty alleviation. The Peruvian economist De Soto, for instance, describes poor people as small entrepreneurs who are stuck in a poverty trap because their wealth is informal. While formalization of informal wealth may likely face opposition from businesses and national elites, a strong government, public funding, an efficient bureaucracy and substantial legal changes may help accomplish this goal.[90]

Not all firms are created equal. In order to achieve higher rates of economic growth and jobs creation, policy incentives need to be established to encourage high-quality or high-expectation companies instead of just firm birth rates. One way to achieve this would be to reduce incentives and support for the establishment of low-quality companies. Some suggest that the government should act like a venture capitalist and encourage only innovative companies.[91]

Finally, an appropriate immigration policy may act as an important driver of innovations and entrepreneurial dynamics. In the US, data from 1950–2000 indicated that a 1.3 percent increase in the share of migrant university graduates led to an increase in the number of patents issued per capita by 15 percent.[92] The 2006–2007 GEM report found that the immigrant population in the US showed more startups than the native-born population consisting of Caucasians and African Americans. It was also found that minorities in the US exhibited higher rates of entrepreneurship than whites.[93]

1.8. Concluding Comments

Despite the GFC-led decline in some types of entrepreneurial activities, the long-term positive outlook for entrepreneurship remains intact. Entrepreneurs contribute to the national economy in several ways. Some of the important mechanisms associated with entrepreneurs' role in generating wealth and income include creating jobs, providing competition to existing businesses, helping to improve productivity by bringing innovations in product and process, introducing new goods and services, reducing the prices of existing products, advancing technological development, and enhancing the competitive position of an economy.

While societal, governmental and economic environments for entrepreneurship have dramatically improved and entrepreneurial activities have exhibited an explosive growth rate worldwide in recent years, significant international differences exist with respect to the availability and structure of entrepreneurial opportunities as well as the impacts, performance measures and various determinants of entrepreneurship.

Considerable variation across population segments can be observed in the willingness and abilities to pursue and respond to entrepreneurial opportunities. In some economies, a large gender gap in participation in entrepreneurial activities exists, which can be attributed to differential access to resources, differential societal expectations and differential opportunities for men and women. It is thus essential to design appropriate policy intervention in light of the fact that increased female participation in entrepreneurial activities has a strong positive impact on the society and economy of any country.

1.9. Review Questions

1. Why is it important to formalize the informal sector?
2. What are the various forms of capitalism? Give an example of a country, which has a prevalence of each form of capitalism.
3. What is oligarchic capitalism? How does it affect a country's economic development?
4. What is destructive entrepreneurship?

1.10. Critical Discussion Questions

1. Select an economy which is among the most friendly to small businesses (e.g., New Zealand) and another economy that is among the least friendly to small businesses (e.g., Indonesia). Do some research on determinants of entrepreneurship in these countries and compare them. What conclusions can you draw?
2. How are the indicators of determinants, entrepreneurial performance and entrepreneurial impacts related?
3. How can unproductive and destructive entrepreneurship be discouraged?

1.11. End-of-chapter Case: Cellular Phones and Micro-entrepreneurship in Developing Countries

Cellular phones are diffusing rapidly in the developing world, which has greatly facilitated entrepreneurial activities. As of 2009, over four billion handsets were in use worldwide and about 75 percent of them were in the developing world. By 2010, mobile cellular penetration rates reached 68 percent in the developing world. India and China alone added over 300 million mobile phones in 2010.

Africa's 41 percent population had a mobile phone in 2010.[94] During 2000–2009, mobile phone usage increased tenfold in Africa, which was a faster rate of increase than in any other region of the world.[95] Mobile phones arguably compensate for inadequate infrastructure, such as poor-quality roads and slow postal services. They thus help boost entrepreneurship by allowing information to move more freely and making markets more efficient. According to the World Bank, an increase in ten phones per hundred people in a developing country leads to a GDP growth of 0.8 percentage points. An executive of a telecommunications company noted in 2005: "Mobile phones have created more entrepreneurs in Africa in the past five years than anything else."[96] Mobile phones have facilitated entrepreneurial activities and created employment and produced a number of multiplier effects by triggering new economic activities.

Facilitation of Micro-entrepreneurship[97]

Facilitation of entrepreneurial activities by cellular phones is especially apparent in micro-enterprises, which account for 50–60 percent of all businesses in the world and nearly 90 percent in Africa.[98] In the cellular phone industry, a key trend has been the development of phone-based services, beyond voice calls and basic text messages. In developed countries, uses of such services are centered around activities such as music downloads and games. In developing countries, some of the popular activities in which mobile phones are used include agricultural advice, health care and money transfer.[99] These activities are providing a number of entrepreneurial, economic and developmental benefits.

One of the important uses of mobile phones in developing countries has been in information search activities. Farmers and small business owners utilize the information gathered via mobile phones to eliminate or reduce the role of intermediaries in the value chain and to lower the risk of their profit margins being squeezed by larger firms or firms from developed countries.[100] For example, mobile phones have enabled Bangladeshi farmers to find the proper prices of rice and vegetables. Similarly, groups of small farmers in remote areas of Côte d'Ivoire share mobile telephones so they can follow hourly fluctuations in coffee and cocoa prices in the international market. Thanks to mobile phones, the farmers can choose to sell their crops when world prices are favorable. Before mobile phones were available, the only way to find out about the market trends was to go to the capital city and the deal making was largely based on unreliable information from buyers.[101] Similarly, fishermen in India use mobile phones to get information about the price of fish at various accessible ports before making decisions about where to land their catch.[102] Mobile data communication methods are enabling farmers to obtain and share information beyond simply prices. In Costa Rica, small farmers in the field employ HP handheld computers, equipped with simple icons, to interact with centralized databases that guide the farmers through the complex steps of growing certified organic coffee beans.[103]

Second, mobile phones have enabled small business owners in developing countries to promote their products and communicate with customers effectively. In the late 1990s, when mobile phones were relatively newer, in Johannesburg, South Africa, one could see many homemade signs in the streets with mobile phone numbers posted by micro-entrepreneurs that offered services ranging from house painting to gardening.[104]

Third, mobile phones have contributed to enhance the efficiency and competitiveness of small business owners. For instance, mobile phones have made taxis in Kampala, the Ugandan capital, more efficient. Similarly, tradesmen traveling on bicycles in Jamaica use mobile phones to communicate with suppliers and customers.[105]

Fourth, mobile phones have reduced the cost of doing business and helped increase the yields of farmers and small business owners by providing safety. A story published by the International Telecommunications Union (ITU) documents how the driver and occupants of a van laden with readymade garments that met an accident in Chittagong, Bangladesh used a mobile phone to avoid the risk of their consignments being looted. Similarly, in Lubumbashi in the Democratic Republic of Congo, mobile phones given by maize farmers to their security guards have been effective deterrents against robbery and have increased farm yields significantly.[106]

Notes

1. DeCarlo, S. 2013, "The World's Biggest Companies", April 17, at www.forbes.com/sites/scottdecarlo/2013/04/17/the-worlds-biggest-companies-2/.
2. Nikitina, O. 2004, "Changing Times, Changing Attitudes: What do Russians Really Think about the Transition to Capitalism?", *Russ Profile*, 1(4), pp. 26–27.

3. Streeter, R. 2010, "Asian Entrepreneurs Are Bullish on the Future", August 3, at http://online.wsj.com/article/SB1000142405274870427180457540 4650983236426.html.

4. Ortmans, J., & Wadhwa, V. 2009, "Why Global Entrepreneurship Week Matters", *BusinessWeek Online*, November 16, 25.

5. "Global Entrepreneurship Week 2012", at www.kauffman.org/entrepre neurship/global-entrepreneurship-week-2012.aspx.

6. Seligson, H. 2010, "Nine Young Chinese Entrepreneurs to Watch", February 28, at www.forbes.com/2010/02/26/young-chinese-entrepre neurs-to-watch-entrepreneurs-technology-china.html.

7. AllWorld Network 2012, "Overview: The Saudi Fast Growth 100 and Arabia 500", www.allworldlive.com/saudi-arabia-100/overview.

8. Sitte, A., & Rheault, M. 2009, "Arab Youth Express Strong Entrepreneur-ial Spirit", *Gallup Poll Briefing*, 9 June, p. 3.

9. Mara, K. 2010, "First-Ever Drop in Filings under Patent Cooperation Treaty Seen in 2009", *Intellectual Property Watch*, 8 February, at www.ip-watch.org/weblog/2010/02/08/first-ever-drop-in-filings-under-patent-cooperation-treaty-in-2009.

10. *Economist* 2010, "The 70–30 nation", June 19, 395(8687), p. 36.

11. Baumöl, W.S., Litan, R.E., & Schramm, C.J. 2007, *Good Capitalism, Bad Capitalism, and the Economics of Growth and Prosperity*, New Haven and London: Yale University Press.

12. Morris, R. 2011, "GEM Endeavor 2011 High Impact Entrepreneur Entrepreneurship Report", at http://gemconsortium.org/docs/295/gem-endeavor-2011-high-impact-entrepreneurship-report.

13. Adly, A. I. 2009, "Politically-Embedded Cronyism: The Case of Post-Liberalization Egypt", *Business and Politics*, 11(4), at www.bepress.com/bap/vol11/iss4/art3.

14. EMF (Emerging Markets Forum) 2009, "India 2039: An Affluent Soci-ety in One Generation", at www.emergingmarketsforum.org/papers/pdf/2009-EMF-India-Report_Overview.pdf.

15. According to Plato, "oligarchy" is governance by a small group of people. In Plato's approach, oligarchs are different from nobles in terms of legality. Whereas nobles are few but rightful rulers, oligarchs rule in an unlawful way. In the contemporary literature, an oligarch is a large business owner controlling sufficient resources to influence national policy making and/or the judiciary to further his/her economic interests.

16. Panahatan, A. 2010, "Entrepreneurship as a Compulsary Subject in the Education of Indonesian", August 8, at http://edukasi.kompasiana.com/2010/08/08/entrepreneurship-as-a-compulsary-subject-in-the-educa tion-of-indonesian/.

17. Cetron, M. J., & Davies, O. 2008, "Trends Shaping Tomorrow's World", *Futurist*, 42(3), pp. 35–50.

18. Frazier, D. 2012, "Indonesia Minister: "We Need Four Million Entre-preneurs", 14 May, at www.forbes.com/sites/donaldfrazier/2012/05/14/indonesian-minister-we-need-four-million-entrepreneurs/.

19. Bosma, N., Jones, K., Autio, E., & Levie, J. 2007, "2007 Executive Report, Global Entrepreneurship Monitor", London: Global Entrepreneurship Research Association.

20. Muravyev, A., Schaefer, D., & Talavera, O. 2008, "Entrepreneurs' Gender and Financial Constraints: Evidence from International Data", at http://ideas.repec.org/p/kse/dpaper/11.html.

21. Bugshan, F. 2012, "Lack of Mentors May Hinder Women's Entrepreneurship in GCC", *Gallup Poll Briefing*, May 15, p. 4–4

22. Frazier, D. 2012, "Indonesia Minister: 'We Need Four Million Entrepreneurs'", at www.forbes.com/sites/donaldfrazier/2012/05/14/indonesian-minister-we-need-four-million-entrepreneurs/.

23. Gandhi, G. 2010, "Indian Entrepreneurs Need a Hug: Google's Gandhi", February 16, at http://blogs.wsj.com/india-chief-mentor/2010/02/16/indian-entrepreneurs-need-a-hug-google percentE2 percent80 percent 99s-gandhi/.

24. World Economic Forum 2011, "Global Competitiveness", at www.wefo rum.org/issues/global-competitiveness.

25. Lewis, G. 2007, "Who in the World is Entrepreneurial?", *FSB: Fortune Small Business*, 17(5), p. 14.

26. Blanchflower, D. G., Oswald, A., & Stutzer, A. 2001, " Latent Entrepreneurship across Nations", *European Economic Review*, 45(4–6), p. 680.

27. ECEI (European Commission Enterprise and Industry) 2010, "Eurobarometer Survey on Entrepreneurship", Brussels: ECEI.

28. Ahmad, N., & Hoffmann, A. N. 2008, "A Framework for Addressing and measuring Entrepreneurship", *OECD Statistics Working Paper*, January, at www.olis.oecd.org/olis/2008doc.nsf/LinkTo/NT000009FA/$FILE/ JT03239191.PDF.

29. Baumol, W. J. 1990, "Entrepreneurship: Productive, Unproductive, and Destructive", *Journal of Political Economy*, 98(5), pp. 893–921.

30. Karabegović, A., & McMahon, F. 2008, "Economic Freedom in North America", at www.fraserinstitute.org/uploadedFiles/fraser-ca/Content/ research-news/research/articles/EconomicFreedominNorthAmerica2008. pdf.

31. New Euorope 2010, "The Change We Need", July 18, 894, at www.neu rope.eu/articles/The-Change-We-Need/101952.php.

32. Hutton, W. 2010. "What the World Needs Now is Definitely Not 1011 Billionaires", *Canberra Times*, March 17, p. 11

33. Baumol, W. J. 2008, "Mega Entrepreneurs: Active Molders and Creators of Key Institutions", mimeo, New York: Berkley Center for Entrepreneurial Studies, New York University.

34. Murphy, K. M., Shleifer, A., & Vishny, R. W. (1993), "Why is Rent Seeking so Costly to Growth?", *American Economic Review*, 83(2), pp. 409–414.

35. Ahmad, N., & Hoffmann, A. N. 2008, "A Framework for Addressing and Measuring Entrepreneurship", OECD Statistics Working Paper, January, at www.olis.oecd.org/olis/2008doc.nsf/LinkTo/NT000009FA/$FILE/JT0 3239191.PDF.

GLOBAL ENTREPRENEURSHIP

36. De Backer, K. 2008, "Definition and Measurement of High Growth Enterprises: The OECD–EUROSTAT Entrepreneurship Indicator Programme", INNO-Views Policy Workshop, Brussels, November 17, at www.proinno-europe.eu/extranet/upload/deliverables/1_1_De_Backer_WS06_Brussels7962.pdf.
37. Audretsch, D. B., & Fritsch, M. 2002, "Growth Regimes over Time and Space", *Regional Studies* 36, pp. 113–124
38. Bains, E. 2009, "Qatar Tackles Region's Jobless Youth", *MEED: Middle East Economic Digest*, June 26, 3(26), pp. 26–27.
39. Dyer, P., & Yousef, T. 2007, "Will the Current Oil Boom Solve the Employment Crisis in the Middle East", Arab World Competitiveness Report, World Economic Forum, 31, at http://belfercenter.ksg.harvard.edu/files/AWCR percent203.pdf.
40. Stangler, D., & Litan, R.E. 2009, "Where Will the Jobs Come From?" Kansas City, MO: Kauffman Foundation, at www.kauffman.org/~/media/kauffman_org/research%20reports%20and%20covers/2009/11/where_will_the_jobs_come_from.pdf.
41. Reynolds, P. D., Bygrave, W. D., Autio, E., Cox, L., & Hay, M. 2002, *Global Entrepreneurship Monitor 2002 Executive Report*. Wellesley, MA/London: Babson College/London Business School.
42. Nickell, S. J., Nicolitsas, D., & Dryden, N. 1997, "What Makes Firms Perform Well?" *European Economic Review* 41, pp. 783–796.
43. Carree, M., & Thurik, A. R. 1998, "Small Firms and Economic Growth in Europe", *Atlantic Economic Journal* 26 (2), pp. 137–146.
44. Country Specific Information, at http://lnweb90.worldbank.org/eca/eca.nsf/1f3aa35cab9dea4f85256a77004e4ef4/ae1f227d6ac1b39085256a940073f4eb?OpenDocument.
45. Schneider, F., & Enste, D. 2000, "Shadow Economies: Size, Causes and Consequences", *Journal of Economic Literature* 38(1), pp. 77–114.
46. De Soto, H. 2000. *The Mystery of Capital*. New York: Basic Books.
47. Prentice, C. 2010, "Shadow Economies on the Rise around the World", at www.businessweek.com/globalbiz/content/jul2010/gb20100728_303459.htm.
48. ILO 2002, "Women and Men in the Informal Economy: A Statistical Picture". Geneva: ILO.
49. South Pacific Island Countries, at www.ilo.org/public/english/region/asro/bangkok/arm/pac.htm.
50. Schneider, F., & Enste, D. 2000, "Shadow Economies: Size, Causes and Consequences", *Journal of Economic Literature* 38(1), pp. 77–114.
51. *Economist* 2009, "Reforming through the Tough Times", September 12, p. 71.
52. Ibid.
53. Klapper, L., Amit, R., & Guillén, M.F. 2010, "Entrepreneurship and Firm Formation across Countries", at www.nber.org/chapters/c8220, pp. 129–158.

54. Smith, W. 2005, "Unleashing Entrepreneurship, the Brookings Blum Roundtable: The Private Sector in the Fight against Global Poverty, Session I: Facilitating Entrepreneurship's Contribution to Development", August 3, at www.brookings.edu/global/200508blum_smith.pdf.
55. Ibid.
56. Malhotra, H. B. 2009, "Oligarchic Capitalism May Take Hold in India", September 22, at www.theepochtimes.com/n2/content/view/22829/.
57. Fonseca, R., Michaud, P., & Sopraseuth, T. 2007, "Entrepreneurship, Wealth, Liquidity Constraints, and Start-up Costs", at http://ftp.iza.org/dp2874.pdf.
58. Smith, W. 2005, "Unleashing Entrepreneurship, the Brookings Blum Roundtable: The Private Sector in the Fight against Global Poverty, Session I: Facilitating Entrepreneurship's Contribution to Development", August 3, at www.brookings.edu/global/200508blum_smith.pdf.
59. commerce.gov 2010, "Fact Sheet—Outreach to Muslim-Majority Countries", April 27, US Department of Commerce, at www.commerce.gov/news/fact-sheets/2010/04/27/fact-sheet-outreach-muslim-majority-countries.
60. *Economist* 2010, "Making a Success of Failure", January 7, p. 68, at www.economist.com/node/15211818.
61. *Economist* 2004, "Measure First, Then Cut", September 11, 372(8392), at www.economist.com/node/3178693.
62. Molinski, D., & Shirouz, N. 2009, "Venezuela's President Threatens Toyota", *GM*, December 26, at http://online.wsj.com/article/SB10001424052748704039704574615990386867578.html?mod=WSJ_hpp_MIDDLTopStories.
63. Baumgartner, E. 2001, "Private Enterprise", *Business Eastern Europe*, June 25, p. 4.
64. Warner, M., & Daugherty, C.W. 2004, "Promoting the 'Civic' in Entrepreneurship: The Case of Rural Slovakia", *Journal of the Community Development Society*, 35(1), pp. 117–134.
65. Hall, E. T. 1976, *Beyond Culture*, New York: Anchor Press.
66. Silatech 2010, "The Silatech Index: Voices of Young Arabs", *Gallup*, November 16, at http://sas-origin.onstreammedia.com/origin/gallupinc/media/poll/pdf/Silatech.Report.2010.Nov.pdf.
67. Ohe, T., Honjo, S., Oliva, M., & Macmillan, I.C. 1991, "Entrepreneurs in Japan and Silicon Valley: A Study of Perceived Differences", *Journal of Business Venturing*, 6, pp. 135–144.
68. Karlan, D., & Valdivia, M. 2006, "Teaching Entrepreneurship: Impact of Business Training on Microfinance Clients and Institutions", Yale University, typescript; Munshi, K. 2007, *From Farming to International Business: The Social Auspices of Entrepreneurship in a Growing Economy*, NBER Working Paper No. 13065, Cambridge, MA: NBER.
69. Tozzi, J. 2012, "China's Next Export: Venture Capital", May 17, at www.businessweek.com/articles/2012-05-17/chinas-next-export-venture-capital.
70. Manchin, A., & Crabtree, S. 2010, "Europeans Don't Think Schools Encourage Entrepreneurs: Americans, Chinese Think their Schools Do

Better Jobs", August 17, at www.gallup.com/poll/142163/Europeans-Dont-Think-Schools-Encourage-Entrepreneurs.aspx.

71. *businessweek.com* 2010, "Mexico's Calderon Seeks Stronger Antitrust Law, Fines (Update1)", at www.businessweek.com/news/2010–04–05/mexico-s-calderon-seeks-stronger-antitrust-law-fines-update1-.html.

72. Hutton, W. 2010. "What the World Needs Now is Definitely Not 1011 Billionaires", *Canberra Times,* March 17, p. 11.

73. *Economist* 2011. "Making the Desert Bloom", August 27, 400(8748), pp. 59–61.

74. Hurst, E. 2003, "Liquidity Constraints, Household Wealth and Entrepreneurship", at http://faculty.chicagobooth.edu/erik.hurst/research/final_entrepreneurship_JPE_sept2003.pdf.

75. Freedman, P. L., & Click, R.W. 2006, "Banks that Don't Lend? Unlocking Credit to Spur Growth in Developing Countries", *Development Policy Review*, 24(3), pp. 279–302.

76. Moreno, L. A. 2007, "Extending Financial Services to Latin America's Poor", *McKinsey Quarterly*, Special Edition, pp. 83–91.

77. *Economist* 2011, "Let a Million Flowers Bloom", March 10, www.economist.com/node/18330120.

78. Ibid.

79. Amsden, A.H. 1991, "Diffusion of Development: The Late Industrializing Model and Greater East Asia", *The American Economic Review*, 81(2), pp. 282–289.

80. Acs, Z., Braunerhjelm, P., Audretsch, D., & Carlsson, B. 2009, "The Knowledge Spillover Theory of Entrepreneurship", *Small Business Economics*, 32(1), pp. 15–30.

81. Kshetri, N. 2008, *The Rapidly Transforming Chinese High Technology Industry and Market: Institutions, Ingredients, Mechanisms and Modus Operandi*, London and Oxford: Caas Business School, City of London and Chandos Publishing.

82. Cappelli, P., Singh, H., Singh, J., & Useem, M. 2010, "The India Way: Lessons for the US", *Academy of Management Perspectives*, 24(2), pp. 6–24.

83. Kaplan, S. 2009, "Faith and Fragile States", *Harvard International Review*, 31(1), pp. 22–26.

84. Kitching, J., Smallbone, D., & Athayde, R. 2009, "Ethnic Diasporas and Business Competitiveness: Minority-owned Enterprises in London", *Journal of Ethnic & Migration Studies*, 35(4), pp. 689–705.

85. Clay, J. 2005, *Exploring the Links between International Business and Poverty Reduction: A Case Study of Unilever in Indonesia*, London: Oxfam GB, Novib, Oxfam Netherlands, and Unilever.

86. United Nation Commission on the Private Sector Development 2004, *Unleashing Entrepreneurship: Making Business Work for the Poor*. New York: Report to the Secretary-General of the United Nations, UNDP.

87. Africa Commission 2009, *Realising the Potential of Africa's Youth*, Accra: UniBRAIN, at www.ddrn.dk/filer/forum/File/About_UniBRAIN.pdf.

88. Ibid.

89. Ibid.

90. Schaefer, P. 2009, "A $9 Trillion Question: Did the World Get Muhammad Yunus Wrong?", *Foreign Policy*, August 18, at www.foreignpolicy.com/articles/2009/08/18/a_9_trillion_question_did_the_world_get_muhammad_yunus_wrong?page=0,0.

91. Shane, S. 2008, *The Illusions of Entrepreneurship: The Costly Myths that Entrepreneurs, Investors, and Policy Makers Live*, New Haven: Yale University Press.

92. Hunt, J., & Gauthier-Loiselle, M. 2008, "How Much Does Immigration Boost Innovation?" *Working Paper No. 14312*, Bonn: IZA.

93. Klein, K.E. 2008, "Taking the Pulse of Entrepreneurship", *BusinessWeek Online*, November 19, 19.

94. ITU 2010, "The World In 2010: The Rise of 3G", at www.itu.int/ITU-/ict/material/FactsFigures2010.pdf.

95. Kapstein, E.B. 2009, "Africa's Capitalist Revolution", *Foreign Affairs*, 88(4), pp. 119–129.

96. *Economist* 2005, "Leaders: Less is More. Mobile Phones and Development", 376(8434), p. 11.

97. A micro-entrepreneur is a business owner with five or fewer employees including the entrepreneur.

98. *Economist* 2009, "Mobile marvels", 392(8650), special section, pp. 3–4.

99. Ibid.

100. Woodall, P. 2000, "Survey: The New Economy: Falling Through the Net?" *Economist*, September 23, pp. S34–S399. "Most farmers from developing countries are commodity producers that come low down in the supply chain. Since e-commerce has shifted power from sellers to buyers, corporate buyers from developed countries are likely to squeeze the profit margins of farmers from developing countries."

101. Lopez, A. 2000, "The South Goes Mobile", *UNESCO Courier*, July/August, March 24 2001, at www.unesco.org/courier/2000_07/uk/con nex.htm.

102. Rai, S. 2001, "In Rural India, a Passage to Wirelessness", *New York Times*, August, C1–C3.

103. See www.hp.com/e-inclusion/en/project/cats.html.

104. *Economist* 1999, "Survey: Telecommunications", October 9.

105. World Bank 2000, "The Role of Science and Technology in Small and Medium Sized Enterprise Development", March 24, 2001, at www.worldbank.org/html/fpd/technet/gk-smes.htm.

106. Lopez, A. 2000, "The South Goes Mobile", *UNESCO Courier*, July/August, March 24 2001, at www.unesco.org/courier/2000_07/uk/con nex.htm.

2

THE ENTREPRENEURIAL ECOSYSTEM AND ITS COMPONENTS

Abstract

This chapter expands the ideas and concepts discussed in Chapter 1 to study interrelationships among key determinants of entrepreneurship development. We start with a discussion of the concept of the natural ecosystem. An ecosystem encompasses a complex set of relationships among the necessary ingredients and components of the system. The study of entrepreneurial ecosystems consists of the study of contexts, mechanisms and processes that link the human and material resources in the ecosystem. The idea is that it is more important to pay attention to the whole system at work rather than individual elements. We also discuss how virtuous and vicious circles develop in an entrepreneurial ecosystem. Finally, some examples of measures taken by governmental and non-governmental agencies to change some of the institutional factors to stimulate entrepreneurship are discussed.

This chapter's objectives include:

1. To demonstrate an understanding of entrepreneurial activities from an ecosystem perspective.
2. To appraise the relative importance and interrelationships among some of the key elements in an entrepreneurial ecosystem.
3. To describe the roles of the government and other actors in bringing changes in an entrepreneurial ecosystem.
4. To identify various types of flows across different entrepreneurial ecosystems.

5. To analyze the determinants of productivity in an entrepreneurial ecosystem.

6. To identify some of the ways to change an entrepreneurial ecosystem.

2.1. Introduction

Entrepreneurship as a whole has much to learn from an understanding of a natural ecosystem. An ecosystem can be defined as a biological environment that consists of living or biotic components (e.g., animals and plants) as well as nonliving or abiotic physical components (e.g., air, soil, water and sunlight) with which the living organisms interact.[1] The study of an entrepreneurial ecosystem involves complex relationships of entrepreneurial firms with key players, contexts and ingredients such as government agencies, industry and trade associations, consumers, investors, financial institutions, capital markets, and national culture as well as natural and geographic factors. Each of these components influences and is influenced by the entrepreneurial ecosystem.

Before turning to the focus of this chapter—key elements of an entrepreneurial ecosystem—it is essential first to discuss the importance of developing a good entrepreneurial ecosystem. A good entrepreneurial ecosystem values creativity, innovation and excellence, facilitates partnerships among key players, and enables the development of good ideas and technologies to reach the market. Such an ecosystem can attract latent high-tech entrepreneurs and other types of high-expectation entrepreneurs because people see a chance to build successful companies. A good entrepreneurial ecosystem also attracts local and foreign investments. All these lead to a noticeable role in promoting economic and social development locally, regionally and nationally.

The entrepreneurial ecosystem provides a practical and holistic approach to understanding the development of the entrepreneurial climate. For instance, policy makers can take actions to align incentives to foster a productive and successful entrepreneurial ecosystem, which nurtures entrepreneurial behavior and enhances entrepreneurship productivity. Likewise, entrepreneurial firms, singly and collectively, take measures to create an entrepreneurial environment that allows them to take calculated risks and become successful.

2.2. Comparing Natural and Entrepreneurial Ecosystems

2.2.1. Productivity of an Entrepreneurial Ecosystem

Ecosystem productivity provides the most appropriate starting point for the treatment of entrepreneurial activities from the ecosystem perspective. One way to measure productivity in an ecosystem is to look at the rate of synthesis of organic materials (e.g., leaf litter and woody material),[2] which principally takes place through photosynthesis by primary producers (e.g., trees and sea grass). Ecosystem productivity determines the population size of herbivores, omnivores, carnivores and other organisms that the ecosystem can support. A related concept is the carrying capacity, which is the maximum population size of a species that can be sustained by the environment given the supply of food, water and other necessities. Put differently, carrying capacity is the environment's maximal load.[3]

The productivity of an entrepreneurial ecosystem may be measured by the extent to which financial, material, human and knowledge resources are used to achieve positive entrepreneurial impacts such as job creation, economic growth and poverty alleviation. An increase in productivity leads to a higher carrying capacity of an entrepreneurial ecosystem, which means more job creation, higher incomes and higher standards of living.

In the natural ecosystem, the rate of photosynthesis is high in the presence of a proper amount and combination of temperature, carbon dioxide, water, sunlight and nutrients (e.g., coral reefs and rain forest). A wrong combination of these factors may lead to a low rate of or no photosynthesis (e.g., unavailability of water in deserts, very low temperature on the tundra and lack of nutrients in the open ocean).[4] This process has a parallel in an entrepreneurial ecosystem. An effective entrepreneurial ecosystem is characterized by the existence of lively and active networks of individuals and organizations to facilitate entrepreneurial activities. For instance, financial institutions provide early-stage funding for sensible ventures. Educational institutions provide the required talents. Local government agencies such as the municipality provide supports for entrepreneurs. Entrepreneurship is culturally supported. That is, being an entrepreneur is viewed as a respected career choice. Moreover, business failure is not viewed negatively. There are also a number of entrepreneurial role models and successful entrepreneurs, who provide advice, support and mentoring to new entrepreneurs.

A common problem with some of the entrepreneurial ecosystems is the lack of the right combination of key ingredients. For instance, many young technology firms with promising ideas lack financial resources to implement their projects. Likewise, as noted in Chapter 1, China reportedly has a large number of venture capitalists interested in funding US startups, but they lack skills and experience to manage venture investments.

2.2.2. Diversity in an Entrepreneurial Ecosystem

Diversity has an important role and function in an ecosystem. A diverse ecosystem containing varied terrain (e.g., caves, mountains, forests and bodies of water) and inhabited by a wide range of native species of flora and fauna is likely to be healthy, and has a higher probability of containing species that are likely to have a strong ecosystem effect. Each species, irrespective of its size and type, has an important role to play and thus boosts ecosystem productivity. Diversity can also increase the efficiency of resource use.[5] Species diversity generally enhances the health of an ecosystem, which is less likely to be seriously damaged by calamities and natural disasters such as extreme weather situations.

The health and productivity of an entrepreneurial ecosystem depend on the diversity of entrepreneurial firms. Mature and healthy entrepreneurial ecosystems are characterized by size, product, market, industry, and the technological and structural diversity of entrepreneurial firms. Firms of each type are likely to have a niche in the entrepreneurial ecosystem that would help keep the entrepreneurial system healthy, resilient and productive. Diversity also allows entrepreneurial firms to establish alliances with other firms that could be complementors.

In order to illustrate this phenomenon, we consider South Korea. In the early stage of development, government-sponsored schemes encouraged the growth of "chaebols" (family-owned conglomerates) such as Hyundai and Samsung, which helped transform the economy. According to the Bank of Korea, the thirty largest chaebols control 40 percent of the South Korean economy.[6] Chaebols have created entrepreneurial opportunities for SMEs. For instance, SMEs make most of the parts for Korean car-makers such as Hyundai, Kia and Daewoo. The chaebols support SMEs in a variety of ways—direct and indirect, formal and informal. For instance, several of the biggest chaebols have launched in-house lending programs that support the financing needs of their SME partners.

Chaebols and SMEs have distinct roles in the country's economic growth and job creation. SMEs are major contributors to the country's job creation. SMEs account for 99 percent of the companies and 88 percent of the manpower in South Korea.[7] Compared to big firms in the country, South Korean SMEs are, however, highly inefficient. For instance, SMEs' operating profits in 2007 were 4.5 percent of sales, compared with large firms' 7 percent. Likewise, small firms' value added per worker is less than half as much as in large ones.[8]

2.2.3. Poor-quality Species and Parasites and their Effects

In a natural ecosystem, prevalence of poor-quality species is one of the main causes of low productivity and destruction of the ecosystem. This phenomenon has a striking and interesting parallel to the functioning of the entrepreneurial ecosystem. Easy availability of government money, which is distributed without carefully looking at the efficiency, depth and quality of entrepreneurial ideas, will encourage the formation of many low-quality firms. This situation will have a negative impact on the pace and rate of deal flow for private equity investors. That is, venture capitalists or private equity investors on the other hand are less likely to receive business proposals/investment offers. One might cite many examples to illustrate this point. One example is Canada's government sponsored Labor Fund Program started in the 1990s, which was largely unsuccessful. The program was mostly managed by people with little knowledge and experience in venture capital. Investment decisions were driven by political processes rather than merit-based considerations. Moreover, the fund was much bigger in terms of size than the private venture capital market. Consequently private venture capitalists were intimidated and scared off by the Labor Fund Program.[9] Another example is Malaysia's BioValley, a US$150 million complex started by the government to attract firms in the biotechnological industry. The proposed cluster lacked the necessary organic development and became a target of criticism and mockery as the "Valley of the BioGhosts".[10] Other high-profile but unsuccessful government funded programs include Dubai's entrepreneurial hub, Australia's BITS (Building on Information Technology Strengths) program, and the European Union's (EU) European Investment Fund (which was started in 2001 with an endowment of more than €2 billion—about US$2.8 billion), Japan's Tsukuba Science City and Egypt's "Silicon Pyramid".[11] In this regard, just as ecosystem productivity can be increased by replacing poor-quality species by nutritious grasses, the quality of an entrepreneurial ecosystem can be improved by encouraging high-growth enterprises.

Even worse is the fact that formal and informal institutions in some economies promote the growth of parasitic entrepreneurs. A journalist noted that parasitic entrepreneurs in Egypt produced low-quality goods which were sold to the state, and that they did not pay taxes.[12] Parasites can bring marked changes in the dynamics of the ecosystem by directly or indirectly modifying the environment of other organisms. Research in natural ecosystem has indicated that parasites' actions lead to the increased mortality and reduced fecundity of the host population. In an entrepreneurial ecosystem, resources and opportunities that enable the parasitic entrepreneurs to pursue their economic goals are likely to scare off high-quality challengers.

2.2.4. Feedback Systems

Ecosystems contain feedback mechanisms which function to maintain the various elements of the system in an equilibrium state. The interaction among various elements of the ecosystem exhibits dynamic exchange processes, which are associated with the circulation of energy or materials. A negative feedback loop tends to slow down a production process in an ecosystem, whereas the positive feedback loop tends to accelerate it.

As entrepreneurs participate in developing and learning in the entrepreneurial ecosystem, they develop an understanding of what must be done to succeed in the environment. The nature and quality of entrepreneurial ecosystems determine the feedbacks that potential and actual entrepreneurs receive, as well as their actual experiences. Entrepreneurial success stories provide positive feedback in the entrepreneurial ecosystem. Moreover, positive feedback systems tend to have a perpetual cycle, which can lead to a further improvement in entrepreneurial performance. High levels of corruption in the government and the proliferation of low-quality entrepreneurial firms and parasitic entrepreneurs, on the other hand, are associated with a negative feedback system, which discourages entry into entrepreneurship and reduces levels of productive entrepreneurial activities.

2.3. The Essential Elements of an Entrepreneurial Ecosystem

In this section we first briefly revisit the three key determinants of entrepreneurship noted in Chapter 1, which constitute the key ingredients that affect the quality of an entrepreneurial ecosystem: (1) regulatory framework, (2) values, culture and skills, (3) access to finance, market, R&D and technology. Here are some additional examples that demonstrate how these factors are linked to the entrepreneurial ecosystem.

1. **Regulatory framework:** First, the existence of a legislative framework that is comprehensible, sensible and stable is the most important prerequisite for the development of a good entrepreneurial ecosystem. A well-developed system of legal and commercial rules and enforcement mechanisms (e.g., commercial code, property law, intellectual property rights protection, bankruptcy legislation, contract law, consumer law) contributes to the development of a high-quality entrepreneurial ecosystem. In top business-friendly countries, starting a business involves only a few steps, which can be completed in a few days and is inexpensive for the entrepreneurs. Especially important for many developing economies are rules and procedures to start a business. For instance, one study indicated that a ten-day reduction in the time taken to start a business can lead to a 0.4 percentage point increase in GDP growth.

2. **Values, culture and skills**: As to values and culture in some parts of the world, entrepreneurs are associated with various negative images. While entrepreneurs are considered to be members of the privileged class in many countries, they are arguably regarded as "déclassé", or ascribed a lower or inferior social status in some economies such as France, Germany and Sweden.[13] Moreover, observers have noted that in countries such as those of Sweden and the UK a business failure is considered to be a family disgrace. At the World Entrepreneur Summit in 2007, an Internet entrepreneur noted: "In the UK, there is a stigma against business failure among the general public, whereas in the US it's almost a badge of honor."[14]

Likewise, despite the high level of entrepreneurial intentions among Arab youths, entrepreneurs have a negative social identity in Arab culture. A 2009 Gallup poll found that about half of young Arabs viewed entrepreneurs as individuals who think only about profits. The proportions of youth with such a viewpoint were 82 percent in Lebanon, 72 percent in Kuwait and 72 percent of Palestine.[15] Arab societies are also described as exhibiting a fairly high degree of hostility towards entrepreneurship education. For instance, when an adviser to the Egyptian Education minister initiated some of the educational reform measures, traditionalists labeled his attempts as "Westernization" of the curriculum.[16]

3. **Access to finance, market, R&D and technology**: Availability of capital influences not only the ability of firms to enter new markets, but also the ability to compete with incumbent firms.[17] In many developing countries financial institutions' unavailability of funds and/or unwillingness to lend to small businesses have led to unfavorable entrepreneurial ecosystem conditions. For most potential entrepreneurs in these countries, a village loan shark is the only available source of capital, whose interest rate is usually 200–300 percent a year.[18] Well-developed

consumer markets bring entrepreneurial opportunities, and help the entrepreneurial ecosystem. In some cases, demanding customers force businesses to be more innovative and thus play a critical role in stimulating entrepreneurial activity. A customer can also make it easier to carry out entrepreneurial and innovative activities by communicating its plans, expectations and intentions. New technologies may create richer and more favorable contexts and conditions in which to develop entrepreneurial ventures.

In addition to the three factors already mentioned, a fourth factor must be considered:

4. **Natural and geographic conditions**: Natural and geographic conditions are important, not only in the natural ecosystem, but also in entrepreneurial ecosystem. Geographic factors such as climate, distance to coastline, landlockedness, availability and type of natural resources, land features (e.g., terrain and topography, the proportions of arable land and land area in the tropics), accessibility to transportation routes, proximity to attractive customers and suppliers affect the pattern and potential for entrepreneurial ventures.

Iceland's Data Islandia   Some entrepreneurial firms and policy makers have utilized a geographic location as a value proposition. For instance, Data Islandia, an Iceland-based company, wants to develop Iceland as the world's data storage center. Data Islandia is responding to the needs of businesses to archive data to comply with various regulations. The company's unique selling propositions included cool climate, geothermal energy and secure remoteness.[19] Renewable energy sources such as hydroelectric and geothermal power plants are used to meet the project's energy needs.

While Iceland has huge renewable energy reserves, the country's remote island location means that the direct export of these reserves to foreign markets has been difficult and expensive. This means that extremely energy-intensive processes that can be performed in the

country such as aluminum smelting, which involves extracting aluminum from its oxide alumina, and data centers are better ways of exporting its energy resources.[20] In addition, the country's cool climate can
be considered to be an asset given that over a quarter of data centers'
operating costs in the US are spent on cooling.[21] Likewise, data centers
in the UK consume 2.2–3.3 percent of the country's total grid power.

Emerald Networks' submarine cable system, which is a 5,200-km,
100-Gbps undersea cable connecting North America and Europe via
Iceland, would further facilitate Iceland's efforts to develop itself as
the world's data center. In an attempt to encourage investment in data
centers and other technology projects, the government has reduced
duties on imports of equipment.

The Automobile Industry in Slovakia   Another example is the development
of the automobile industry in Slovakia. Being centrally located in
Europe, it has easy access to 350 million customers (within a radius of
1,000 km). Slovakia also acts as the gateway to the Balkan countries.
The *Financial Times* described Slovakia as the "Detroit of the East"
(February 20, 2007). Others refer to the country as a "Mecca for
car production". Automobile manufacturing accounts for 25 percent
of industrial production and 30 percent of exports.[22] The country
produced an estimated 900,000 cars in 2008, which makes it the
world's top per-capita car producer.[23]

One example of a company benefiting from Slovakia's location is
Kia, which has a production capacity of 300,000 vehicles in Zilina.
Kyu Bae, CEO of Kia Motors Slovakia, noted that the location gives
the company easy access to both Western Europe and Russia. Russia
has become a larger market for Kia than Germany.[24] Watch the video
"Slovakia" (www.youtube.com/watch?v=hPjsAbZ3P_s).

Israel's Evolution as a Clean Technology Hub   As a further example,
consider Israel's evolution as a clean technology (CT) hub in recent
years. Israel has the advantage of being well endowed with plenty of
sun, which makes it a fertile ground for solar innovations. The lack
of water and oil increases the value proposition of CT. In 2009 and
2010, eight Israeli companies made it to the Global Cleantech 100

(www.cleantech.com/global-cleantech-100/), consisting of the world's top one hundred CT companies. Only the US and the UK had more companies named. Similarly, in the Global Cleantech Innovation Index 2012, which evaluated the world's top thirty-eight countries investing in CT, Israel ranked second behind Denmark. The rank was based on the establishment of startups in proportion to the overall financial strength.

Rare Earth Elements in China   Availability of natural resources such as farm land, minerals, hydroelectric power, oil and timber is likely to influence the amount and type of entrepreneurial opportunity. For instance, China has the advantage of being well endowed with natural resources required for the CT industry. One estimate suggests that China produces 97 percent of the world's rare earth elements (REE).[25] Likewise, Africa accounts for 60 percent of the world's uncultivated arable land, providing abundant opportunities for creating entrepreneurial ventures.[26]

2.4. The Roles of Policy and Regulation in Enhancing the Quality and Productivity of an Entrepreneurial Ecosystem

The government is considered to be the most powerful institutional actor and thus can become an important force in shaping an entrepreneurial ecosystem. Regulative frameworks not only exert direct influence on entrepreneurial activities, but also affect other determinants of entrepreneurship such as market conditions, infrastructures, human capital and access to finance.

In the Iceland example, the country has regulations and policy in place to provide strong data security and privacy protection. In general, the EU has no restriction on its member countries to move their data to Iceland.[27] This can be contrasted with some economies such as India, which are not considered data secure by the EU. The fact that India has not achieved the status of a data secure country prevents flow of sensitive data, such as patient information, to India.

The Slovakian government's incentives for entrepreneurs include cash grants to obtain tangible and intangible assets, corporate income tax relief, contributions for newly created jobs and transfer of real estate from the municipality ownership for a discounted price. The country has a flat tax of 19 percent, there is no dividend tax to shareholders and foreign companies can repatriate all their profits. Slovakia's labor unions have little power. In the World Bank Group's *Doing Business 2010* report, Slovakia ranked first in the Central and Eastern European region.

In Israel's case, the transparent laws for establishing companies provide a favorable and supportive environment to entrepreneurial activities. While foreign investments involving sensitive sectors need prior approval, the country gives equal treatment to domestic and foreign investors in most sectors. Likewise, 80 percent of the first US$500,000 for every idea identified is funded by the government.[28]

Israel has especially favorable policies towards the CT industry. For instance, import tax in the country has dropped to 10 percent for electric vehicles and increased to 72 percent for gas-powered cars.[29] Israel wants to generate 10 percent of its electricity by alternative means by 2020 in contrast with its present complete reliance on imported coal and natural gas.

Governments can also play a key role in the development of a better corporate governance system, which is one of the most important mechanisms contributing to entrepreneurial success of an economy. Note that corporate governance entails the systems, principles, rules, laws and processes by which businesses are operated, regulated and controlled. The idea here is that good corporate governance plays a key role in the integrity of corporations, financial institutions and markets. Key elements of good corporate governance practices include a high level of transparency, respect for minority shareholders, and strong and independent boards of directors. For instance, in some economies, controlling shareholders engage in siphoning off company funds by various means.[30] In countries characterized by poor corporate governance, underdeveloped financial and legal systems and higher corruption, the growth rate of the smallest firms is most adversely affected, and fewer new firms, particularly small firms, are created.[31]

Poor enforcement—rather than absence—of existing regulatory safeguards is one of the main constraints to the development of an effective corporate governance mechanism in India. For instance, following the 1991 Indian liberalization and reform of capital markets, a new regulatory body, Securities Exchange Board of India (SEBI) was established in 1992 in order to protect the interests of investors and promote the development of the securities market. However, the SEBI has been accused of not punishing the guilty.[32]

It should be noted that the various determinants of entrepreneurship discussed above, however favorable they may be to entrepreneurship in themselves, may be counteracted in practice by flawed policies and corrupt institutions. In some emerging economies ambiguous wording and frequent changes in tax laws allows tax inspectors to engage in corrupt behavior and increase uncertainty for businesses. Moreover, the processes involved in determining whether an entrepreneur has violated the tax law, such as the tax inspector's examination of the tax payments and submission of a report to the authorities for verification, lack transparency. There is little, if any, supervision of tax inspectors. The upshot of these tendencies is tax inspectors' lack of accountability and substantial discretionary power to determine whether an entrepreneur has violated a tax law. In these economies, there is thus a firmly held belief among entrepreneurs that paying bribes demanded by a tax inspector is the only way to avoid more serious troubles.[33]

Politicians' and bureaucrats' engagement in corrupt behavior has been a major concern in many economies. Corruption is the abuse of public authority for private gain. It is a transaction that usually takes place between government officials or representatives and profit-oriented organizations. Corruption may take various forms. Analysts argue that Russia is trapped in a predatory and corrupt system that has slowed the growth of an entrepreneurial class.[34] Likewise, a private coal miner in China's Shanxi Province told a journalist that corruption accounted for 20 percent of his operating costs. The proportion is expected to be higher in illegal mines.[35]

2.4.1. Two African Success Stories on the Policy Front

Despite their authoritarian character, the governments of Rwanda and Ethiopia have been able to improve their countries' entrepreneurial outlooks drastically in a fairly short period of time.

Rwanda   Rwanda has been among the most successful countries in fostering new private firms and attracting foreign investment due primarily to peace and political stability maintained by President Paul Kagame's government. President Kagame came to power in 2000, and set Rwanda's goal to increase the GDP seven times over a generation. His government's Vision 2020 plan aimed at transforming the coffee- and tea-growing country into a middle-income, service-based economy by 2020.

Due to the Rwandan genocide of 1994, most people in foreign countries had a negative view of the country. The negative news coverage, which was mainly produced by people living outside the country, had a profound effect on foreign investors' opinion. In this regard, the Rwandan online newspaper igihe.com launched a campaign to change the negative international image of the country. The number of visitors on igihe.com increased from thirty a day in 2008 to over seventy-thousand in 2012.[36] Rwanda has opened strategic business offices in Turkey, Canada, the UK, the US, South Africa, Singapore and China to promote investments in those countries.[37] In addition, billboards and posters in Kigali encourage visitors to invest in the country.

Rwanda has introduced various initiatives to facilitate entrepreneurial development. In 2008, mandatory entrepreneurship classes were added to secondary school curricula. The Rwanda Education Board has also developed a strong entrepreneurship curriculum with assistance from the UN's Industrial Development Organization.[38] As of 2012, the Rwanda Development Board (RDB) had established over thirty business development centers, which offer services to improve enterprise performance, competitiveness and market access.[39]

In 2010, Rwanda was named as the best East African country to do business. It is the one of the world's fastest places to start a business (eighth overall in 2013). Likewise, Rwanda's economic freedom score of 64.9 in 2012 made it the world's fifty-ninth freest economy and third out of forty-six countries in SSA.

These initiatives have produced measurable improvements. The country's per capita GDP has quadrupled in the fifteen-year period since the mid-1990s. Rwanda attracted US$230 million in foreign investment by 2009, which increased to US$626 million in 2011.[40] Total investment in 2012 passed US$1.1Billion. Most of its foreign investment is in the tourism, energy, construction and real estate sectors.

Ethiopia Ethiopia is another good example that illustrates how regulations to ease entry barriers for entrepreneurial firms can stimulate the entrepreneurial ecosystem. Until 2003, registering a business in Ethiopia cost five years' average income. In addition, an entrepreneur was required to publish costly notices in two newspapers. The government abolished the rule and reduced the registration cost to nine months' income. The number of new businesses registered in the country increased by half.[41] According to the UN Economic Commission for Africa (ECA), the country was the second-fastest-growing economy in Africa for 2011, after Ghana.

2.5. A Systems Approach to Understanding the Entrepreneurial Ecosystem: Moving from Parts to the Whole

To take an "ecosystem approach" means that it is important to pay attention to the whole system at work rather than individual elements. That is, instead of analyzing individual components or aspects of the entrepreneurial processes, such as government policy or R&D, we holistically examine all the components and the interactions among them, as part of one system.

While the roles of factors such as geography and policy in shaping an entrepreneurial ecosystem are discussed in detail above, these factors' synergistic interaction with other elements is what makes the entrepreneurial ecosystem more or less productive. For instance, Slovakia's rapid emergence as an industrial and entrepreneurial powerhouse, in the automobile industry as well as in a diverse range of industries, can be attributed not only to favorable geographic and friendly policy-related factors but also to their interaction with other elements. According to the World Bank's Student Learning Assessment Database, Slovaks scored higher in math than any other Central and Eastern European students and were placed third in science. Despite this, there is a weakness in the labor market. The average labor cost per month in 2009 in Slovakia was €723 (US$1,078) compared to €942 (US$1,405) in the Czech Republic.[42] This interaction has offered attractive enough incentives for foreign firms to locate in the country despite some problems related to a lack of qualified specialists in commercial technology.

The development of the CT industry and entrepreneurship in general in Israel can be attributed to more than just favorable and supportive government policies and its sunny climate. The tiny country of seven million people has over seventy nationalities represented. Public- and private-sector organizations in the country have made a conscious effort to create a virtuous circle of entrepreneurship development. In terms of venture activity, Israel's Tel Aviv is the second largest hub worldwide after San Francisco.[43] Israel attracts as much venture capital as France and Germany combined. In 2009, venture capital investments in Israel amounted 0.18 percent of GDP, which ranked it highest among all the economies in the world.

Religions and ethical systems have facilitated economic growth. Like Confucianism and some forms of Christianity, Judaism arguably has played a role in shaping habits and values that promote economic success, including the belief that people can influence their destinies. The Jewish faith is arguably learning-based, not rite-based, which encourages a belief in progress and personal accountability.[44]

One way to understand inventive entrepreneurial activity around the world would be to look at the distribution of patents awarded to inventors in the US. In this regard, between 1980 and 2000, Israelis registered 7,652 patents in the US, which compares with Egyptians' 77 and Saudis' 171.[45] Strong university–industry linkages and a large pool of highly trained scientists and engineers have driven Israel's entrepreneurial performance. By the early 2010, Israel had twenty-four technology incubators.[46]

As to the culture and value system, the entrepreneurial spirit of the Jews is considerable. For instance, Jews account for 0.2 percent of the world population, but 54 percent of the world chess champions, 27 percent of the Nobel Prize winners in physics and 31 percent in medicine. In the US, they represent 2 percent of the population, but account for 21 percent of Ivy League students. Similarly, 26 percent of Kennedy Center honorees and 37 percent of Academy Award-winning directors are Jews. Likewise, among a *Business Week* list of leading philanthropists, 38 percent were Jews. They also represent 51 percent of the Pulitzer Prize winners for nonfiction.[47]

Unsurprisingly, Israel has more high-tech startups per capita than any other nation. The country also adds two hundred startups every year. The country ranks second behind the US in the number of NASDAQ-listed companies. Israel has more companies in NASDAQ than Europe, Korea, Japan, India and China combined. By the early 2010, Israel had over 3,000 entrepreneurial technology firms and the annual revenue of 500 of them had crossed US$20 million.[48]

Non-government actors are sometimes more effective than the government in effecting favorable change in the entrepreneurial eco-system. For instance, entrepreneurial success is not socially admired in Scandinavia (see Jante's Law, Chapter 4). In Sweden, the think-tank Timbro is working to bring a long-term shift in "public opin-ion in favor of free markets, entrepreneurship, private property, and an open society".[49] The institute is funded mostly by large Swedish corporations. Likewise, the NGO Injaz al-Arab (www.injazalarab. org/), which was formed in 2004 and operated in thirteen countries in the Middle East and North Africa in 2010, sends volunteers to teach work readiness, financial literacy and entrepreneurship in schools. As of mid-2010, Injaz al-Arab programs engaged 10,000 private-sector volunteers and reached over 500,000 students.[50]

There are also instances of news media and the popular press devoting substantial space to promoting entrepreneurship. In an attempt to support and encourage local entrepreneurship, Puerto Rico's largest daily newspaper, *El Nuevo Día*, devoted a weekly page of startup success stories. The stories promoted new forms of social dialogue and created awareness about the ingredients and effects of entrepreneurship.[51]

Corporate governance mechanisms differ across contexts due to differences in culture and history, in addition to local power rela-tions, policies and regulations, as discussed above. While the US and Western European economies have well-developed corporate gover-nance systems, cross-cultural differences in their corporate governance mechanisms are observed, especially in family businesses. For instance, US businesses are less likely to give senior positions to non-family members than their European counterparts. This difference can be attributed to the fact that US family businesses can grow by focusing only on the large US market, while European companies are forced to internationalize their business at a much earlier stage due to their small national markets.[52]

While all the above factors are important in having a role to play in an entrepreneurial ecosystem, different factors may dominate the system under different conditions that shape incentives and challenges in establishing certain types of firm. Consider, for instance, ForShe, which is an all-women-driver taxi service in Mumbai, India. The company was founded in 2007 with nine vehicles. The company's target customers are women who travel alone and prefer an all-female service. Businesses, hotels and call centers showed an interest in these taxis for their women employees. However, taxi driver is a very rare occupation for women in India and other Asian countries. The ForShe founder noted that a major challenge for her is to find female drivers that are well versed in the geography of Mumbai city.[53]

2.6. Concluding Comments

A favorable entrepreneurial ecosystem is characterized by factors such as entrepreneurship-friendly formal institutions, supportive informal institutions, a strong orientation towards innovation and state-of-the-art technologies, a good geographic location and high-quality infrastructures. These conditions are associated with a high rate of firm creation and help existing entrepreneurial firms to survive, thrive and grow. These factors also help to attract foreign firms, which can stimulate the entrepreneurial ecosystem by contributing considerably to quality, diversity and competition.

To take an "ecosystem approach" means that various actors interested in entrepreneurship development shift their focus from the part to the whole. The sustainability, health and productivity of the entrepreneurial ecosystem and firms can be enhanced by the implementation of a more holistic strategy for assessing, monitoring and managing the entrepreneurial ecosystem. The above discussion indicates that government has the most important role to play in this process.

2.7. Review Questions

1. Among the key elements of the entrepreneurial ecosystem discussed above, which one do you think is the most important in driving entrepreneurial activities?
2. Can state or non-state actors change an entrepreneurial ecosystem? If so, how?
3. Why are policy-related factors important for a high-quality entrepreneurial ecosystem?
4. How does corruption influence entrepreneurship?
5. What types of skill are needed to promote entrepreneurship?

2.8. Critical Discussion Questions

1. Select a developing country and critically examine how key elements of the entrepreneurial ecosystem discussed in this chapter have influenced entrepreneurship in the country.
2. Are factors related to the access to market, finance, R&D and technology more important than policy and culture in promoting entrepreneurship? Why or why not?

2.9. End-of-chapter Case: The Colombian Entrepreneurial Ecosystem

Colombia serves as a good example to illustrate how the government in an economy can improve the quality of the entrepreneurial ecosystem and the nature of the barriers it is likely to face. Despite its deep long-term embroilment in a war with guerrilla paramilitary groups and drug cartels, Colombia has made drastic improvement in its entrepreneurial performance in recent years. According to a BBC World survey, the country was rated among the twenty-four "most entrepreneur-friendly nations". It is a high-defense-spending, family-business-dominated culture, but a low level of investment in R&D has severely constrained the efficiency and productivity of its entrepreneurial ecosystem. Moreover, foreigners' perception of the country as "lawless" and "violent" has been difficult to change.

Colombia's entrepreneurial revolution is a result of a number of diverse, contradictory and conflicting forces. Many paradoxes thus exist in the Colombian entrepreneurial ecosystem as well as its various components and processes. Colombian entrepreneurship-related institutions, for instance, are characterized by a recombination of old institutional elements with the introduction of new elements in a process of institutional change.[54]

Indicators Related to Entrepreneurial Performance and Impact

Indicators related to entrepreneurial performance and impact are mixed. Colombia has become one of the most dynamic economies in Latin America. In 2011, Colombia was represented in Forbes' Global 2000 list of the world's biggest companies. The country's unemployment decreased from 17.3 percent in 2002 to 12.1 percent in 2009.[55] During 2002–2007, Colombia's average annual economic growth rate exceeded 5 percent thanks to improved domestic security, greater foreign investment inflows, export growth and sound monetary policy.

Colombia is Latin America's fourth biggest oil producer as well as fifth biggest coal exporter in the world. It is a top producer of mild, washed arabica coffee. It also is a major flower exporter and textile producer. However, most Colombian companies have not been able to move beyond natural-resource-based industries. Commodities make up more than 50 percent of Colombia's exports, while exports account for about 20 percent of its GDP.[56]

A significant informal economy has been a major challenge faced by the Colombian entrepreneurial ecosystem. One estimate suggested that Colombian informal economy employs about 60 percent of the country's population.[57] Moreover, the size of the informal sector is expanding. The country also performs poorly with respect to poverty reduction. A Gini coefficient of 58.5 puts it among economies with the highest income inequalities between the rich and the poor.[58]

Externalities Generated by Violence, Insecurity and Drug Entrepreneurship

By the early 2000s, about 4 percent of the country's population, mostly from rural areas, was forced to leave their homes due to violence.[59] Likewise, during 2000–2005, about one million Colombians migrated to the US, Spain and Costa Rica.[60] However, an institutional framework for entrepreneurship has emerged through the stable coexistence of violence and democracy. Entrepreneurship-friendly institutions have emerged and operate in an environment characterized by violence and insecurity.

Stereotypes and a negative perception of the country have been nurtured and sustained by many foreign investors. A *Business Week* article notes: "The handful of Wall Street analysts who cover Colombia supply their clients with charts of murder rates and kidnappings."[61]

A major challenge facing Colombia is related to a fertile ecosystem developed around unproductive and destructive entrepreneurship. Colombia arguably has the world's most powerful drug cartels and the illegal drug industry in the country has more dramatic social, political and economic effects on Colombia than any other country. Guerrilla fighters as well as counter-guerrilla and paramilitary groups benefited tremendously from entrepreneurial activities in the drug economy. They employed the unemployed and semi-employed workforce of the country. One estimate suggests that drug cartel groups owned about one-third of the country's agricultural land in the early 1990s.[62]

Drug entrepreneurship took place in Colombia in all shapes, sizes and forms. Estimates suggest that about ten million acres (four million hectares) have been taken from peasants by paramilitaries, drug lords and ranchers.[63] Traditionally, drug entrepreneurship allowed peasants and everyone else involved to reap the rewards with little effort. For instance, for many peasants in remote parts of Colombia, coca yielded much higher returns than corn, rice, potatoes and vegetables. Some suggest that cocaine in Colombia has been a "small entrepreneur's dream". As in the case of Afghanistan, drug eradication campaigns in Colombia had little effect on drug production but alienated the local population, which has led to a higher political capital to insurgents.

Experts say that Colombia's illegal drug industry was the result of the weakness of the state and its institutions, and the delegitimation of the governmental system. It is also argued that the development of the illegal drug industry is an effect rather than a cause of the structural and institutional weaknesses of the country.

Regulatory Framework

While significantly improved, laws and enforcement mechanisms in Colombia are weak due primarily to the fact that defense spending is draining the civilian economy in general and entrepreneurial development in particular. In the 1990s, the defense budget averaged 1.35 percent of GDP. Even until the early 2000s, the country's defense spending was significantly lower compared to most other countries in conflict and even other Latin American countries at peace.

After Alvaro Uribe was elected as the country's president in 2002, he significantly increased defense spending to intensify military actions against the guerrillas. Colombia's spending on defense increased from US$2.6 billion in 2001 to over US$9 billion in 2009.[64] Laws and enforcement mechanisms, however, are often ineffective due to a lack of funding for police forces and civil law enforcement.

According to the World Bank's Doing Business 2011 report (www. doingbusiness.org/reports/global-reports/doing-business-2011/), Colombia ranked third in Latin America for the ease of doing business. The country's performance is better than the average for Latin America in terms of time taken, costs and the number of procedures for starting a business. Colombia is the best country in the region to protect an investor.

Colombia has also implemented some pro-SME policies that are based on direct government support of SMEs. The government has increased the availability of micro credit for small entrepreneurs. In a study of fifty-three countries in terms of their friendliness to small businesses, Colombia ranked twenty-ninth.[65]

Signs of Oligarchic Capitalism

Compared to other South American countries, multinationals and state enterprise played a much smaller role in Colombia in the twentieth century. Revenues of the four largest Colombian business groups (*grupos*) were estimated at 12.5 percent of the country's GDP, compared to the Latin American average of 9.6 percent.[66] Likewise, revenue from the ten largest business groups in 1995 was 28 percent of GDP in Colombia compared to 11 percent in Argentina, 10 percent in Mexico and 8 percent in Brazil, and 14 percent in Latin America.[67]

These *grupos*, which are mostly family-owned, had close ties with high government officials and relied on the state for various resources such as credit, contracts and favorable regulation, thrived in the closed system and dominated several industries.[68] Politicians, on the other hand, depend on the *grupos* for campaign supports. This dynamic formed the basis of mutual interdependence and the ongoing institutional partnership relationship between them. In addition, the state relies on the *grupos* for jobs, investment, and taxes. Not only the *grupos* but also the paramilitary groups are able to penetrate state institutions.

Banking, Financial and Capital Markets

The Colombian stock market is small with low market capitalization, has a few listed companies, a low volume of transactions and is shallow with few types of fund. Colombia's principal stock exchange, the Bolsa de Valores de Colombia was created in 2001. By 2007, the Bolsa's stock market capitalization was US$59 billion.[69] As of 2010, the Bolsa had about twenty shares actively traded, with market capitalization 60 percent of GDP compared with 100 percent in Chile.[70] The Bolsa was also criticized on the grounds that it lacked proactivity, was inward-looking in orientation, failed to go beyond simply fulfilling its institutional mandate, and contributed very little to economic development. In May 2011, Chile, Peru and Colombia created a common trading platform—the Latin American Integrated Market (Mercado Integrado Latinoamericano, or Mila)—by formally combining the operations of their stock markets. This development is expected to contribute to the development of the Colombian equity market by drawing more liquidity.

According to Venture Equity Latin America (VELA), Colombia is highly underrepresented in venture capital transactions. For instance, Colombia represented only 37 transactions of the 1403 in VELA.[71] The environment, however, is improving. According to the Latin American Venture Capital Association (LAVCA), Colombia ranked fourth among Latin American economies, with the most favorable environment for private equity investment (only behind Chile, Brazil and Mexico).

The underdevelopment of the Colombian stock market can be attributed to the demand and supply sides. In terms of the structure of corporate Colombia, the largest firms in the country have shown reluctance and resistance to list on the stock market. Being mostly family-owned, they are characterized by a conservative mindset, and thus tend to avoid volatility in equity markets. As in Mexico, the Colombian middle classes are much more inclined towards real-estate investments than putting their money in the stock market.[72] Due primarily to an underdeveloped capital market, Colombia-bound foreign investors do not have a lot of investment choices other than in the property market.

Colombia's small businesses and people have traditionally lacked access to banking and finance. One estimate suggested that in 2007 even in the capital city, Bogotá, fewer than 40 percent of families had access to the financial system.[73]

While banks in many developing countries have adopted lending policies that are too conservative, Colombian banks have been reasonably well managed. One indicator to look at is the liquidity ratio of liquid assets to total deposits. Banks in most developing countries tend to exhibit a high propensity to maintain high proportions of their assets in liquid forms such as cash, deposits with other banks, central bank debt and short-term government securities. For instance, in a study of a sample of thirty-five developing countries, the mean of liquidity ratio was 45 percent and the ratio was to 126 percent in Argentina compared to 2 percent in the UK and 6.5 percent in the US.[74] The liquidity ratio for Colombia was 33 percent.

Colombia's foreign remittances are higher than those of most Latin American countries. In 2006, Colombia ranked third among Latin American countries in total remittances received, just behind Brazil and Mexico. As a proportion of GDP, remittances accounted for 3.3 percent of GDP in Colombia compared to 0.3 percent in Brazil and 2.9 percent in Mexico.[75]

Big multinationals such as Citibank and McDonald's have entered the country. Call centers serving the world are proliferating in the capital city, Bogotá. Foreign direct investment (FDI) in Colombia averaged US\$9.1 billion a year between 2005 and 2008 and was US\$9.5 billion in 2010.[76] This surge in FDI can be primarily attributed to an improvement in security. The FDIs were market access-seeking types, focusing on national as well as regional market. The focal points of FDI in Colombia included financial services, electricity and gas distribution. During the 1990s, foreign ownership increased from 10 percent to 24 percent in the Colombian banking sector.[77]

Access to Market

For many Colombian firms, maximum potential is reached in their home market. The domestic market thus offers little growth opportunity. Firms have realized that the only way to grow would be to expand into foreign markets, possibly through mergers and acquisitions (M&A). An underdeveloped equity market has been a major challenge. The country reached a free trade agreement with the US in 2011, which has increased market access for its firms.

R&D and Technology

Colombians have an abundance of entrepreneurial curiosity and interest. For instance, the world's top two cities from where per capita Google searches for the management thinker "Peter Drucker" originated were Bogotá and Medellín.[78] An article published in *Brand Strategy*[79] even goes so far as to say that Medellín has "the most dynamic and professional business culture". Colombia also has an advantage in the development of business process outsourcing. Analysts point out that Colombians speak "clear, unaccented Spanish".

One observation is that Colombia lacks absorptive capacity and has failed to develop its technological capabilities effectively to utilize FDI inflows as well as foreign development assistance. The country spends very little on innovation and technology. Colombia's R&D spending is estimated at around 0.3 percent of GDP.[80] According to a study conducted by Microsoft across thirty countries, investment in IT was the lowest in Colombia.[81] Among the BBC World Service's twenty-four "most entrepreneur-friendly nations", Colombia was found to have "the least well-developed culture of innovation and entrepreneurship".[82] About two-thirds of the Colombian respondents surveyed by the BBC World Service disagreed with the statement that innovation and creativity were valued in the country.

For many Colombian businesses local diversification was traditionally the only way to grow due to factors such as protectionism and foreign-exchange restrictions. One upshot of this tendency, as in many other Latin American countries, is that Colombia lacks a mature corporate governance culture. Many industries in Colombia are dominated by pre-modern traditional patriarchal family-owned businesses, which are characterized by concentrated ownership structures. They tend to have an expectation of family succession. The country's businesses are adopting responsible business practices and codes of conduct.

Case Conclusion

Various elements of the Colombian entrepreneurial ecosystem have witnessed dramatic progress in the past decade. To some extent, a whole ecosystem developed around drug entrepreneurship has made it challenging to develop productive entrepreneurship in the country. Dismantling the ecosystem is not an easy task. On the plus side, the security situation in Colombia has drastically improved, which is an important precondition for entrepreneurial development. Most potential foreign investors, however, have not yet realized this progress has been made. Policy makers, entrepreneurs and other institutional actors need to take measures to change the country's image as a lawless, violent and dangerous place.

Notes

1. Campbell, N.A., Reece, J.B., Taylor, M.R., Simon, J.E., & Dickey, J.L. 2009, *Biology Concepts & Connections*, 6th edn, San Francisco: Cummings Benjamin, pp. 2, 3.
2. Helms, D.R., Helms, C. W, & Kosinski, R.J. 1997, *Biology in the Laboratory*, London: Macmillan.
3. Hui, C. 2006, "Carrying Capacity, Population Equilibrium, and Environment's Maximal Load", *Ecological Modeling*, 192, pp. 317–320.
4. Helms, D.R., Helms, C. W, & Kosinski, R.J. 1997, *Biology in the Laboratory*, London: Macmillan.
5. Chapin, III, S. F, Walker, B.H., Hobbs, R. J, Hooper, D.U., et al. 1997, "Biotic Control over the Functioning of Ecosystems", *Science*, 277 (5325), pp. 500–504.
6. Fackler, M. 2008, "Samsung Scandal May Herald End of Chaebol's Grip on South Korean Economy", April 23, at www.nytimes.com/2008/04/23/business/worldbusiness/23iht-samsung.4.12281759.html.
7. *Korea Times* 2010, "Korea Times: Korea Has Competitive Support System for Small Firms", June 4.

8. *Economist* 2011, "What Do You Do when You Reach the Top?", November 12, 400(8759), pp. 79–81
9. Dan Richards' interview with Josh Lerner, "Why Public Funding of Venture Capital Has Failed", *Advisor Perspectives*, February 1, 2011, at http://advisorperspectives.com/newsletters11/pdfs/Why_Public_Funding_of_Venture_Capital_Has_Failed.pdf.
10. "Fish Out of Water: Policymakers are Turning their Minds to the Tricky Subject of Promoting Entrepreneurship", October 29, 2009, at www.economist.com/node/14743944.
11. "Prospects Bright for UK's 'Silicon Roundabout'", December 16, 2010, at http://blogs.reuters.com/great-debate-uk/2010/12/16/prospects-bright-for-uks-silicon-roundabout/.
12. Kaplan, R.D. 1996, "War after Peace", *New Republic*, 214(18), pp. 22–23.
13. Isenberg, D.J. 2010, "Entrepreneurship in Haiti", July 18, at www.huffingtonpost.com/daniel-isenberg/entrepreneurship-in-haiti_b_650519.html.
14. Singleton, A. 2008, "The Stigma of Failure is Bad for Britain", January 15, at http://blogs.telegraph.co.uk/alex_singleton/blog/2008/01/15/the_stigma_of_failure_is_bad_for_britain.
15. Sitte, A., & Rheault, M. 2009, "Arab Youth Express Strong Entrepreneurial Spirit", *Gallup Poll Briefing*, June 9, p.3.
16. Theil, S. 2007, "Teaching Entrepreneurship in the Arab World", *Newsweek International*, August 14, 2007, German Marshall Fund of the United States, at www.gmfus.org/publications/article.cfm?id=332.
17. Ho, Y.P., & Wong, P.K. 2007, "Financing, Regulatory Costs and Entrepreneurial Propensity", *Small Business Economics*, 28, pp. 187–204.
18. Gross, D. 2008, "Poverty: Cheap Loans at Insanely High Rates? Give Us More", *Newsweek*, September 20, at www.newsweek.com/id/160074.
19. *Economist* 2008, "Computers without Borders", October 25, at www.economist.com/node/12411854.
20. *Icenews* 2008, "Iceland Green Data Centre Dream still Alive", November 13, 2008, at www.icenews.is/2008/11/13/iceland-green-data-centre-dream-still-alive/.
21. Browning, J., & Valdimarsson, O.R. 2012, "Iceland, Data-center Hub?" March 29, at www.businessweek.com/articles/2012-03-28/iceland-data-center-hub.
22. Samson, I., & Pänke, J. 2009, "Slovakia's Sonderweg to Normalcy", *IP Journal*, June 1, at https://ip-journal.dgap.org/en/article/slovakia%E2%80%99s-sonderweg-normalcy-1.
23. Prysm Group 2010, "Starting a Business in Slovakia", at www.startupoverseas.co.uk/starting-a-business-in-slovakia.
24. Ewing, J. 2009, "The Auto Slump Hits Slovakia", *Zilina Slovakia*, June 19, at www.spiegel.de/international/business/detroit-east-the-auto-slump-hits-slovakia-a-631388.html.
25. Rare earth elements (REE) or rare earth metals are a collection of seventeen chemical elements in the periodic table: scandium, yttrium and the

fifteen lanthanoids. REE are used in technologies such as wind turbine generators, electric vehicle motors, fuel cells and energy-efficient lighting.

26. McKinsey Global Institute, 2010, "Sizing Africa's Business Opportunities", July, at www.mckinseyquarterly.com/Economic_Studies/Productiv ity_Performance/Sizing_Africas_business_opportunities_2633.
27. Hamilton, D. 2010, " Q&A: Verne Global's Lisa Rhodes on Iceland Data Centers", September 2, at www.thewhir.com/web-hosting-news/qa-verne-globals-lisa-rhodes-on-iceland-data-centers.
28. Shah, H.J. 2010, "Valuate the India Opportunity through Incubators, Demographics and PEG", March 9, at http://blogs.wsj.com/india-chief-mentor/2010/03/09/valuate-the-india-opportunity-through-incu bators-demographics-and-peg/.
29. Johnson, M.W., & Suskewicz, J. 2009, "How to Jump-start the Clean Tech Economy", *Harvard Business Review*, 87(11), pp. 52–60.
30. Bertrand, M., Mehta, P., & Mullainathan, S. 2002, "Ferreting out Tunneling: An Application to Indian Business Groups", *Quarterly Journal of Economics*, 117(1), pp. 121–148.
31. Beck, T., Demirgüç-Kunt, A., & Maksimovic, V. 2002, "Financial and Legal Constraints to Firm Growth: Does Size Matter?" World Bank Working Paper 2784. Washington, DC: World Bank.
32. Goyal, A. 2005, "Regulation and De-regulation of the Stock Market in India", September 8, at http://papers.ssrn.com/sol3/papers.cfm?abstract_id=609322.
33. International Consortium for Law and Development, 2004, "Knowledge in the Service of Democratic Social Change", Kyrgyz Workshop on Drafting Anti-corruption Legislation, November 22–26, at www.iclad-law.org/ Country percent20Projects/KyrgyzAlt.html.
34. Fish, S. 2005, *Democracy Derailed in Russia: The Failure of Open Politics.* New York: Cambridge University Press.
35. Epstein, G. 2009, "The Price of Corruption", October 30, at www.forbes. com/2009/10/30/china-coal-corruption-communist-party-beijing-dispatch.html/
36. Whitford, R. 2012, "Why Building Entrepreneurial Capacity is Important to Rwanda", October 16, at http://en.igihe.com/opinions/why-building-entrepreneurial-capacity-is.html.
37. Butera, S. 2012, "Rwanda's Foreign Investments Surge to $476.5million", July 27, at www.newtimes.co.rw/news/index.php?i=15066&a=56391.
38. Whitford, R. 2012, "Why Building Entrepreneurial Capacity is Important to Rwanda", October 16, at http://en.igihe.com/opinions/why-building-entrepreneurial-capacity-is.html.
39. IGIHE 2010, "2012 Investments in Rwanda reached US$1.1Billion", December 22, at http://en.igihe.com/news/2012-investiments-in-rwanda-hit-us-1-1billion.html.
40. Jacobs, S. 2010, "Paul Kagame and the Rwandan Elections: Learning the Lessons of History", *Foreign Policy Journal*, August 13, at www.foreignpol

icyjournal.com/2010/08/13/paul-kagame-and-the-rwandan-elections-learning-the-lessons-of-history/.

41. *Economist* 2004, "Measure First, Then Cut", September 11, 372(8392), at www.economist.com/node/3178693

42. Cerralbo, Y. 2009, "Slovakia a 'Korean-friendly' country", *Korea Herald*, November 17.

43. Dan Richards' interview with Josh Lerner, "Why Public Funding of Venture Capital Has Failed", *Advisor Perspectives*, February 1, 2011, at http://advisorperspectives.com/newsletters11/pdfs/Why_Public_Funding_of_Venture_Capital_Has_Failed.pdf.

44. Pease, S.L. 2009, *The Golden Age of Jewish Achievement*, Deucalion.

45. Brooks, D. 2010, "The Tel Aviv Cluster", January 11, at www.nytimes.com/2010/01/12/opinion/12brooks.html.

46. Shah, H.J. 2010, "Valuate the India Opportunity through Incubators, Demographics and PEG", March 9, at http://blogs.wsj.com/india-chief-mentor/2010/03/09/valuate-the-india-opportunity-through-incubators-demographics-and-peg/.

47. Brooks, D. 2010, "The Tel Aviv Cluster", January 11, at www.nytimes.com/2010/01/12/opinion/12brooks.html.

48. Shah, H.J. 2010, "Valuate the India Opportunity through Incubators, Demographics and PEG", March 9, at http://blogs.wsj.com/india-chief-mentor/2010/03/09/valuate-the-india-opportunity-through-incubators-demographics-and-peg/.

49. Lehrer, E., & Hildreth. J. 2002, "Scandinavia's Surprising Turn from Socialism", *American Enterprise*, 13(8), pp. 42–44.

50. Zawya 2010, "Injaz Al-Arab Board Convenes in Qatar", June 3, at www.zawya.com/story/ZAWYA20100603071642/.

51. Isenberg, D.J. 2010, "How to Start an Entrepreneurial Revolution in Six Months", *Huffington Post*, July 7, at www.huffingtonpost.com/daniel-isenberg/how-to-start-an-entrepren_b_637555.html.

52. Cambieri, G. 2011, "Family Business Challenges Differ between the US and Europe", September 28, at www.campdenfb.com/article/family-business-challenges-differ-between-us-and-europe.

53. Chadha, M. 2007, "Mumbai's Women-only Taxi Service", *BBC News*, May 8, at http://news.bbc.co.uk/2/hi/south_asia/6623211.stm,

54. Campbell, J.L. 2004. *Institutional Change and Globalization*, Princeton, NJ: Princeton University Press.

55. Datamonitor 2010, "DATAMONITOR: Colombia", *Colombia Country Profile*, pp. 1–75.

56. Lesova, P. 2009, "Interested in Colombia? A new ETF Offers Access", *Market Watch*, March 24, at www.marketwatch.com/story/interested-colombia-a-new-etf-offers.

57. Mance, H. 2010, "Waiting Game for Colombia's Informal Workers", BBC News, January 19, at http://news.bbc.co.uk/2/hi/business/8458019.stm.

58. UNDP 2010, *Human Development Report 2010*, at http://hdr.undp.org/en/media/HDR_2010_EN_Complete_reprint.pdf.
59. Arboleda, J., & Correa, H. 2002, "Forced Internal Displacement", in *Colombia: The Economic Foundation of Peace*, ed. Marcelo M. Giugale, Oliver Lafourcade and Connie Luff, Washington, DC: World Bank.
60. Inter-American Development Bank 2006, *Remittances 2005: Promoting Financial Democracy*. Washington, DC: Inter-American Development Bank.
61. Farzad, R. 2007, "Extreme Investing: Inside Colombia", May 28, at www.businessweek.com/stories/2007-05-27/extreme-investing-inside-colombia.
62. *Economist* 1994, "The Wages of Prohibition", December 24, 1994.
63. Rosenberg, M. 2011, "Colombia Shifts from Drugs to Food in Farm Expansion", May 23, at www.reuters.com/article/2011/05/23/us-colombia-agriculture-idUSTRE74M4OQ20110523.
64. US Department of State 2011, "Background Note: Colombia", July 15, Bureau of Western Hemisphere Affairs, at sharing.govdelivery.com/bulletins/GD/USSTATEBPA-159DC7.
65. Lewis, G. 2007, "Who in the World is Entrepreneurial?", *FSB: Fortune Small Business*, 17(5), p. 14.
66. Wilson, P. 1998, *Grandes empresas y gnipos indtistriales latinoam,ericanos: expansion y desajtos en la era de la apertura y la globalizadon*. Mexico City: Siglo Veintiuno.
67. Schneider, B. R. 2009, "A Comparative Political Economy of Diversified Business Groups, or How States Organize Big Business", *Review of International Political Economy*, 16(2), pp. 178–201.
68. Andrade, L.F., Barra, J.M., & Elstrodt, H.-P. 2001, "All in the Familia", *McKinsey Quarterly*, 4, pp. 81–89.
69. Farzad, R. 2007, "Extreme Investing: Inside Colombia", May 28, at www.businessweek.com/stories/2007-05-27/extreme-investing-inside-colombia.
70. Rathbone, J.P. 2010, "Capital Markets: Investors Require Patience More than Nimble Financial Footwork", April 6, at www.ft.com/intl/cms/s/0/53e3395e-4042-11df-8d23-00144feabdc0.html#axzz1VLe1OWo0.
71. Charvel, R. 2009, "Is Private Equity Out of Control in Latin America?", *Journal of Private Equity*, 13(1), pp. 80–88.
72. Portes, A., & Smith, L. 2008, "Institutions and Development in Latin America: A Comparative Analysis", *Studies in Comparative International Development*, 43(2), pp. 101–128.
73. Moreno, L.A. 2007, "Extending Financial Services to Latin America's Poor", *McKinsey Quarterly*, special edition, pp. 83–91.
74. Freedman, P.L., Click, R.W. 2006, "Banks that Don't Lend? Unlocking Credit to Spur Growth in Developing Countries", *Development Policy Review*, 24(3), pp. 279–302.

75. International Fund for Agricultural Development 2007, *Sending Money Home: Worldwide Remittance Flows to Developing Countries*. Rome: International Fund for Agricultural Development.
76. Markey, P. 2011, "Colombia Sees FDI Rising to $10 billion in 2011", March 31, at www.reuters.com/article/2011/03/31/us-latam-summit-colombia-trade-idUSTRE72U5EJ20110331.
77. Andrade, L.F., Barra, J.M., & Elstrodt, H.-P. 2001, "All in the Familia", *McKinsey Quarterly*, Special Edition, Issue 4, pp. 81–89.
78. Farzad, R. 2007, "Extreme Investing: Inside Colombia", May 28, at www.businessweek.com/stories/2007–05–27/extreme-investing-inside-colombia.
79. Clifton, D. 2007, "Mas y mejor for Latino brands", *Brand Strategy*, 217, pp. 54–55.
80. Datamonitor 2010, "DATAMONITOR: Colombia", *Colombia Country Profile*, pp. 1–75.
81. Bahree, M. 2008, "Knitters without Windows", *Forbes*, 182(5), pp. 74–77.
82. Alsema, A. 2011, "Colombia Lacks 'culture of Innovation and Entrepreneurship': BBC", May 25, at colombiareports.com/colombia-news/economy/16532-colombia-lacks-culture-of-innovation-and-entrepreneurship-bbc.html.

3

SOURCES OF ENTREPRENEURIAL FINANCE AND THEIR VARIATION ACROSS THE WORLD

Abstract

Not everyone who wants to become an entrepreneur is able to achieve the goal. A lack of access to capital is often the biggest roadblock for latent entrepreneurs to materialize the goal of owning a business. Availability and the cost of a given source of finance vary across countries, types of ventures and phases of businesses. This chapter examines some of the important sources of entrepreneurial finance for potential and existing entrepreneurs, and international variation of such sources and availability. Specifically, this chapter examines various financing sources such as informal investments, bank financing and other forms of credits, venture capital financing, the capital market, microfinance, supply chain financing and economic aids from non-governmental organizations and international agencies. Also discussed in this chapter is crowdfunding as an alternative financial source.

This chapter's objectives include:

1. To demonstrate an understanding of various types of entrepreneurial financing.
2. To analyze international variations and their sources in the availability of funds as well as types of funds to meet financial needs of potential and existing entrepreneurial ventures.
3. To evaluate the impact of disruptive economic events such as the 2008 global financial crisis and the IT bubble burst on the availability of various types of entrepreneurial finance.
4. To assess the effects of microfinance on the entrepreneurial activities of the poorest people in developing economies.

5. To demonstrate an understanding of motivations of investors associated with various forms of entrepreneurial financing.
6. To assess the appropriateness of various sources of financing for entrepreneurs with different levels of needs and different phases of business operations.
7. To demonstrate an understanding of some of the recent innovations in entrepreneurial financing such as crowdfunding.

3.1. Introduction

Not everyone who wants to start a business venture is able to do so. Lack of access to capital is often the biggest obstacle for latent entrepreneurs to materialize the goal of starting their own business. Economies worldwide vary widely in terms of the availability of funds to meet the financial needs of entrepreneurial ventures, types of available funds and the relative availability of such funds across various phases of a venture. A country's entrepreneurial finance environment is shaped by the diverse motivations of various players such as investors, entrepreneurs, regulatory agencies and non-governmental organizations (NGOs).

For most potential entrepreneurs, business financing is not a problem in most industrialized countries. In these countries, policies, structures and strategies are in place in banks to reduce the risk of lending to SMEs. For instance, SMEs in OECD countries benefit from the fact that financial markets in these countries are highly competitive. Market-based banking in these economies forces banks to achieve high returns. For many banks, financing SMEs is becoming attractive. They are also developing effective techniques which distinguish high- and low-risk SME borrowers, and identify those likely to expand and survive. Banks in industrialized countries have also come up with new business models and products, which derive an increasing proportion of revenue from fees for services rather than interest on loans. Such models favor lending to SMEs. There are also well-established systems for raising money through capital markets.[1]

SMEs in developing countries are more likely to be impeded by the lack of financing than those in developed countries. For many commercial banks in these countries, revenues from fees for services are insignificant. Due primarily to the lack of competition, banks in many emerging markets have been laggards in implementing models which provide incentives to lend to SMEs. This shortage of financing has special implications on the size distribution of firms. Compared with developed countries, firms in emerging markets tend to be heavily concentrated at the top and the bottom. In many cases, big firms are powerful oligarchs, as discussed in Chapter 1, or state-owned enterprises, which have access to bank loans. For instance, some Russian oligarchs received huge loans from state banks and invested in big state companies. Many Western banks have also provided loans to Russia's oligarchs. Likewise, in China, a large proportion of loans from large commercial banks that are state owned go to state-owned enterprises primarily to finance public infrastructure projects.[2]

The characteristics of the banking system in these markets work against SMEs. Many banks are state owned and their credit may be allocated on the basis of government guarantees or in line with government targeting to develop specific sectors. Often banks are subject to ceilings on the interest rates they can charge, which makes it difficult to price credit in a way that reflects the risk of lending to SMEs. Lending to SMEs involves special risks for financial institutions. This means that if banks are earning acceptable returns on other lending, there is no incentive to develop necessary skills to serve SMEs.

For many potential entrepreneurs, the only way to finance their venture would be to rely on informal sources. As explained in Chapter 1, micro-enterprises that are funded through informal sources of capital lack growth opportunities. The shortage of SMEs, also known as the "missing middle", is arguably related to the low rate of economic growth.[3] The availability and composition of formal and informal finances explain the phenomenon of the missing middle.

Despite the ease with which SMEs receive bank loans in OECD economies, innovative SMEs, which create value through the development of technology and innovation, face problems accessing finance in these economies. Such SMEs are perceived as more risky than traditional SMEs or large firms. They often do not meet the criteria for traditional bank loans. Moreover, banks have exhibited higher perceptions of risks with regard to financing innovative SMEs following the so-called dot.com bubble burst which mainly hit the IT and closely related industries between the late 1990s and early 2000s.[4]

3.2. Availability and Costs of Bank Financing

Many entrepreneurs prefer bank loans over other forms of financing as such loans allow them full control of their firms and so give them more incentive to exert their efforts. Traditional bank financing is more important to SMEs because they have fewer alternative options available compared to large enterprises. For instance, large South Korean firms are increasingly using the capital market for financing and have thus dramatically reduced their dependence on bank credit.

As noted earlier, economies worldwide differ widely in terms of the availability and costs of bank loan financing. First, there are significant differences worldwide in the cost of lending (Fig. 3.1). A comparison of annual lending rates (ALR) for the short- and medium-term financing needs of businesses across countries would help us understand the variability of the costs of entrepreneurial finance. ALR would serve as an indicator to assess how easy or difficult it is to access the financial resources or capital for starting and/or continuing a business. The high ALRs (Fig. 3.1) in Brazil and Zaire (now the Democratic Republic of the Congo) are a response to the legacies of their hyperinflationary pasts. For instance, during 1980–1994, Brazil went through hyperinflation with three- to four-digit annual inflation rates. Likewise, the DRC's inflation peaked at about 24,000 percent in 1993–1994.

The real issue for most potential entrepreneurs, however, concerns the availability rather than the cost of capital. In this regard, many OECD countries have realized that focused government intervention is necessary to improve SMEs' access to finance. They have launched a number of programs to use public funds to facilitate SME lending. One example is the European Commission's SME guarantee facility (SMEG) (http://ec.europa.eu/enterprise/policies/finance/cip-financial-instruments/index_en.htm), which encourages banks to make more debt finance available to SMEs such as microcredit and mezzanine finance (which is typically debt capital that is used to finance existing SMEs' expansion; the lender has the right to convert to ownership or equity if the loan is not paid back in time and in full).

The SMEG program reduces the banks' risk exposure by providing co-guarantees, counter-guarantees or direct guarantees. Consequently, large proportions of SMEs have access to bank financing. For instance, in the EU economies, commercial banks are the main source of finance for 79 percent of SMEs.[5]

Perhaps unavailability of financing is a more critical barrier faced by most entrepreneurs in developing countries. For instance, despite high interest rates, there is a demand for credit in most developing economies. For instance, banks in the DRC reject over one-third of credits and loans applications. The fact that they cannot enforce their legal rights as lenders has led to the risk-averse behavior of the banking industry. This situation is a manifestation of a broader structural problem in developing economies such as the DRC, in which a large proportion of the population lacks access to formal banking institutions. A country of sixty-eight million people, the DRC is estimated to have between 60,000 and 100,000 bank accounts. There are about sixty bank branches in the country, which translates to fewer than one branch per one million inhabitants. The total banking sector assets accounted for around 10 percent of GDP in 2006, which is below the average ratio of 25 percent in the rest of SSA. Total credit to the private sector was at 3 percent of GDP in 2006 in the DRC, compared to 12.3 percent for SSA.

The situation is not much different in other SSA countries or developing countries in general. For instance, in Africa, only 20 percent of families have bank accounts—10 percent in Kenya, 5 percent in Tanzania and 15 percent in Liberia.[6] Looking outside Africa, less than 15 percent of the population has access to formal savings or credit products in Pakistan. In Haiti, there are only two banks for every 100,000 people.

On the other hand, in addition to excessive interest rates, some small businesses in the DRC offered several reasons for their unwillingness to borrow from financial institutions including unacceptable credit conditions such as short credit repayment periods and the requirement of high collateral.[7] The constraints associated with loans may also create a barrier to expansion. For instance, micro-loans in the DRC are mainly used for production activities rather than for capital investment, due to their small size and their short-term nature.[8]

Part of the problem also lies in the fact that many developing economies are characterized by the lack, or poor performance, of credit rating agencies providing information about the creditworthiness of SMEs. A national credit bureau would collect and distribute reliable credit information and hence increase transparency and minimize the banks' lending risks. Many emerging economies lack such an agency and some have a poorly functioning one. This situation puts SMEs in a disadvantaged position in the credit market. SMEs tend to be more informationally opaque than large corporations because they often lack certified audited financial statements and thus it is difficult for banks to assess or monitor their financial conditions.

Due to the rapidly increasing internationalization of banking, many foreign banks are active in emerging markets. There is, however, a common accusation that foreign banks "cherry pick" the best borrowers, and lend more to large transparent firms at the expense of SMEs.[9]

Many developing countries also have government-supported programs to help SMEs finance their businesses. For instance, due to its history of high interest rates, Brazil's development bank, the Banco Nacional de Desenvolvimento Econômico e Social (BNDES), dominates long-term debt business. The BNDES provides low-interest

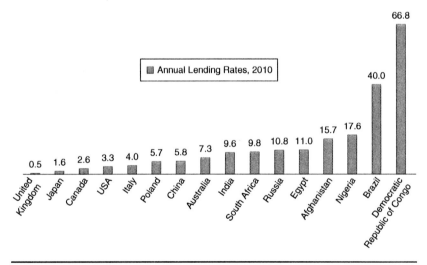

Figure 3.1 Annual lending rates in selected economies (2010)
Source: Annual Lending Rates: International Monetary Fund (IMF), International Financial Statistics–Euromonitor International

loans for longer periods compared to banks or institutional investors. However, due to many bureaucratic red-tape processes, such as the need to notarize signatures for several declarations and certificates, there are significant costs and the process often takes more than six months.[10]

3.3. The Capital Market

Entrepreneurial firms can also raise money through capital markets by issuing debt or equity securities. An initial public offering (IPO), which occurs when a company first sells common shares to the public, is often a major goal for many SMEs. In addition to raising capital to finance growth, a publicly traded company is more likely to gain the trust of their customers, as it is more closely monitored than private corporations.

Some indicators of capital market development include market capitalization (which is the share price times the number of outstanding shares) of listed companies, the number of listed firms, and the size of IPOs. Economies across the world vary widely in the development of the capital market. For instance, according to the World Bank (http://data.worldbank.org/indicator/CM.MKT.LCAP.GD.ZS), market capitalization as a proportion of GDP in 2011 varied from 0.4 percent in Armenia to 358 percent in Hong Kong.

Developing economies such as Armenia lack the appropriate legal and regulatory framework required for the development and functioning of the capital market. There is a lack of effective supervisory and monitoring systems, and bankruptcy regulations, in addition to features that are hostile specifically to entrepreneurs: a lack of transparent accounting and disclosure standards, and poor protection of minority shareholders' rights.[11] Moreover, some emerging markets have unfavorable regulations for foreign investors. For instance, in China, foreign investors require a license under the qualified foreign institutional investor program to access the financial markets.

In some developing economies, raising money through the capital market represents an undesirable option because of socioeconomic, cultural and other structural features. For instance, as stated in Chapter 2, the largest firms in Colombia and some other Latin American countries have shown reluctance and resistance to list on the stock market.

Their family-owned structure means that they tend to reflect more conservative views and to avoid more unpredictable equity markets.[12] At the same time, there is also a low degree of willingness of people to invest in the capital market. In Mexico and Colombia, for instance, the middle classes are much more likely to make property investments than investments in the stock market.[13]

Some emerging economies, however, have experienced strong growth in the capital markets (Fig. 3.2). For instance, the BRIC countries (Brazil, Russia, India and China) accounted for 40 percent of the global IPO proceeds in 2007.[14] Likewise, in 2008, fifteen of the twenty largest IPOs worldwide were from the emerging markets, which included four each from China and Saudi Arabia. China's state-owned Agricultural Bank of China's IPO in 2010, which raised over US$22 billion, had been the largest IPO up until then. In 2010, IPOs' emerging markets raised close to US$200 billion (69 percent of the global total) in 983 deals (71 percent of the global total).

According to Ernst & Young's *Global IPO Trends 2012* report, venture-capital-backed firms' strong preference for IPO has been one factor contributing to the rapid growth of IPOs in emerging markets such as China and India. This trend is in contrast with markets such as Israel, Europe and the US, where mergers and acquisitions (M&As) account for more than 90 percent of exits for VC-backed firms.

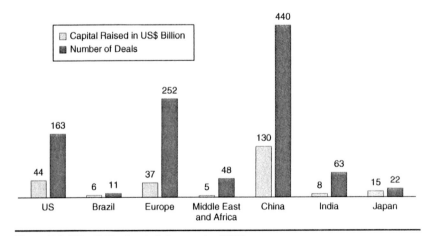

Figure 3.2 IPO activities in selected economies (2010)

Source: ey.com 2011, "Outlook: Global IPOs Continue to Rebound", in *Global IPO Trends 2011*, http://drivkraft. ey.se/wp-content/uploads/2011/06/Global_IPO_trends-report_2011.pdf

3.4. Venture Capital

Venture capital (VC or Venture) is a form of private equity capital, which is normally provided to immature capital-intensive companies that have high growth potential. The investor may be a person or an investment firm. The investor hopes to generate a return through events such as an IPO or trade sale of the company. In a VC-financed company, the entrepreneur is thus likely to benefit from the VC investor's entrepreneurial experience and managerial input. However, the entrepreneur is required to surrender partial ownership of the venture. In a VC-financed project, there are problems related to adverse selection and two-sided moral hazard. Note that adverse selection (anti-selection, or negative selection) arises from information asymmetry between the investor and the entrepreneur. In such a case, one party is unable to determine if the other party is lying. Moral hazard is the problem of not being able to determine if the other party (the entrepreneur or the VC investor in this case) is cheating or acting dishonestly. They cannot verify each other's efforts.

VC is especially attractive for new and innovative companies, which have limited history of operation. They tend to be too small to raise capital in the public markets and as noted above face difficulty in securing a bank loan. VC funds are important not because a large proportion of entrepreneurs receive them but because they are important funding sources for high-growth firms or SMEs with innovative ideas, products, services or new technologies (innovative SMEs). Indeed, less than 1 percent of all startups get VC funding, which makes the VC availability irrelevant for most entrepreneurs. In the US, for instance, most businesses are created as sole proprietorships and service companies. These businesses tend to be less capital-intensive and thus do not seek or obtain VC funding.

The US attracts more VC funding than any other economy. Of the "fastest-growing and most successful companies" in the US, about 16 percent have VC backing.[15] Returns on VC funds to investors in the country have been about 20 percent annually or twice as much as the average of stocks.

Business Angels Business angels or angel investors, who are individuals that provide financial backing through seed money for small-startups usually founded by their family members or friends, are becoming

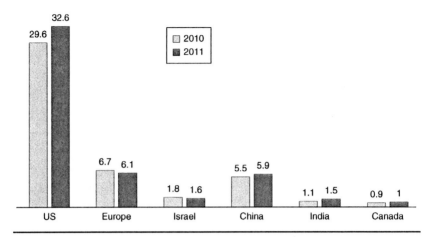

Figure 3.3 Venture capital investments in major economies (in US$ billion)

Source: ey.com 2011, *Globalizing Venture Capital: Global Venture Capital Insights and Trends Report 2011,* http://tinyurl.com/c4p4n72

increasingly important investors in many countries. In particular, the US has dense networks in which successful entrepreneurs mentor startups and play the roles as "business angels", or general partners of VC firms.

One thing that should be noted is that available data and statistics on the VC industry mainly cover formal private equity investments in the industry, that is, funds raised and investments that circulate through "intermediary" VC companies. While there is a lack or limited availability of hard and reliable data on direct investments made by business angels, such investments are believed to be several times higher than formal VC investment in the early stages. According to Konstantin Fokin, President of the National Business Angels Association of Russia, business angels invest in young businesses about US$100 billion annually worldwide, which is 90 percent of all the investment in early-stage businesses.[16]

The VC Industry in Developing Countries   VC and angel investments are a relatively new phenomenon in the developing world. In most of the economies of Middle East and North Africa (MENA), there is the lack of institutional investors that are capable of investing in the VC industry. Likewise, the banks are not interested in being players in the VC industry.[17] Global venture firms, on the other hand, are reluctant to invest in emerging markets due to various challenges such as unfamiliar local laws and accounting standards, stock exchanges that have little experience in technology listings and different negotiating styles.

Some developing economies are, however, becoming increasingly attractive destinations for VC. In a 2009 survey by Deloitte, most (42 percent of) US VC investors considered China to be the most attractive market. It was followed by the US (24 percent) and India (12 percent).[18] According to Ernst & Young, VC in China reached the same level as in Europe in 2011 (Fig. 3.3). Global venture capitalists are also showing increasing interests in Former Soviet Union economies such as Ukraine, Moldova, Latvia and Lithuania as well as other Central and Eastern European economies such as Poland, especially for technology-related VC. These economies have an abundance of young people with math and engineering expertise due to these economies' legacy of highly technical academic institutions. At the same time, angel groups are widening their spread and reach in economies such as China and India thanks to the stock of large numbers of experienced entrepreneurs who have exited their successful ventures.[19]

3.5. Microfinance

Microfinance was started in the 1970s to provide small working capital loans to poor people in the developing world to start a business. A microfinance institution (MFI) typically borrows funds at a low cost and tries to keep loan defaults and overhead expenses very low. Loans are made to entrepreneurs without physical collateral. As discussed above, small-scale entrepreneurs in the DRC are often unable to provide the collateral and security demanded by banks and other lending institutions. In this regard, many entrepreneurs in the rural area of the country have benefited from micro-credit loans offered by NGOs.[20]

The Grameen Bank in Bangladesh founded in 1983 by Muhammad Yunus, who was awarded the Nobel Peace Prize in 2006, was probably the earliest successful example of an MFI. Even before the establishment of the Grameen Bank, Yunus had developed a microfinance program in Jobra village in Bangladesh. In 1976, his program gave a micro-loan of US$27 to a group of forty-two bamboo furniture makers, which was probably the world's first micro-loan.[21]

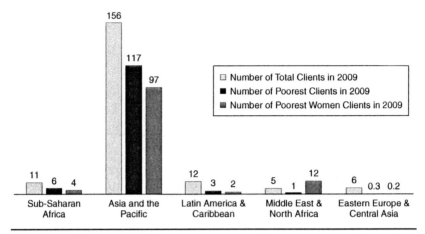

Figure 3.4 Number of families (in millions) served by microfinance programs in various regions
Source: Reed, L.R. 2011, *State of the Microcredit Campaign Report 2011,* Washington, DC: Microedit Campaign Report, p. 47, www.microcreditsummit.org/uploads/resource/document/socr-2011-english_41396.pdf

3.5.1. Size and Structure of the Global Microfinance Industry

The current microfinance industry consists of a wide variety of organizations, which provide microfinance capital in the forms of grants (philanthrocapitalism) as well as pure ventures. In recent years, expanding the spread of microfinance services has also been a focus of national governments, international NGOs, such as the US-based NGO Mercy Corps, supranational organizations, such as the UNDP and Asian Development Bank (ADB), and aid and development agencies funded by Western governments, such as Central Asia Microfinance Alliance (CAMFA–USAID).[22] In the late 1990s, Western donors provided US$400–500 million per year of microcredit.[23] According to the CGAP (Consultative Group to Assist the Poor), foreign-capital flows into the microfinance industry tripled during 2004–2006. During 2004–2007, funding to microfinance from the International Finance Corporation (IFC), which is part of the World Bank Group, grew by 55 percent annually.

Despite the above initiatives, demand exceeds supply by a large factor in the global microfinance industry and market. One estimate suggested that as of 2010, 2.5 billion of the world's adults did not use formal or semiformal financial services (e.g., MFI).[24] A 2007 report from the Deutsche Bank indicated that due to MFIs' funding limitations, only 10 percent of potential borrowers get loans. It was reported that one MFI in India had a waiting list of 50,000 clients that were seeking but unable to find loans.[25] According to the Grameen Foundation, over sixty-five million poor households in India have no access to microfinance.

One estimate suggested that the Grameen Bank model of micro-credit has been replicated in over sixty-five countries including the US. According to the Microcredit Summit Campaign, about 3,700 MFIs reached over 205 million clients by the end of 2010. About 138 million of the clients were among the poorest when they took their first loans, and of the poorest clients, 82 percent were women.[26] An estimate suggested that the size of the global microfinance industry was US$70 billion in 2009.[27]

The latitude in terms of products offered by microfinance companies has also expanded. Nowadays, microfinance provides people on low incomes with diverse financial services such as various types of loan (student loans, home loans), savings, money transfers and insurance. Microfinance is described as one of the highest-profile and most effective examples of the anti-poverty program.[28]

Most microfinance activities are concentrated in the Asia Pacific region (Fig. 3.4). India and Bangladesh together account for about half of all borrowers in the world. As of 2012, MFIs in Bangladesh served about 23 million borrowers.[29] In Central Asian economies, microfinance was only started in the mid-1990s, and thus the penetration rates are small. A study conducted in 2004 indicated that less than 0.5 percent of people in Kazakhstan, the Kyrgyz Republic, Tajikistan and Uzbekistan were served by MFIs.[30]

3.5.2. Profit-seeking Microfinance Programs

The flow of massive private investment highlights the increasing popularity of profit-seeking microfinance programs. Microfinance provided by private investment funds grew from US$600 million in 2004 to US$2 billion in 2006.[31] Compartamos, Mexico's largest MFI, which raised US$400 million from an IPO in 2007, is reported to make a 40 percent return on equity.[32] In India, private-equity firms and other investors have poured billions of dollars into microfinancing. Global investors, venture capitalists and local entrepreneurs have backed SKS Microfinance, which is India's largest MFI, and the second pure MFI, after Mexico's Compartamos Bank, to go for an IPO.

Large multinational banks have also been attracted to the microfinance industry. For instance, Citigroup, Deutsche Bank and HSBC have separate microfinance divisions. As of 2009, Citibank worked with eighty-five MFIs in thirty-five countries.[33] Microfinance has a clear "double bottom line for these multinational banks, social as well as financial, as it allows them to show their corporate social responsibility and to realize attractive returns on investments".[34]

Some countries have relaxed regulations to allow commercial banks to enter into this business. In the Philippines, in 2010, the central bank introduced a policy that allows all banks to lend directly to farmers. Before that, only rural banks that were part of the Micro Enterprises' Access to Banking Services (MABS) program could provide direct loans to farmers.[35]

3.5.3. Repayment Rates and Interest Rates in Microfinance Programs

Despite the fact that loans are made without any physical collateral, the repayment rates in microfinance are reported to be in the 97–98 percent range. MFIs typically rely on a system of peer pressure. In such a system, an individual's success is a function of the responsible behavior of the overall group.

There is also evidence that microfinance customers borrow money from traditional moneylenders to pay off the debts with an MFI. Proof of that claim is evident in the growth of both microfinance as well as traditional moneylending in India. Data from a government survey indicated that, in the 1990s, traditional moneylenders' share in the rural Indian household debt increased from 18 percent to 30 percent.[36] There is peer pressure within microfinance groups to pay back loans. A field observation in Andhra Pradesh state in India indicated that women who borrowed from MFIs needed to rotate loans from other sources, including local moneylenders, to pay to the MFIs.[37]

Interest rates charged by MFIs vary widely and there is no agreement as to what a reasonable rate would be. The average interest rate worldwide is 26 percent. The Indian MFI SKS charges a 28.3 percent annual interest rate.[38] Mexico's Compartamos charges interest rates of around 85 percent.[39] For most poor people who lack access to credit, however, micro-lenders are a better option than the village loan sharks.

3.5.4. Microfinance and Women

One of the most inspiring aspects of microfinance programs is that a significantly higher proportion of women than men are served by these programs. For instance, according to Microcredit Summit Campaign, of the 138 million clients, who were among the poorest when they took their first loan, 82 percent were women.[40] In Eastern Europe and the Commonwealth of Independent States, 62 percent of microfinance clients are women.[41] Likewise, about 70 percent of Uzbekistan's MFI clients are estimated to be women. There are several projects established and implemented to support women's entrepreneurship in the Karakalpakstan Autonomous Region of Uzbekistan. For instance, the NGO, Karakalpakstan Branch of Business Women Association (BWA), which was established in 1997, has 100 percent women clients. The BWA launched SME development and microfinance projects with UNDP's financial and technical support. By 2004, it had 1,000 active borrowers who took loans of an average size of US$35 for producing livestock and poultry, cultivating agricultural products and engaging in petty trade such as selling vegetables and tailoring.

It is easy to see how microcredits can inspire, empower and equip women, especially the poorest ones, to enrich their lives and those of their families. Studies have shown various benefits of microfinance to women such as financial empowerment, increase in self-confidence and reduction in behaviors related to HIV risk.[42] Some observers go as far as to note: "Microfinance has done more to bolster the status of women and to protect them from abuse than any laws could accomplish."[43] The roles of microfinance programs to improve women's standard of living both economically and socially have begun to be recognized at national and international levels. For instance, the year 2005 was promoted as the UN's Year of Microfinance. The idea was to empower women "to improve not only their own lives, but, in a widening circle of impact, the lives of their families, their communities, and their nation".[44]

3.5.5. Some Challenges to Microfinance Programs

There are some drawbacks to microfinance in general as well as to the way such programs are managed. Too small loans, unrealistic and oppressive repayment conditions and a lack of proper business training and other entrepreneurial skills may hinder the borrower's ability productively to utilize microcredits. As for microfinance credits towards women, sufficient training and large enough loans to buy meaningful assets to engage in entrepreneurial activities are critical for the success of such credits.[45]

The microfinance industry mainly exists to meet the investment needs of poor people. However, many observers think that some microfinance loans have been used by borrowers to finance consumption instead of investment. It is also suspected that some borrowers use new loans from an MFI to pay off debts with another MFI.

A downside of microfinance is that poor people who borrow from MFIs are susceptible to exploitation and harassment by the lenders. There is a widespread impression that many MFIs are profiteering at the expense of poor and vulnerable groups. In December 2010, the prime minister of Bangladesh, Sheik Hasina Wazed, noted that MFIs in the country were "sucking blood from the poor in the name of poverty alleviation".[46] She also ordered an investigation into Grameen Bank. Some MFIs in India have been reported to engage in activities that violate human rights. For instance, women borrowers who were not able to repay their loans were reportedly forced to stand outside all day in the sun by some MFIs in India. In other cases, MFI employees were reported to detain the whole group if some members in the group failed to make payments.[47] It was reported that more than eighty micro-loan recipients in India had committed suicide during a few months in 2010 after they defaulted on loans.[48]

3.6. Economic Aid from NGOs and International Agencies

As noted earlier, the investment needs of potential entrepreneurs are not fully met in the developing world. For instance, the needs of some entrepreneurs, such as street vendors who want to own a shop, are beyond the scope of micro-credit and are unbankable for commercial banks. A complaint that is often heard about micro-credit is that the loans are too small. For instance, loans made by microfinance organizations in Uzbekistan average US$145.[49]

Many observers expect that double-bottom-line-motivated "hybrid funding" approaches involving government, non-profit organizations and businesses, which measure success in terms of social benefits as well as financial returns, are likely to have a real impact in reducing poverty.[50] There have been some initiatives on this front. Some NGOs and international agencies have come up with alternative forms of financing to meet some of the need. In May 2009, the Africa Commission, which is an initiative by the Danish government, launched a US$3-billion "guarantee facility" to mobilize loans for small businesses.[51]

3.6.1. Acumen Fund's Combination of Venture Capital and Economic Aid

In the context of entrepreneurial projects targeted at poor people, the New York-based Acumen Fund's (www.acumenfund.org) philanthropic VC fund deserves mention. Acumen is a non-profit organization, which provides profit-motivated "patient capital" with returns that are below the market rate. As of 2012, Acumen invested US$75 million in India, Pakistan, Kenya, Tanzania, Uganda and Rwanda in mosquito netting, drinking water, affordable housing and other projects.

In April 2011, Acumen invested US$1.9 million in NRSP Microfinance Bank Limited, a Pakistani microfinance bank, which is majority owned by the country's National Rural Support Program. Acumen's financial injection enabled the bank to lend amounts of up to US$350 to farmers. While the bank charges an average annual interest rate of 28 percent, this rate is much lower than those charged by the local moneylenders.[52] As another example, Acumen has provided management help in an anti-malaria bed nets company in Tanzania. Note that about thirty-five million people in Tanzania are at risk from malaria. About 100,000 deaths are attributed to malaria every year in the country, about 80,000 of which are the deaths of children under 5.[53]

In India, Acumen Fund has teamed up with HLL to fight maternal mortality among the low-income population. HLL and Acumen Fund have formed LifeSpring Hospitals Private Limited as a 50/50 equity partnership joint venture. LifeSpring Hospitals aims to provide low-cost health care services, especially in the area of reproductive health. The first LifeSpring Hospital was launched in Hyderabad in 2005. The hospital serves the bottom 60 percent of the Indian population.[54]

Acumen has also invested in WaterHealth International's (WHI) clean drinking water projects. WHI's rural community water systems have provided access to safe, clean and affordable water to one million people in India alone. Acumen provided a loan guarantee, which helped WHI establish a US$1 million debt facility from the Indian bank, ICICI.[55]

In many ways, Acumen's business model functions in the same manner as those of micro-lenders. A major difference, however, is that the loans and projects are bigger than those that are typically funded by microfinance companies.[56] Acumen argues that its businesses models are more sustainable than "giveaways" for two reasons. First, Acumen's businesses earn profits. Second, they treat poor people as customers.[57]

3.7. Crowdfunding

Crowdfunding, which involves raising small amounts of capital from a large number of individuals, is considered to be a major disruption in entrepreneurial financing. Key elements of crowdfunding include an online platform, an individual or an entity that needs funding, and a community willing to contribute to the funds. Due primarily to the current regulatory restrictions, most crowdfunding investments may not involve equity or profit sharing for the contributors, and there may not be a guarantee of interest or that the money is to be paid back. According to *Massolution*, 170 crowdfunding platforms, which accounted for about 38 percent of the total number of platforms, raised US$1.5 billion to fund over 1 million projects in 2011.[58] Another study suggested that the amount of money raised by crowdfunding platforms during 2012 would reach US$2.8 billion.[59]

Economies worldwide are rapidly adjusting their regulatory frameworks to take advantage of the opportunities offered by crowdfunding. For instance, in 2012, the US passed the Jumpstart Our Business Startups (JOBS) Act, which was signed into law by President Obama in April 2012. The JOBS Act allows small firms to sell equity stakes online to a large number of investors. Businesses will not face a wide array of rules and red tape involved with larger equity offerings as long as they are looking to raise less than US$1 million. This is important, as most entrepreneurs are unable or unwilling to take the time to complete a huge amount of paperwork.

The New York-based website, Kickstarter (www.kickstarter.com/) was started in 2009, which is among the most well-known crowdfunding websites. As of August 2012, over a million contributors had funded US$274 million to more than 28,000 ideas.[60] Average project size was reported in the range of US$5,000. The company is backed by Union Square Ventures and other firms and takes 5 percent of the money raised on its site. Other well-known crowdfunding platforms include Indiegogo, and Crowdfunder.

Since the laws in many economies do not allow selling equity stakes to crowdfunding backers, they may receive token gifts, rewards and recognition. Some crowdfunding platforms such as Indiegogo and Kickstarter are training consumers to commit to buy goods even before their existence.

In the past few years, crowdfunding sites have mushroomed. Crowdsourcing.org estimated that there would be more than 530 crowdfunding platforms (CFPs) by the end of 2012. As of August 2012, the US had 191 CFPs, the UK had 44, the rest of the Europe had 100. Analysts suggest that it is important for an entrepreneur to make sure that the platforms are reliable and comply with legal requirements. Sherwood Neiss, co-founder of Startup Exemption, emphasized that in order to minimize the risks of fraud, crowdfunding must begin with the entrepreneur's personal social networks.

3.7.1. Some Examples of Successful Ventures that Raised Money by Crowdfunding

Eric Migicovsky's Pebble watch Venture in the US Eric Migicovsky, the founder of Pebble watch, thought he had a great idea. His app-supported "smartwatch" would connect to an iPhone or Android phone via Bluetooth to provide a number of useful functions including messaging notifications, music control, distance and pace calculations for runners, swimmers or bikers. His idea, however, was rejected by a number of venture capitalists. On April 11, 2012, Migicovsky posted his idea on Kickstarter. He had set his fundraising goal at US$100,000. Within about twenty-four hours, he had raised US$1 million. As of May 3, the project had raised over US$8.3 million from about 56,000 contributors who pledged from US$100 to US$10,000.[61] As of August 2012, he had raised US$10.3 million.[62]

The contributors who supported Migicovsky's project will get a "cool" watch, but no equity in his company. This is because the Securities and Exchange Act of 1934 limits the number of investors a company can have before it goes public and makes this type of exchange illegal. Thus a Kickstarter pledge may be an expression of confidence or a preorder, but it cannot be an investment. This means that Kickstarter projects have "backers" but no investors.

Choi Yong-bae's Film 26 Years in South Korea   Choi Yong-bae is a seasoned South Korean film producer. He wanted to make a film entitled *26 Years*, about the South Korean president, who allegedly ordered the massacre of democracy protesters in Gwangju city in the late 1970s. He bought the film rights in 2006 and made investment pitches to the top four South Korean entertainment companies, which together account for over 90 percent of the country's film investment and distribution. He was turned down for four years. Yong-bae said: "Some said their companies can't invest in such a politically sensitive movie ahead of the presidential election this year [in 2012]. Others initially said yes but then changed their mind without giving any reasons."

In early 2012, Choi set up a crowdfunding website for *26 Years*. In less than three months, over 12,000 people contributed about US$404,000 in exchange for movie tickets and small gifts. Some of the donors reportedly said that they felt a sense of indebtedness and obligation to the Gwangju citizens who had risked their lives for democracy.

Word of mouth and social media helped the continuous growth in contributions. While donations he received accounted for only a small proportion of the movie's US$4.1 million budget, the crowdfunding project created a lot of buzz, which helped attract the attention of rich individuals who were willing to invest in the movie. By October 2012, about 90 percent of the entire budget was secured.[63] The movie opened in theaters in December 2012 and took the number one spot.

3.8. Supply Chain Financing

Supply chain financing is a new mode of financing in which companies collaborate with financial institutions to provide financing and other related services such as technical assistance, management, corporate governance and legal compliance to small firms in the company's supply chain. For instance, the Brazilian company VCP has collaborated with the bank ABN AMRO Real in its Poupança Florestal (Forest Savings Account) program, which provides farmers with financial resources. VCP also provides seedlings and technical assistance to plant eucalyptus, and has committed to buying the timber at a fair price after seven years. The Forest Savings Account program is supported by local partnerships with governmental agencies and universities.[64]

Another example is PepsiCo, which started supply chain financing in India in the 1990s through a contract farming arrangement with farmers in the Punjab state to buy tomatoes and chilies. Subsequently the company extended this model to other states and diverse agricultural commodities. It has collaborated with State Bank of India (SBI), which has provided credits at low interest rates to over 12,000 farmers in six states in India. In addition, PepsiCo has also collaborated with another Indian bank, ICICI, to provide farmers with weather insurance.[65]

South Africa's Anglo American provides a further example of a company which has managed three funds—the Supply Chain Fund, the Anglo Khula Mining Fund and the Small Business Start-Up Fund—through Anglo Zimele, its enterprise development and empowerment initiative. Anglo Zimele provides financing to small firms and provides support in diverse areas such as management, corporate governance, legal compliance, accounting, administration, public relations, and environment, health and safety.[66]

3.9. Informal Financing Sources

In addition to the number of formal financing sources discussed above, informal financing sources also exist. The importance of informal sources is readily understood within the context of the lack of access to formal financing. According to the Global Financial Inclusion Database, which covers 184 countries, 59 percent of adults and 55 percent of borrowers in developing countries have no bank accounts.[67]

GEM estimates indicated that several million entrepreneurial firms in forty-two countries received US$600 billion from 208 million informal investors in 2006.[68] This amount is significantly bigger than investments made by formal venture capitalists, which amounted to US$37.3 billion in 11,066 companies in all the eighty-five countries included in GEM in 2005.

Informal financing often involves small short-term loans to borrowers in rural areas. Informal financial institutions often serve the lower end of the market and are complementary to the formal financial system. Two important questions arise: the first is how informal sources of finance can exist where formal sources cannot. The second concerns the financing gap. The answer to the first question involves considering informal investors' superior information about the entrepreneur or enforcement possibilities that reduce problems such as adverse selection and moral hazard. Informal financial institutions rely on relationships and thus have advantages that enable them to lend, efficiently monitor and enforce repayment to the entrepreneurs that formal investors such as commercial banks may not trust. The answer to the second question lies in the lack of availability of sufficient funds and the relatively high cost of capital. The limited and costly funds constrain growth.[69] Moreover, monitoring and enforcement mechanisms of informal financial institutions are ill equipped and ineffective, which makes them unprepared to scale up investments or to move to the formal sector.[70]

3.9.1. Informal Equity Funding

A potential entrepreneur's own savings as well as help from friends and family are among the first sources of capital for the majority of entrepreneurial activities. These informal investments are among the largest and most popular sources of finance for entrepreneurs. A report from the Kauffman Foundation and Babson College noted: "Small investments primarily by the so-called 4Fs—founders, family, friends and foolhardy strangers—are crucial in funding not only micro-companies but also future superstars."[71] Funding from the first 3Fs are also known as "love money". An estimate suggested that, in 2007, informal funding to new firms in thirty-seven countries was US$298 billion.[72]

A study conducted in Canada identified three main types of informal investor in private equity markets: relationship investors, opportunity-based investors and angel investors.[73] We discussed in detail the concept of angel investors earlier in this chapter. Here we will focus on the first two of these three categories of informal investors.

Friends, family members, business associates, employees and consultants are some of the major sources of relationship capital. These investors may lack knowledge related to market opportunity or the technological risk of the firm in which they are investing. These investors' pre-existing relationships with the entrepreneur would help minimize agency risk, i.e., the risk associated with the entrepreneur's pursuance of his or her own interests instead of that of the firm. Some also have the ability to engage in long-term monitoring of the company.

Opportunity-based capital is drawn from individuals or firms that have no relationship to the entrepreneurs. They often have a limited pool of capital to invest and are presented with opportunities by the entrepreneurs. Opportunity-based investors often prefer to invest in earlier-stage investments. They tend to have limited knowledge about the firm they are investing in as well as its investment prospects. They also have limited ability to engage in effective monitoring.

Studies conducted in Canada and the US have indicated that the first two investor types—relationship investors and opportunity-based investors—are a major total source of capital. They often invest smaller amounts than angel investors and do so close to home. According to GEM, 5.3 percent of the US adult population made informal investments during 2008–2010. US informal investments amounted to about US$51 billion in 2010, of which US$9.4 billion was angel investment and US$41.6 billion was from friends and family.[74] Informal investments in the US are significantly more prevalent compared to venture capital funds, which amounted to US$11.6 billion in 2010.[75]

3.9.2. Informal Sources of Debt Financing

While formal sources such as commercial banks are often the most popular sources for debt financing for entrepreneurs in the industrialized countries, the informal sector is considered a competitor to the formal.[76] Informal financial institutions refer to non-market institutions in various forms that make little or no use of the formal legal system for contract enforcement. Some examples include credit cooperatives, moneylenders, informal credit and insurance, and rotating savings and credit associations (ROSCAs). Credit cooperatives collect money from members and lend at low interest rates. While ROSCAs are found all over the world, they are especially prevalent in the developing countries of Asia, Africa and Latin America. In ROSCAs, typically the members pool their savings and make regular cyclical contributions to a common fund, which is given to one member as a lump sum in each cycle.

In most developing countries, informal institutions are a means to overcome the limitations of the formal institutions. For instance, a high degree of reliance on informal financial institutions in China can be attributed to the fact that the government uses the equity markets as a means for privatizing the state-owned enterprises. Most of China's large IPOs are former SOEs.[77] Most private firms thus rely on the informal institutions to raise capital.

Informal arrangements often work better than formal systems in developing countries' settings, because relationships are important to people and in this process they do not risk losing them. Several of these institutions also operate as loan sharks in developing countries, charging extremely high interest rates.

3.10. International Remittances as Sources of Entrepreneurial Financing

International remittances are an important source of financing in many developing countries (Fig. 3.5). A study of the International Fund for Agricultural Development (IFAD) indicated that there are 150 million migrants worldwide. An estimate of the World Bank suggested that remittance flows to developing countries would reach US$406 billion in 2012 and US$534 billion in 2015.[78] In most SSA economies, remittances sent by emigrants are almost as high as export earnings or official development assistance.[79] Likewise, in Latin America, remittance flows are higher than foreign direct investment and official development assistance combined.[80]

While some studies have shown that remittances are mainly used for consumption rather than investment activities, research has also indicated that households receiving international remittances tend to invest more in entrepreneurial activities than those not receiving them.[81] Remittances contribute to entrepreneurship by increasing savings and promoting credit mobilization and other forms of investment. Remittance-receiving families often receive funds that are much larger than required for immediate expenditure. They thus deposit the excess funds in the formal banking system, which enhance banking system liquidity. In India, which is the highest remittance-receiving country, remittances have led to the establishment of new businesses and social service organizations such as nursing homes and educational institutions.[82] In January 2010, India's Gujarat state's chief minister noted that the state's economy was growing despite the global financial crisis due to "record-breaking investments made by the Indian diasporas".[83]

Use of international remittances to stimulate entrepreneurship development is becoming a central focus of some international institutions. In 2004, the G8 adopted the Action Plan "Applying the Power of Entrepreneurship to the Eradication of Poverty". This Plan recognized the important role of remittances in the development of the private sector in developing economies.[84]

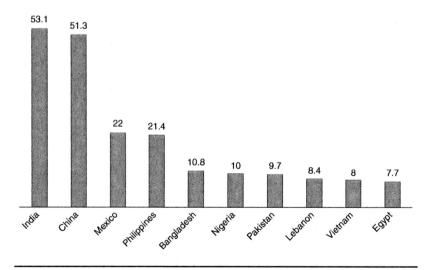

Figure 3.5 Remittance inflows in the top ten recipients (2010, US$ billion)

3.11. Concluding Comments

A variety of sources exist to meet the financial needs of existing and potential entrepreneurs. Availability and affordability of a given source vary across countries, types of ventures and the phases of a business. While in recent years there has been a dramatic increase in the availability of different sources of finance for potential entrepreneurs in emerging economies, supplies are insufficient to meet the financing needs of potential entrepreneurs. Financing SMEs is a risky proposition for many banks in emerging markets. While the largest firms use formal sources of finance (e.g., bank loans in China mostly go to SMEs), the smallest tend to rely more on informal finance.

Microfinance deserves special attention in the context of emerging economies. In many cases, what seems to be happening, however, is that MFIs are focusing more on increasing repayment rates rather than on encouraging productive utilization of micro-credits. In this regard, one way to increase the success rate of microfinance programs is to provide trainings that can address the lack of business and entrepreneurial skills.

Given the important roles of microcredit and microfinance among the poorest of the poor, efforts should be made to boost their effectiveness and diffusion. Many potential entrepreneurs are unaware of the diverse financing options that they may access. Improving awareness is also important.

3.12. Review Questions

1. What are some of the potential barriers that MFIs are likely to face in industrialized countries?
2. What are some of the barriers for the development of the VC industry in the developing world?
3. What are some of the key factors that have led to the phenomenon of the "missing middle" in developing economies?

3.13. Critical Discussion Questions

1. Do you think that there should be an appropriate interest rate that MFIs can justify charging to potential borrowers? What factors would determine such rates?

2. Do you agree with the following statement: "Microfinance has done more to bolster the status of women and to protect them from abuse than any laws could accomplish"? Why?

3.14. End-of-chapter Case: Microfinance Programs and Village Phone Ladies

When Iqbal Quadir was putting together his project of providing mobile phones to rural Bangladeshis, his idea was not well received by development agencies and telecommunications companies.[85] In fact, until not long ago, governments in many developing countries viewed mobile phones essentially as the communication tools of rich business people.

Quadir and Grameen Foundation teamed up to establish GrameenPhone (GP), the village-phone model in Bangladesh. Grameen Foundation is the not-for-profit organization set up by Muhammad Yunus, the founder of Grameen Bank (GB). GB provided small loans without collateral to the Bangladeshis who were "unbankable" for other financial institutions.[86] Telenor AS of Norway also collaborated in the establishment of GP.

Entrepreneurial Activities and Multiplier Effects Associated with Mobile Phones

Mobile phones have facilitated micro-entrepreneurship and brought multiplier effects as well as social changes in Bangladesh. The following are some representative examples:[87]

- One woman thought of raising a large number of chickens. She had not been able to undertake the project earlier because she was afraid that if the chickens developed diseases, she would not be able to call a veterinarian on time.
- Another woman reported that she was able to save her child who was running a high fever by contacting the doctor on time.
- A man reported that he was planning to cultivate bananas on a large scale because mobile phones would enable him to obtain the market price on time to make effective selling decisions.

- Immigrant workers throughout the world with roots in Bangladeshi villages call home to find out how their families are doing and if the money they sent is reaching its destination.

The Phone Lady: Social and Economic Success

The cell phone lady in Bangladesh is considered to be the classic case of a successful microfinancing project in the developing world. By 2009, there were about 360,000 village phone ladies, who had taken loans of BDT 2.57 billion (US$40 million). In 2009, village telephone ladies accounted for 2.6 percent of total cellular phone subscribers of GP but accounted for 33 percent of all calls.[88]

One of the challenges for many women in Bangladesh becoming village phone operators concerned literacy in the English language. One of the criteria for selecting a GP village phone operator is that at least one member of the family knows English letters and numbers. For those interested in becoming operators but lacking such knowledge, however, GP provides training and education services.

Phone ladies sell their minutes to individual callers. Their phones are thus used by many people. Research conducted in the early 2000s indicated that each phone served an average of nearly seventy customers in Bangladesh.[89]

With the increase in income and participation in family decision-making, women have become more socially empowered in Bangladesh. Because villagers have to travel to the phone ladies' homes to make or receive calls, their homes have become an important place in the village. Moreover, unlike in other public places, women can go to the village phone office unescorted by a male relative.[90]

Cell phone ladies in Bangladesh have been able to buy houses and send their children to schools and colleges. The village phone model has been replicated in a number of countries such as Afghanistan, Cameroon, Indonesia, Rwanda and Uganda. In Afghanistan, on average, the village phone ladies pay off the micro-loan required to buy their equipment in eight months and then are able to earn US$50–100 a month.

The International Finance Program has reported many success stories related to the village phone model across the world. In one such story in Rwanda, Marie Claire runs her village phone business from her restaurant's private room. Her income from the phone business allowed her to pay school fees for her children. She has bought land and started constructing a house for her family. She has plans to start a second phone business. Her future plans also included buying a truck and selling local produce in Kigali, the capital city of Rwanda.[91] Overall, the phone business substantially improved the living standards of the families of Marie Claire and many other village phone ladies.

Notes

1. OECD 2013, "Financing SMEs and Entrepreneurs 2013: An OECD Scoreboard", April 17, at www.oecd.org/cfe/smes/.
2. Yan, L. 2012, "Development Finance", *Chinese Economy*, 45(1), pp. 8–27.
3. Lee, S., & Persson, P. 2012, Financing from Family and Friends, *NYU Stern Working Paper FIN-12-007*, August 30, at http://papers.ssrn.com/sol3/papers.cfm?abstract_id=2086625.
4. OECD 2006, "Financing SMEs and Entrepreneurs", *Policy Brief*, November, at www.oecd.org/cfe/37704120.pdf.
5. Ibid.
6. Dovi, E. 2011, "Boosting Domestic Savings in Africa", *Africa Renewal*, 22(3), at www.un.org/africarenewal/magazine/october-2008/boosting-domestic-savings-africa.
7. Ulloa, A., Katz, F., & Kekeh, N. 2009, "Democratic Republic of the Congo: A Study of Binding Constraints", at www.hks.harvard.edu/fs/drodrik/Growth%20diagnostics%20papers/DRC_Growth_Diagnostic.pdf.
8. Ibid.
9. Degryse, H., Havrylchyk, O., Jurzyk, E., & Kozak, S. 2009, "Foreign Bank Entry and Credit Allocation in Emerging Markets", at www.imf.org/external/pubs/ft/wp/2009/wp09270.pdf.
10. *The Brazil Business* 2011, "7 Challenges SMES Face in Brazil", December 13, at http://thebrazilbusiness.com/article/7-challenges-smes-face-in-brazil.
11. De la Torre, A., Gozzi, J., & Schmukler, S. (2007) "Capital Market Development: Whither Latin America?", Policy Research Working Paper No. 4156, Geneva: World Bank.
12. Rathbone, J.P. 2010, "Capital Markets: Investors Require Patience More than Nimble Financial Footwork", April 6, at www.ft.com/cms/s/0/53e3395e-4042-11df-8d23-00144feabdc0.html#axzz2mRxvfhT7.
13. Portes, A., & Smith, L. 2008, "Institutions and Development in Latin America: A Comparative Analysis", *Studies in Comparative International Development*, 43(2), pp. 101–128.
14. Ernst & Young 2008, "Global IPO Trends Report", at www.ey.com/GL/en/Services/Strategic-Growth-Markets/SGM_IPO_Trends_2008.

15. Kedrosky, P. 2009, *Right-Sizing the U.S. Venture Capital Industry*, Kansas City, MO: Ewing Marion Kauffman Foundation.
16. National Business-angels Association 2012, "European Business Angel Network Congress", at http://rusangels.ru/en/congress/y2012/home/european-business-angel-network-congress/.
17. OECD 2006, "MENA Investment Policy Brief", 1, April, at www.oecd.org/mena/investment/37256468.pdf.
18. Deloitte 2009, *Global Trends in Venture Capital: 2009 Global Report*, Deloitte Touche Tohmatsu.
19. Ernst & Young 2012, *Globalizing Venture Capital: Global Venture Capital Insights and Trends Report 2011*, at www.ey.com/GL/en/Services/Strategic-Growth-Markets/Global-venture-capital-insights-and-trends-report-2011—-Paradigm-shifts-in-global-capital.
20. Ulloa, A., Katz, F., & Kekeh, N. 2009, "Democratic Republic of the Congo: A Study of Binding Constraints", at www.hks.harvard.edu/fs/drodrik/Growth%20diagnostics%20papers/DRC_Growth_Diagnostic.pdf.
21. Robertson, T. 2010, "Dean's Column: A Force for Good", *Financial Times*, January 25, at www.ft.com/cms/s/2/86064f60-ffd4–11de-ad8c-00144feabdc0.html.
22. Gulnoz, B., & Malohat, G. 2009, "Impact of Microfinance on Alleviating Rural Poverty in Uzbekistan", *Problems of Economic Transition*, 52 (2), pp. 67–85.
23. Dokmo, C. L., & Reed, L. 1998/1999, "Building Blocks", *Harvard International Review*, 21(1), pp. 66–67.
24. Chaia, A., Goland, T., & Schiff, R. 2010, "Counting the World's Unbanked", *McKinsey Quarterly*, 2, pp. 98–99.
25. Engen, J. 2009, "Microfinance: Ready for its Next Big Leap?", *American Banker*, at.www.americanbanker.com/magazine/119_2/-372021–1.html.
26. Maes, J.P., & Reed, L.R. 2012, "State of the Microcredit Summit Campaign Report 2012", at www.microcreditsummit.org/resource/46/state-of-the-microcredit-summit.html.
27. Bajaj, V. 2011, "Microlenders, Honored with Nobel, Are Struggling", January 5, at www.nytimes.com/2011/01/06/business/global/06micro.html?pagewanted=all.
28. Hubbard, G., & Duggan, W. 2009, *The Aid Trap*, New York: Columbia University Press.
29. Rhyne, E. 2012, "Microfinance in Bangladesh: It's Not What You Thought", February 2, www.huffingtonpost.com/elisabeth-rhyne/microfinance-in-banglades_b_1266759.html.
30. The World Bank 2004, *Microfinance and the Poor in Central Asia: Challenges and Opportunities*, Agriculture and Rural Development Discussion Paper 6, World Bank, Europe and Central Asia Region, May 2004, at http://siteresources.worldbank.org/INTARD/825826–1111400636162/20431907/CentralAsiaMicrofinanceStudyFinalPrint.pdf.

31. *Economist* 2009, "Sub-par but not Subprime", May 19, at www.economist. com/node/13342261.
32. Evans, J. 2010, "Microfinance's Midlife Crisis", March 1, at http:// online.wsj.com/article/NA_WSJ_PUB:SB100014240527487033 15004575073510472268430.html.
33. Engen, J. 2009, "Microfinance: Ready for its Next Big Leap?", *American Banker*, at.www.americanbanker.com/magazine/119_2/-372021–1.html.
34. Hermes, N., Lensink, R., & Meesters, A. 2011, "Outreach and Efficiency of Microfinance Institutions", *World Development*, 39(6), pp. 938–948.
35. Remo, M. 2010, "Big Banks Can Now Lend Directly to Farmers", *Philippine Daily Inquirer*, January 24, at http://business.inquirer.net/money/ topstories/view/20100124–249251/Big-banks-can-now-lend-directly-to-farmers.
36. Gokhale, K. 2009, "As Microfinance Grows in India, So Do Its Rivals", *Wall Street Journal – Eastern Edition*, December 15, pp. A17–A18.
37. Young, S. 2010, "The 'Moral Hazards' of Microfinance: Restructuring Rural Credit in India", *Antipode*, 42(1), pp. 201–223.
38. Economist.com 2010, "SKS Comes to Market: Microfight", July 29, at www.economist.com/node/16702063?story_id=16702063.
39. Evans, J. 2010, "Microfinance's Midlife Crisis", March 1, at http:// online.wsj.com/article/NA_WSJ_PUB:SB10001424052748703315004 575073510472268430.html.
40. Maes, J.P., & Reed, L.R. 2012, "State of the Microcredit Summit Campaign Report 2012", at www.microcreditsummit.org/resource/46/state-of-the-microcredit-summit.html.
41. Molenaar, K. 2009. "Microfinance, its concepts and development, lessons to draw for Europe", Paper prepared for the conference on "Implementing the EU Microcredit Initiative What can be learned from developing and transforming countries?" European Microfinance Network, www. chabal.eu.
42. Agnes, Y. 2002, "Engendering Microfinance Services: Beyond Access", Paper Presented at a Workshop on Women's Empowerment or Feminisation of Debt? Towards A New Agenda In African Microfinance Organised by One World Action, held at Carlton House Terrace, London, March 21–22.
43. Kristof, N.D., & WuDunn, S. 2009, *Half the Sky: Turning Oppression into Opportunity for Women Worldwide*, New York: Knopf Doubleday.
44. UNCDF 2005, *Microfinance and the Millennium Development Goals. A reader's guide to the Millennium Project Reports and MDGs*, Geneva: UNCDF, at www.yearofmicrocredit.org/docs/mdgdoc_MN.pdf.
45. Agnes, Y. 2002, "Engendering Microfinance Services: Beyond Access", Paper Presented at a Workshop on Women's Empowerment or Feminisation of Debt? Towards A New Agenda In African Microfinance Organised by One World Action, held at Carlton House Terrace,

London, March 21–22, at www.genfinance.info/Case%20Studies/CEEWU.pdf.

46. Bajaj, V. 2011, "Microlenders, Honored with Nobel, Are Struggling", January 5, at www.nytimes.com/2011/01/06/business/global/06micro.html?pagewanted=all.

47. Young, S. 2010, "The 'Moral Hazards' of Microfinance: Restructuring Rural Credit in India", *Antipode*, 42(1), pp. 201–223.

48. Biswas, S. 2010, "India's Micro-finance Suicide Epidemic", December 16, at www.bbc.co.uk/news/world-south-asia-11997571.

49. worldbank.org 2007, "Microfinance Development in Uzbekistan: Technical Note", at http://siteresources.worldbank.org/INTUZBEKISTAN/Resources/294087–1246601504640/Policy_Note_on_Microfinance_FINAL_eng.pdf.

50. Engen, J. 2009, "Microfinance: Ready for its Next Big Leap?", *American Banker*, at.www.americanbanker.com/magazine/119_2/-372021–1.html.

51. Smith, A.D. 2009, "Is Trade, Not Aid, the Answer for Africa?", *Guardian*, May 25, at www.theguardian.com/business/2009/may/25/africa-entrepreneurs-charity.

52. Coster, H. 2011, "Can Venture Capital Save The World?", *Forbes.com*, November 30, at www.forbes.com/sites/helencoster/2011/11/30/novogratz/.

53. poverty.ch 2009, "Tanzania's Successful Malaria Bednets Programme", at www.poverty.ch/malaria-bednets/successful-bednet-programme-tanzania.html.

54. LifeSpring Hospitals 2012, "Impact", at www.lifespring.in/impact.html.

55. acumenfund.org. 2009, "WaterHealth International (WHI): Safe Drinking Water for the Poor", at www.acumenfund.org/investment/waterhealth-international.html.

56. Weidner, D. 2009, "Meet Gordon Gekko's Grandchildren: Finding Market-based Solutions to Social and Economic Ills", December 10, at http://online.wsj.com/article/SB10001424052748704240504574586171127809520.html.

57. Kristof, N.D. 2009b, "A Most Meaningful Gift Idea", December 23, at www.nytimes.com/2009/12/24/opinion/24kristof.html.

58. techcrunch.com 2011, "Crowdfunding: $1.5B Raised, 1M Campaigns Funded in 2011; Figures Set To Double in 2012", at http://techcrunch.com/2012/05/08/crowdfunding-state-of-the-union/.

59. Prive, T. 2012, "Top 10 Benefits of Crowdfunding", October 12, at www.forbes.com/sites/tanyaprive/2012/10/12/top-10-benefits-of-crowdfunding-2/2/.

60. Milian, M. 2012, "After Raising Money, Many Kickstarter Projects Fail to Deliver", August 21, at www.businessweek.com/news/2012–08–21/kickstarter-s-funded-projects-see-some-stumbles.

61. Gobble, M.A.M. 2012, " Everyone Is a Venture Capitalist: The New Age of Crowdfunding", *Research Technology Management*, 55(4), pp. 4–7.

62. Milian, M. 2012, "After Raising Money, Many Kickstarter Projects Fail to Deliver", 21 August 2012, at www.businessweek.com/news/2012–08–21/kickstarter-s-funded-projects-see-some-stumbles.
63. Youkyung, L. 2012, "Crowdfunding Rescues Provocative SKorean Film", Associated Press, October 1, at http://finance.yahoo.com/news/crowd funding-rescues-provocative-skorean-film-085601557.html.
64. Boechat, C., & Mokrejs, R. 2008, "Paro Votorantim Celulose e Papel (VCP) in Brazil: Planting Eucalyptus in Partnership with the Rural Poor", at http://growinginclusivemarkets.org/media/cases/Brazil_VCP_2008.pdf.
65. "Activating Collaborative Farming", at http://tinyurl.com/q4g23mb.
66. "Business Linkages: Enabling Access to Markets at the Base of the Pyramid, Report of a Roundtable Dialogue", March 3–5, 2009, Jaipur, India, at http://c.ymcdn.com/sites/www.gbsnonline.org/resource/collection/0814 C059–1ABC-4D1F-B774-A01A9014CF79/BusinessLinkages_Base OfPyramid.pdf.
67. Franklin, A., Qian, J., & Qian, M. 2005, "Law, Finance, and Economic Growth in China", *Journal of Financial Economics*, 77(1), pp. 57–116.
68. Bygrave, W.D., & Quill, M. 2006, "Financing Report", GEM, at www.gemconsortium.org/docs/download/274.
69. Lee, S., & Persson, P. 2012, "Financing from Family and Friends", *NYU Stern Working Paper FIN-12-007*, August 30, at http://papers.ssrn.com/sol3/papers.cfm?abstract_id=2086625.
70. Ayyagari, M., Asli, D., & Maksimovic, V. 2010, "Formal versus Informal Finance: Evidence from China", *Review of Financial Studies*, 23(8), pp. 3048–3097.
71. Cook, J. 2003, "Venture Capital: Start-ups Know What Friends Are For", seattlepi.com, August 15, at www.seattlepi.com/venture/135102_vc15.html.
72. Alhorr, H.S., Moore, C.B., & Payne, G.T. 2008, "The Impact of Economic Integration on Cross-Border Venture Capital Investments: Evidence From the European Union", *Entrepreneurship: Theory & Practice*, 32(5), pp. 897–917.
73. Robinson, M.J., & Cottrell, T.J. 2007, "Investment Patterns of Informal Investors in the Alberta Private Equity Market", *Journal of Small Business Management*, 45(1), pp. 47–67.
74. Shane, S. 2011, "How Much Do Informal Investors Put into Start-ups?", September 8, at www.forbes.com/sites/scottshane/2011/09/08/how-much-do-informal-investors-put-into-start-ups/.
75. Schonfeld, E. 2011, "Venture Funds Raised 14 Percent Less in 2010", January 12, at http://techcrunch.com/2011/01/12/venture-funds-14-per cent-less-2010/.
76. Ayyagari, M., Asli, D., & Maksimovic, V. 2010, "Formal versus Informal Finance: Evidence from China", *Review of Financial Studies*, 23(8), pp. 3048–3097.
77. Ibid.

78. worldbank.org 2012, "Remittances to Developing Countries Will Surpass $400 Billion in 2012", November 20, at http://siteresources.worldbank.org/INTPROSPECTS/Resources/334934–1288990760745/Migration DevelopmentBrief19.pdf.

79. Aderanti, A. 2008, *Migration in Sub-Saharan Africa*, Current African Issues no. 37, Uppsala: Nordic Africa Institute.

80. Amuedo-Dorantes, C., & Mazzolari, F. 2010, "Remittances to Latin America from Migrants in the United States: Assessing the Impact of Amnesty Programs", *Journal of Development Economics*, 91(2), pp. 323–335.

81. Adams, R.H., Jr 2006, "International Remittances and the Household: Analysis and Review of Global Evidence", *Journal of African Economies*, 15(Suppl. 2), pp. 396–425.

82. Abdelal, R., Khan, A., & Khanna, T. 2008, "Where Oil-Rich Nations Are Placing their Bets", *Harvard Business Review*, 86(9), pp. 119–128.

83. mangalorean.com 2010, "Gujarat Gained from Investments by Indian Diaspora", January 9, at http://twocircles.net/2010jan09/gujarat_gained_investments_indian_diaspora.html.

84. Kristof, N.D., & Kunz, R. 2008, "Remittances are Beautiful? Gender Implications of the New Global Remittances Trend", *Third World Quarterly*, 29(7), pp. 1389–1409.

85. Boyle, D. 1998, "A Mobile Phone is a Cow", *New Statesman*, July 31, p. 33.

86. Chowdhury, A. 2001, "Local Heroes", *New Internationalist*, March, pp. 22–23.

87. Dholakia, N., & Kshetri, N. 2002, "The Global Digital Divide and Mobile Business Models: Identifying Viable Patterns of E-Development", *Proceedings of the IFIP WG9.4 Conference*, Bangalore, India, May 29–31, pp. 528–540.

88. *Economist* 2009, "The Power of Mobile Money", September 26, at www.economist.com/node/14505519.

89. Businessweek.com 2001, "Providing Rural Phone Services Profitably in Poor Countries", at http://adsections.businessweek.com/digital/profit.htm.

90. Dholakia, N., & Kshetri, N. 2003, "Mobile Commerce as a Solution to the Global Digital Divide: Selected Cases of e-Development", in S. Krishna and S. Madon (eds), *The Digital Challenge: Information Technology in the Development Context* (pp. 237–250), Aldershot: Ashgate.

91. IFC 2008, "The Village Phone Program, Connecting Communities, Creating Opportunities, Improving Lives", International Finance Program, World Bank, at http://siteresources.worldbank.org/EXTEDEVELOP MENT/Resources/20080225_VillagePhoneOverview_Gender&IT. pdf?resourceurlname=20080225_VillagePhoneOverview_Gender%26IT.pdf.

4

ENTREPRENEURSHIP IN OECD ECONOMIES

Abstract

The reasons and motivations underlying the formation of the Organization for Economic Co-operation and Development (OECD) are tightly linked to the development of entrepreneurship and improvement in the entrepreneurial climate in its member as well as non-member countries. OECD economies, however, show remarkable similarities as well as striking differences in various entrepreneurship-related indicators. While all OECD economies are characterized by democratic institutions at all levels, they differ on some of the key ingredients of entrepreneurial ecosystems. In this chapter, we examine key factors related to entrepreneurship in OECD economies such as policy, culture, market, technology and finances. We also discuss initiatives, and measures that contributed to the new members' full membership in the OECD.

This chapter's objectives include:

1. To demonstrate an understanding of determinants, performance indicators and impacts of entrepreneurship in OECD economies.
2. To analyze the variation in the patterns of entrepreneurship across OECD economies.
3. To demonstrate an understanding of various forms of entrepreneurial financing in OECD economies.
4. To understand the causes, contexts, mechanisms and processes associated with economic and political reform activities undertaken by the newly joined OECD members.

Table 4.1 OECD member countries

Australia	France	Korea	Slovenia
Austria	Germany	Luxembourg	Spain
Belgium	Greece	Mexico	Sweden
Canada	Hungary	Netherlands	Switzerland
Chile	Iceland	New Zealand	Turkey
Czech Republic	Ireland	Norway	UK
Denmark	Israel	Poland	US
Estonia	Italy	Portugal	
Finland	Japan	Slovak Republic	

4.1. The OECD in Relation to Entrepreneurship

The reasons and motivations underlying the formation of the Organization for Economic Co-operation and Development (OECD; www.oecd.org/) relate to the development of entrepreneurship and improvement in the entrepreneurial climate in its member as well as non-member countries that are committed to democracy and the market economy. The organization's missions include supporting sustainable economic growth, improving living standards, boosting employment, maintaining financial stability, assisting non-member countries' economic development and contributing to the growth in world trade.[1] As of 2013, the OECD had thirty-four member countries (Table 4.1). The OECD is also strengthening partnership with key non-member economies such as Brazil, China, India, Indonesia, Russia and South Africa.

4.2. The Newly Accessed and Candidate Countries

A review of some of the newly accessed and candidate countries would help illustrate the importance of economic and political climate reforms in order to be qualified for OECD membership. Accession talks to join the OECD had begun with Estonia, Israel and Slovenia along with Chile and Russia in May 2007. Their readiness to join

the OECD was assessed by the progresses made by these economies in political and economic reform activities, especially in areas
such as combating corruption, ensuring high standards of corporate
governance, and protecting intellectual property rights (IPRs).[2] As
explained in Chapters 1 and 2, these factors are critical foundations
for entrepreneurial development.

Chile, Slovenia, Israel and Estonia joined the OECD in 2010.
Below we discuss the economic and political reforms undertaken by
these newly joined members in the three areas noted above: combating
corruption, enhancement of corporate governance and IPR protection.
Table 4.2 presents some of the key indicators in these areas for the new
members and compares them with Russia, which has not yet achieved
full OECD membership. The Economic Freedom Index covers ten
components: business freedom, trade freedom, fiscal freedom, government spending, monetary freedom, investment freedom, financial
freedom, property rights, freedom from corruption and labor freedom.
IPR protection is a component of the Economic Freedom Index. The
Corruption Perceptions Index measures the perceived levels of public
sector corruption. The Regulatory Quality Index measures the "perceptions of the ability of the government to formulate and implement
sound policies and regulations that permit and promote private sector
development".[3] This index can be used to evaluate overall economic
and political reforms including the regulatory environment related to
corporate governance.

Chile   Following the accession talks, an Accession Roadmap was
adopted in November 2007, which set out the terms, conditions and
process for Chile's accession to the OECD. In the Roadmap, the
OECD Council requested a number of OECD committees to provide
it with a formal opinion. In light of the formal opinions received from
OECD committees and other relevant information, the OECD
Council decided to invite Chile to become an OECD member in
December 2009. After completion of its internal procedures, Chile
became a member of the OECD in May 2010.

As is clear from Table 4.2, Chile outperforms the other four economies in terms of all the indicators considered. While Chileans have

shown concerns about massive and endemic corruption in government and state institutions, Chile has seen rapid and phenomenal progress in anticorruption efforts following the end of Augusto Pinochet's dictatorship in 1990.[4] Despite some instances of corruption and criminal activity, the levels are low by regional standards. A number of high-profile corruption scandals served as a spurt to anticorruption efforts. For instance, the Chilean economic development agency (CORFO), the Ministry of Public Works (MOP), the Central Bank, the Sports and Recreation Department (ChileDeportes) and a number of other state-owned enterprises (SOEs) were embroiled in huge corruption scandals. ChileDeportes' use of state funds for political campaigns in 2006 was the most noted scandal to prompt the Chilean government to introduce a number of regulatory reforms.

Key elements of the new regulatory frameworks include clarification and modernization of the way public employees are paid, new campaign finance legislation, the establishment of a budget commission for monitoring and overseeing government spending, and the establishment of ethical guidelines for public employees. There have also been reforms in the way the MOP awards government contracts. These measures have produced the anticipated effects. In Transparency International's 2011 Corruption Perceptions Index, Chile ranked 22 out of 182 economies, which compares with the US rank of 24. Chile is also the least corrupt country in Latin America.

A concentrated ownership structure with conglomerates and business groups controlling most firms and the capital market's limited liquidity were major challenges facing Chile's corporate governance landscape. Minority shareholders are often vulnerable in such settings due to the controlling shareholders' tendency to engage in irregular practices to extract private benefits. In this regard, Chile has made considerable progress on the corporate governance front, mainly through laws adopted in 2000 on Public Tender Offers and on Corporate Governance, and a Corporate Governance law approved by Congress in 2009.[5] Adequate safeguards are put in place through the new laws to protect minority shareholders which include enhanced transparency standards and restrictive rules regarding the use of privileged information, related party transactions and conflicts of interest. Major changes have been made to the definition of independent directors as well as their role in reviewing sensitive issues. The 2009 law has also strengthened the governance of Chile's largest SOE, the copper mining company Codelco. The OECD has noted that this is a significant step, which is likely to result in momentum to further reform in the country's other SOEs.

Commercial operations are aided by efficient regulations that support open-market policies.[6] Chile's economic freedom score of 78.3 in 2012 (Table 4.2) made it the seventh freest economy in the world, and its score was the highest in South and Central America and the Caribbean region. The 2012 score was 0.9 points higher than in 2011 due to its improved scores in property rights, freedom from corruption and monetary freedom. Especially impressive is the country's progress in the property rights component, in which Chile scored 90 percent. In the 2010 International Property Rights Index, Chile ranked thirty-fourth out of 125 countries and was among the highest-ranked emerging economies. Private property is well protected and contracts are secure. Except for some areas, such as coastal trade, air transport and the mass media, there is no restriction of private ownership.[7] The laws provide for compensation in the case of property expropriation. Foreign investors can own up to 100 percent of a Chilean-based company.

The key to Chile's success on this front is also a highly transparent and efficient court administration. For instance, as of 2004, 99 percent of court proceedings were open to the public and out of every hundred crimes reported to law enforcement agencies, eighty-nine cases were closed. In 2004, the average time to process a case varied from eleven to 307 days, which was much quicker compared to the old system.[8]

Israel   The adoption and implementation of the 2000 Companies Law and its subsequent upgrades have strengthened Israel's corporate governance. Corporate transactions that are viewed as potentially abusive are required to go through stringent approval at board level and in shareholder meetings. The Israeli authorities are considering tightening the rule further.[9] Virtually all large companies except for those in public utilities and the military have been privatized, and measures to promote a level playing field between public and private enterprises have been introduced.

The Review of Corporate Governance in Israel conducted by the OECD in 2011 made some recommendations for policy changes to further improve the quality of corporate governance. A main recommendation was to enhance the autonomy of the Israeli securities regulator, including giving the right to issue secondary regulations and levy fines. The OECD viewed that these measures would provide better protection to investors than the current system's reliance on legislation and legal enforcement. Other recommendations were to monitor the quality of the auditing of listed companies and to establish specialized courts for hearing commercial cases. The OECD report, however, noted that the country had made progress in several of these areas.

The Israeli court system is independent, and bribery as well as other forms of corruption are illegal. In 2008, the offence of bribery of a foreign public official was introduced to the Israeli Penal Law; it prohibits offering or paying a bribe to a foreign public official for the purpose of obtaining business or other advantages.[10] Israel has also launched a campaign to increase awareness of the OECD Convention on Combating Bribery of Foreign Public Officials and the foreign bribery offence. The Inter-ministerial team on Combating Bribery has coordinated this effort and the Ministry of Justice (MOJ) has intended to work with the State Comptroller's Office. The MOJ has also established a website, which is dedicated to fighting corruption and international bribery (http://index.justice.gov.il/Pages/default.aspx).[11]

Protections for property rights and contracts are enforced effectively. Israel's broader efforts specifically aimed at increasing its ability to benefit from an enhanced IPR regime deserve mention. The country has increased the resources of the patent office, upgraded enforcement activities as well as implemented programs to bring ideas funded by government research to the market.[12] In March 2008, the MOJ submitted a statement on IPR in Israel to the Office of the US Trade Representative (USTR) as part of USTR's annual "Special 301" review process. Note that the Special 301 reports identify trade barriers to US companies and products due to the lack of "adequate and effective" IPR protection in other countries. Israel defended its IPR regime as adequate, effective and in conformance with all relevant international obligations, and requested removal of Israel from the "watch list".[13] A 2011 OECD report suggested the importance of improvement in a number of areas including enhancing protection in specific areas of copyright and patent protection and improving administrative efficiency.[14]

Estonia According to the annual surveys of Transparency International (TI), Estonia is the least corrupt country in Eastern Europe. Indeed, Estonia is cleaner than some West European countries, something that can be attributed to the proactive measures taken by the country to fight corruption. The Estonian MOJ invited TI to take a lead role in the drafting of the country's new anticorruption strategy.[15]

The principles of the "Honest State" program started in 2004 have been an integral part of the government of Estonia's best practices to fight corruption. The program has a number of components designed to reduce corruption in the government, including auditing local governments, which have been viewed as the greatest source of corruption. The program also requires public servants to file electronic declarations of economic interest. Additional components of the program include the establishment of the National Ethics Council, an increase in the number of specialized investigators and prosecutors who focus on corruption, and an anonymous hotline to report corruption cases.[16] Estonia has been a signatory of the OECD Convention on Combating Bribery of Foreign Public Officials in International Business Transactions since 2005. As a signatory of the Convention, Estonia is obligated to criminalize bribery of foreign public officials in conducting international business.

Estonia has committed to the development of a superior corporate governance practice. It revised legal frameworks several times based on EU directives. Issues identified earlier, such as audit requirements and standards and the lack of institutional arrangements for SOE oversight and monitoring, have been addressed. There are voluntary guidelines in issues such as the role of independent directors. These are important because the small size of the market for listed companies and low liquidity means that market mechanisms are less likely to provide incentives for good corporate governance. Observers have noted that Estonian companies closely follow legal corporate governance requirements.[17]

Estonia's economic freedom score was 73.8 in 2012, which put it ahead of many OECD members. Especially impressive is its investment freedom component of 90. Only a small number of the country's enterprises in strategic sectors such as main port, the power plants, the postal system, railway, airports and the national lottery are state-owned. SOEs operate on the same legal bases as private enterprises. Foreign and local investors are treated equally in Estonia. The regulatory frameworks in Estonia have been well developed adequately to protect property rights, including intellectual property such as copyrights, patents, trademarks, industrial design and trade secrets.

Slovenia Not long ago Slovenia was plagued with a number of corruption scandals. Some argue that effectiveness of anticorruption institutions is hampered by factors such as the country's small size, a history of close interaction between the public and private sectors, and an important role of personal contacts in business relations. Contrary to these observations, Slovenia has made significant progress on the anticorruption front, as reflected in its position as the least corrupt state in Central and Southeastern Europe.

As is the case with other transition countries in the region, Slovenia was constantly monitored as part of the process of attaining full membership of international organizations such as the EU, NATO and the OECD. In response to the Council of Europe's critical report, Slovenia initiated various efforts including the establishment of a coordinating anticorruption commission in 2001. Slovenia has also established specialized law enforcement units to combat serious economic crimes.

A major feature of the Slovenian economy concerns the prevalence of SOEs, both in the listed as well as in the unlisted sectors. It is thus of paramount important to ensure that there are consistent and transparent ownership policies. Moreover, it is important for the state to act as an informed and responsible shareholder, and to make sure that SOE board members possess the skills and authority to exercise their functions.[18] In this regard, the accession process led to the country's adoption of key legislation to improve the corporate governance framework for SOEs, minority shareholder protection and securities regulation. In April 2010, the Slovenian parliament adopted legislation that established a central ownership agency to manage all of the state's direct interests in SOEs. In addition, the country is also

Table 4.2 Indicators related to political and economic reforms in the four newest OECD members

	CHILE	ESTONIA	ISRAEL	SLOVENIA	RUSSIA
Corruption Perceptions Index (rank) (2012)[a]	72(20)	64 (32)	60 (39)	61 (37)	28 (133)
Economic Freedom Index (2012)[b]	78.3	73.2	67.8	62.9	51.1
Regulatory Quality Index (2011) [c]	1.54	1.4	1.35	0.63	-0.35

[a]Corruption Perceptions Index 2012, www.transparency.org/cpi2012/results/#my Anchor1 (0–100, highly corrupt to very clean)

[b]2012 Index of Economic Freedom, www.heritage.org/index/default

[c]The World Bank Group, http://info.worldbank.org/governance/wgi/index.aspx#home. The indicators are rated on a −2.5 to +2.5 scale, a higher number indicating a higher regulatory quality

preparing legislation to define the relationship between the new central ownership agency and two key state institutions overseeing the pension fund (KAD) and the restitution fund (SOD).[19]

In Slovenia's Index of Economic Freedom, the property rights component was 60 in 2012, which puts it ahead of many other OECD members. The country made significant amendments and modifications, particularly during the process of accession to the EU.[20] More specifically, the IPR-related regulatory framework underwent several changes between its declaration of independence in 1991 and EU accession in 2004. As it is an EU member, the legal standards related to Slovenia's IPR regime are similar to those of most OECD countries. Slovenia grants protection to copyright and related rights, trademarks, geographical indications, patents, industrial designs, topographies of integrated circuits and undisclosed business secrets.[21]

Russia's Barriers to Full OECD Membership   In order to provide further insights into the requirements necessary for becoming an OECD member, we describe the situation facing Russia. Russia made an official request for OECD membership in 1996. While Russia is reported to have made some progress, progress overall has been insufficient to become an OECD member. As shown in Table 4.2, Russia lags behind the newly accessed OECD members in the Corruption Perceptions Index, the Economic Freedom Index and the Regulatory Quality Index.

Russia is plagued by bribery and other forms of corruption (watch the video, "Russia corrupt from top to bottom": www.youtube.com/watch?v=BLTY-dzjlfA). Russian Prime Minister Dmitry Medvedev claimed that Russia suffers from "legal nihilism", and that investors in the country feel unsafe due to concerns regarding law enforcement agencies' ability and willingness to protect them and the legal system's inefficiency. Factors such as the weak rule of law, the inefficient bureaucracy and public officials' corrupt practices pose a serious challenge to entrepreneurship in the country.

Russia also suffers from unsatisfactory corporate governance practices, which have created a further barrier to full OECD membership. Investors have complained about instances in which insiders and major shareholders have engaged in fraud such as transfer pricing and asset stripping. They allegedly do so by selling output, assets or additional securities to another firm they own at below market prices.[22] Russia also adopted a corporate governance code in April 2002. However, the Business and Industry Advisory Committee (BIAC) to the OECD, which consists of the industrial and employers' organizations in the OECD member countries, are concerned about the lack of respect for and compliance with the code.[23]

In reports submitted to the OECD in 2008 and 2009, BIAC expressed concerns about the lack of strong IPR protection and its inadequate enforcement in Russia. For fifteen consecutive years (1998–2012), Russia has been on the US Priority Watch List of countries with serious deficiencies in IPR protection. A BIAC report made the accusation that Russia's Internet infrastructure primarily serves as a channel for illegitimate e-commerce involving the distribution of pirated content and software. The report noted that a number of illegal peer-to-peer services and pay-per-download websites hinder the development of the legitimate online market.[24] The BIAC also expressed concerns regarding the law's inadequacy to address Internet piracy due to the lack of clear provisions on Internet service provider (ISP) cooperation and third party liability, thus failing to provide incentives for intermediaries to assist in curbing piracy.

Despite the above criticisms, Russia has taken a number of positive steps in recent years. In 2011, the Russian Parliament passed a law that prohibits Russian companies from bribing foreign officials. Following this, Russia was invited to join the anti-bribery convention in May 2011—a step toward OECD membership for Russia as acceptance into the convention is a requirement for the membership.

Russia has also taken measures to address the significant losses of foreign companies due to IPR infringement. It has enacted a law to establish a special court for intellectual property disputes by February 2013. Russia has also amended its criminal code to revise criminal thresholds for copyright piracy. The country's law enforcement authorities have taken criminal and civil action against some serious copyright infringers.

4.3. Determinants of Entrepreneurship in OECD Economies

While all the economies in Table 4.1 belong to the club of OECD, they differ widely in entrepreneurial performance. This section discusses the key determinants of entrepreneurship in these economies and illustrates key intra-OECD differences in terms of these factors: (1) laws, regulations and policy, (2) values, culture and skills, (3) access to finance, market, R&D and technology.

4.3.1. Regulatory Framework

The OECD economies differ on various components of regulatory framework. As presented in Fig. 4.1, procedures for starting a business are far more difficult and time-consuming in Japan and Chile than in Canada and Australia. Too many rules and regulations, bureaucracy and red tape are the primary disadvantages of Chile and Japan. For instance, despite the progress noted above, inefficient and conservative government bureaucracy is widely recognized as a major problem facing Chile.[25] It has been suggested that Japan had more than 11,000 rules to regulate businesses in the mid-1990s, which cost the Japanese economy US$75–110 billion a year.[26] Among the eight procedures involved in starting a business, the third step, registering at the Legal Affairs Bureau of the Ministry of Justice, takes one to three weeks. The authorities can return the filed documents for revision.

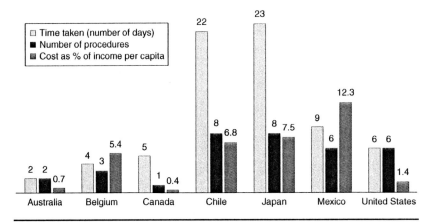

Figure 4.1 Regulations related to starting a business in selected OECD economies
Source: World Bank Group, "Doing Business", www.doingbusiness.org/data/exploretopics/starting-a-business

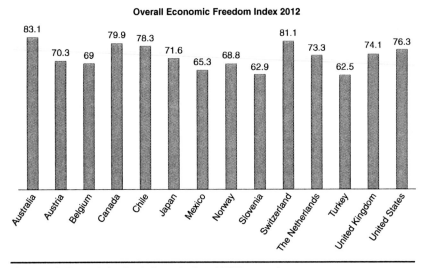

Figure 4.2 Economic freedom indices of selected OECD economies
Source: Euromonitor international database

Compared to most other OECD economies, Turkey's regulatory frameworks have been ineffective in driving entrepreneurial outcomes. It is among the OECD countries with the lowest economic freedom (Fig. 4.2). Despite its progress in areas such as trade and fiscal freedom, its relatively inefficient judicial system has driven down

the economic freedom overall. According to the US State Department's 2010 Human Rights Report: Turkey (www.state.gov/j/drl/
rls/hrrpt/2010/eur/154455.htm), the close relationship between
judges and prosecutors has been an obstacle to the right to a fair trial.
Another problem concerns long trials. A related issue is the high rate
of infringement of intellectual property rights despite the improvement in the IPR regime. In addition to the overburdened and slow
court system, the lack of judges with proper training for commercial
cases makes enforcement of property rights difficult. Inflexible labor
regulations have also hindered Turkey's entrepreneurial development.
The Turkish labor market is characterized by a high non-salary cost of
employing and difficulty in firing an employee. Turkey also has lengthy
and unnecessarily burdensome bankruptcy proceedings.[27] In particular, the legal fees associated with bankruptcy proceedings are notori-
ously high.[28]

In light of the above discussion about Turkey, available data and statistics show that poor regulatory quality, weak rule of law and corruption
are even bigger problems in Mexico (Figs 4.3 and 4.4). Mexico has the
lowest Corruption Perceptions Index, that is, the highest public sector corruption among OECD economies (Fig. 4.5). One observation
is that excessive regulation in Mexico has been a means of punishing

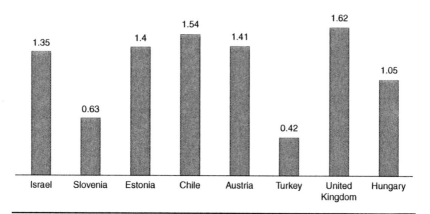

Figure 4.3 The regulatory quality of selected OECD economies (2011)
Source: World Bank Group (2009): regulatory quality measures "the ability of the government to provide sound policies and regulations that enable and promote private sector development"

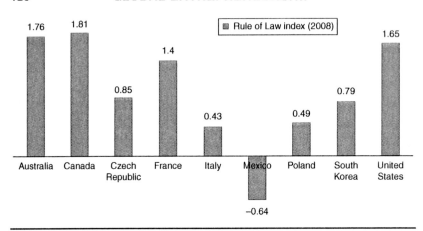

Figure 4.4 Rule of law indices of selected OECD economies
Source: World Bank Group (2009): rule of law measures "the extent to which agents have confidence in and abide by the rules of society including the quality of property rights, the police, and the courts, as well as the risk of crime"

private sector firms. For instance, local governments have been found to use the regulations as a tool to extort and to blackmail private sector firms. One example to illustrate this point would be regulations in the transport industry prior to 1990, known as *regreso vacio* or empty return cargo, which prohibited two-way merchandise transportations. That is, private firms in the transport industry could transport from the point of origin to the destination, but not from the destination to the point of origin. If a firm did not want to make a return trip with an empty truck, it needed to bribe state and federal officials.[29]

Congestion in the law enforcement system caused by drug trafficking and related violence has also led to a decline in respect for the rule of law in Mexico. For most types of crime, the rates of arrest and successful prosecution are low. In a few cases, suspects are detained, but they are put through lengthy criminal proceedings and the court is often unable or unwilling to adhere to due process standards, which hampers trials.[30]

Tax Policy and Entrepreneurship Among OECD economies, Luxembourg and Switzerland have formulated favorable tax policies to stimulate entrepreneurship. Luxembourg has a low effective corporate tax rate of 21 percent. Likewise, in 2010, Switzerland's federal corporate tax rate was 8.5 percent. Even after adding states (known as cantons) and municipal taxes, Switzerland has one of the lowest tax rates in the world.

The average corporate tax rate in Switzerland in 2010 was 21.2 percent, compared to 30 percent in Germany and 25.5 percent in the Netherlands. The top corporate tax rates in the country in 2010 varied from 11.8 percent to 24.2 percent depending on the location. These rates compare with the UK's 28 percent and 35 percent in the US. Switzerland had budget surpluses in 2009 while other European countries were severely affected by the global financial crisis and faced debt crises.

These initiatives have paid off brilliantly. According to McKinsey & Co., during 1998–2008, Switzerland attracted the regional headquarters of over 180 large foreign companies. Companies such as Kraft Foods, Yahoo and Google have established European headquarters in Switzerland. As of 2010, over 150 US companies have a presence in Switzerland.

Note too that Switzerland's cantons have more autonomy than states in the US. The cantons enjoy autonomy on important issues such as social security contributions, business and residency permits and construction codes. The Canton of Zug has been the most attractive location in terms of taxation, and attracted 1,600 new businesses in 2007 alone. Other cantons are competing with Zug.

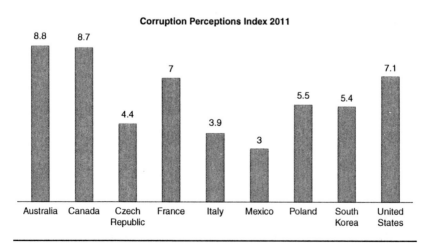

Figure 4.5 Corruption perception indices of selected OECD economies
Source: Euromonitor International from Transparency International

Corporate Bankruptcy Laws It is an overriding reality that most new firms fail during their first five years. For instance, according to the OECD, 62.3 percent of new firms in the Netherlands and 53.1 percent of new firms in Hungary that were started in 2007 died within three years. Due to the high potential failure rate of startups, policies that penalize failed entrepreneurs keep most people away from entrepreneurship. On the other hand, a country with regulations that are friendly to failed entrepreneurs and a high tendency to forgive entrepreneurial failure is likely to attract more people in entrepreneurship.

The US has been a global role model for its favorable and lenient corporate bankruptcy law. If an entrepreneurial firm is troubled but potentially viable, Chapter 11 allows entrepreneurs and managers to retain control of the firm, obtain protection from creditors and develop a reorganization plan. The situation is different in Japan, where secured creditors, who, as lenders, hold legally enforceable claim on the company's assets, are given the control rights.[31] The Japanese system is thus more likely to lead to premature liquidation of the firm than the US system. Companies that are "terminally ill", on the other hand, can file for "Chapter 7", which involves liquidation and distribution of available assets among creditors. Debtors filing Chapter 7 bankruptcy can retain certain exempt assets such as household and personal goods, automobiles and homesteads.

Another important difference is whether or not there is an automatic stay on assets. Among OECD economies, Canada and the US have the provision of an automatic stay on assets, which means that creditors cannot seize the company's assets used as collateral for loans after the bankruptcy proceedings have commenced. In South Korea, on the other hand, regulations do not provide such provision.[32]

4.3.2. Values, Culture and Skills

Values and Culture

While OECD economies exhibit a high degree of homogeneity in political institutions, they are culturally heterogeneous. OECD economies differ significantly in the entrepreneurs' own view of themselves and preference for entrepreneurship as a career and societal attitudes towards entrepreneurs. According to a survey released by the European Commission, 45 percent of Europeans would prefer to start their own business instead of working as an employee, which compared with 55 percent in the US. In the US, 73 percent view businessmen favorably compared to 49 percent in Europe. The research also indicated that entrepreneurs in Europe are viewed as exploiters of workers, whereas they are considered to be job creators in the US.

The lack of respect for entrepreneurs as well as the lack of social appreciation of their work is of special concern in OECD countries with a socialist past. For instance, according to the Global Entrepreneurship Week Policy Survey conducted in 2012, only 28 percent of entrepreneurs in Hungary thought that people who successfully start new firms have at least the same level of status and respect as a manager in a medium-sized company. Hungary ranked thirty-fourth out of thirty-four countries surveyed.[33]

Entrepreneurs are regarded as "déclassé" in some OECD countries and are not socially admired in others. Jante's Law, which comes from the Norwegian/Danish author Aksel Sandemose's novel, helps explain the lack of social admiration for entrepreneurial success in the Scandinavian communities. The Law is an unspoken code of ethics and explains the pattern of group behavior observed in these communities. It is centered around encouraging people to act less arrogantly and more modestly and humbly. Jante's Law teaches people that flaunting their wealth or achievements is unworthy and inappropriate. Commenting on Danish culture, a report observed that due to the prevalence of Jante's Law, "which condemned the attempt of an individual to do better than others", entrepreneurial success is not socially admired in the country.[34]

That said, in some OECD economies, there has been a drastic change in entrepreneurship-related cultural values. Ireland and Chile are probably the two most spectacular examples to demonstrate how entrepreneurship-related social norms can emerge in a short period. Until the 1980s, Irish youths were attracted to jobs in government and financial services. Defaulting on loans was judged as an immoral practice for businesses. The social norms also stigmatized bankruptcy.[35] The Irish economy produced a number of multi-millionaire businessmen in the 1980s. As of 2008, Ireland had over 30,000 Euro millionaires and most of them were self-made.[36] Entrepreneurs gradually started treating entrepreneurial failure as a learning opportunity, not as a personal failure or a stigma.

Similarly, entrepreneurs in the past had a negative social image as "greedy exploiters" in Chile, a view that has changed. Until the 1980s, well-educated middle classes in the country avoided opportunity-driven entrepreneurship.[37] However, according to the Chile 2008 GEM Report, 80 percent of the country's economically active population considered entrepreneurship to be a desirable career option. It was estimated that 12.9 percent of the adult population in Chile consisted of early-stage entrepreneurs. Sixty-eight percent of entrepreneurs were opportunity-based (seeking real opportunities for business and not driven by necessity).[38]

Skills   In terms of education, even in the worst-performing OECD countries, the proportion of tertiary-education-age cohort enrolled in tertiary institutions is higher than the global average of 26 percent and SSA economies' 6 percent[39] (Fig. 4.6). But the real issue is whether students develop entrepreneurship skills in universities. An even more relevant indicator concerns successful entrepreneurs' views regarding the development of entrepreneurial skills and capabilities in colleges and universities. In this regard, entrepreneurs in OECD economies have generally expressed dissatisfaction and frustration with the lack of entrepreneurship-related skills among university graduates. For instance, according to the EU Entrepreneurship Survey, entrepreneurial skills were among the most important barriers to entrepreneurship in Denmark. Twenty-eight percent of respondents indicated the supply of skills and entrepreneurial capabilities as the main obstacle to entrepreneurship, which was the highest proportion in the EU.[40]

In terms of college and tertiary education entry rates, for example, Australia and Poland perform better than most other OECD economies (Fig. 4.6). In international comparison, however, university education systems in these two economies do not have good standing in relation to the development of entrepreneurial skills and capabilities. For instance, according to the Global Entrepreneurship Week Policy Survey conducted in 2012, only 6 percent of Australian high-impact

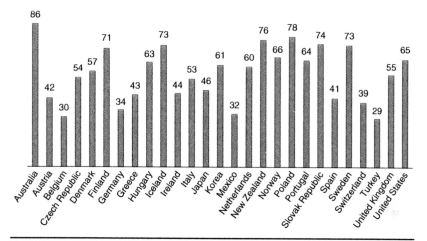

Figure 4.6 First-time entrants in tertiary education as a percentage of the population in the corresponding age group in selected OECD economies (2007)
Source: OECD, www.oecd-ilibrary.org/education/tertiary-education-entry-rates_20755120-table2

entrepreneurs and 8 percent of Polish high-impact entrepreneurs thought that university-level educational systems in their countries did a good job in teaching entrepreneurial skills.[41] These two countries ranked respectively thirty-first and twenty-ninth out of the thirty-four countries surveyed.

Openness to Immigration and Availability of Entrepreneurial Skills A country's openness to immigration is tightly linked to entrepreneurial performance, innovation and economic growth.[42] The US is an obvious example of an economy that has benefited greatly from immigrants' entrepreneurial activities. A quarter of technology and engineering companies launched in the US between 1995 and 2005 had at least one foreign-born founder. These enterprises generated US$52 billion in sales and provided jobs to 450,000 workers in 2005.[43] Likewise, according to the Partnership for a New American Economy, over 40 percent of Fortune 500 businesses in the US were started by immigrants or their children.[44]

Immigrants have also made a significant contribution to innovation. In 2006, foreign nationals living in the US were inventors or co-inventors in 26 percent of patent applications filed in the US. This proportion was only 8 percent in 1998. Some US corporations with the highest proportions of foreign nationals' contribution to patent applications include Qualcomm (72 percent), Merck (65 percent), GE (64 percent) and Cisco (60 percent). Likewise, over 40 percent of the international patent applications filed by the US government had foreign authors.

4.3.3. Access to Finance, Market, R&D and Technology

Market Access

While most OECD members have well-developed institutions to facilitate market access, some show many clear instances of barriers to market access related to antitrust and unfair competition laws and enforcement. In Chapter 1, we discussed the anticompetitive consequences of barriers to new firms in Mexico. As a further example, there have been many instances of bid-rigging, in which competitors collude so that a competing business can secure a government contract at a predetermined price, which is increased artificially. Most businesses and consumers suffer the consequences of these anticompetitive and illegal practices.

Mexico's Social Security Department spends about US$2.5 billion each year on pharmaceutical products and other goods and services. In order to fight against these anticompetitive acts by improving rules and procedures, and training procurement officers, the Mexican Competition Authority and the Mexican Social Security Institute (IMSS) signed a cooperation agreement with the OECD in 2011 to implement the OECD guidelines. Since then, the OECD and the Mexican Competition Authority have been working with the IMSS to address these issues.[45]

In the OECD's product market regulation index, Japan performed poorly in the "barriers to competition" sub-category, which included areas such as entry barriers and antitrust issues.[46] The real issue is related to the lack of effective enforcement rather than the existence of law. Critics and skeptics have argued that the Japan Fair Trade Commission (JFTC) has not been effective in enforcing the Antimonopoly Act. The JFTC is often viewed as "a watch dog that does not bite".[47] Likewise, notwithstanding the progress France has made on this front, regulatory barriers to entry exist in the retail trade, professional service and other sectors.[48] While some regulations are necessary to protect the consumer, barriers to entry in the country are arguably higher than needed for such purpose in general professions such as accountants, architects and lawyers; regulated professions such as physiotherapists, veterinarians, pharmacists and hairdressers; and partially substitutable professions such as conventional physicians and practitioners of alternative medicine.[49]

Access to Finance

Compared to less developed economies, OECD economies are characterized by greater availability of and easier access to financial resources for potential entrepreneurs. That said, intra-OECD differences can be observed in the availability and affordability of credits. Of the thirty-four OECD members, twenty-one belong to the EU. In this regard, as discussed in Chapter 3, thanks to focused government intervention such as the European Commission's SME guarantee facility, large proportions of SMEs in the EU have access to bank financing.

In some countries the governments are facing pressures to increase SMEs' access to financing. For instance, in South Korea, the government encouragement for banks to shift lending away from chaebol and towards consumers and SMEs is likely to increase in 2012–2016 in response to public pressure.

In the US in 2007, loan requests of 72 percent of SMEs were approved. The proportion decreased to 67 percent in 2008, due to the GFC.[50] In addition, many entrepreneurs such as the founders of Cisco Systems took second mortgages on their homes in order to finance their entrepreneurial ventures.[51] Some entrepreneurs also use their credit cards for short-term operating funds.

Due to the substantial size of the informal economy in Mexico, potential entrepreneurs are less likely to borrow from formal financing sources. According to the 2002 employment census in Mexico, the country's informal economy employed twenty-four million people compared to fifteen million employed in the formal economy.[52] Most informal sector workers are unable to fulfill the requirements necessary to get loans from banks. A taco seller in Mexico City said that he is unable to get a loan from a bank: "The banks have a lot of requirements that I can't meet."[53] Looking at a broader indicator, the country's bank claims on the private sector are the lowest among OECD countries. According to the Economist Intelligence Unit, domestic bank credit to the private sector was estimated at 18 percent of GDP in 2011, which is among the lowest levels in the region and significantly lower than Brazil's 50 percent and Chile's over 80 percent.

A related problem is that compared to the urban areas, individuals and micro-enterprises in rural and semi-rural communities in the country have significantly lower access to formal financial institutions. There are no incentives for banks to expand their geographical coverage. As of 2009, only 36 percent of municipalities had at least one bank branch. According to a household survey conducted in 2011 by the World Bank and Gallup, only 27 percent of Mexico's adult population has an account in a financial institution.

Venture Capital   Venture capital covers a vanishingly small share of total financing needs in most OECD economies. VC funding is less than 0.05 percent of GDP in most of these countries. OECD countries with more developed venture capital markets include Israel, Sweden, Switzerland, the UK and the US. According to Ernst & Young, the US accounts for about 70 percent of global VC investment.[54] In 2009, Europe's VC investment as a share of GDP was about a quarter of that of the US. As a proportion of GDP in 2009 VC investments in Israel were equal to 0.18 percent of GDP, which was the highest in the world.[55]

The performance of European VC funds has been poorer compared to those in the US. In the 2000s, for instance, an investor in the average European VC fund lost 1.9 percent annually compared to a gain of 8.4 percent by a US VC fund.[56] A problem facing European members of the OECD is the lack of an integrated European venture capital market. VC regulations vary widely from country to country.

As to the development of the VC industry in Japan, a commonplace observation is that Japanese consumers' share in savings accounts is more than double compared to other industrialized economies, and they have a significantly lower share in more risky assets, which can be taken as an indication of their risk averse behavior. Second, pension funds, which have been a major source of VC in the US, account for only 4 percent of total investments in Japan. Third, Japanese universities have played limited roles in the development of the venture sector.[57]

Business angels are becoming increasingly important investors in many OECD countries. In the US, they play a more important role than formal investors. One estimate suggested that there are about 60,000 angel investors in the US.[58] According to the University of New Hampshire's Center for Venture Research, more than 66,000 companies received US$23 billion through angel investors in 2011, compared to 36,000 receiving US$15.7 billion in 2002.[59] Likewise, according to the European Business Angels Network (EBAN), Europe had 125,000 active investors and one million potential investors. At that time, the investment pools of available business angels finance was estimated at between €10–20 billion. Looking at individual countries, investments made by angels were €3 billion in the UK, €1.5 billion in the Netherlands, €300 million in Finland and €20 million in Ireland.[60]

There are also important differences in the sources of VC funds. In the US, institutional investors such as pension funds, which manage pooled contributions from pension plans set up by employers, unions or other organizations, are key actors for VC funding. Pension funds and insurance companies together account for as much as 40 percent of VC finance. These investors control a large share of national assets and have long-term liabilities. They thus possess the necessary liquidity and the ability to absorb risk, which make them capable of participating in VC. Due to the dominance of bank-based financial systems, VC financing in Europe mainly comes from the banks. For instance, in Austria, Germany and Italy, about 50 percent of VC funds between 1992 and 2002 came from banks.[61]

Microfinance   Compared to less developed economies, microfinance in the OECD economies has low relative effectiveness vis-à-vis the other well-established and well-known sources of financing discussed above. Nonetheless, microfinance obviously holds tremendous potential in OECD economies if we consider the fact that an estimated 60 million adults (8 percent of the adult population) do not use formal or semi-formal financial services in these economies.[62] Among OECD countries, MFIs have an especially notable presence in Mexico. As of

2008, MFIs in Mexico had 3.9 million active borrowers with a gross loan portfolio of US$2.1 billion.[63]

In the US, microcredit is becoming a growing source of credit for small businesses that are unbankable in the conventional credit market. Estimates suggest that the size of the unbanked population in the US is 28 million and about 45 million people have only limited access to the services of financial institutions.[64]

Organizations such as ShoreBank in Chicago and Women's Economic Development in Montana, which operate on the same principle as MFIs, have existed in the US since the 1980s. Microfinance in the US started to be noticed when Acción, a Latin American microfinance institution, entered the country in 1991. The nonprofit MFI, Grameen America (www.grameenamerica.com/) launched its first branch in the US in 2008 in New York. The peer-to-peer lending site Kiva, which facilitates micro-loans to low-income entrepreneurs, has been partnered with US-based microfinance institutions such as Accion USA and Opportunity Fund since 2009. In 2011, the US had 362 home-grown and foreign MFIs. Accion USA is the largest microlender in the US, and had disbursed 19,500 small business loans worth over US$119 million as of January 2010.[65]

There are some success stories of entrepreneurship facilitated by microfinance in the US. For instance, in 1991, Accion provided a loan of US$1,000 to Brooklyn New York-based entrepreneur, Uvalda Alvarado, which enabled her to exchange her taco truck for a small kitchen in a storefront. Subsequently, she turned the storefront café into a popular restaurant, Antojitos Mexicanos. Alvarado noted how the loan transformed her life: "It wasn't just the economic help. It was the moral support. That someone believes in you, that belief encourages you to keep pushing forward."[66]

Crowdfunding As discussed in Chapter 3, crowdfunding is becoming increasingly popular in OECD economies. As of 2012, Australia, France, Ireland, the Netherlands, Switzerland, and the UK were the only OECD countries that permitted crowdfunding platforms to sell equity shares to small investors.[67] As noted in Chapter 3, the US passed the JOBS Act in 2012. However, as of May 2013, the Securities and

Exchange Commission had not issued regulations that implement the procedural requirements of the JOBS Act. Some compare crowdfunding investors with angel investors and suggest that crowdfunding would create 60 million new angel investors in the US alone.[68]

R&D and Technology

Since R&D is a key driver of a new and innovative product or service, the likelihood of launching a successful product by an entrepreneurial firm, while not guaranteed, is greatly enhanced by the firm's engagement in R&D. R&D activities in an industry would benefit other firms in the same industry as well as in related industries by intra-industry and inter-industry and R&D spillovers, leading to an increase in total factor productivity.

OECD economies differ in their emphasis on R&D. Israel's civilian R&D per capita is the highest in the world. The Israeli government has pursued an effective R&D policy. Attention has been focused on a policy of commercialization of new ideas and technologies. The Office of the Chief Scientist (OCS) (www.matimop.org.il/ocs.html) in the Ministry of Industry, Trade and Labor is a unique government agency for promoting industrial R&D and innovation. It provides a wide range of support to build and strengthen the innovation ecosystem's links from "idea" to "market". Successful entrepreneurs from the private sector are recruited to manage government programs that were launched to support innovation and entrepreneurship.[69]

R&D activities in Israel are also greatly facilitated by the fact that many foreign companies have located their R&D centers in the country. One estimate suggested that by 2010, multinationals such as Alcatel, Deutsche Telecom, Cisco, Google, HP, Merck, Microsoft and IBM had set up 220 R&D centers in the country.[70]

R&D expenditure as a proportion of GDP is among the lowest in Mexico, Turkey, Greece and economies in Central and Eastern Europe (CEE) such as Poland, Hungary and the Slovak Republic (Fig. 4.7). Comparatively low R&D investments in these economies has led to low productivity per worker. For instance, according to the OECD   (http://stats.oecd.org/Index.aspx?DatasetCode=LEVEL), the amount of GDP generated per worker in 2012 as a proportion of the US was 29 percent in Mexico, 54 percent in Slovakia and 45 percent

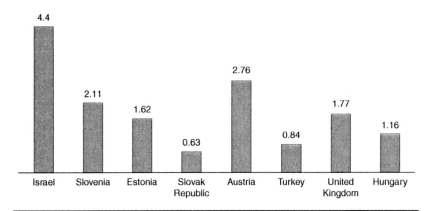

Figure 4.7 Gross domestic expenditure on R&D as a percentage of GDP in selected OECD economies (2010)
Source: OECD, www.oecd-ilibrary.org/science-and-technology/gross-domestic-expenditure-on-r-d_2075843x-table1

in Turkey. For example, while Turkey is making attempts to shift from an economy largely based on a low-skilled labor force towards an industrial economy, agriculture accounted for about a quarter of the total employment in 2012.[71] Some problems facing Turkey include business R&D expenditure that is lower than the EU average, and insufficient commercialization of R&D. For instance, according to the OECD Science, Technology and Industry Scoreboard 2011, while the business sector accounts for about 70 percent of R&D spending in the OECD and 80 percent in Israel, Turkey is one of the three OECD economies (along with Greece and Poland) in which the business sector's R&D spending is lower than that of the higher education sector.

4.4. Concluding Comments

Entrepreneurial performance varies widely across the OECD economies. Heterogeneity in performance and indicators of entrepreneurship indicates that the local social, cultural and political contexts constrain the roles that international organizations such as the OECD play in modern world affairs.

In response to the intra-OECD regulatory differences, some entrepreneurial firms have engaged in arbitrage among national regulations by moving their activities in order to exploit such differences. For instance, it is reported that an increasing number of Czech companies have moved their headquarters to other OECD and some non-OECD economies with more favorable fiscal environments. By the end of 2009, 4,551 Czech-owned companies were headquartered in Netherlands. Cyprus and Luxembourg were the other top two destinations for Czech companies to house their operations.[72]

In addition to the above differences, OECD economies' entrepreneurial patterns exhibit differences in the relative emphasis on small and big businesses. Countries that are friendliest to small businesses include New Zealand, the US, Canada and Australia.[73] On the other hand, Japan and the Nordic countries have exhibited a tendency to favor big businesses. Some of the world's leading brands such as Ericsson, Ikea, Lego and Nokia are from the Nordic countries. Likewise, big businesses have driven the Japanese economy.

The OECD accession process has been a catalyst for bringing reforms in the four newly joined countries. Especially for small countries with limited natural resources such as Israel, economic and political reforms are of paramount significance and importance to drive entrepreneurial growth. For Estonia and Slovenia, the reforms required for EU accession also helped them prepare for OECD accession. They had achieved substantial progress on many of the fronts mentioned earlier to join the EU. Chile especially has overcome significant cultural barriers. While the old system based on patronage, cronyism and regionalism has hindered the efforts to develop modern reform-oriented institutions in most Latin American economies such as Brazil and Mexico, Chile has been able to overcome such barriers.

A transparent and stable business climate with no barriers to free trade can create a dynamic environment for entrepreneurs. In this regard, the newly joined OECD members have had more success than countries with longer membership records in areas such as anticorruption and the fight against poor corporate governance, and have encouraged the development of a climate that promotes entrepreneurship. In the Corruption Perceptions Index, for instance, the newly joined members outperform some countries which have been OECD members for longer: Hungary (4.6, rank = 54), Czech Republic (4.4, rank = 58), Turkey (4.2, rank = 61), Mexico (3, rank = 100).

4.5. Review Questions

1. What are some of the reforms needed in Russia to become a full OECD member?
2. Select an OECD economy which has among the lowest per capita incomes and examine the entrepreneurial ecosystems in the economy you selected.

4.6. Critical Discussion Questions

1. Which OECD countries perform the best in terms of major entrepreneurial indicators? What are the main reasons behind their superior performance?
2. During the past three decades, which OECD countries have made the fastest progress in enhancing their entrepreneurial ecosystems?
3. How do the new OECD members differ from the old ones in terms of various determinants of entrepreneurship?

4.7. End-of-chapter Case: Governments' Export Promotion Strategies in EU Economies

Governments' export promotion measures, which entail providing supports to exporting firms, are condemned as violations of global trade rules and are sharply criticized by anti-poverty campaigners. The opponents of this approach maintain that government supports to exporting firms in rich countries to tap the export market potential could adversely affect the developing world's indigenous firms' capability to compete. Nonetheless, governments across the world have utilized numerous and varied approaches to export promotions.

Export promotion strategies have been employed by almost all governments in industrialized economies and by some developing economies. The four Asian Tigers—Hong Kong, South Korea, Singapore and Taiwan—are some of the most remarkable examples of economies that have achieved a high level of economic growth primarily through export promotion. Many OECD economies have devoted considerable attention and resources and have employed varied strategies and techniques for export promotions, especially SMEs' foreign market access.

Governments' export promotion measures are based on the basic idea that compared to larger firms, SMEs perform poorly in exporting. In the US, for instance, companies with fewer than five hundred employees account for 50 percent of the private non-farm outputs but only 30 percent of exported goods. It is thus easy to see why the US government is providing subsidies and other supports to facilitate SMEs' export activities. The Obama administration asked the Export-Import Bank to increase export financing by more than a third to US$6 billion in 2010.

Some European members of the OECD spend higher proportions of GDP on export promotion than the US government. For instance, the French government's expenditure on export promotion per thousand dollars of GDP in the mid-1990s was estimated to be six to ten times that of the US. Likewise, in 1995, as a proportion of GDP, the UK government outspent US export promotion activities by a factor of eight.[74] In EU economies, export policies to increase firms' access to foreign market have been a cornerstone of the governments' SME policies. In some cases, the EU economies have also developed a collective approach towards export promotion (e.g., the European Commission's export promotion campaign "Gateway to Japan").[75]

As to the rationale behind EU governments' spending on export promotion activities, they have argued that the US government's increased export promotion activities have forced them to promote domestic firms through government intervention. The French, for instance, think that US successes abroad threatened the country's exports and forced them to take more promotional efforts. In May 2004, the EU's trade commissioner noted that the EU countries would eliminate agricultural export subsidies if the US and other countries would take similar measures.[76]

OECD governments have implemented and utilized a wide range of export promotion tools and activities. Some of the most popular tools include lobbying and visits to the target countries by high-level government officials, financing trade shows, and other types of government-supplied financing packages. Some export promotion tools also entail supplying actual and potential exporters with specific information. Certain countries (e.g., Italy, Japan and Spain) have tied their development aids to developing countries with export promotion programs.[77] Likewise, South Korea's export promotion measures also include the establishment of specialized banks for the development of "strategically important" sectors.[78] Some countries have developed free trade zones and provided incentives to attract export-producing manufacturers.

Some OECD countries have their export promotion strategies geared toward certain geographical markets. For instance, Germany launched an "East Asia Initiative" and a "Latin America Concept" in the mid-1990s. These programs were developed to improve the long-term performance of German exporters in these regions. Another example is France's "Initiative for Asia", which was announced in 1994.[79]

The UK probably offers the most spectacular examples of well-coordinated and well-funded export promotions campaigns. The UK prime minister, Cabinet officials and the royal family advocate British firms' products in foreign countries. In the mid-1990s, about one-fifth of British diplomats in foreign countries worked full-time in export promotion. Of particular interest is the idea of involving the country's royal family in these activities. In 1997, the UK government promised to spend US$97 million to buy a new yacht for the royal family. It was argued that the queen's visit to foreign countries on the "Buybritish" yacht would help attract foreign businesses.[80]

Among EU economies, German export promotion efforts are arguably broadly similar to those of the US. For instance, in 1995, Ronald H. Brown, then US Secretary of Commerce, wrote to the president and speaker of the house: "The Germans are emulating the US approach to export promotion."[81] Among other things, German export promotion strategies entail supplying actual and potential exporters with specific information. France, on the other hand, extensively utilizes varieties of lobbying strategies such as phone calls, letters and high-level visits. In addition, the French government finances trade shows and provides other finance packages to companies involved in exporting. Italy and Spain also use high-level visits and trade missions as export promotion tools. In addition, these two countries' development aids to developing countries are also tied in with export promotion programs.[82]

Export Promotions in Large vs Small Countries

In a large country, the central government's export promotion efforts face various difficulties, especially in promoting SMEs' exports. The EU's biggest economies—Germany, Italy, France, the UK and Spain—tend to implement most policies specifically targeted at SMEs. To take one example, the Baden-Wuerttemberg state of Germany helped set up distribution centers in China.[83] The state did so because at that time German firms' most important entry barriers in the Chinese market centered on distribution arrangements.

Regional Focus

EU economies also launched special programs for regions with high export potential. As mentioned above, in the mid-1990s, Germany launched the "East Asia Initiative" to increase its exports to the region. High-level delegates paid a visit to major East Asian economies such as Vietnam, Malaysia and Indonesia. To promote exports, the country's economic minister also emphasized enlarging German embassies in Asia. German diplomats with industrial policy expertise were assigned to work on expanding the country's business in China. In the mid-1990s, Germany also started a "Latin America Concept" to promote exports in that region. Likewise, in 1994, France announced an "Initiative for Asia". French officials, including the prime minister, foreign affairs, industry, post, and telecommunications and foreign trade ministers, visited a number of Asian countries. They were accompanied by representatives from French firms.[84]

Notes

1. oecd.org 2010, "About the OECD", at www.oecd.org/about/.
2. OECD 2010, "Accession: Estonia, Israel and Slovenia invited to join OECD", October 5, at www.oecd.org/document/57/0,3746,en_215713 61_44315115_45159737_1_1_1_1,00.html.
3. http://info.worldbank.org/governance/wgi/pdf/rq.pdf.

4. BMI 2011, "Business Environment", in *Chile Business Forecast Report 2010*, 2nd quarter, pp. 23–30.

5. OECD 2011, *Corporate Governance in Chile*, at www.oecd.org/corpo rate/ca/corporategovernanceofstate-ownedenterprises/corporategovernan ceinchile.htm.

6. heritage.org, 2013 Index of Economic Freedom, Chile, at www.heritage. org/index/country/chile.

7. BMI 2011, "Business Environment", in *Chile Business Forecast Report 2010*, 4th quarter, pp. 33–40.

8. chile-usa.org 2005, "Ministry of Justice Reforms Underway", February, at www.chile-usa.org/minjustice.htm.

9. OECD 2011, *Corporate Governance in Israel 2011*, March 8, at www. oecd-ilibrary.org/governance/corporate-governance-in-israel-2011_ 9789264097698-en.

10. Ministry of Justice, Israel, n.d., "Israel Strengthens the Battle against Bribery and Corruption", at www.justice.gov.il/MOJEng/Mankal/Cor ruption/.

11. OECD 2011, "Convention on Combating Bribery of Foreign Public Officials in International Business Transactions", at www.oecd.org/daf/anti-bribery/ConvCombatBribery_ENG.pdf.

12. OECD 2011, *Enhancing Market Openness, Intellectual Property Rights, and Compliance through Regulatory Reform in Israel*, at www.oecd.org/ israel/48262991.pdf.

13. Israel Ministry of Foreign Affairs 2008 "Israel's Intellectual Property Law", March 16, at www.mfa.gov.il/MFA/Government/Law/Legal+ Issues+and+Rulings/Israel%20intellectual%20property%20law% 2016-Mar-2008.

14. OECD 2011, *Enhancing Market Openness, Intellectual Property Rights, and Compliance through Regulatory Reform in Israel*, at www.oecd.org/ israel/48262991.pdf.

15. US Department of State, Bureau of Economic Energy and Business Affairs, 2011, "2011 Investment Climate Statement: Estonia", at www. state.gov/e/eb/rls/othr/ics/2011/157274.htm.

16. Ibid.

17. OECD 2011, *Corporate Governance in Estonia 2011*, at www.oecd-ilibrary.org/governance/corporate-governance-in-estonia-2011_ 9789264119079-en.

18. OECD 2011, *Corporate Governance in Slovenia 2011*, at www.oecd-ilibrary.org/governance/corporate-governance-in-slovenia-2011_ 9789264097704-en.

19. "Background Note: Slovenia's Accession to the OECD", www.oecd.org/ document/53/0,3746,en_21571361_44315115_45161781_ 1_1_1_1,00. html.

20. OECD 2011, *Enhancing Market Openness, Intellectual Property Rights, and Compliance through Regulatory Reform in Slovenia*, at www.oecd.org/slove nia/48263001.pdf.

21. WIPO 2008, "Country Profile from WIPO Guide to Intellectual Property Worldwide", at www.wipo.int/about-ip/en/ipworldwide/pdf/si.pdf.

22. OECD Observer 1999, "Corporate Governance: Getting it Right in Russia", at www.oecdobserver.org/news/archivestory.php/aid/21/Corporate_governance:_getting_it_right_in_Russia.html.

23. BIAC 2012, "Russia-OECD Accession Discussions: Improving the Russian Business Environment, BIAC Statement to the OECD", May 14, at www.biac.org/statements/nme/12–06_FIN_BIAC_BIAC_RUSSIA_PAPER_2012.pdf.

24. BIAC 2011, "OECD-Russia Accession Discussions: Improving the Russian Business Environment: BIAC Statement to the OECD", March 9, at www.biac.org/statements/nme/08%2003%202011%20FINAL%20BIAC%20DRAFT%20BIAC%20RUSSIA%20PAPER%202011.pdf.

25. *Economist* 2012, "The Lure of Chilecon Valley", October 13, at www.economist.com/node/21564589.

26. *BusinessWeek* 1995, "Score One More for Japan's Bureaucrats", (International Edition) April 2, at www.businessweek.com/stories/1995– 04–02/score-one-more-for-japans-bureaucrats-intl-edition.

27. heritage.org, 2010 Index of Economic Freedom, "Turkey", at www.heritage.org/index/country/Turkey.

28. *Economist* 2010, "Making a Success of Failure", p. 68.

29. Gamboa-Cavazos, M., Garza-Cantu, V., & Salinas, E. 2007, "The Organization of Corruption: Political Horizons and Special Interests", at http://sitios.itesm.mx/egap/que_es_egap/inv_pub/EGAP_AP_07_01.pdf.

30. Shirk, D.A. 2011, "Criminal Justice Reform in Mexico: An Overview", *Mexican Law Review*, at http://info8.juridicas.unam.mx/pdf/mlawrns/cont/6/arc/arc1.pdf.

31. Franks, J., Nyborg, K., & Torous, W. 1996, "A Comparison of US, UK, and German Insolvency Codes", *Financial Management*, 25, pp. 86–101.

32. Peng, M.W., Yamakawa, Y., & Lee, S.-H. 2010, "Bankruptcy Laws and Entrepreneur-Friendliness", *Entrepreneurship Theory and Practice*, 34(3), pp. 517–530.

33. Global Entrepreneurship Week 2012, "Global Entrepreneurship Week Policy Survey Turns Up Unexpected Results", November 14, at www.unleashingideas.org/policysurvey.

34. OECD 2008, "Raising Labor Supply to Sustain Strong Potential Growth", in *OECD Economic Surveys: Poland*, pp. 19–45.

35. Isenberg, D.J. 2010, "How to Start an Entrepreneurial Revolution", *Harvard Business Review*, 88(6), pp. 40–50.

36. Brown, J.M. 2008, "Lucre of the Irish", *Prospect*, 142, at www.prospectmagazine.co.uk/magazine/lucreoftheirish/.

37. Isenberg, D.J. 2010, "How to Start an Entrepreneurial Revolution", *Harvard Business Review*, 88(6), pp. 40–50.

38. Chile 2008, "GEM Report, 2009. Chileans See Entrepreneurship as Desirable Career Option", May 10, 2009, at www3.babson.edu/Newsroom/Releases/Chile-GEM-2009.cfm.

39. UIS 2010, "Trends in Tertiary Education: Sub-Saharan Africa", UIS Fact Sheet no. 10, at www.uis.unesco.org/FactSheets/Documents/fs10–2010-en.pdf/

40. European Commission 2007, *Entrepreneurship Survey of the EU (25 Member States), United States, Iceland and Norway: Analytical Report*, Geneva: Eurobarometer.

41. Global Entrepreneurship Week 2012, "Global Entrepreneurship Week Policy Survey Turns Up Unexpected Results", November 14, at www.prweb.com/releases/2012/11/prweb10132456.htm.

42. Zachary, G.P. 2000. *The Global Me: New Cosmopolitans and the Competitive Edge: Picking Globalism's Winners and Losers*, London: Nicholas Brealey.

43. Pofeldt, E. 2007, "Is the US Winning Back its Competitive Edge?", *FSB Magazine*, at http://money.cnn.com/2007/06/08/magazines/fsb/immigrant_universities.fsb/index.htm.

44. Bahl, N. 2011, "Smarter Immigration Laws Would Boost Economy", *The Tennessean*, November 6, www.tennessean.com/article/20111106/OPINION03/311060040/Smarter-immigration-laws-would-boost-economy.

45. OECD 2011, "Fighting Bid Rigging in Government Contracts: Mexico-OECD Partnership", at www.oecd.org/competition/cartelsandanti-competitiveagreements/fightingbidrigginginvestmentcontractsmexico-oecdpartnership.htm.

46. OECD 2008, "Enhancing the Productivity of the Service Sector in Japan", in *Economic Survey of Japan 2008*, pp. 125–170.

47. Shogo, I. 2001, "Competition in Japan's Telecommunications Sector: Challenges for the Japan Fair Trade Commission", October 11, at www.jftc.go.jp/en/policy_enforcement/speeches/2001.files/011011speech.pdf.

48. OECD 2009, "Strengthening Competition to Boost Efficiency and Employment", in *Economic Survey of France 2009*, pp. 101–130.

49. Ibid.

50. OECD 2007, *Financing SMEs and Entrepreneurs: Scoreboard for the United States*, October 2007, Paris: OECD, doi: 10.1787/9789264166769-table 106-en.

51. Schramm, C.J. 2004, "Building Entrepreneurial Economies", *Foreign Affairs*, 83(4), pp. 104–115.

52. Becker, K.F. 2004, *The Informal Economy, Fact Finding Study*, Stockholm: Sida, at www.eldis.org/vfile/upload/1/document/0708/DOC15233.pdf.

53. Comlay, E. 2012, "Small Banks Target Lending at Mexico's Informal Sector", *The European*, March 13, at www.the-european.eu/story-335/small-banks-target-lending-at-mexicos-informal-sector.html.

54. Ernst & Young 2012, *Globalizing Venture Capital: Global Venture Capital Insights and Trends Report 2011*, 2, at www.ey.com/Publication/vwLUAssets/Globalizing_venture_capital_VC_insights_and_trends_report_CY0227/$FILE/Globalizing%20venture%20capital_VC%20insights%20and%20trends%20report_CY0227.pdf.

55. OECD 2011, "Access to Finance: Venture Capital", in *Entrepreneurship at a Glance 2011*, at http://dx.doi.org/10.1787/9789264097711-25-en.
56. Yiannopoulos, M. 2012, "Why European Venture Loses So Much Money", May 3, at www.kernelmag.com/yiannopoulos/2066/gurgle-gurgle-gurgle/.
57. OECD 2006, *Economic Survey of Japan 2008*, Paris: OECD.
58. Kitchens, R., & Torrence, P.D. 2012, "The JOBS Act: Crowdfunding and Beyond", *Economic Development Journal*, 11(4), pp. 42–47.
59. St. John, Oliver, 2012 "Angel Sites: Match.com for Start-ups and Investors", *USA Today*, November 26, at www.cnbc.com/id/49982917.
60. Baygan, G., & Freudenberg, M. 2000, *The Internationalisation of Venture Capital Activity in OECD Countries: Implications for Measurement and Policy*, OECD Science, Technology and Industry Working Papers, Paris: OECD, at www.oecd-ilibrary.org/science-and-technology/the-internationalisation-of-venture-capital-activity-in-oecd-countries_084236411045.
61. OECD 2006, "Venture Capital Development in MENA Countries: Taking Advantage of the Current Opportunity", *MENA Investment Policy Brief*, 1, at www.oecd.org/mena/investment/37256468.pdf.
62. Chaia, A., Goland, T., & Schiff, R. 2010, "Counting the World's Unbanked", Insights & Publications, at www.mckinsey.com/insights/financial_ser vices/counting_the_worlds_unbanked.
63. mixmarket.org 2010, "Microfinance in Mexico", at www.mixmarket.org/mfi/country/Mexico.
64. Grameen America 2008, "Grameen America", http://grameenamerica.org/about-us.
65. Knowledge@Wharton 2011, "American Offshoots: Will Microfinance Ever Really Take Root in the U.S.?", June 17, at http://knowledge.whar ton.upenn.edu/article.cfm?articleid=2797.
66. *Washington Post* 2012, "A Glance at Microcredit in the US", August 8.
67. Ahlers, G.K.C., Cumming, D., Guenther, C., & Schweizer, D. 2012, "Signaling in Equity Crowdfunding", October 14, at http://papers.ssrn.com/sol3/papers.cfm?abstract_id=2161587.
68. Kitchens, R., & Torrence, P.D. 2012, "The JOBS Act: Crowdfunding and Beyond", *Economic Development Journal*, 11(4), pp. 42–47.
69. Seker, M. 2012, "Lessons from a Start-Up Nation", July 11, at http://blogs.worldbank.org/psd/lessons-from-a-start-up-nation.
70. "The Danish Enterprise and Construction Authority Profile of Israel: An Entrepreneurial Country", at www.erhvervsstyrelsen.dk/publikationer/ivaerksaettere/Entrepreneurship%20Index%202010/kap05.htm.
71. OECD 2012, "Science and Innovation: Turkey", at www.oecd.org/turkey/sti-outlook-2012-turkey.pdf.
72. Heijmans, P. 2010, "EU Sets its Sights on Tax Havens", *Prague Post*, January 27.
73. Lewis, G. 2007 "Who in the World is Entrepreneurial?", *FSB: Fortune Small Business*, 17(5), p. 14.

74. Donovan, R.J. 1996, "The National Export Strategy: Generating Jobs through Exports", *Business America*, 117(5), pp. 8–10.
75. EU News 2001, "EU Gateway to Japan Export Promotion Campaign: Trade Mission to Include Technical Seminar Featuring EU Medical and Home Care and Rehabilitation Equipment Manufacturers", at www.euin japan.jp/en/media/news/news2001/20010920/110000/.
76. Center for International Development 2004, "European Union Summary", May, at www.cid.harvard.edu/cidtrade/gov/eugov.html (accessed August 19, 2010).
77. Freres, C. 2000, "The European Union as a Global 'Civilian Power': Development Cooperation in EU–Latin American Relations", *Journal of Interamerican Studies and World Affairs*, 42(5), pp. 63–86.
78. Soh, C. 1997, *From Investment to Innovation? The Korean Political Economy and Changes in Industrial Competitiveness*, Seoul: International Trade and Business Institute.
79. Brown, R.H. 1995, "Letter from Secretary Brown", *Business America*, October, 116(10), p. 6.
80. *Economist* 1997, "Thoroughly Modern Mercantilists", February 1, pp. 23–25.
81. Brown, R.H. 1995, "Letter from Secretary Brown", *Business America*, October, 116(10), p. 6.
82. Freres, C. 2000, "The European Union as a Global 'Civilian Power': Development Cooperation in EU–Latin American Relations", *Journal of Interamerican Studies and World Affairs*, 42(5), pp. 63–86.
83. Dichtl, E., Koeglmayr, H., & Mueller, S. 1990, "International Orientation as a Precondition for Export Success", *Journal of International Business Studies*, 21(1), pp. 23–40.
84. *Business America* 1995, "Washington Advocacy: Supporting US Jobs in Global Competition", *The National Export Strategy: Third Annual Report to the United States Congress*, 116(10).

5

ENTREPRENEURSHIP IN POST-SOCIALIST ECONOMIES IN THE FORMER SOVIET UNION AND CENTRAL AND EASTERN EUROPE

Abstract

There is growing recognition among post-socialist (PS) economies in the Former Soviet Union and Central and Eastern Europe (FSU&CEE) that free-market entrepreneurship is essential for ultimately improving their economic future. As a result of external pressures from a number of international organizations as well as a realization on the part of policy makers of the benefits of a free economy, these economies have initiated a series of measures to facilitate entrepreneurship. The promotion of market entrepreneurship, however, has been a challenging experience for most of them. FSU&CEE economies also vary in the rate at which they are transitioning to market economies. This chapter examines key determinants of entrepreneurship in PS economies and their various forms of entrepreneurship. A special focus of this chapter is on the clear contexts and attendant mechanisms associated with the institutions–entrepreneurship nexus in the context of FSU&CEE economies. Looking at entrepreneurial development in various FSU&CEE states, we find success stories as well as major failures.

This chapter's objectives include:

1. To demonstrate an understanding of the natures of entrepreneurial activities in FSU&CEE economies.
2. To analyze the drivers of entrepreneurship in FSU&CEE economies.

3. To evaluate some of the barriers to transition to market economies in FSU&CEE economies.
4. To assess the extent of productive, unproductive and destructive entrepreneurship in FSU&CEE economies.
5. To demonstrate an understanding of the sources of heterogeneity in entrepreneurial activities in FSU&CEE economies.

5.1. Introduction

In this chapter, we shift our attention to entrepreneurship in the formerly socialist countries of the Former Soviet Union and Central and Eastern Europe (FSU&CEE). Note that during the socialist economic systems of the past, all these countries were characterized by a pervasive hostility to entrepreneurship. Among the FSU&CEE economies, the Czech Republic, Estonia, Hungary, Poland, Slovakia and Slovenia are OECD members. In Chapter 4 we discussed at length the importance of economic and political reforms in order to qualify for OECD membership. Some other FSU&CEE economies, while not yet OECD members, have joined NATO and the EU, and thus institutional reforms in these economies were constantly monitored as part of the process of attaining full membership of these international organizations.

In general there is growing recognition among post-socialist (PS) economies in FSU&CEE that free-market entrepreneurship is ultimately essential to improving their economic future. Even countries which lack membership in any of the above international organizations have demonstrated their commitment and willingness to encourage and promote free-market entrepreneurship. One example to illustrate this point is Russia's Skolkovo project announced by then President Dmitry Medvedev in 2009 to reduce the country's reliance on commodities and develop a globally competitive knowledge-based economy. The plan is to transform 400 hectares of farmland near Moscow into Silikonnovaya Dolina or Russia's Silicon Valley. The Skolkovo project includes five "clusters" specializing in IT, energy, nuclear technologies, biomedicine and space technologies. As of mid-2012, the government had allocated about US$4.2 billion for the project.[1] As of February 2012, the project had approved US$220 million in grants to 330 startups.[2]

Corporate and personal tax breaks and other incentives are promised for investors and about two hundred laws had been amended as of mid-2012 to encourage high-tech investment in Skolkovo. High-level government officials have visited foreign countries to promote the Skolkovo project. In 2010, Medvedev met with a group of US venture fund managers in an attempt to attract VC in Silikonnovaya Dolina.[3] Likewise, in February 2012, executive directors of the five clusters of the Skolkovo project visited the UK to raise awareness of the opportunities available for researchers and companies, and to attract partners and investors. These incentives have already attracted multinationals such as Microsoft, IBM, Siemens, Intel, Cisco and Nokia. As of the early 2013, participant status was granted to over three hundred companies. In 2012, Skolkovo announced its intention to open a similar innovation city in Vladivostok.

While many examples of promoting entrepreneurship in FSU&CEE economies exist, there are various inertia effects that have posed difficulties. One obvious problem concerns the absence of and difficult-to-construct key ingredients of an entrepreneurial ecosystem such as the appropriate political, legal, economic and commercial structures needed for a free-market economy. These problems are even prevalent in some FSU&CEE economies that are considered to be successful. For instance, in Poland, which is viewed as among the most successful FSU&CEE economies, small firm size, lack of innovative capacity, limited access to capital, underdeveloped management skills and a lack of experience in conducting businesses in foreign countries have hindered entrepreneurial development.[4] Polish SMEs also complain about the complexity of the legal system, high administrative costs and high corporate tax rates.[5]

5.2. Variation across FSU&CEE Economies in Different Forms of Entrepreneurship

The positive impacts of entrepreneurship are felt across most FSU& CEE economies. Most economies in the region have experienced positive economic growth in recent years. For instance, every country in the CEE region except for Romania experienced positive GDP growth in 2010. These economies have also made a significant progress in reducing poverty. For instance, according to the Federal State Service for Statistics (Rosstat), absolute poverty in Russia fell from 29 percent in 2000 to 13.4 percent in 2007.[6]

Formal and informal institutions needed to support market entre-preneurship have not developed at the same rate across the FSU&CEE economies. There is more variation across FSU&CEE economies' reforms than many analysts predicted. While some FSU&CEE economies have made significant progresses, the reform process has been relatively slow in others. The Czech Republic, Estonia, Hungary and Poland are described as some examples of successful FSU&CEE economies.

Hungary, an EU member with a population of ten million, is described as an example of a post-1989 success. It has one of the most developed VC markets among CEE economies. It has a well-developed entrepreneurial ecosystem consisting of successful serial entrepreneurs, business angels, entrepreneurial infrastructures and services, all of which provide entrepreneurs with access to skills and expertise.[7] Local government, local firm development centers such as the Hungarian Foundation for Enterprise Development, private firms and profes-sional organizations have teamed up to establish business incubators. Hungary has been successful in producing globally successful firms in leading-edge, technology-intensive sectors. For instance, LogMeIn (which allows Internet users to connect remotely), Prezi (a provider of cloud-based software) and Ustream (a provider of a live video stream-ing service) started from Hungary and globalized their businesses within a few years. As of the mid-2012, these three companies had over 110 million users worldwide.[8]

Economies such as those of Russia and Ukraine, on the other hand, have been slow to develop institutional supports needed to promote productive free-market entrepreneurship. For one thing, political entrepreneurship, in which entrepreneurs use political power, capital and social networks to maximize economic rewards, is more readily apparent in Russian and some other FSU&CEE economies.[9] More-over, as is the case in other developing economies, the ruling elites and their families, friends and clients have lived a parasitic existence in some FSU&CEE economies. It is argued that the Russian economy is a hybrid between Soviet capitalism and feudalism. In the Forbes' list of 1,011 billionaires (March 2010) sixty-two were Russian oligarchs, which may serve as an indication of the lack of free-market competi-tion in the country.[10] A similar point can be made about many other

FSU&CEE economies. It has been reported that Kazakh President Nursultan Nazarbayev allegedly transferred at least US$1 billion dollars of oil export revenues to his private accounts.[11] His family members control many key enterprises in the country. Likewise, an estimate suggested that thirteen Ukrainian oligarchs control about 40 percent of the Ukrainian economy.[12] Three top oligarchs[13] in Ukraine played a key role in supporting former President Leonid Kuchma's regime. One of the oligarchs, Pinchuk, is Kuchma's son-in-law. In 2004, the businessmen's favor gravitated toward the opposition candidate Viktor Yushchenko, who benefited enormously. This shows that governments failing to direct efforts towards buttering up businesses may face severe consequences.

5.3. Productive, Unproductive and Destructive Entrepreneurship in FSU&CEE Economies

Individuals in FSU&CEE economies do not necessarily have a lower propensity to engage in entrepreneurial activities than those in mature market economies. According to the International Social Survey Program data set, the proportion saying "I would prefer to be self-employed" was the largest in Poland—80 percent.[14] As noted in Chapter 1, people in FSU&CEE economies have also accepted the idea of the free market and capitalism.

The concept of entrepreneurship, however, is quite broad in FSU&CEE economies. Indeed, as noted earlier, entrepreneurs in FSU&CEE economies have come in various forms. One way to classify entrepreneurial activities is in terms of their legalities. There have been an increasing number of businesses within the legal boundary. In rapidly changing environments like those of FSU&CEE economies, however, entrepreneurs find attractive economic niches from outside the current institutional boundaries.[15] A significant proportion of entrepreneurial activities in these economies have been in quasi-legal and extralegal areas.

A related point is that the inertia effects of socialism influence entrepreneurial activities in FSU&CEE economies. One scholar noted: "capitalism is built not *on* but *with* the ruins of socialism".[16] Socialism's ruins come in various forms including the influence of

Table 5.1 Entrepreneurship in post-socialist economies: a typology

LEGALITY ⇒ IDEOLOGY ⇓	LEGAL	NON-LEGAL/ILLEGAL
Socialism dominated	• Collective entrepreneurship	• Elite entrepreneurship • Political entrepreneurship • Red hat entrepreneurship
Capitalism dominated	• Market entrepreneurship	• Institutional entrepreneurship

Marxist-Leninist philosophy and the prominence of communist party members and bureaucrats in the entrepreneurship landscape.

Based on the two dimensions discussed above—legality and the inertia effects of socialism—we have developed a 2 x 2 typology of entrepreneur types in FSU&CEE economies (Table 5.1). Our observations above also raise the interesting possibility that institutions in some FSU&CEE economies may do better in promoting entrepreneurship in unproductive and destructive forms than those in mature market economies. Note that free-market entrepreneurship, which relies on competition, supply, and demand, is likely to add to the social product and is productive. Some forms of political entrepreneurship are also associated with criminal and quasi-criminal activities,[17] which are inefficient, unproductive or even destructive.

5.3.1. Productive Market Entrepreneurship

Market entrepreneurs in FSU&CEE economies depend upon the newly created market institutions. While economic systems in mature market economies are characterized by private enterprise and market entrepreneurship, this form of entrepreneurship is at its early stages of development in most FSU&CEE economies.

Contrary to the stereotypically different expectations that surround FSU&CEE economies, however, market entrepreneurship is growing rapidly in some FSU&CEE economies. A significant proportion of small and self-employed firms in FSU&CEE economies have the ingredients of market entrepreneurship in their functioning. For instance, traditional Russian business values have changed gradually and are becoming more and more consistent with free-market entrepreneurship.[18]

5.3.2. Unproductive and Destructive Entrepreneurship

Compared to more mature market economies, unproductive and destructive forms of entrepreneurship tend to be more prevalent in FSU&CEE economies. For one thing, the introduction of market forces in FSU&CEE economies pushed a great deal of economic activity underground. One scholar notes: "One of every five workers in Eastern and Central Europe labors off the books and receives under-the-table payments."[19] The underground economy as a proportion of GDP is significantly bigger in CEE economies than corresponding figures for EU member countries and a sizeable proportion of them are also associated with criminal and quasi-criminal activities.[20]

In 1997, the black market accounted for 95 percent of retail activity in Tajikistan and 50–60 percent in Ukraine.[21] According to Goskomstat, Russia's State Statistics Service, unreported income accounted for 30 percent of wages paid in the late 1990s in the country. The corresponding figure for Bulgaria is estimated at about one-third.[22] Similarly, according to the Romanian Information Service, unofficial economic activity in the country is about 30–40 percent of GDP and in 1998, smuggling was 12 percent higher than official imports.[23] Other estimates suggest that the "shadow economy" accounts for about 24 percent of GDP in Lithuania and 40 percent in Russia.[24] Formalization of the informal economy is a critical practical challenge facing FSU&CEE economies.

Finally, a remarkable example of parasitical existence of entrepreneurs upon the economy is the creation of firms to support criminal activities in some FSU&CEE economies. There are, for instance, companies whose primary purpose is to provide money-laundering services for criminal organizations.[25] Organized crime groups in Russia have been the driving force behind the rapid rise of the global cybercrime industry.

Political Entrepreneurship   One scholar makes an intriguing argument as to how political entrepreneurs emerge in FSU&CEE economies: post-socialist transition is not a transition from *plan* to *market* but from *plan* to *clan*.[26] The essence of the argument is simple: political entrepreneurs take advantage of their positional power to maximize economic rewards. They receive state subsidies and contracts in various forms. This emphasis on the exploitation of positional power is echoed in the political capitalism thesis, which argues that major winners of the PS transformations are the former nomenklatura.[27] Political entrepreneurship goes against the idea of capitalism and describes a paradoxical situation of "making capitalism without capitalists".[28]

Russia differs from other transition economies in the CEE in several important aspects, inter alia its vast natural resources, which provides enormous opportunities for rent-seeking.[29] Unsurprisingly, state managers and new entrepreneurs benefited tremendously from rent-seeking in the transition.

While political entrepreneurship also exists in mature market economies, this form of entrepreneurship is more readily apparent in FSU&CEE economies. A central feature of the privatization of state enterprises in CEE economies is that privileged elites converted "limited de facto use and income rights into more de jure alienable rights".[30] In Russia, for instance, following the mass privatization, former nomenklatura appointees accounted for about two-thirds of the top positions in businesses and the government.[31] Likewise, beginning in the mid-1980s in Hungary and Poland and in the late 1980s in Romania, political and administrative elites capitalized on their positional power to start their own businesses.

That is not to say that political entrepreneurship is absent in mature market economies such as the US. The concept of manifest and latent functions[32] can be very helpful in understanding how the nature of political entrepreneurship differs in FSU&CEE and more mature market economies. Manifest functions are explicitly stated and understood by the participants in the relevant action and the consequences can be observed or expected. Latent functions are those that are not explicitly stated, recognized or intended by the people involved. In the US, for instance, the manifest posture is of private enterprise, but deeply ingrained below the surface are a wide range of firms that are politically dependent. For instance, according to the Center for Responsive Politics, candidates for the US congress and presidency received over US$12 million between 1989 and 2000 from the sugar industry.[33] Observers have pointed out the possibility that these political contributions might have an adverse effect on regulatory efforts to revise national nutritional policy. Likewise, large firms in the US textile industry have received institutional favors in various forms, such as subsidies and barriers to trade in textile products, and have thus benefited from political entrepreneurship.[34] In China, on the other hand, the manifest posture is that of collective enterprise while the latent reality is privatized enterprise owned by political entrepreneurs.

There are, however, important differences between political entrepreneurship in FSU&CEE economies and mature market economies. Part of the fascinating character of political entrepreneurship in FSU&CEE economies stems from the fact that there is a symbiosis between economic and political elites, where political entrepreneurs take advantage of positional power to maximize economic rewards.[35] In some cases, bureaucrats are also capitalists and possess the capacity to penetrate into the government apparatus.[36] This situation is similar to economies in the Middle East[37] and is different from more mature market economies, in which economic and political elites tend to be different groups.

Studies conducted on FSU&CEE economies have found that the most important barrier to the transition to free-market economy centered on Communist Party bureaucrats' resistance. This phenomenon is similar to that in the Middle East, where bureaucrats discourage policies favoring institutional reforms and remain a strong anti-reform force.[38]

Another way of viewing political entrepreneurship is in terms of the entrepreneurs' engagement in central vs peripheral positions. Political entrepreneurs in FSU&CEE economies tend to possess economic and non-economic resources and are central players. In more mature market economies, on the other hand, political entrepreneurs tend to be peripheral players.[39]

A final issue that deserves mention relates to nepotism's influence on political entrepreneurship. As is the case of the Arab world (Chapter 6), such a tendency can be attributed to the culture (e.g., strong kinship ties and obligations to family and friends). While some degree of nepotism is involved everywhere, influences of favoritism, nepotism, and personal connections are more readily apparent in some FSU&CEE economies.

Institutional Entrepreneurship   To understand the differences in entrepreneurial activities in FSU&CEE economies and mature market
economies, we introduce the concept of institutional entrepreneurship.
Actors with key strategic resources or power, who can play an important
role in the creation of new institutions related to entrepreneurship,
are called institutional entrepreneurs. Institutional entrepreneurs are
driven by interests that they value, aware of the possible effects on
new institutions they seek to create and calculate.[40] They can change
existing models of social or economic order in the process of starting
or expanding businesses.

In the FSU&CEE economies' context, the most relevant issue concerns institutional holes. In many cases, institutional entrepreneurs
benefit from such holes—structural gaps between diverse institutional
actors that control complementary resources.[41] In general, such holes
tend to be more prevalent in transitional economies such as FSU&CEE
economies, than in more mature market economies because institutional rules in the former group are incomplete and ambiguous. In many
emerging economies', institutional entrepreneurs' access to political
resources facilitates their attempts to create new market institutions.[42]

Institutional entrepreneurship in FSU&CEE economies may entail
illegal activities and represent a significant component of political
entrepreneurship. An example is the *ex ante investment with ex post justification* approach to institutional entrepreneurship.[43] In this form of
entrepreneurship, an entrepreneur starts or expands a business, which
may violate existing laws or regulations. When the business becomes
successful and generates social benefits, the entrepreneur reports the
business to the government and persuades it to change existing laws
and regulations. In such cases, access to political resources is critical
to success.

5.4. Determinants of Entrepreneurship in FSU&CEE Economies

5.4.1. Regulatory Framework

One encouraging trend in FSU&CEE economies concerns the governments' shifting basis of legitimacy. In most FSU&CEE economies, governments are moving from coercive control over the state

and the legitimacy of Marxism-Leninism to economic legitimacy based on growth. Unsurprisingly, these economies have undertaken public policies to promote entrepreneurship as indicated by favorable regulatory climates to start new businesses. According to the World Bank's Ease of Doing Business Index 2013, Poland was the global top improver in the entrepreneurial climate from June 2011 to May 2012. Of the world's top ten economies that were recognized for making most improvement in the ease of doing business five were FSU&CEE economies: Poland, Ukraine, Uzbekistan, Serbia and Kazakhstan.[44]

As noted earlier, an important challenge in promoting entrepreneurship in FSU&CEE economies concerns the deficiency of formal institutions to support the functioning of the market. In overly politicized states, entrepreneurial efforts are diverted away from wealth creation into non-market behaviors, which entails securing protection from market forces. In many FSU&CEE economies, because of ineffective legal enforcement of private property rights, entrepreneurs considered it important to acquire political and administrative protection or depend on informal networks for security.[45] The absence of institutions to protect property rights and the lack of a strong judicial system hinder the growth of private entrepreneurship. In the absence of mechanisms to protect intellectual property and discourage monopolies and unfair trade practices, market entrepreneurship cannot thrive. The existence of appropriate regulative institutions determines whether potential entrepreneurs are likely to engage in new wealth creation through productive entrepreneurship or transfers of existing wealth through unproductive political entrepreneurship.

The government's inability to strengthen the rule of law also raises the interesting possibility that some market entrepreneurs may go underground and that many others will move into political entrepreneur and rent-seeking activities.[46] Most private actors may be tempted to exploit short-term profit-making opportunities under the existing institutional arrangement rather than engaging in long-term efforts at building new institutions. This is the obvious challenge for promoting market entrepreneurship in most FSU&CEE economies.

As noted above, Russia and Romania are often cited as unsuccessful examples of FSU&CEE economies in promoting market entrepreneurship. Earlier we discussed the roles of supra-national institutions or outside anchors such as the EU and OECD in facilitating the formation of market institutions. The significant improvements made by Romania in the past decade further illustrate this point (Fig. 5.1). Romania's development was often referred to as "stalled" or even "de-developed".[47] One expert observed that "the former party bosses are alive and, to the despair of many Romanians, well".[48] In 2000, there were at least thirteen institutions involved in the process. It was observed that state officials in Romania lack accountability, it was impossible to sue them, and that formal complaints have no effects.[49] Barriers to starting a business in recent years are less evident in Romania than in some economies that are entrepreneurially more successful. For instance, in terms of number of procedures, time and costs, it is much easier to start a business in Romania or Bulgaria than in Poland or the Czech Republic (Fig. 5.1).

Russia, on the other hand, is not an EU member, which may explain less developed market institutions. It is suggested that the Russian government arguably acted like a "grabbing hand" and discouraged entrepreneurial activities. The "merchant capitalism" thesis suggests that the dominant direction of change in the former Soviet Union would be "backward" or towards a more primitive merchant capitalism rather than a free-market-based more advanced capitalism.[50]

We can use the example of the Skolkovo project to illustrate barriers facing entrepreneurship in Russia. Progress in the project has been slower than expected. Observers have noted that after Vladimir Putin's return for a third presidential term in 2012, the project was relegated to a low priority list.[51] Whereas Medvedev has placed a higher priority on innovation and economic development, Putin's priorities have been about fulfilling his campaign promises, such as increasing the availability of emergency housing and public kindergartens.[52] There are also alleged engagements in corruption by government officials.[53] In February 2013, criminal cases against two high-ranking officials of the Skolkovo project were filed. The two officials allegedly embezzled US$800,000 from the project, money that was provided by the government to develop the infrastructure and support local startups.[54]

5.4.2. Values, Culture and Skills

Entrepreneurial Culture

The battle to promote market entrepreneurship is about more than just creating market-friendly political and economic institutions. In this regard, it is important to note that socialism was characterized by a negative social perception of entrepreneurs and market entrepreneurship. Attempts to promote entrepreneurship in some FSU&CEE economies face crucial cultural, social and cognitive challenges related to skills and psychology. Societal norms and networks that provide support for entrepreneurial risk-taking in mature markets are lacking in PS economies. For instance, Russian managers with experience in state-owned enterprises tend to avoid risk.[55] In addition, overcoming institutional inertia such as that related to a lack of accountability, initiative and trust to others has been a problem.[56]

Some have suggested the degree of religious-secular differentiation explains the heterogeneity in the FSU&CEE economies' entrepreneurial performance. Note that as a result of their communist history, some FSU&CEE economies have large populations of non-practicing

Table 5.2 Some examples of barriers to entrepreneurship in economies in the Orthodox group

COUNTRY	INSTITUTIONAL BARRIERS TO ENTREPRENEURSHIP IN CEE ECONOMIES
Belarus	• Businesses are dominated by Soviet-era managers that lack free-market mindsets.
Bulgaria	• Bulgarians did not experience twentieth-century capitalist production methods and work habits, risks and rewards.[78] • After the fall of the communist system in the late 1980s, secret service agents were reported to be engaging in organized crime.
Romania	• Beginning in the late 1980s, political elites started converting their positional power into starting businesses.[79]
Russia	• Following mass privatization, former nomenklatura appointees accounted for two-thirds of the top positions in businesses and the government.
Ukraine	• Predatory actions of state officials hinder rural entrepreneurship. • Powerful oligarchs have a strong influence on government policies. • Businesses are dominated by Soviet-era managers who lack free-market mindsets. • The regulatory burden on business takes 14% of a manager's time.

believers and non-believers. Among the believers, however, the dominant religions in economies in Belarus, Bulgaria, Romania, Russia and Ukraine are various forms of Orthodox Christianity, which lack the religious-secular differentiation.[57] On the other hand, Roman Catholicism is the dominant religion in Croatia, the Czech Republic, Estonia, Hungary, Lithuania, Poland and Slovakia. It is argued that in the Orthodox countries, informal institutions did not change at the same rate as formal institutions. The Orthodox tradition viewed entrepreneurship negatively and socialism further reinforced the stereotypes. Table 5.2 presents some examples of barriers to entrepreneurship in economies that have Orthodox Christianity as their dominant form of religion.

Entrepreneurial Capabilities The growth of new enterprise hinges critically upon the availability of entrepreneurial skills to carry out business functions effectively. Some FSU&CEE economies severely lack these skills. Russian managers with experience and training gained under the communist system in state-owned enterprises lack the management and business skills needed for free-market entrepreneurship. For instance, observers have noted that the majority of managers who are still running most Russian enterprises have values from the Soviet period, as well as values passed on from the previous tsarist era.[58] In general, in CEE economies, while there is no dearth of technology talent, management and marketing skills have been in a short supply. As to the lack of marketing skills, it is important to note that, traditionally, a central plan rather than the consumer was the driving force of national production in these economies.

Measures are being taken at various levels to improve entrepreneurial capabilities in most FSU&CEE economies. For instance, by 1995, Poland had fifty business incubators owned by foundations, associations or local governments, which offered offices for entrepreneurs at lower rents. In order to raise long-term entrepreneurial awareness, Poland's Ministry of Education has introduced an entrepreneurship curriculum at all education levels.[59] The country has also developed policies to attract the diaspora. Poland has identified that one of its main tasks is to establish a feedback mechanism between Poland and its diaspora living in other countries.[60] These efforts are reflected in Poland's SME-friendly environment. SMEs account for 30 percent of GDP in Poland compared to 10–15 percent in Russia.[61]

Observers have also noted that international practices such as international accounting standards, transparency standards and corporate governance rules are diffusing rapidly in the region. Likewise, Western professional service providers are operating throughout the area to provide various skills needed for carrying out entrepreneurial activities.

5.4.3. Access to Finance, Market, R&D and Technology

Access to Market

As noted earlier, institutional reforms in FSU&CEE economies which are members of international organizations such as the OECD, the EU and the NATO were constantly monitored. In particular, the EU members have well-developed competition and antitrust laws in place, which make it easy for a new company to enter the market. Moreover, the EU members also have easy access to the combined population of over 500 million EU inhabitants. Entrepreneurial firms in economies that are not EU members, however, face problems related to access to market.

R&D and Technology Some FSU&CEE economies have made a significant progress in R&D and technology creation. For instance, many investors think that Russians, Poles and Romanians outperform China and India in the creation and operation of high-tech startups needed for breakthrough innovations.[62] CEE economies' superior performance in R&D and IT can be attributed to the region's traditional emphasis on science and engineering. Speaking of the emphasis on mathematics in Romania, a scientist in Bucharest put the issue this way: "The respect for math is inside every family, even simple families, who are very proud to say their children are good at mathematics."[63]

Access to Finance   The infrastructures for the financial and capital markets such as banks, stock exchanges and various sources of venture capital were destroyed in most FSU&CEE economies under communism. Nonetheless, most CEE economies have made significant progress in reforming and developing the financial sector.

Due to CEE economies' superior performance in R&D, some VC investors consider the region more attractive than India and China. This is especially the case for high-tech startups with global potential. By 2007, OpenView Venture Partners, an expansion-stage VC fund focusing on high-growth technology companies, had invested 30 percent of the company's US$100-million global technology fund in the CEE region. Scott Maxwell, co-founder of the company noted: "Central and Eastern Europe are already a better play [than China and India]. The technologies are more sophisticated."[64]

According to European Private Equity & Venture Capital Association, CEE economies attracted €645 million (US$ 900 million) in private equity and venture capital in 2010, which was 60 percent higher than in 2009. Poland, the Czech Republic, Romania, Ukraine, Bulgaria and Hungary accounted for 94 percent of the total private equity for the CEE region.[65]

While a weak financial sector and a lack of entrepreneurial skills has hindered the inflow VC and other forms of foreign investments in

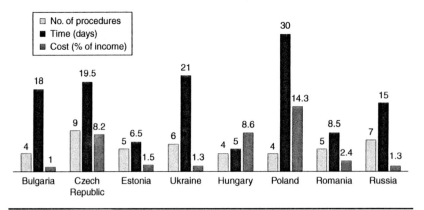

Figure 5.1 Time, costs and procedures required to start a new business in some CEE economies
Source: World Bank Doing Business Survey 2014, "Understanding Regulations for Small and Medium-Size Enterprises", www.doingbusiness.org/reports/global-reports/doing-business-2014

Russia, there have been many success stories. For instance, as early as in the mid-1990s, Russia had VC-funded companies in the technology sectors that employed high-profile scientists.[66] The domestic VC industry is also developing rapidly. In a meeting with US venture capitalists in 2010, then Russian President Dmitri Medvedev noted there were about twenty venture funds in the country with combined assets of about U$2 billion. Some companies have also raised substantial funds from international IPOs. In May 2011, Yandex NV, also known as "the Russian Google", raised US$1.3 billion on NASDAQ.[67]

5.5. Concluding Comments

FSU&CEE countries are undergoing a fundamental shift from a centrally planned economy to an entrepreneurial economy. Due to institutional inertia, formal and informal institutions in many FSU&CEE economies are currently less supportive of free-market entrepreneurship than in mature market economies. In many cases, the existing institutions tend to contribute to ineffective entrepreneurial thinking, behavior and decision making. Thus, the issue here is not that FSU&CEE economies lack entrepreneurship talents but that a significant proportion of entrepreneurial ventures in these economies lack the characteristics of productive free-market entrepreneurship. The promotion of productive free-market entrepreneurship in FSU&CEE economies requires drastic changes in formal and informal institutions.

Transition from central plan to free market is a complicated process requiring economic, political and social transformations for FSU&CEE economies. We noted above that FSU&CEE economies vary in terms of the development of free-market entrepreneurship as well as institutions to support private enterprises such as protection of property rights. While some economies have made a quantum leap on that front, institutional changes seem to be more of an upward drift than a surge in others. At the same time, there is no clear definition of the type of market economy desired by these economies.

The differences between the entrepreneurially successful and unsuccessful economies, for instance, can be attributed to entrepreneurial traditions during the communist and pre-communist eras. For instance, in contradistinction from the Czech Republic, Poland and Hungary, in Russia the state was the principal entrepreneur, and private entrepreneurship had had a weak tradition even before the revolution. Moreover, during the communist era, while some form of private entrepreneurship was permitted in Hungary and Poland, Russia and Romania depended entirely on central planning.[68] Russia, in particular, spent eight decades under communism, longer than any other FSU&CEE economy. In the process the critical elements of the infrastructure of modern capitalism were destroyed. It lacks an impartial court system and secure private property rights. Commercial organizations lack transparency and accountability. Consequently, there has been a higher degree of resistance to construct market institutions.

We also discussed the existence of parasitic entrepreneurs in some FSU&CEE economies. If there is any analogy that biological parasites' actions in environmental ecology teach, it is that parasites (entrepreneurs) adversely affect the host (the state) and may also mediate the influence the host (state) has on other components of the (entrepreneurial) ecosystem.[69] The presence of these parasitic entrepreneurs may negatively affect the health of the economy, economic growth, as well as the formation of new firms and their growth, and may increase firm mortality rates.

What conditions can transform the rules of the game so that various forms of unproductive and inefficient forms of entrepreneurship can be converted into productive and efficient free-market entrepreneurship? In most cases, formal institutions are easier to change than informal institutions. De-institutionalization and re-institutionalization of social practices, cultural values and beliefs occur very slowly.[70] A related point is that formal institutions affect informal institutions and vice versa. For instance, entrepreneurship-friendly laws and regulations may erode hostility toward entrepreneurship and profit-making at the societal level. Likewise, with the development of skills and expertise needed for free-market entrepreneurship, the psychology of risk-taking as well as social networks to provide support for entrepreneurship, governments are likely to face pressures to enact new laws and regulations.

One final but no less important aspect of informal institutions in FSU&CEE economies that is of interest to us is the fact entrepreneurs can take measures to change them in favor of private entrepreneurship.

Indeed, as the cases of Chile and Ireland discussed in Chapter 4 suggest, the negative social perception of profit-making behavior is not a phenomenon observed only in FSU&CEE economies. In this regard, FSU&CEE economies may also borrow a page from Timbro's lesson book (Chapter 2) to change the negative social perception of entrepreneurs and entrepreneurship.

5.6. Review Questions

1. In terms of legality and ideology, what are the different types of entrepreneurial activity in FSU&CEE economies?
2. How are formal and informal institutions affecting entrepreneurial activities in FSU&CEE economies?
3. Give some examples of productive, unproductive and destructive forms of entrepreneurship in FSU&CEE economies.
4. Give some examples of positive externalities generated by criminal and illegal enterprises.
5. Why do FSU&CEE economies differ in terms of their transition to market economies?

5.7. Critical Discussion Questions

1. Select a FSU&CEE economy. What are the natures of formal and informal institutions for entrepreneurial activities in the economy you selected? How have they changed in recent years?
2. How can productive entrepreneurship be promoted in FSU&CEE economies?

5.8. End-of-chapter Case: Kaspersky Lab – from Russia with Antivirus

Our growth strategy bases on several pivotal points, those are: deliver best protection to all our customers, be they consumers or corporate clients and develop best of breed technologies that ensure reliable protection. Our growth rates prove that it is a good strategy and it will bring us to the leading position on the marketplace.

These are the words of Moscow-based Kaspersky Lab's (KL) CEO and Chairman Eugene Kaspersky, outlining his vision and strategy for the company he co-founded in 1997.[71] Headquartered in Russia, KL provides IT security software such as antivirus, anti-spam, and network security software to protect computer users against viruses, spam and hackers. In 2010, KL was the world's fourth biggest IT security company. Due to KL's success in developing innovative products to fight cybercrime, the company was ranked thirty-second in Fast Company's 2011 list of the World's 50 Most Innovative Companies.[72]

The company lagged behind its chief rivals substantially. The two US household names Symantec and McAfee as well as Japan's Trend Micro were much bigger than KL. Symantec and McAfee were described as "an elephant to Kaspersky's mouse" in the global software security market, which was estimated at US$16.6 billion in 2010.[73] KL's other top competitors included Finland's F-Secure, Britain' Sophos, Spain's Panda Software and Norway's Norman, Czech Republic's AVG Technologies, Romania's BitDefender, Israel's Check Point and the Slovak Republic's ESET.

KL's Inception and the Early Years

Eugene Kaspersky studied at the A.N. Kolmogorov School in Moscow; it specializes in physics and mathematics. In 1987, he graduated with a degree in mathematical engineering from Moscow's Institute of Cryptography, Telecommunications and Computer Science. After graduation, he worked for the Russian defense department as a cryptologist and then in the KAMI Information Technologies Center. In 1994 Natalya Kaspersky joined him in KAMI, and in 1997 they co-founded an independent company.

Before starting KL, Eugene Kaspersky had developed some antivirus products to pursue his hobby of capturing computer viruses. A complete virus protection package, AntiViral Toolkit Pro was the first product he developed. In a series of independent tests conducted by Germany's Hamburg University, this product won top marks. A virus encyclopedia was among Eugene Kaspersky's early works, which provided analysis and descriptions of tens of thousands of viruses and how they functioned. KL developed many technological standards for the antivirus industry.

KL is Russia's largest software company and the only Russian firm among the world's top one hundred software companies. In 2009, a study from the market research firm IDC indicated that KL was the world's seventy-sixth biggest packaged software vendor (ranked by 2008 revenue). As of 2011, KL was Europe's largest antivirus company and the world's largest privately held Internet security company.

Tables 5.3 and 5.4 present some indicators related to KL's growth and reputation. While the company performed most of its R&D activities in Russia, its R&D centers were also located in some regional offices—in the US and in China. In 2010, about 84 percent of KL's sales were made outside Russia.[74]

KL had various incentives to attract and retain qualified employees. In 2000, the firm's turnover rate was less than 3 percent.[75] A survey conducted by the Boston Business Journal in 2010 also named KL as one of the best places to work in Massachusetts. Roger Wilson, KL Vice-President, Marketing, noted that the company provided stock options to employees and helped them find housing, as well as deal with Russian bureaucracy on obtaining residency permits.[76] This was in stark contrast with most Russian companies, which paid their employees poorly and with no link to productivity. Moreover, compensations in most Russian firms rarely included bonuses or stock options.[77]

The Russian Business Environment

Speaking of the barriers in the development of productive entrepreneurship in Russia, Eugene Kaspersky recently put the issue this way: "Russia has a lot of talented software engineers but not a lot of successful businesses. People still have an iron curtain in their minds."[80] When KL was launched, there was no government incentive program in Russia.[81] The lack of proper incentives had also led to a brain drain. According to AmBar, the Russian business association, 30,000–60,000 Russian-speaking professionals worked in the San Francisco Bay Area.[82]

When a KL office was opened in Tianjin, China in 2003, the company benefited from the Chinese government's incentives for startups

Table 5.3 KL's workforce and revenue growths

YEAR	NO. OF EMPLOYEES	REVENUE (MILLION, US$)	GEOGRAPHIC BREAKDOWN OF KL REVENUE	COMPETITORS' PERFORMANCE
2004		24		
2006		67		
2007	900	130	Russia: US$23.4 million, CIS & Baltic countries: US$5 million	Symantec: $2.8 billion from security
2008	1250	274	Russia: US$49.1 million Consumer products: 55%, businesses: 33%	Symantec: $2.31 billion and McAfee: US$1.13 billion
2009	1787 (631 in R&D)	391	Europe: US$188 million, Eastern Europe Middle East Africa (EEMEA): US$97 million, Americas: US$80 million, Asia and Pacific (APAC): US$26 million Consumer: US$255 million, corporate: US$109 million, technology alliances: US$27 million	Symantec: $2.39 billion and McAfee: US$1.19 billion
2010	2,338 (1,500 in Russia) 818 in R&D	538	Europe: US$218 million, Americas region: US$134 million, Asia-Pacific region and Japan: US$55 million, CIS, Eastern Europe, the Middle East and Africa: US$131 million	Symantec: $3.1 billion and McAfee: $1.85 billion

Kshetri, N. 2011, "Kaspersky Lab: From Russia with Anti-virus", *Emerald Emerging Markets Case Studies*, 1(3), pp. 1–10.

Table 5.4 KL's major milestones

TIME	EVENT
1994	The AntiViral Toolkit Pro by Eugene Kaspersky was recognized as the best antivirus scanner in the world by Hamburg University test lab.
1997	KL was founded.
2003	KL entered China.
2005	Independent US entity Kaspersky Lab Inc. was established.
May 2008	KL had twelve offices worldwide and a partner network of over 500 companies in 100 countries.
Oct. 2008	KL opened an office in Hong Kong.
Oct. 2008	KL opened a Melbourne office (for Oceania) and a Southeast Asia office in Selangor, Malaysia.
Early 2009	KL opened an office in Dubai Internet City.
Sep. 2009	Kaspersky received the National Friendship Award of China.
2009	Kaspersky received the Russian state prize from President Medvedev for improving state security.
2010	KL opened its first Indian office in Hyderabad.
Feb. 2010	KL was named one of the Top 10 Power Brands by PC.com, and voted "Best Antivirus Software" by the magazine's readers.
Apr. 2010	KL had a direct presence in twenty-nine countries.
Apr. 2010	KL won the Security Brand of the Year award at the Channel Awards.
Jun. 2010	Boston Business Journal's survey found KL to be one of the best places to work in Massachusetts.
Jun. 2010	Kaspersky won the Asia Entrepreneur Alliance (AEA) International Distinguished Entrepreneur as CEO of growth and expansion.
Nov. 2010	KL was honored with the Strategic Brand Leadership Award in India.
Feb. 2011	KL ranked no. 32 in Fast Company's 2011 list of the World's 50 Most Innovative Companies.
May 2011	Ninety patent applications related to IT security technologies filed by KL were being processed in the US, Russia, China and Europe.

Kshetri, N. 2011, "Kaspersky Lab: From Russia with Anti-virus", *Emerald Emerging Markets Case Studies*, 1(3), pp. 1–10.

in a special economic zone, which included free office space for a year and a tax holiday.[83] Pointing out the impact of a well-developed infrastructure, tax incentives and other support networks on the development of the Chinese IT industry, Natalya Kaspersky noted that a similar technology park would stimulate entrepreneurship in Russia.[84]

Since KL relies heavily on IP for its success, it faced a unique challenge in Russia due to weak IP protection laws and enforcement mechanisms. In most industrialized countries, duties and obligations to one's former employer, confidentiality clauses and non-compete agreements would prohibit a departing worker from taking valuable information with them. Natalya Kaspersky noted that such agreements were ineffective in Russia.[85] When an employee in the Russian Internet advertiser, System.ru, reportedly took the firm's entire client database to a newly formed rival, it was an eye-opener for IT firms such as KL.[86]

Trends in the IT Security Industry

The growth of the IT security industry is associated with and facilitated by a rapid rise in the cybercrime industry. Some estimates suggest that the global cybercrime industry generated US$1 trillion in 2009.[87] According to IDC, the secure content and threat management sector was worth US$15.1 billion in 2007, which is expected to increase to US$21 billion in 2011.

Another important trend has been global technology developers' business models based on open innovation and open source. Such models facilitated individuals and enterprises worldwide to develop applications. For instance, Google created an open environment for Android. Developers such as KL could sign up to the Android Marketplace and develop software. The rapidly transforming cybercrime landscape also provided opportunities for Kaspersky Lab and other developing world-based firms to use their technical expertise to expand their markets. The Romanian IT firm, BitDefender, for instance, was the first to develop a clean-up tool for the Sasser worm in May 2004.[88]

KL benefited greatly from Soviet-era investments in science and engineering. KL considered Russia to be an appropriate location in which to develop IT security products due to the country's skilled

Table 5.5 KL's performance and indicators related to the size/growth of the antivirus market in selected economies[89]

ECONOMY/REGION	KL MARKET SHARE/POSITION	INDICATORS RELATED TO THE DEMAND OF ANTIVIRUS PRODUCTS	REMARKS
Russia	50% (2001) 45–60% consumer market, 30% of the corporate market (2004) 47.4% (2008) 59.9% (2010)	Endpoint security market: grew by 10% in 2010 to reach US$137 million, grew by 10% in 2009	Prominent clients: the presidential administration, the Central Bank
The US	2.7% (2009), 3.5% (2010)	Endpoint security market: grew by 4% in 2010 to reach US$3015 million	
Australia	2.1% of market share in 2010	Endpoint security market: grew by 24% in 2010 to reach US$209million	
China	In top 3 in 2010 with 14.8% market share	Endpoint market declined by 39% in 2010	
Malaysia	14.3% (2009), 17.3% (2010)	2010: Endpoint market grew by 15%	
UAE	16.3% by volume (2010)		
Middle East	10.6% (2010)		Corporate customers: 87% (2010) in terms of value Endpoint revenues grew by 12% (2010)
Worldwide	5.5% (2009) 7.2% (2010)	No. of new malicious programs (e.g., viruses, worms, and Trojans) > 3 million (2007), about 20 million (2010) No. of botnets: 45,000 (2007)	Symantec: 34.1% in (2009), 33.1% (2010) and McAfee: 17.0% in (2009), 17.2% (2010)

workforce and a prevalence of the computer hacking culture. Eugene Kaspersky notes:

> There are technical universities in every major city and with one million students graduating every year, and there is a big labor market for software engineers. . . . Russian engineers are much more expensive than in China or India, who are good if you just want something programmed, but if it's about research, then it has to be Russia.[90]

The Russian environment provides a fertile ground for hackers. Experts say that Russian hackers possess the capacity to perform sophisticated operations with limited computer power and inexpensive software. Eighty-two percent of respondents participating in a worldwide poll conducted on a hacker-oriented website indicated that Russia had the world's best computer hackers. Only 5 percent of the respondents believed that American hackers were the best.[91] In the US National Security Agency-backed "hacking" competition of 2009, among the 4,200 participants, ten finalists were from Russia, compared to two from the US. Noting that the company had no plans to move its R&D to locations such as the Middle East, Eugene Kaspersky noted: "What we really need is the pool of talented engineers and I think Russian software engineers are the best, which is why our core R&D is in Moscow."[92]

KL's Product-market Strategy and Performance

The company had a stronger competitive position in the consumer market compared to the business market. According to Gartner, KL was the world's third largest vendor of consumer IT security software and the fifth largest vendor of Enterprise Endpoint Protection based on 2010 revenues. In addition, dozens of original equipment manufacturers (OEMs) such as Microsoft, IBM and Cisco used Kaspersky Lab's antivirus engine through licensing.[93]

KL's top consumer products in 2010 were Kaspersky Internet Security and Kaspersky Anti-Virus. In 2009, over 250 million consumers worldwide used KL's products and services (including Technology Alliances) and the company added 50,000 new users every day.[94] As of December 2010, KL's products were used by over 300 million people and about

200,000 organizations.[95] The company had a strong foothold in Russia. The company also occupied strong competitive positions in major emerging markets (Table 5.5). In China, KL had 100 million users in 2010.[96] The company's growth markets in Asia also include Thailand, Vietnam, the Philippines, Singapore and Indonesia.[97]

While KL had an indirect presence through OEM in the US market for some time,[98] the company was a relative latecomer in the US market. KL made visible efforts to make up for its late start. In 2006, KL's Internet Suite and Anti-Virus titles began selling through CompUSA, Fry's Electronics and Office Depot.[99] KL also recruited retailers and distributors such as Best Buy and Staples. In North America (the US and Canada), the number of retail stores selling KL products increased from 200 in 2006 to 15,000 in 2008.[100] KL gave these retailers more attractive profit margins than its competitors. KL also provided marketing and technical supports. Jon Oltsik, senior analyst at Enterprise Strategy Group (ESG) commented that KL's approach was based on a "tender, loving care model". The major target market consisted of consumers who were willing to pay extra for high-quality security programs.[101] Stephen Orenberg, KL's Chief Sales Officer, noted that the company targets "savvier" users interested in results rather than a low price or loyalty to other brands.[102]

Looking Forward

The company had an IPO plan, which was postponed due to the 2008 global financial crisis. Regarding the motivations behind an IPO, Eugene Kaspersky commented:

> The main reason is not to get money—we have enough—but to raise corporate profile and become more transparent, that contributes a lot into company's positions on corporate market, especially in the US and the UK. Gaining market share in corporate segment is one of the key priorities of KL business development.[103]

It is also important to note that KL's two largest competitors, McAfee and Symantec, are public companies. Symantec was founded in 1982 and went public in 1989 (NASDAQ: SYMC). McAfee was founded in 1987 and is a wholly owned subsidiary of Intel Corporation

(NASDAQ: INTC). John Bernstein, General Atlantic Managing Director and KL board member, expected that KL would go for an IPO by 2016. Bernstein said: "We intend to help them with all the steps towards that."[104]

Case Questions

1. Perform a SWOT analysis for KL.
2. What were some of the technological developments that made it possible for emerging economy-based companies such as KL to compete with industrialized world-based firms?
3. How would you segment the potential market for antivirus products? Evaluate KL's performances in each of the segments.
4. Did KL's Russian origin lead to an adverse perceived impact on its brand image? What were some of the activities KL pursued to enhance its brand and overcome its negative country of origin (COO)? What other activities would you suggest to strengthen its brand globally?
5. Would an IPO strengthen KL's market position vis-à-vis its rivals? How?

Notes

1. Corcoran, J., & Galouchko, K. 2012, "Russian Silicon Valley Plans First IPO as Venture Capital Booms", Bloomberg, July 20, at www.bloomberg.com/news/2012–07–20/russian-silicon-valley-plans-first-ipo-as-venture-capital-booms.html.
2. Neate, R. 2012, "Russia Reaches for the Stars with its own Silicon Valley", Observer, February 18, www.guardian.co.uk/business/2012/feb/19/russia-investment-drive-skolkovo-silicon-valley.
3. Fedynsky, P. 2010, "High Risk for Venture Capital in Russia", Voice of America, May 26, at www.voanews.com/english/news/economy-and-busi ness/High-Risk-for-Venture-Capital-in-Russia-94929299.html.
4. OECD 2010, "Making the Most of Globalization", in OECD Economic Surveys: Poland 2010, 8, pp. 95–147.
5. Ibid.
6. OECD 2009, "Stabilisation and Renewed Growth: Key Challenges", in OECD Economic Surveys: Russian Federation, 6, pp. 19–51.

7. Wright, M., Karsai, J., Dudzinski, Z., & Morovic, J. 1999, "Transition and Active Investors: Venture Capital in Hungary, Poland and Slovakia", *Post-Communist Economies*, 11(1), pp. 27–47.
8. Karasz, P. 2012, "Hungarian Start-Ups Defy Economic Climate", *New York Times*, May 22, at www.nytimes.com/2012/05/23/business/global/hungarian-start-ups-defy-economic-climate.html.
9. Stoica, C.A. 2004, "From Good Communists to Even Better Capitalists? Entrepreneurial Pathways in Post-socialist Romania", *East European Politics and Societies*, 18(2), pp. 236–277.
10. Hutton, W. 2010, "What the World Needs Now is Definitely Not 1011 Billionaires", *Canberra Times*, March 17, p. 11.
11. Kramer, A.E., & Norris, F. 2005, "Amid Growing Wealth, Nepotism and Nationalism in Kazakhstan", *New York Times*, December 23, atwww.nytimes.com/2005/12/23/business/worldbusiness/23kazakh.html?pagewanted=all.
12. Gorodnichenko, Y., & Grygorenko, Y. 2005. "Are Oligarchs Productive? Theory and Evidence", mimeo, University of Michigan.
13. According to Plato, "oligarchy" is governance by a small group of people. In Plato's approach, oligarchs are different from nobles in terms of legality. Whereas nobles are few but rightful rulers, oligarchs rule in an unlawful way. In the contemporary literature, an oligarch is a large business owner controlling sufficient resources to influence national policy making and/or the judiciary to further his/her economic interests.
14. Blanchflower, D.G., Oswald, A., & Stutzer, A. 2001, "Latent Entrepreneurship across Nations", *European Economic Review*, 45(4–6), p. 680.
15. Yang, K. 2002, "Double Entrepreneurship in China's Economic Reform: An Analytical Framework", *Journal of Political and Military Sociology*, 30(1), pp. 134–148; Yang, K. 2004, "Institutional Holes and Entrepreneurship in China", *Sociological Review*, 52(3), pp. 371–389.
16. Stark, D. 1996, "Recombinant Property in East European Capitalism", *American Journal of Sociology*, 101, pp. 993–1027.
17. Warner, M., & Daugherty, C.W. 2004, "Promoting the 'Civic' in Entrepreneurship: The Case of Rural Slovakia", *Journal of the Community Development Society*, 35(1), pp. 117–134.
18. McCarthy, D.J., & Puffer, S.M. 2008, "Interpreting the Ethicality of Corporate Governance Decisions in Russia: Utilizing Integrative Social Contracts Theory to Evaluate the Relevance of Agency Theory Norms", *Academy of Management Review*, 33(1), pp. 1–31.
19. Williams, C.C. 2009, "The Hidden Economy in East-Central Europe: Lessons from a Ten-Nation Survey", *Problems of Post-Communism*, 56(4), pp. 15–28.
20. Warner, M., & Daugherty, C.W. 2004, "Promoting the 'Civic' in Entrepreneurship: The Case of Rural Slovakia", *Journal of the Community Development Society*, 35(1), pp. 117–134.

21. O'Rourke, P.J. 2000, "The Godfather Decade", *Foreign Policy*, 121, pp. 74–81.
22. Ibid.
23. Szilagyi, G. n. d., "Harmonization of Regional Economic and Social Policies within the Romanian-Hungarian-Ukrainian Border Area", at www.policy.hu/szilagyi/respaper.htm.
24. O'Rourke, P.J. 2000, "The Godfather Decade", *Foreign Policy*, 121, pp. 74–81.
25. Kuznetsov, A., McDonald, F., & Kuznetsova, O. 2000, "Entrepreneurial Qualities: A Case from Russia", *Journal of Small Business Management*, 38(1), pp. 101–108.
26. Stark, D. 1996, "Recombinant Property in East European Capitalism", *American Journal of Sociology*, 101, pp. 993–1027.
27. The nomenklatura were people within the former Soviet Union and other Eastern Bloc countries who occupied key administrative positions. The communist party of the country needed to approve the positions. Hankiss, E. 1990, *East European Alternatives*, Oxford: Clarendon Press.
28. Eyal, G., Szelényi, I., & Townsley, E. 1998, *Making Capitalism without Capitalists: The New Ruling Elites in Eastern Europe*, London: Verso.
29. Guriev, S., & Rachinsky, A. 2006, "The Evolution of Personal Wealth in the Former Soviet Union and Central and Eastern Europe", http://siteresources.worldbank.org/INTDECINEQ/Resources/Evolution_of_personal_wealth.pdf.
30. Feige, E. 1997, "Underground Activity and Institutional Change: Productive, Protective, and Predatory Behavior in Transition Economies", in Nelson, J., Tilly, C., & Walker, L. (eds), *Transforming Post-communist Political Economies*, Washington, DC: National Academy Press.
31. Lazarev, V. 2005, "Economics of One-party State: Promotion Incentives and Support for the Soviet Regime", *Comparative Economic Studies*, 47(2), p. 346.
32. Merton, R. 1968, *Social Theory and Social Structure*, New York: Free Press.
33. Ebbeling C., Pawlak D., & Ludwig D. 2002, "Childhood Obesity: Public-health Crisis, Common Sense Cure", *Lancet*, 360(9331), pp. 473–482.
34. Rivoli, P. 2005, *The Travels of a T-shirt in the Global Economy: An Economist Examines the Markets, Power, and Politics of World Trade*, Hoboken, NJ: Wiley.
35. Stoica, C.A. 2004, "From Good Communists to Even Better Capitalists? Entrepreneurial Pathways in Post-socialist Romania", *East European Politics and Societies*, 18(2), pp. 236–277.
36. Chen, A. 2002, "Capitalist Development, Entrepreneurial Class, and Democratization in China", *Political Science Quarterly*, 117(3), pp. 401–422.
37. Kshetri, N., & Ajami, R. 2008, "Institutional Reforms in the Gulf Cooperation Council Economies: A Conceptual Framework", *Journal of International Management*, 14(3), pp. 300–318.
38. Atkine, N.B.D. 2006, "Islam, Islamism and Terrorism", *Army*, 56(1), pp. 55–62.

39. Greenwood, R., & Suddaby R. 2006, "Institutional Entrepreneurship in Mature Fields: The Big Five Accounting Firms", *Academy of Management Journal*, 49, pp. 27–48.
40. Greenwood, R., & Suddaby, R. 2006, "Institutional Entrepreneurship in Mature Fields: The Big Five Accounting Firms", *The Academy of Management Journal*, 49(1), pp. 27–48.
41. Yang, K. 2004, "Institutional Holes and Entrepreneurship in China", *Sociological Review*, 52(3), pp. 371–389.
42. Groenewegen, J., & van der Steen, M. 2007, "The Evolutionary Policy Maker", *Journal of Economic Issues*, 41(2), pp. 351–358.
43. Daokui Li, D., Feng, J., & Jiang, H. 2006, "Institutional Entrepreneurs", *American Economic Review*, 96(2), pp. 358–362.
44. World Bank, Ease of Doing Business Index 2013, at http://data.world bank.org/indicator/IC.BUS.EASE.XQ/countries/1W?display=default.
45. Yang, K. 2002, "Double Entrepreneurship in China's Economic Reform: An Analytical Framework", *Journal of Political and Military Sociology*, 30(1), pp. 134–148.
46. Alexeev, M. 1999, "The Effect of Privatization on Wealth Distribution in Russia", *Economics of Transition*, 7(2), pp. 449–465.
47. Negoita, M. 2006, "The Social Bases of Development: Hungary and Romania in Comparative Perspective", *Socio-Economic Review*, 4(2), pp. 209–238.
48. Stoica, C.A. 2004, "From Good Communists to Even Better Capitalists? Entrepreneurial Pathways in Post-socialist Romania", *East European Politics and Societies*, 18(2), pp. 236–277.
49. OECD 2002, *OECD Economic Surveys: Romania*, Paris: OECD.
50. Burawoy, M., & Krotov, P. 1992, "The Soviet Transition from Socialism to Capitalism: Worker Control and Economic Bargaining in the Wood Industry", *American Sociological Review*, 57, pp. 16–38.
51. Agence France-Presse 2013, "Russian Investigators Search Skolkovo Hi-tech Hub", April 18, at www.globalpost.com/dispatch/news/afp/130418/russian-investigators-search-skolkovo-hi-tech-hub.
52. Barry, E. 2013, "Video Shows an Angry Putin Threatening to Dismiss Officials", *New York Times*, April 17, www.nytimes.com/2013/04/18/world/europe/video-shows-putin-threatening-to-dismiss-officials.html.
53. RIA Novosti 2013, "Investigators Search Russian 'Silicon Valley'", April 18, http://en.ria.ru/crime/20130418/180707737.html.
54. Ibid.
55. Taylor, T.C., & Kazakov, A.Y. 1997, "Business Ethics and Civil Society in Russia", *International Studies of Management & Organization*, 27(1), pp. 5–18.
56. Ibid.
57. Pipes, R. 1992, *Russia under the Old Regime*, New York: Collier.
58. Taylor, T.C., & Kazakov, A.Y. 1997, "Business Ethics and Civil Society in Russia", *International Studies of Management & Organization*, 27(1), pp. 5–18.

59. OECD 2010, "Making the Most of Globalization", in *OECD Economic Surveys: Poland 2010*, 8, pp. 95–147.
60. Baygan, G., & Freudenberg, M. 2000, 'The Internationalisation of Venture Capital Activity in OECD Countries: Implications for Measurement and Policy', *OECD Science, Technology and Industry Working Papers*, July, Paris: OECD Publishing.
61. Goldman, M. 2006, "Russia's Middle Class Muddle", *Current History* 105(693), pp. 321–327; Euro-East 2000, "Euro-East: Training for Enterprise in Transition Economies", *Euro-East*, December 19, p. 1.
62. *Business Week* 2007, "Where the VCs Are Flocking Now", June 11, www.businessweek.com/magazine/content/07_24/b4038056.htm.
63. Wylie, I. 2007, "Romania home base for EBay scammers", *Los Angeles Times*, December 26, at http://articles.latimes.com/2007/dec/26/business/fi-ebay26.
64. *Business Week* 2007, "Where the VCs Are Flocking Now", June 11, www.businessweek.com/magazine/content/07_24/b4038056.htm.
65. Trade and Investment Promotion Section in Montreal 2011, "Poland no. 1 in Central&Eastern Europe in Private Equity and Venture Capital Investment in 2010", at http://montreal.trade.gov.pl/en/aktualnosci/article/a,18280,.html.
66. Starikov, E.N. 1996, "The Social Structure of the Transitional Society (an Attempt to 'take inventory')", *Russian Social Science Review*, 37(2), p. 17.
67. Kolyandr, A. 2011, "Russian Firm Holds Biggest Virtual IPO So Far", *Wall Street Journal*, June 3, http://blogs.wsj.com/emergingeurope/2011/06/03/russian-firm-holds-biggest-virtual-ipo-so-far/.
68. Stoica, C.A. 2004, "From Good Communists to Even Better Capitalists? Entrepreneurial Pathways in Post-socialist Romania", *East European Politics and Societies*, 18(2), pp. 236–277.
69. Wood, C.L., Byers, J.E., Cottingham, K.L., Altman, I., Donahue, M.J., et al. 2007, "Parasites Alter Community Structure", *Proceedings of the National Academy of Sciences*, www.pnas.org/content/104/22/9335.short.
70. Zweynert, J., & Goldschmidt, N. 2006, "The Two Transitions in Central and Eastern Europe as Processes of Institutional Transplantation", *Journal of Economic Issues*, 40(4), pp. 895ff.
71. Hennigan, M. 2012, "Irish Innovation: Ireland's Faith-based Goal to Create World-class Knowledge Economy by 2013: Success or Failure?, Finfacts, October 15, at www.finfacts.ie/irishfinancenews/article_1025039.shtml.
72. fastcompany.com 2011, "The World's Most Innovative Companies 2011", at www.fastcompany.com/most-innovative-companies/2011/profile/kaspersky-lab.php.
73. Rapooza, K. 2011, "Kaspersky's Market Share Rises as Symantec and McAfee's Falls", Forbes Blogs, April 13, at http://blogs.forbes.com/kenrapoza/2011/04/13/kasperskys-market-share-rises-as-symantec-mcafees-falls/.

74. Arnold, M. 2011, "GA Buys 20% Kaspersky Stake", January 20, at www.ft.com/cms/s/2/b7cc912a-24d7–11e0-a919–00144feab49a. html#axzz1Q4gxlyjn.
75. Baumgartner, E. 2001, "Private Enterprise", Business Eastern Europe, June 25, p. 4.
76. Ibid.
77. Ivanenko, V. 2005, "Markets and Democracy in Russia", BOFIT Discussion Papers 16, Bank of Finland, Institute for Economies in Transition, at http://papers.ssrn.com/sol3/papers.cfm?abstract_id=1002866.
78. Spenner, K.I., & Jones, D.C. 1998, "Social Economic Transformation in Bulgaria: An Empirical Assessment of the Merchant Capitalism Thesis", *Social Forces*, 76(3), pp. 937–965.
79. Stoica, C.A. 2004, "From Good Communists to Even Better Capitalists? Entrepreneurial Pathways in Post-socialist Romania", *East European Politics and Societies*, 18(2), pp. 236–277.
80. Kramer, A.E. 2010, "Russia Aims to Create a Silicon Valley of its Own", *International Herald Tribune*, April 12, p. 5.
81. Bentley, E. 2009, "Russian IT Companies Let Down by Education", November 26, at www.telegraph.co.uk/sponsored/russianow/business/6661659/ Russian-IT-companies-let-down-by-education.html.
82. Kramer, A.E. 2010, "Innovation, by Order of the Kremlin", April 9, 2010, at www.nytimes.com/2010/04/11/business/global/11russia.html? pagewanted=all.
83. Kramer, A.E. 2010, "Russia Aims to Create a Silicon Valley of its Own", International Herald Tribune, April 12, p. 5.
84. Morris, B. 2010, "Russia Creates its own Silicon Valley", BBC News, at http://news.bbc.co.uk/1/hi/8638222.stm.
85. Baumgartner, E. 2001, "Private Enterprise", *Business Eastern Europe*, June 25, p. 4.
86. Ibid.
87. Harris, S. 2009, "Digital Security in an Analog Bureaucracy", *National Journal*, June 9, p. 15, at www.nationaljournal.com/njmagazine/ nj_20090613_8035.php.
88. Schenker, J.L. 2004, "Europe's Virus Fighters are Gaining Attention", *International Herald Tribune*, May 13, p. 18.
89. Kshetri, N. 2011, "Kaspersky Lab: From Russia with Anti-virus", *Emerald Emerging Markets Case Studies*, 1(3), pp. 1–10.
90. Ibid.
91. CNN.com 2000, "Russia's Hackers: Notorious or Desperate?", November 20, at www.cnn.com/2000/TECH/computing/11/20/russia.hackers.ap/ index.html (accessed 27 October 2004).
92. Menon, V. 2010, "Kaspersky Lab Eyes No. 3 Position in Endpoint Security", February 2, at www.itp.net/579148-kaspersky-lab-eyes-no–3-position-in-endpoint-security.

93. fastcompany.com 2011, "The World's Most Innovative Companies 2011", at www.fastcompany.com/most-innovative-companies/2011/profile/kaspersky-lab.php.

94. Luxoft 2009, "Rapid Growth Compels Leading Antivirus Software Company to Identify and Streamline Operating Efficiencies", October, at www.luxoft.com/upload/iblock/47b/case_study_rapid_growth_compels_leading_antivirus_software_company_software_luxoft_for_kaspersky_lab.pdf.

95. Ranger, S. 2010, "Photos: Inside Kaspersky Lab's antivirus HQ", December 2, www.zdnet.com/photos-inside-kaspersky-labs-antivirus-hq- 3040153923/.

96. McMillan, R. 2010, "Kaspersky: Google Hack Takes Spotlight From Russia", February 4, at www.pcworld.com/businesscenter/article/188590/kaspersky_google_hack_takes_spotlight_from_russia.html.

97. Singh, R. 2009, "Kaspersky Banks on SMEs to Increase Market Share", *New Straits Times (Malaysia)*, November 16, p. 8.

98. Claburn, T. 2005, "From Russia with Security Help", *InformationWeek*, February 16, www.informationweek.com/from-russia-with-security-help/d/d-id/1030489?.

99. Olenick, D. 2006, "Kaspersky Bows Web Security SW at Retail. TWICE", *This Week in Consumer Electronics*, 21(11), p. 6–5.

100. Swartz, J. 2008, "Russian Kaspersky Lab Offers Antivirus Protection in U.S.", *USAToday*, November 24, at http://usatoday30.usatoday.com/money/companies/management/profile/2008–11–23-kaspersky-lab-pc-security_N.htm.

101. Ibid.

102. Olenick, D. 2006, "Kaspersky Bows Web Security SW at Retail. TWICE", *This Week in Consumer Electronics*, 21(11), p. 6–5.

103. Kshetri, N. 2011, "Kaspersky Lab: From Russia with Anti-virus", *Emerald Emerging Markets Case Studies*, 1(3), pp. 1–10.

104. Arnold, M. 2011, "GA Buys 20% Kaspersky Stake", January 20, at www.ft.com/cms/s/2/b7cc912a-24d7–11e0-a919–00144feab49a.html#axzz1Q4gxlyjn.

6

ENTREPRENEURSHIP IN THE GULF COOPERATION COUNCIL ECONOMIES

Abstract

Entrepreneurial ecosystems of the Gulf Cooperation Council (GCC) economies have many unusual and idiosyncratic features. Institutions promoting
entrepreneurship are slow to change in these economies. A lack of institutions
supporting free-enterprise economy has resulted in an ineffective entrepreneurial ecosystem. There is some evidence that capitalism and entrepreneurs
are viewed negatively in Arab society. These economies' heavy reliance on
foreign labor has also acted as a barrier to the development of entrepreneurship. Despite this, the ingredients of an effective entrepreneurial ecosystem
are beginning to develop in some GCC economies. This chapter reviews
various determinants of entrepreneurship in GCC economies. It also identi-
fies clear contexts and attendant mechanisms associated with institutional
changes in GCC economies. The explanations shed light on the nature of
the entrepreneurial ecosystem as well as on the power balance among various institutional actors associated with GCC economies and their cognitive
frameworks.

This chapter's objectives include:

1. To demonstrate an understanding of the natures of entrepreneurial activities in GCC economies.
2. To analyze the facilitators of and hindrances to entrepreneurship in GCC economies.
3. To evaluate some of the barriers to changes in institutions
   needed to promote entrepreneurship in GCC economies.
4. To assess the roles of various institutional agents in GCC economies in bringing institutional changes related to entrepreneurship.

5. To demonstrate an understanding of the various sources of
   finance in GCC economies and their differences with the rest
   of the world.

6.1. Introduction

Entrepreneurship in the six Gulf Cooperation Council (GCC) member states—Bahrain, Kuwait, Oman, Qatar, Saudi Arabia and the United Arab Emirates (UAE)—faces various political, social and cultural challenges. Institutional reforms required to promote productive entrepreneurship have been slow. Although GCC regimes have agreed on the necessity to strengthen the rule of law and move towards a free enterprise economy, there have been only superficial reforms. Political and economic liberalizations, which have been insignificant in most cases, have been responses to crises rather than the systematic pursuit of stated reform objectives, and reluctantly carried out. The Third Wave of democratization, which started with the fall of the last dictatorships in Western Europe—Portugal, Greece and Spain in the mid-1970s—and continued in Latin America in the 1980s, has failed to touch the Arab world. There is not a single full-fledged democracy in the GCC region and some new repressive institutions have also emerged.

GCC economies are also characterized by a symbiosis of political and economic elites. Observers refer to the 1990s as the lost decade for these economies and state the importance of enhancing institutional quality by emphasizing accountability in government practices, strengthening the rule of law, and controlling bureaucracy and corruption.[1] Experts argue that a genuinely entrepreneurial class, which is lacking in the region, would be the single most important force for change. GCC economies' reform is likely to have far-reaching implications for their own populations as well as those outside the region.

6.2. A Survey of Entrepreneurship in the GCC Region

To start with, there is no equivalent word for "entrepreneurship" in Arabic. Unsurprisingly, GCC economies lack the essential ingredients for the creation of an effective ecosystem for entrepreneurship and innovation. Indeed, entrepreneurial propensity among youth is found to be higher in Lebanon and North Africa, which are less economically prosperous than the GCC economies.[2]

Probably the biggest challenge facing the region is the low level of involvement of women in economic and entrepreneurial activities. A World Bank survey conducted in the Middle East and North Africa found that a woman is the principal owner of only about 13 percent of the businesses. This proportion is much lower than in other comparable middle-income economies in East Asia, Latin America and the Caribbean, and Europe and Central Asia.[3] An important benefit that stems from female-owned firms is that such firms in the region tend to hire more women and in higher positions than male-owned firms. For instance, female workers accounted for about 25 percent of the workforce in female-owned firms compared with 22 percent in male-owned firms. The qualitative differences are even more remarkable as female-owned firms employ a higher proportion of female workers at professional and managerial levels while male-owned firms employ more women in unskilled positions.[4]

In some cases, the direction of change from the perspective of women's participation in entrepreneurial activities has been regressive rather than progressive. A visible example to illustrate institutional change in Saudi Arabia is the Jeddah Economic Forum, which has been held annually every winter since 1999 during winter in Jeddah city. In 1999, women were not allowed at the forum. In 2000, fifty women were allowed to watch the forum's proceedings. In 2001, there were over a hundred women, who were also allowed to ask questions. About two hundred women attended the forum in 2002. In 2003, women had their own forum. In 2004, a Saudi businesswoman delivered the keynote speech. However, in 2004, members of religiously conservative groups vigorously opposed and protested against women's taking center stage at the forum. Consequently, at the sixth Jeddah Economic Forum of 2005, women participants had a separate entry to the hall and were only allowed to ask questions from a different room without being seen.

While GCC economies have been able to achieve sustained economic growth and macroeconomic stability, development of entrepreneurship and job creation has remained a challenge. The public sector has been the main source of employment for their citizens. Some estimates suggest that foreign expatriate workers account for at least 80 percent of the private sector jobs in these economies.[5] The preference for public sector jobs acts as a barrier to entrepreneurship in GCC economies. For instance, compared to working in the private sector or being self-employed, public sector jobs are preferred by 60–73 percent of youths in the region.[6] Moreover, public sector jobs seriously lack productivity. A Kuwaiti female entrepreneur noted: "by doing this [becoming an entrepreneur] I'm not working in the public sector where . . . there's nothing to do. For every 20 people in government, 18 sit around doing nothing."[7]

While some GCC economies have undertaken some successful mega-projects, these economies have failed to promote the development of SMEs. This is a serious problem since small companies account for most of the job creation as well as the production and innovation of mature economies, especially in the service sector. Moreover, a significant proportion of small enterprises grow into medium-sized players. SMEs are likely to play a critical role in the region, as most GCC economies are experiencing unemployment rates in double digits, which are higher among young people. In 2011, 39 percent of Saudis in the 20–24 age group were unemployed.[8] Likewise, in 2009, 27 percent of youth in Bahrain were unemployed, the highest rate among GCC economies.[9] Until recently, GCC governments have not made serious efforts to create jobs for women or to encourage female entrepreneurship. Women represent a significant pool of qualified human capital.

A considerable proportion of SMEs in some GCC economies are owned by foreigners. A manager of the Kuwait Small Developments Project Company noted that most small businesses in Kuwait are run by expatriates. The domination of the small business landscape by foreigners has led to a reluctance on the part of Kuwaiti nationals to launch their own firms. Moreover, there is easy availability of government employment for Kuwaiti nationals.

GCC economies' oil-fuelled prosperity has acted as a barrier to entrepreneurship development. An expert summarized this dynamic: "There is a dominant business class in the Middle East, but it owes its position to oil or to connections to the ruling families. Its wealth is that of feudalism, not capitalism, and its political effects remain feudal as well."[10] Some GCC governments, however, have realized the need to encourage entrepreneurship. For instance, to reduce its reliance on the oil industry, the Kuwaiti government wants to increase the number of Kuwaiti-run enterprises and broaden the base of the country's economy. Kuwait Small Developments Project Company announced a plan to lend up to 80 percent of the capital needed for starting a venture. The borrower doesn't need to pay service charges or interest. Potential entrepreneurs are also provided with viability studies, and their business plans and ideas are looked at by experts.[11]

6.3. Determinants of Entrepreneurship in GCC Economies

6.3.1. Regulatory Framework

As in the case of most developing countries, GCC states implemented import substitution policies for several decades. In recent years, in most of the GCC economies the tasks related to starting a business have been vastly simplified and eased in comparison to how they used to be (Fig. 6.1).

The speed of economic reform measures in the GCC economies has, however, been slower than potential entrepreneurs would like

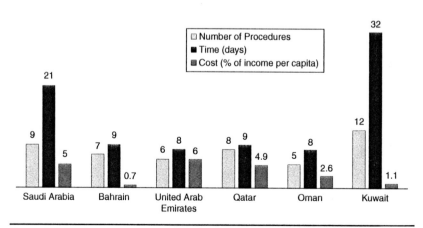

Figure 6.1 Starting a business in the GCC economies
Source: World Bank Group Doing Business Survey 2013, www.doingbusiness.org/~/media/GIAWB/Doing%20 Business/Documents/Annual-Reports/English/DB13-full-report.pdf

to see. Institutions promoting a free enterprise system and economy are severely lacking. There is no minimum wage law in most
of the GCC economies. Some argue that the introduction of such
a law may force firms to be more efficient and that associated jobs
are likely to be perceived better. While some GCC economies have
recently introduced minimum wage laws, these are only for their
nationals. For instance, Oman has introduced a regulation that has
set a minimum wage for Omani workers in the private sector but not
for non-Omanis.[12]

Unsurprisingly, GCC economies, and Arab countries in general,
scored the lowest in a comparison of legal reform across the world's
regions. Likewise, while the business climate in the region was above
the world average and it outperformed other emerging markets on
indicators related to infrastructure and some institutional dimensions,
the region stood second last to Africa on market orientation.[13]

The International Country Risk Guide (ICRG) index, which considers political, economic and financial indicators, is probably the most
comprehensive indicator for studying institutional changes. During
the 1990s, the region narrowed the ICRG index gap with East Asia
and surpassed SSA. Out of 140 countries ranked by the ICRG in
January 2010, GCC economies' ranks were: Qatar: 10, Kuwait: 20, the
UAE: 25, Bahrain: 30, Saudi Arabia: 43, and Oman: 61. Having said
that, some argue that these economies' natural openness may be driving the ICRG index. Controlling for factors such as trade interdependence and locations, the GCC region is behind East Asia on policies
of oriented openness.[14]

6.3.2. Values, Culture and Skills

Entrepreneurial Culture
Entrepreneurship development faces various social issues and cultural
challenges in the Arab region. First, many of the consumption habits
associated with global capitalism are considered to be "antithetical" to
Islamic ethical traditions.[15] Observers note that people in the region
look down on capitalism. There is also a widespread negative attitude towards entrepreneurship involving small businesses as well as
towards menial and low-paying work. Since private sector jobs in these

economies suffer from an image problem, entrepreneurs face barriers to hiring qualified employees.

Some concepts related to entrepreneurship are considered to be too Western and face strong resistance. For instance as "angel investors" sounded too Christian for many Arabs, the promoters needed to replace it with a more neutral term—"uncles' network".[16]

Social norms impose restrictions on female employment, which has led to a low rate of female participation in economic activities in general and entrepreneurship in particular (Fig. 6.2). Observers have noted that most women in the region do not consult financial advisors.[17] The GCC tradition of family businesses has also been a barrier to entrepreneurship development and economic growth. Experts say that governments in these economies need to do more to broaden entrepreneurship.

While expatriates constitute a significant proportion of the population in most GCC economies, their involvement in high-quality entrepreneurship is limited. One problem is that GCC economies often view immigrants merely as an extra source of labor.[18] Recruiters organize most of the movements of workers on fixed-term contracts, and in most cases, contract workers are required to depart the receiving country upon completion of the contract.[19] In this regard, compared to the rest of the GCC and the Middle East, the Dubai Emirate UAE has pursued more liberal social and economic policies. The emirate has attracted foreigners for more than a century. Dubai thus performs well in terms of the availability of the key ingredients of an entrepreneurial ecosystem like wealthy investors and skilled workers.[20]

Entrepreneurial Skills and Capabilities

GCC economies are making significant progress in education. Progress in women's education in the region has been especially impressive. Women outnumber men in most of the Arab universities. Gender gaps in literacy rates and enrollment in primary and secondary schools has fallen dramatically since the 1970s (Fig. 6.2). In 2005, the Saudi government announced plans to establish seventeen women-only technical colleges that would provide skills needed for the job market.[21]

In order to reduce their dependence on foreign workers, GCC economies are putting more efforts into improving the education

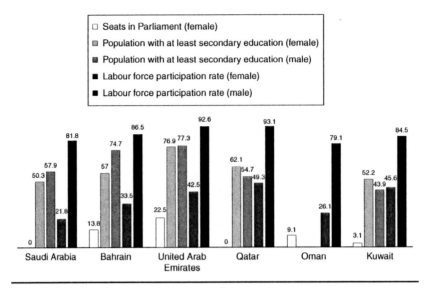

Figure 6.2 The gender gap in some key areas in GCC economies
Source: UNDP, 2010, Human Development Report, Gender Inequality Index, http://hdr.undp.org/en/media/
HDR_2010_EN_Complete_reprint.pdf

levels and skills of their own nationals. Some measures are being taken by NGOs as well. The NGO Injaz al-Arab (www.injazalarab.org/), which was formed in 2004 and operated in thirteen countries in the Middle East and North Africa in 2010, sends volunteers to teach work readiness, financial literacy and entrepreneurship in schools. As of mid-2010, Injaz al-Arab programs engaged 10,000 private sector volunteers and reached over 500,000 students.[22]

That said, GCC economies are facing major human capital constraints. GCC entrepreneurs are not well versed in supporting skills such as those related to forecasting techniques, market research and business models.[23] The GCC economies perform poorly in international student achievement tests. The educational system emphasizes preparing the citizens for luxury work rather than for productive employment.

If there is a lesson to be learned from entrepreneurship development in mature economies, it is that providing vocational training and adopting strict professional standards leads to the professionalization of blue-collar workers which leads to their working at a higher level of prestige. Short-term certificate and diploma programs also help.

6.3.3. Access to Finance, Market, R&D and Technology

Access to Market

Some argue that the GCC economies' political and economic systems resemble and can be accurately described as feudalism rather than capitalism.[24] One upshot of this approach is that big businesses dominate the markets in the region, especially in vital and important productive sectors. Market access barriers continue to pose serious obstacles for the growth of SMEs and new firms. The antitrust laws in these economies are not well equipped to deal with the problem of dominance by big businesses. In 2012, a prominent Saudi attorney called for a stronger antitrust law to eliminate business monopolies in the country.[25]

However, entrepreneurial firms in the region are in a favorable position to gain access to major foreign markets. Factors related to natural openness to international trade, such as distance from major economies in the world (their location near Europe) and the common language of Arabic, which is spoken by over 160 million people and is the official language of twenty-two countries, facilitate these economies' entrepreneurial firms' access to foreign market.

R&D and Technology Related Factors

GCC economies have exhibited a culture of heavy reliance on low-cost and low-skilled imported labor, mainly in the labor-intensive industries of construction and services. This culture has favored low-quality entrepreneurship in the region by encouraging inefficient production techniques. Due to the easy availability of cheap labor, organizations in the GCC region have faced little pressure to reform their organizational structures, develop the skills of their workforce or introduce superior technologies.

R&D is virtually non-existent in the region. According to the World Bank, Saudi Arabia's R&D expenditure in 2007 was 0.07 percent of GDP, which contrasts with Israel's 4.9 percent and Finland's 3.5 percent.[26] The region also performs poorly in some of the key ICT indicators (Fig. 6.3). Due to their lack of emphasis on R&D and technology adoption, GCC economies remain in a low productivity trap.

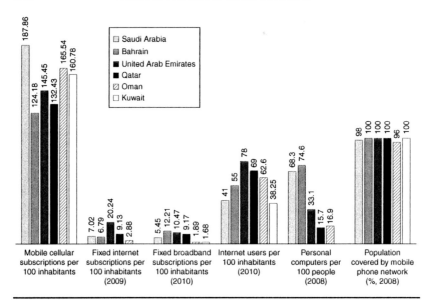

Figure 6.3 Key ICT indicators in the GCC economies

Source: For mobile cellular subscriptions, fixed Internet subscriptions, fixed broadband subscriptions, Internet users per 100 inhabitants: ITU, 2011, ICT data and statistics, www.itu.int/ITU-D/ict/statistics/. For personal computers per 100 people, population covered by mobile phone: UNDP, Human Development Report, ICT Data, 2010, http://hdr.undp.org/en/media/HDR_2010_EN_Complete_reprint.pdf

Access to Finance

Given their prosperity levels, GCC economies perform poorly in most indicators related to access to finance. Although there has been an increase in foreign direct investment (FDI) inflows, this can be attributed to the attractiveness of the oil industry rather than to institutional reforms.[27] Microfinance institutions as a source of capital account for less than 2 percent of women entrepreneurs in GCC economies.[28]

The establishment of the Gulf Venture Capital Association (GVCA) is a key development. The GVCA was formed by a consortium of institutions and professionals in GCC economies. The GVCA is "committed to supporting the growth of a strong venture capital and private equity industry within the Arabian Gulf".[29] Likewise, in July 2011, the Omani Centre for Investment Promotion and Export Development launched a VC fund of US$135 million to be spent by 2020. The goal is to promote investment in science and technology in the GCC region. The fund is expected to attract foreign high-tech firms and R&D facilities. It also expects to support local SMEs in the technology sector. The services provided include finance for five years, access to IT and energy, and mentoring. In July 2011, the UAE-based Arab Science and Technology Foundation also announced a plan to set up a US$15 million VC fund. Its objective is to distribute US$500,000 to technology startups.[30]

GCC economies also differ widely in the proportion of VC-funded businesses. A survey indicated that while 10 percent of women business owners in Bahrain had venture capital financing, no women-owned business had received VC financing in the UAE.[31]

A unique characteristic of GCC economies concerns a large number of high-net-worth individuals. An estimate of the Gulf Investment House suggested that the private wealth of the GCC region was US$1.5 trillion in 2007. Experts argue that GCC's high-net-worth individuals are in a strong position to provide VC financing. In this way, they can play the roles played by institutional investors or banks in the US and Europe.[32]

The capital markets of the region have many contradictory features. The ratio of market capitalization to GDP for the GCC region is similar to that of many mature markets. There have been some high-profile examples of IPOs in the region in recent years. For instance, in 2008, of the twenty largest IPOs worldwide, four were from Saudi Arabia. During the period mid-2002 to mid-2005, Dubai's stock market rose by 768 percent. The corresponding rates for Qatar, Kuwait and Saudi Arabia were 600 percent, 225 percent and 290 percent respectively.[33] Nonetheless, the region's stock markets are not well developed in some important aspects. The ratio of traded equity to GDP for the GCC region remains lower than in many emerging markets. The GCC stock markets have also experienced wide fluctuations, which have undermined investor confidence and created difficulties for fund managers at the exit stage.[34] Moreover, exchanges specializing in high-growth companies (such as NASDAQ) are lacking in the region.

6.4. Formal and Informal Institutions in Relation to Entrepreneurship

This section explores formal and informal institutions in the GCC economies in greater detail. Notwithstanding some institutional reforms in GCC economies, a close look indicates a lack of substantiveness. For instance, in most cases, holding elections has been the only measure taken to promote democracy and the elections arguably tend to be merely "rubber-stamp affairs".[35]

Institutional reform attempts in the region are facing various roadblocks. At the *Forum of the Future*'s 2005 meeting of the intergovernmental initiative for reform in the broader Middle East, three GCC economies—Bahrain, Oman and Saudi Arabia—supported Egypt's approach to restrict independence of NGOs.[36] In Saudi Arabia, in 1999 women were allowed for the first time to attend sessions of the Shura as observers. The Shura's chairman, however, reminded them that Islam denies women's right to public offices. Likewise, in Bahrain, the king emphasized the necessity to resume democracy, but critics doubt whether democratic moves are genuine. Those challenging the rulers to engage in dialogue were banned from public gatherings. In 2005, authorities closed a leading human rights organization. A leader who called on the prime minister to resign for human rights violations and failure to restore growth was arrested. Organizations such as the Bahrain Center for Human Rights, the General Organization for Youth and Sports and Al-Uruba are viewed as cultural establishments and barred from political activities. In February 2011, the country's Shi'ite Muslim majority organized a protest on the street seeking more jobs and a greater voice in government. A crackdown and martial law forced an end to the protest.

To take yet another example of institutions shifting into reverse gear, consider Kuwait. In the early 2000s, more women were wearing the veil than before and university classes were segregated by gender.[37] While the rulers are in favor of empowering women, there have been oppositions from Islamic groups. These groups also voted against women's right to vote on social and religious grounds. While Kuwaiti rulers promised genuine democratization, progress has been insufficient.

Among GCC rulers, those with a Western education or with Western-educated advisors have introduced substantial institutional measures. In Kuwait, Western-educated members, who gained posts in the cabinet, introduced an economic package in 2001 to attract foreign investment.[38] Similarly, Sheik Mohammad, the crown prince of Dubai, who has played a critical role in modernizing the country, has a team of Western-educated economic advisors. GCC regimes are also facing institutional reform pressure from citizens with access to Western-style education. Some notable examples include Kuwait's first open political party formed by Western-educated liberals, the protest by Western-educated Kuwaiti women during the 1992 election and the candidacy of twenty-eight women—mostly Western-educated— in the 2006 parliamentary elections, as well as Saudi intellectuals' 2003 petition to the king calling for a constitution and bill of rights.

6.4.1. The Governments' Reform Measures

The government is the most powerful institutional actor and is in a special position to create market institutions, change the legal rules and enforce private actors' behavior. In the GCC region, a free enterprise economy is far from being fully institutionalized. Even if the governments want to institute reform measures, they have to appease actors with disparate purposes and conflicting interests such as bureaucrats, entrepreneurs, financial, corporate and economic elites; intellectuals, opinion makers, religious spokespersons, multinationals, foreign governments, international agencies, interest groups, labor unions and ordinary citizens.

6.4.2. Institutional Change Agents

It would be erroneous, however, to conclude that the government is the only actor associated with institutional changes. More broadly, it may be helpful to consider the roles of institutional change agents or institutional entrepreneurs. Institutional entrepreneurs challenge or disrupt particular models of social or economic order and construct new institutions. They are effective in identifying opportunities, frame issues and problems, and mobilize various type of resource in an attempt to change societal beliefs, norms and value systems. They also engage in activities related to deinstitutionalization (the dissolution of existing logic or governance structure) as well as institution formation, which entails the birth of a new logic or governance structure.[39]

Institutional entrepreneurs come in many shapes and sizes. In GCC economies, some examples of institutional entrepreneurs include Western-educated professionals, Western-educated liberals who formed Kuwait's first open political party, Kuwaiti women's groups who protested during the

1992 election for their voting rights, women candidates in Kuwait's 2006 elections; and Saudi intellectuals, who submitted a petition to the king in 2003 calling for a constitution and bill of rights.

Institutional entrepreneurs' positions need to be dominant in order to allow them to gain wider legitimacy, bridge diverse stakeholders and compel other actors to change practices.[40] It is important for them to be able to mobilize external and internal constituents, have financial resources and be able to communicate with other institutional actors in the system so that their initiatives can be perceived favorably.[41]

6.4.3. Selective Adaptation

Social, political and economic contexts can limit the actions that the government and institutional entrepreneurs may undertake. The idea of selective adaptation can be helpful in understanding this dynamic. Selective adaptation entails balancing local needs with the pressure to comply with practices (institutional reforms) imposed from outside. Selective adaptation is typically framed as a process by which exchanges of non-local rules across cultural boundaries are mediated by and interpreted in terms of local practices, conditions, imperatives and norms.[42]

The nature of selective adaptation is a function of perception, complementarity and legitimacy. First, the processes and results of selective adaptation depend on how policy makers and other institutional change agents perceive the content and effect of foreign and local institutional arrangements. Complementarity describes a situation in which seemingly contradictory phenomena can be combined so that they reinforce each other effectively while at the same time the essential characteristics of each component are preserved. Legitimacy concerns the extent to which local communities support the purposes and consequences of selective adaptation. The effectiveness of selectively adapted legal forms and practices depends to an important degree on local acceptance. Institutional reform pressures, for instance, may face opposition by actors benefiting from the existing institutional arrangements.

6.4.4. The "Triple Embeddedness" Thesis

The gist of the "triple embeddedness" thesis[43] is that in determining institutional changes, it is important to examine the interaction and interdependence of economy, polity and society. To put things in context, elements of political institutions such as democracy and the rule of law and the nature of the civil society are tightly linked to the business climate.

Society-related factors include the nature of social organizations— "the holistic order" and "the extended order" and society's orientation towards the West (e.g., the presence of Western-educated leaders, technocrats and citizens). Polity-related variables include the government's dependence on businesses and on Western countries. Finally, resource-based economic development is an economy-related variable. Table 6.1 presents some factors facilitating or hindering institutional changes in the region.

Table 6.1 Factors facilitating and hindering institutional reforms in GCC economies

FACTOR	EFFECTS ON THE GOVERNMENT'S SUBSTANTIVENESS OF REFORM MEASURES	EFFECTS ON PROGRESSIVE/ REGRESSIVE INSTITUTIONAL CHANGES
The "holistic order" of society	• Economic and political logic for reform may face difficulties. The government may be unwilling to take substantive reform measure.	• Institutional change processes that are against the "general binding moral prescripts" face resistance.
The presence of Western-educated leaders, technocrats and citizens	• Open to Western-style reforms and can influence policy makers to take substantial measures.	• Support to reform measure. • Externality effects.
The government's dependence on businesses	• Governments that are vulnerable to capital dependence are likely to adopt pro-business policies.	
Bureaucrats' involvement in businesses	• The government may not take substantial reforms that go against bureaucrats' interests.	• Institutional reforms may adversely affect bureaucrats' utility functions. They may be unwilling to direct attention and provide supports and resources to reforms.

(Continued)

Table 6.1 (Continued)

FACTOR	EFFECTS ON THE GOVERNMENT'S SUBSTANTIVENESS OF REFORM MEASURES	EFFECTS ON PROGRESSIVE/ REGRESSIVE INSTITUTIONAL CHANGES
Dependence on Western countries	• Pressures to bring institutional reforms.	
Ability to achieve economic development without reforms	• The regimes can hold their citizens at bay by providing some welfare. • Institutional entrepreneurs may face communicating need for change.	

6.4.5. The "Holistic Order" and the "Extended Order"

Institutionalists and historians have argued that institutions' propensity to change can arguably be described with two ideal types of social organizations—the holistic order and the extended/functionally differentiated order. A holistic society is often characterized by an ideology, mostly in the form of a religion, that "claims validity for all spheres of action and thought", and an action's legitimacy is evaluated on the basis of "general binding moral prescripts imposed by a superior authority" rather than by economic, political or juridical logic.[44] To take an example, conservative Islamist factions such as the Islamic Salvation Front view Islam "as a holistic order whose societal organization is perfect and does not allow individual beliefs".[45] In some cases, ideology concerns a value system such as the system of Asian values.

As noted above, the government and institutional entrepreneurs engage in selective adaptation of foreign practices. This means that practices incompatible with local conditions and norms are less likely to be introduced or likely to fail if they are introduced. In a holistic society, selectively adapted practices become ineffective because they lack legitimacy or local community support. The government's and institutional entrepreneurs' attempts to bring changes may face difficulty in going beyond pre-institutionalization.

From the standpoint of institutional reforms in the GCC region, the most relevant issue concerns the notion of a holistic society. As we have said, the more conservative version of Islam views it as "as a holistic order whose societal organization is perfect".[46] This emphasis is echoed in other recent perspectives on Islam. The secular/religious distinction is less likely to exist in the Islamic approach. To take one example, whereas Western governments do not provide assistance to religious-related charities, there is no such restriction in some Islamic governments. The Islamic mission (*da'wa*) in Saudi Arabia, for instance, is state-sponsored. Islam propagates "a holistic conceptualization of life, embracing politics, economics and society".[47] One scholar observes: "Extremists exploit the common misunderstanding of Muslims' holistic view of life; everything is religion and everything is Islam; financial, social, intellectual, theological, military, and political."[48]

The upshot of these tendencies is that institutional changes that go against Islam's logic face resistance. Citizens in these economies think that Islam is inherently democratic and thus perceive no distance between Islam and democracy.[49] They express simultaneous support for democracy and Islam. In these economies, a significant amount of time is devoted to Islamic instruction in educational institutions.[50] Religious and cultural influences make educational reform a sensitive topic. Islam is thus providing the foundation for the politics of the GCC economies. In the ideological arena, Islamic World is one of the notable exceptions to the observation that democracy is the "spirit of the times". A scholar defined the issue regarding the influence of Islam's holistic nature on politics as follows: "The rhetoric of religious movements refuses to recognize the autonomy of politics and instead attempts to put the state under the control of religion. Such religious movements . . . leave no room for cultural, intellectual or ideological differences."[51]

Islam's influence is readily apparent in businesses and economics. Islamic economics, which differs from Western capitalism by several measures, claims that Islam provides an "all-encompassing model for social, economic, and political life".[52] Commercial shariah, for instance, differs drastically from Western business law in several notable respects. It is probably hard to imagine democracy in the GCC region involving English common law, which would most likely bring some disruption to society.

Islam's holistic order has been a barrier to Western-style institutional reforms and a driving force behind regressive changes in the

GCC economies. This pattern is powerfully illustrated in the chairman of the Shura's argument against women's right to public offices in Saudi Arabia, the ban from political activities of organizations such as the Center for Human Rights, the General Organization for Youth and Sports and Al-Uruba in Bahrain, and Islamic groups' opposition to empowering women in Kuwait. Observers have noted that in some GCC economies such as Oman, Qatar and Bahrain, on most political issues, the monarchs are arguably more liberal than the societies they rule.[53] For instance, deliberations in the Bahrain parliament focus more on social than political issues.

The absolute monarchies possessing both religious and political power also benefit from the holistic order (Table 6.2). Accordingly, most GCC rulers lack accountability, can survive through repression, co-optations and manipulation, and maintain control over opponents.[54] Beyond all that, being a "reformist" by complying with the West is an unpopular option for GCC rulers. For instance, in the Arab world, Qatar is perceived as "little more than an American military base".[55]

Table 6.2 Political and religious landscapes of GCC economies: major highlights

ECONOMY	POLITICAL	RELIGIOUS	REMARKS
Bahrain	• Started political liberalization in 2002. In a referendum, the electorate voted to create a parliament and an appointed Majlis al Shura. • 2005: Closed a leading human rights organization.	• Political Islam moderate; Islamist groups dominate parliament. • Five women (a Christian, a Jew) are appointed to the Shura Council.	• The least oil reserve among the GCC economies and thus forced to liberalize the economy.
Kuwait	• Most political power with the ruling Sabah family. • Ahead of most GCC economies on reform.	• Religious fundamentalism is increasing.	• Influence of Saudi Arabia becoming stronger.

(Continued)

Table 6.2 (Continued)

ECONOMY	POLITICAL	RELIGIOUS	REMARKS
Oman	• 1996: "Basic Law" – provided a Bill of Rights, guaranteed freedom of the press, encouraged religious tolerance, insisted on equality of race and gender.	• Constitution is "grounded" in Islamic tradition. • The Sultan convened a Majlis al Shura, or Consultative Council.	• Critics claimed that the 1996 initiatives were the result of an attempted coup two years earlier.
Qatar	• 2003: Qataris (including women) voted and approved a new constitution – called for the establishment of a parliament. • First Gulf state to permit unrestricted free press.	• Follows strict Wahabi sect of Islam (like Saudi Arabia) but has been more flexible in religious ideology.	• Critics argue that the new constitution institutionalized the absolute power of the emir and his family.
Saudi Arabia	• Shura: king appointed and only representative institution. • Considering letting male citizens elect regional councils	• The Shura's chairman reminded that Islam denies women right to public office.	• The most conservative GCC country in many aspects.
United Arab Emirates	• Moderate political culture.	• No religious extremism. • Tolerance for other religions.	• Moderate foreign policy.

6.4.6. Western-educated Leaders, Technocrats and Citizens

A growing number of studies have suggested that governments controlled by "coalitions with strong internationalist links" tend to carry economic reform measures early and consistently.[56] Evidence consistent with this proposition emerged from Mexico, Thailand and Korea in the 1980s, as well as from the Middle East.[57] Such internationalist coalitions are typically dominated by a team of technocrats that have extensive foreign training and experience.

Actors with internationalist links exist at various levels of the political and social structure. Leaders and politicians with internationalist links at the highest level of policy making are more likely to take reform measures compared to those without such links.[58] Western-educated leaders such as Morocco's King Mohamed VI and Jordan's King Abdullah seem to be more open to reforms than most Arab leaders.

At the next level, bureaucrats help precipitate institutional changes by directing attention and providing supports and resources. There is growing recognition that internationalist links provide technocratic and educational expertise necessary for reform. Technocrats with extensive foreign training and experience are more open to Western-style reforms.

But there is another point that is perhaps even more important. Outsiders lack broad legitimacy and thus can do little to bring changes. Some governments also oppose institutional reform pressures from outside. Morocco's King Mohammed VI put the issue this way: "Self-reform is an internal process. Just as we refrain from giving lessons to others, we will not tolerate being told what to do. No one . . . shall impose their views on us."[59] A narrow set of attributes that is attractive with only one group of institutional actors is not sufficient to mobilize the wider cooperation needed to bring institutional changes. Western-educated technocrats' subject position allows them to acquire a wide legitimacy and bridge diverse stakeholders. As they are insiders, the institutional reforms supported by them are likely to possess high face validity. They are thus expected to play a prominent role in change.

Many old GCC leaders are not open to social, technological and economic ideas. Western-educated GCC leaders, on the other hand, seem to be bringing institutional reforms. For instance, Western-educated Qatari Emir Sheikh Hamad introduced the country's first popular elections in 1999, which also allowed women to vote and run for office. He has a team of Western-educated advisors. Unlike most Arab rulers, Western-educated GCC rulers or those with Western-educated advisors seem to emphasize economic gain more than political order. This pattern is powerfully illustrated in Kuwait's 2001 introduction of an economic packageto attract foreign investment and Sheik Mohammad's measurers to modernize Dubai.

Western-educated GCC technocrats are energetic, disciplined, qualified and competent to carry out reforms. They have become important institutional change agents or institutional entrepreneurs.

In 1991, mostly Western-educated Kuwaiti liberals formed the first open political party. In 2003, 104 Saudi intellectuals, many of them Western-educated, presented a petition to the king. The petition, "A Vision for the Present and Future of the Homeland", called for a constitution and bill of rights.[60] It proposed an elected legislature; local and regional elections; an independent judiciary; and a guarantee of "freedom of expression, association, assembly, the right to vote and to participate, as well as human rights". It urged the king to confront corruption, bribery and power abuse and argued that a constitutional monarchy would help counter Muslim extremism.

Reform also depends on populations with a democratic culture. Citizens with a strong desire for democratic participation are likely to exert pressure for progressive change. During the 1992 election in Kuwait, groups of women—mostly Western-educated—protested against their exclusion from voting. In the 2006 parliamentary elections, women were allowed to vote and there were twenty-eight women candidates, mostly Western-educated.

6.4.7. Governments' Dependence on Businesses, and the Merger of Economic and Political Elites

Political institutions tend to have built-in biases that systematically favor specific classes. In a discussion of the dynamics of class forces and state-level policies, businesses deserve special attention. The capital-dependence theory argues that governments that are constrained by the need to generate private investment face structural pressures to adopt policies favoring businesses.[61] Research indicates that governments with capital dependence are likely to adopt pro-business policies even without businesses' pressures.

Rulers' control over economic decision making influences the success of a reform. In an economy characterized by a high degree of dependence of the government on domestic businesses, the businesses can exert a strong grip on state policies. What seems to be happening in such economies is businesses regulating the state rather than vice versa. On the other hand, governments ignore interests of businesses with low economic importance which lack "veto points".[62] Jordan, which depends on foreign aid with the government as the direct aid

recipient, is an example of such an economy. The state allocates investment and employs 50 percent of the workforce.[63]

Of equal importance in the discussion of the government–businesses
nexus is bureaucrats' involvement in businesses. A cohesive reform
team involving bureaucrats is a defining feature of a successful
reform.[64] Academic research conducted in China, Mexico, Russia and
other Eastern European countries has indicated that the most important barrier to transition to a market economy centers on resistance by
the bureaucracy.

Theoretically, the government can control bureaucrats through laws
and by specifying the details of implementation. If bureaucrats are
taking advantage of positional power to maximize economic rewards,
institutional reforms adversely affect their utility function. Moreover,
bureaucrats, who are also capitalists, possess power to penetrate into
the government apparatus.[65] Bureaucrats in such cases are against the
deinstitutionalization of existing institutions and the formation of new
institutions. One would not expect the government to take substantial
reform measures that go against bureaucrats' interests.

While there is some degree of nepotism everywhere, the influences
of favoritism, nepotism and personal connection are more readily
apparent in the GCC, a tendency that can be attributed to the culture (e.g., strong kinship ties and obligations to family and friends).
One scholar goes even further, saying: "In the Arab world nepotism
has none of the negative associations it has in the West."[66] Another
observes: "Corruption and nepotism [prevail], and the concept of the
state [isn't] fully understood . . . as a guardian and representative of
individual and community interests."[67]

To understand the infancy of capitalism in the GCC, it may be
helpful to consider shared mutual interests between merchant and
ruling families. Big businesses play influential roles in political decision making and remain a strong anti-reform force. Note too that the
management principles of these businesses have very few elements of
Islamic economics.

In Saudi Arabia, the royal family entered into business in the 1960s
and has benefited from the status quo. Similarly, in Oman, the sultan
received resources to run the state from merchant families and provided them with institutional favor as well as security and protection.[68]

For the ruling elites, the arbitrary application of business laws provides an important access to resources.

There has also been a colossal increase in bureaucrats' involvement in business. Bureaucrats thus discourage policies favoring institutional reforms and outside investments and remain a strong anti-reform force. An expert notes: "It's just that bureaucracy, corruption and uncertainty make it difficult to build a business bigger than a market stall."[69]

6.4.8. Dependence on Western Countries

As noted above, selective adaptation is a function of how policy makers perceive the "purpose, content and effect" of foreign and local institutional arrangements.[70] The content of Western countries' institutional arrangements in administering aid and loans affects developing countries' reforms. Western countries, especially the US, and international agencies such as the International Monetary Fund and the World Bank have governance criteria[71] for aid and lending decisions.[72] The US has helped friendly regimes develop into "regional showpieces of globalization" and provided them with military support.[73]

In highlighting the role that dependence on aid can play in institutional reforms, consider the Middle East. From this standpoint, there are two groups of economies. The countries of the first group (Tunisia, Morocco, Egypt and Jordan) have benefited from foreign aid and have been consistent in implementing reforms. The countries of the second group (post-1981 Syria, Iran and Sudan, pre-1994 Algeria and pre-2003 Iraq), on the other hand, were hostile to the US and resisted reform.[74]

The countries in the first group, which desperately needed aid, met World Trade Organization (WTO) entry requirements in record time. Ironically, it is the aid that remains a major motivation behind reforms. For instance, a main benefit of joining the WTO highlighted by Jordanian officials was the "massive aid" that the country would receive; the US, the EU and Japan provided assistance to "ease the pain and political costs" of reform.[75]

Some GCC governments depend on Western powers, particularly the US, for external security as well as on technology and economic fronts. For example, the US arguably provides Saudi Arabia with defense against external threats. Saudis have used the US as a "shield" to counter external threats and US troops protect ruling sheikhs' oil fields.[76] The Saudi–US relationship grew to include the exchange of US technology for Saudi cash. While there is some evidence of US influence on societal practices and institutions in Saudi Arabia, the changes are insignificant.

Unsurprisingly, compared to many developing economies, GCC economies are less dependent on the West. GCC regimes' responses with respect to Western powers and foreign multinationals are largely symbolic. Indeed, GCC states face virtually no pressures from OECD countries. For instance, observers have noted that the US has relied on Saudi Arabia to provide a long-term oil supply and is unwilling to push the Saudi regime for institutional reforms. At the same time, the Saudis are "unbribable and unmaneuverable".[77] One scholar notes: "Because of its dependency on Middle East gas and oil, Europe's high talk about human rights doesn't apply much to Arab extremists with energy-rich patrons in the Gulf. America is in a war against Islamic fascism, yet treads carefully around Saudi Arabia, despite the kingdom's subsidies to America-hating madrasahs."[78]

6.4.9. Ability to Achieve Economic Development without Reforms

Economic performance is positively related to a regime's legitimacy. The economic performance–legitimacy nexus is stronger for authoritarian regimes than democratic ones. While some view authoritarian regimes' economic-performance-based legitimacy as superficial, this strategy is producing results for some rulers. Reform-based growth may produce complementarity for authoritarian regimes as essential characteristics of both authoritarianism and reform exist side by side.

The term "performance legitimacy" is often used to describe a justification for political repression by governments delivering high growth.[79] Poor economic performance, on the other hand, may result in the loss of legitimacy. Asia provides a robust example to illustrate this form of legitimacy. Most of the past and present authoritarian Asian regimes (e.g., Singapore, Malaysia and China) acquired legitimacy through high economic growth. In Indonesia, Suharto's legitimacy was based on the country's improved living standards during his rule. In sum, if an economy performs well, institutional entrepreneurs face difficulty in communicating the need for change and value of the proposed changes.

Most GCC governments' ideologies entail different forms of nationalism. Economic failure erodes a government's legitimacy and fosters an ideological vacuum, as old ideologies (e.g., nationalism) are perceived as failures.[80] Falling oil/gas production and growing youth unemployment are among powerful factors pushing reform in GCC economies. Unsurprisingly, achieving growth has been at the top of the agenda. In this regard, the impact of oil revenue on institutional change deserves special attention.

Oil and gas account for 70 percent of government revenue in the GCC economies and for over 80 percent in Kuwait.[81] By meeting citizens' economic expectations and providing some welfare, GCC regimes have reduced resentment toward them. They have been able to hold their citizens at bay. As it happens, a major reason behind GCC economies' poor performance on the institutional reform front is the region's lack of interest in attracting FDI. They have large current account surpluses and are net capital exporters. While reform is producing complementarity effects for some Asian authoritarian regimes, GCC governments have been able to deliver growth without reform.

Unsurprisingly, political, economic and financial crises have induced an appetite for reform. When oil prices declined in the 1980s, GCC regimes offered wider political participation to ensure peace and legitimacy. In 1998, the then Kuwaiti oil minister put the issue this way: "The . . . decline in oil prices may be a blessing in disguise . . . Although it has been difficult for us to do in the past politically, may be we can search for alternative sources of income."[82] When oil prices were low in the early 1990s, Kuwait and Saudi Arabia moved towards economic reforms. The Kuwaiti government talked about turning the country into a free trade zone while "acknowledging the need to prepare their citizens for painful changes". The then Kuwaiti oil minister went on: "Every walk of life has been subsidized . . . We have to see how we're going to work through this."

Kuwait and Saudi Arabia were thus searching for new solutions or were in the pre-institutionalization phase of reform. Broad institutional support rather than economic and technical efficiency is, however, critical to move beyond pre-institutionalization. With higher oil prices and the absence of such support, the whole reform process pretty much stopped right there.

Among GCC economies, per capita oil and gas production is among the lowest in Bahrain, arguably the most diversified GCC economy. It has a history as an important financial center. It took substantive measures (e.g., extensive banking sector reform) to attract industries such as ship repair and financial services.

6.5. Concluding Comments

While some positive steps have been taken toward increasing investments in education, developing entrepreneurship and capital markets, and reforming economic and political institutions, there is an urgent need to intensify these efforts. Compared to the successful East Asian economies, GCC economies have failed to take a sensible and considered approach to the development of human and physical capital. Heavy reliance on imported labor has led to a negative perception of many jobs as unattractive, due primarily to the fact that they are associated with poor working conditions. At the same time, employers try to gain as much as possible from the expatriate workers.

Institutions arguably have a higher propensity to change when they are characterized by contradictions which "create conflicting and irreconcilable incentives and motivations".[83] Nowhere is this characteristic more evident than in the GCC region. In this regard, there are some well-founded rationales for and against doing business in the GCC region as well as a number of misinformed and ill-guided points of view. Many foreign investors, for instance, see the GCC region as a breeding ground for terrorists and underestimate the region's importance despite its GDP of about US$1 trillion.

As is the case in many authoritarian regimes, GCC rulers have been able to acquire "performance legitimacy" by meeting their citizens' economic expectations. Unlike many developing economies, they do not need foreign aid and loans. Oil-based growth has also reduced their dependence on FDI. This means that GCC economies are less dependent on foreign multinationals, Western governments and international agencies. Second, merchant families, royal entrepreneurs and elite entrepreneurs, who have an extremely close and mutually advantageous relationships with the government and are benefiting from the status quo, and government bureaucracies have been a strong anti-reform force.

A third aspect of GCC economies is "the holistic order" of society, which tends to shift the balance of power towards anti-reform groups. Institutional change processes that go against Islam's logic face resistance. Islam's influence is readily apparent in politics (e.g., the perception that there is no distance between Islam and democracy) and in business (e.g., commercial shariah). Moreover, Islam has provided credibility and added legitimacy to GCC regimes because of absolute monarchies' possession of religious power.

Despite the above observations, some encouraging signs are emerging. As of 2007, the UAE's eight campuses of the Higher College of Technology required students to take entrepreneurship training. In 2007, over 60 percent of the campuses' engineering students were women.[84] Even in Saudi Arabia, which is considered to be one of the most conservative societies, institutional changes are taking place which have facilitated females' participation in entrepreneurial endeavors and enhanced their status in the business world. Estimates suggest that women account for 0.8 percent of total private sector employees.[85] While most women work as teachers, the female workforce is diversifying in other occupations such as doctors, journalists, news anchors and television presenters. In 2007, the Saudi government announced plans to reserve one-third of all government jobs for women.[86]

The following observations can be made about mechanisms to achieve effective institutional changes and operate successfully in the GCC region:

The Principle of Minimal Dislocation

The above analysis indicates that transition to a Western form of capitalism is a big jump from the current institutional arrangements of GCC economies. Progressive institutional changes are sustainable only if there is "minimal dislocation". Put differently, the incorporation of a new behavior must have a minimally disruptive effect in the community. In this regard, transition of GCC businesses to the principles of Islamic economics is likely to be a more feasible option than transition to a Western form of capitalism.

Bricolage or Complementarity as a Strategy to Operate in GCC Economies
For foreign entrepreneurial firms, combining components from the existing institutional environment and reorganizing them strategically—also known as bricolage[87]—can be an important way to operate in the GCC region. Western financial institutions, for instance, operate according to the principle of commercial shariah and have helped boost GCC regimes' performance legitimacy by bringing jobs and FDI in the region. This approach can also be viewed as complementarity, as two seemingly contradictory phenomena (Western capitalism and commercial shariah) are combined and the essential characteristics of each component are preserved.

Decline in Production/Price of Oil as a Possible Jolt to the Existing Institutions
The interesting question for the GCC region is what factors could give a jolt to existing institutions. Decline in production and/or price of oil is probably the single most important force that can threaten the GCC regimes' performance-based legitimacy. As noted above, in the early 1990s, Kuwait and Saudi Arabia were at the pre-institutionalization phase but subsequent increased oil prices reduced their incentive to take substantive action towards the full institutionalization of reforms. In the current interaction pattern of institutional actors in the GCC context, a decline in oil price is likely to shift the power balance in favor of pro-reform actors such as foreign multinationals and Western governments.

Western-educated Leaders and Technocrats as Agents of Institution Change
Western-educated leaders and technocrats have introduced and facilitated reform measures. If a GCC economy with an internationalist coalition develops a reformist showcase economy, other GCC regimes may consider reform to be an appropriate arrangement. Note that currently being "reformist" is an unpopular option in the Arab world.[88]

Need for Pro-reform Actors to be Organized and Vocal

Pro-reform constituents tend to be "generally unorganized, silent, and nearly invisible politically", whereas anti-reform actors are "frequently organized and vocal".[89] Obviously, the political process is likely to respond to those with a voice. In the GCC region, pro-reform actors such as political parties, interest groups and unions need to be more organized and vocal in order to bring more entrepreneurship-friendly institutional change.

6.6. Review Questions

1. Why are there low incentives for GCC policy makers to take measures to change institutions in favor of entrepreneurship?
2. What are some of the characteristics of GCC rulers that are more open to institutional reforms? Explain with examples.

6.7. Critical Discussion Questions

1. Select a GCC country. Comment on the quality of its entrepreneurial ecosystem.
2. Do Western governments differ in terms of their orientation towards institutional reforms in GCC economies compared to other developing countries?
3. What are some of the barriers facing a promoter of entrepreneurship in GCC countries?

6.8. End-of-chapter Case: Cellular Phones and Entrepreneurship in the GCC Economies

Cellular phones have greatly facilitated the stimulation of entrepreneurial activities in the GCC region. For instance, women entrepreneurs in the region use cellular phones and other ICT at much higher rates than the world average. As early as in 2005, among the businesses owned by women, 89 percent in Bahrain and 79 percent in the UAE used cell phones compared to the worldwide average of 32 percent.[90] Some social enterprises in the GCC region have used cell phone technologies to connect youth with job opportunities.[91]

Public as well as private sector organizations offer various services through mobile applications. In this regard, mobile apps targeting the

Arab world are proliferating at an unprecedented rate, which is likely to stimulate further entrepreneurship in the region. For instance, by 2010, there were over ninety iPhone apps in Arabic.[92] Local investors are also encouraging the development of apps for the region. AppsArabia, which provides investments for developing and marketing promising app ideas for the Middle East and North Africa, is one example.[93]

Cellular phones were introduced in the GCC economies in the early and mid-1990s. GCC economies have some of the highest mobile penetration rates in the world. Telecommunications companies in the region have launched several 3G and 3.5G products and services such as mobile Internet, video calling and mobile TV. The UAE-based Emirates airline has become the world's first carrier commercially to launch an in-flight mobile telephone service.

Mobile infrastructures cover most of the populations in GCC econ-omies (Fig. 6.3). In particular, Bahrain, Kuwait, Qatar and the UAE are among the top world economies for cell phone use. According to the International Telecommunications Union, mobile penetration rates in the GCC economies in 2012 (www.itu.int/en/ITU-D/Statis tics/Pages/stat/default.aspx) were 156 percent in Bahrain, 191 percent in Kuwait, 181 percent in Oman, 134 percent in Qatar, 184 percent in Saudi Arabia, and 169 percent in the UAE.

The third-generation (3G) cellular market is rapidly taking off. In Saudi Arabia 3G applications such as wide-area wireless voice tele-phony and broadband wireless data are widely used.[94] The 3.5G stan-dard in the country has helped companies to achieve ADSL broadband speeds over the mobile network.

Mobile Government (M-government) Applications

M-government is facilitating entrepreneurship in GCC economies. A typical m-government application involves smart phones that tie in voice communications with computer, network and e-mail functional-ity, or a PDA, which combines the functionality of a computer, a cell phone, a music player and a camera.[95]

In 2003, the Dubai government launched SMS services. "Push" SMS services are available for such services as driving license renew-als, trade license renewals, information about traffic jams and health card renewals. By September 2006, the number of customers for these services had reached over 7 million.[96] Dubai also launched the Middle East's first mobile portal in September 2005. As of February 2007, the Dubai mobile portal offered access to 81 percent of the 1,900 public services offered by the government. They included payment of utilities bills and traffic fines, job searches, flight information and public transport information. The portal has partnered with industry and business communities for airline bookings, stock quotes, entertainment and Dubai city information.[97]

In Oman, Muscat Municipality has developed an m-parking system which enables motorists to pay parking fees via SMS. Likewise, higher secondary school students in the country can receive their grades by sending their seat numbers via SMS to a designated phone number.[98] This is a component of the broader Education Portal, which provides services to parents, students and teachers.[99] Muscat Securities Market has enabled investors to receive updates on market and stock alerts via SMS. Likewise, the Civil Aviation and Meteorology's weather forecast service is available for most towns in the country. It allows consumers to receive weather reports on their cell phones.

Conclusion

Women's inclusion in entrepreneurship could be among the most important benefits of cellular technology diffusion in GCC economies. In some GCC countries, women are not permitted to drive cars, and open and public interactions between men and women are highly constrained outside of marriage and the family. Anecdotal evidence indicates that the Internet has helped overcome such barriers in these economies. In the late 1990s, it was reported that the Internet facilitated Saudi women's operation of home-based businesses.[100] Early evidence clearly indicates that women-owned businesses in the region are benefiting tremendously from cell phones.

Notes

1. Azzam, H.T. 1999, "Arab States Urged to Liberalize Trade, Lure Investment to Bolster Growth", *Middle East Newsfile*, September 2; Reed, O.L. 2001, "Law, the Rule of law, and Property: A Foundation for the Private Market and Business Study", *American Business Law Journal*, 38(3), pp. 441–473.

2. Bains, E. 2009, "Qatar Tackles Region's Jobless Youth", *MEED: Middle East Economic Digest*, 53(26), pp. 26–27.

3. World Bank 2007, *The Environment for Women's Entrepreneurship in the Middle East and North Africa Region*, Washington DC: World Bank, at http://siteresources.worldbank.org/INTMENA/Resources/Environ ment_for_Womens_Entrepreneurship_in_MNA_final.pdf.

4. Ibid.

5. Jarmo Kotilaine 2011, "Comment: Labour Reform Key to Development", *Financial Times*, March 23, at www.ft.com/cms/s/0/04f08dec–5563–11e0–87fe–00144feab49a.html#axzz1Z2bM9tr6.

6. Bains, E. 2009, "Qatar Tackles Region's Jobless Youth", *MEED: Middle East Economic Digest*, 53(26), pp. 26–27.

7. Atkinson, S. 2011, "Kuwait Hands out Cash to Bridge Small Business Gulf", BBC News, July 3, at www.bbc.co.uk/news/business-14006885.

8. Arnold, T. 2011, "Oman Raises Minimum Wage for Nationals", February 17, at www.thenational.ae/news/worldwide/middle-east/oman-raises-minimum-wage-for-nationals.

9. Bains, E. 2009, "Qatar Tackles Region's Jobless Youth", *MEED: Middle East Economic Digest*, 53(26), pp. 26–27.

10. Zakaria, F. 2004, "Islam, Democracy, and Constitutional Liberalism", *Political Science Quarterly*, 119(1), p. 1.

11. Atkinson, S. 2011, "Kuwait Hands out Cash to Bridge Small Business Gulf", BBC News, July 3, at www.bbc.co.uk/news/business-14006885.

12. The minimum wage including salary and benefits was 140 RO (about US$363) per month. Bureau of Economic, Energy and Business Affairs, US Department of State 2011, *Investment Climate Statement 2011*, at www.state.gov/e/eeb/rls/othr/ics/2011/157339.htm.

13. Business Monitor International 2006, *Egypt Business Forecast Report 2006*, chap. 3, "Special Report", 4th quarter, pp. 26–38.

14. Elbadawi, I.A. 2005, "Reviving Growth in the Arab World", *Economic Development and Cultural Change*, 53(2), pp. 293–326.

15. Heftier, R.W. 2006, "Islamic Economics and Global Capitalism", *Society*, 44(1), pp. 16–22.

16. Theil, S. 2007, "Teaching Entrepreneurship in the Arab World", *Newsweek International*, August 14, at www.gmfus.org/archives/teaching-entrepre neurship-in-the-arab-world/.

17. Maceda, C. 2010, "World of Wealthy Women", August 14, http://gulfnews. com/business/your-money/world-of-wealthy-women–1.667819.

18. Simon, G. 1998, "Who Goes Where?", *UNESCO Courier*, 51(11), pp. 23–25.

19. Lucas, R.E.B. 2001, *Diaspora and Development: Highly Skilled Migrants from East Asia, Report Prepared for the World Bank*, at http://citeseerx.ist. psu.edu/viewdoc/download?doi=10.1.1.147.6620&rep=rep1&type=pdf.

20. Balasubramanian, A. 2010, "Rebuilding Dubai", *Harvard International Review*, 31(4), pp. 10–11.

21. *Saudi Gazette* 2010, "Saudi Women: A Major Growth Driver for the Country's Diversification Policy", December 7, at www.saudigazette.com. sa/index.cfm?method=home.regcon&contentID=2010080379929.
22. zawya.com 2010, "Injaz Al-Arab Board Convenes in Qatar", June 2, at www.zawya.com/story/ZAWYA20100603071642/.
23. KNOWLEDGE@Wharton 2010, "Opportunities Mixed with Challenges: Creating Technology that Resonates in the Arab World", November 2, at http://knowledge.wharton.upenn.edu/arabic/article.cfm?articleId=2559.
24. Zakaria, F. 2004, "Islam, Democracy, and Constitutional Liberalism", *Political Science Quarterly*, 119(1), p. 1.
25. *Arab News* 2012, "Saudi Attorney Calls for New Antitrust Law", August 13, at http://arabnews.com/economy/saudi-attorney-calls-new-antitrust-law.
26. World Bank Group 2011, "Research and Development Expenditure (% of GDP)", http://data.worldbank.org/indicator/GB.XPD.RSDV.GD.ZS.
27. Business Monitor International 2006, *Egypt Business Forecast Report 2006*, chap. 3, "Special Report", 4th quarter, pp. 26–38.
28. World Bank 2007, *The Environment for Women's Entrepreneurship in the Middle East and North Africa Region*, Washington DC: World Bank, at http://siteresources.worldbank.org/INTMENA/Resources/Environ ment_for_Womens_Entrepreneurship_in_MNA_final.pdf.
29. OECD 2006, "Venture Capital Development in MENA Countries: Taking Advantage of the Current Opportunity", *MENA Investment Policy Brief*, 1, at www.oecd.org/mena/investment/37256468.pdf.
30. scidevnet 2011, "Venture Capital to Boost Innovation in Arab World", July 25, at www.scidev.net/global/capacity-building/news/venture-capital-to-boost-innovation-in-arab-world.html.
31. International Finance Corporation and Center of Arab Women for Training and Research 2004, "Women Entrepreneurs in the Middle East and North Africa: Characteristics", June, at www.ifc.org/wps/wcm/connect/e3a45180488553abaff4ff6a6515bb18/MENA_Women_Entrepreneurs_ExecSum_English.pdf?MOD=AJPERES&CACHEID=e3a451804885 53abaff4ff6a6515bb18.
32. OECD 2006, "Venture Capital Development in MENA Countries: Taking Advantage of the Current Opportunity", *MENA Investment Policy Brief*, 1, at www.oecd.org/mena/investment/37256468.pdf.
33. Ibid.
34. Ibid.
35. Hudson, M.C. 2002, "Imperial Headaches: Managing Unruly Regions in an Age of Globalization", *Middle East Policy*, 9(4), pp. 61–74; Jamal, A.A. 2006, "Reassessing Support for Islam and Democracy in the Arab World? Evidence from Egypt and Jordan", *World Affairs*, 169(2), pp. 51–63.
36. Gershman, C., & Allen, M. 2006, "The Assault on Democracy Assistance", *Journal of Democracy*, 17(2), pp. 36–51.
37. Kristof, N.D. 2003, "Running for the Exits", *New York Times*, April 18, p. A.15.

38. CountryWatch 2006, "Political Overview", in *Kuwait Country Review 2006*, Houston: CountryWatch, pp. 7–31.
39. Scott, B.R. 2001, "The Great Divide in the Global Village", *Foreign Affairs*, 80(1), pp. 160–177.
40. Hoffman, A.J. 1999, "Institutional Evolution and Change: Environmentalism and the U.S. Chemical Industry", *Academy of Management Journal*, 42(4), pp. 351–371.
41. Groenewegen, J., & van der Steen, M. 2007, "The Evolutionary Policy Maker", *Journal of Economic Issues*, 41(2), pp. 351–358.
42. Potter, P.B. 2001, *The Chinese Legal System: Globalization and Local Legal Culture*, London: Routledge.
43. Boettke, P., & Storr, V. 2002, "Post Classical Political Economy", *American Journal of Economics & Sociology*, 61, pp. 161–191.
44. Zweynert, J., & Goldschmidt, N. 2006, "The Two Transitions in Central and Eastern Europe as Processes of Institutional Transplantation", *Journal of Economic Issues*, 40(4), pp. 895ff.
45. Zoubir, Y.H. 1996, "Algerian Islamists' Conception of Democracy", *Arab Studies Quarterly*, 18(3), pp. 65–85.
46. Ibid.
47. Kadir, S. 2004, "Islam, State and Society in Singapore", *Inter-Asia Cultural Studies*, 5(3), pp. 357–371.
48. Zuhur, S. 2005, *A Hundred Osamas: Islamist Threats and the Future of Counterinsurgency*, Carlisle Barracks, PA: US Army War College, Strategic Studies Institute, p. 26.
49. Jamal, A.A. 2006, "Reassessing Support for Islam and Democracy in the Arab World? Evidence from Egypt and Jordan", *World Affairs*, 169(2), pp. 51–63.
50. In Bahrain and Kuwait, about 10 percent of total class hours are devoted to Islamic instruction. In Saudi Arabia Islamic instruction consumes 32 percent of class time for grades 1–3 and decreases for higher grades (about 15 percent for grades 10–12). The figures for Qatar are 8–17 percent.
51. Ergil, D. 2000, "Identity Crises and Political Instability in Turkey", *Journal of International Affairs*, 54(1), pp. 43–63.
52. Heftier, R.W. 2006, "Islamic Economics and Global Capitalism", *Society*, 44(1), pp. 16–22.
53. Zakaria, F. 2004, "Islam, Democracy, and Constitutional Liberalism", *Political Science Quarterl*, 119(1), p. 1.
54. Hudson, M.C. 2002, "Imperial Headaches: Managing Unruly Regions in an Age of Globalization", *Middle East Policy*, 9(4), pp. 61–74.
55. Kéchichian, J.A. 2004, "Democratization in Gulf Monarchies: A New Challenge to the GCC", *Middle East Policy*, 11(4), pp. 37–57; Power, C. 2003, "Hillary Clinton Stand Back", *Newsweek*, November 10, pp. 31–32.
56. Stallings, B. 1992, "International Influence on Economic Policy: Debt, Stabilization and the Crisis of Import Substitution", in Haggard, S., &

Kaufman, R. (eds), *The Politics of Economic Adjustment*, Princeton, NJ: Princeton University Press, p. 75.

57. Marr, P. 2003, "Iraq 'the day after': Internal Dynamics in Post-Saddam Iraq", *Naval War College Review*, 56(1), pp. 12–29.

58. Glasser, B.L. 1995, "External Capital and Political Liberalizations: A Typology of Middle Eastern Development in the 1980s and 1990s", *Journal of International Affairs*, 49(1), pp. 45–73.

59. Fattah, H.M. 2005, "Conference of Arab Leaders Yields Little of Significance", *New York Times*, March 24, p. A.12.

60. Ignatius, D. 2003, "Home-grown Saudi Reform", *Washington Post*, March 7, p. A.33.

61. Lindblom, C. 1977, *Politics and Markets*, New York: Basic Books.

62. Hicks, A. 1999, *Social Democracy and Welfare Capitalism*, Ithaca: Cornell University Press.

63. Reiter, Y. 2004, "The Palestinian-Transjordanian Rift: Economic Might and Political Power in Jordan", *Middle East Journal*, 58(1), pp. 72–92.

64. Haggard, S., & Kaufman, R.R. 1995, *The Political Economy of Democratic Transitions*, Princeton, NJ: Princeton University Press.

65. Chen, A. 2002, "Capitalist Development, Entrepreneurial Class, and Democratization in China", *Political Science Quarterly*, 117(3), pp. 401–422.

66. Lewis, R. 1995, "How Peace Can Come to the Middle East", *Management Today*, July, pp. 80–81.

67. Khashan, H. 1997, "The New World Order and the Tempo of Militant Islam", *British Journal of Middle Eastern Studies*, 24(1), pp. 5–24.

68. Al-Haj, A.J. 1996, "The Politics of Participation in the Gulf Cooperation Council States: The Omani Consultative Council", *Middle East Journal*, 50(4), pp. 559–571.

69. Pollock, R.L. 2002, "Mideast Peace? Let's Start with the Rule of Law", *Wall Street Journal*, November 27, p. A.10.

70. Potter, P.B. 2004, "Legal Reform in China: Institutions, Culture, and Selective Adaptation", *Law & Social Inquiry*, 29(2), pp. 465–495.

71. The US has created a Millennium Challenge Account (MCA), which has strict standards related to governance and economic reform measures for recipients.

72. Krasner, S.D., & Pascual, C. 2005, "Addressing State Failure", *Foreign Affairs*, 84(4), p. 153.

73. *Economist* 2002, "Murder, and its Consequences: How Safe an Anti-Iraq Ally is Jordan?" October 31.

74. El-Said, H., & Harrigan, J. 2006, "Globalization, International Finance, and Political Islam in the Arab World", *Middle East Journal*, 60(3), pp. 444–466.

75. Pfeifer, K. 1999, "How Tunisia, Morocco, Jordan and Even Egypt Became IMF Success Stories", *Middle East Report*, 29(210), pp. 23–26.

76. Seznec, J. 2005, "Business as Usual", *Harvard International Review*, 26(4), pp. 56–60.

77. Rosner, S. 2007, "Selling Arms to the Saudis", Slate, at www.slate.com/articles/news_and_politics/foreigners/2007/07/selling_arms_to_the_saudis.html.
78. Hanson, V.D. 2006, "How Oil Lubricates our Enemies", *American Enterprise*, 17(6), p. 44.
79. Acharya, A. 1999, "Realism, Institutionalism, and the Asian Economic Crisis", *Contemporary Southeast Asia*, 21(1), pp. 1–29.
80. Richards, A. 2002, "Socioeconomic Roots of Middle East Radicalism", *Naval War College Review*, 55(4), pp. 22–38.
81. Lancaster, J. 1998, "Gulf States Hurt by Oil-price Slump; Kuwaitis, Saudis May Face Spending Cuts in Popular Programs", *Washington Post*, June 14, p. A.21.
82. Ibid.
83. Campbell, J.L. 2004, *Institutional Change and Globalization*, Princeton, NJ: Princeton University Press.
84. Theil, S. 2007, "Teaching Entrepreneurship in the Arab World", *Newsweek International*, August 14, at www.gmfus.org/archives/teaching-entrepreneurship-in-the-arab-world/.
85. *Saudi Gazette* 2010, "Saudi Women: A Major Growth Driver for the Country's Diversification Policy", December 7, at www.saudigazette.com.sa/index.cfm?method=home.regcon&contentID=2010080379929.
86. Ibid.
87. Campbell, J.L. 2004, *Institutional Change and Globalization*, Princeton, NJ: Princeton University Press.
88. Kéchichian, J.A. 2004, "Democratization in Gulf Monarchies: A New Challenge to the GCC", *Middle East Policy*, 11(4), pp. 37–57
89. Kikeri, S., & Nellis, J. 2004, "An Assessment of Privatization", *World Bank Research Observer*, 19(1), p. 87.
90. ifc.org 2007, Women Entrepreneurs in the Middle East and North Africa: Characteristics, International Finance Corporation Gender Entrepreneurship Markets, Center of Arab Women for Training and Research, June 2007, International Finance Corporation and Center of Arab Women for Training and Research 2004, "Women Entrepreneurs in the Middle East and North Africa: Characteristics", June, at www.ifc.org/wps/wcm/connect/e3a45180488553abaff4ff6a6515bb18/MENA_Women_Entrepreneurs_ExecSum_English.pdf?MOD=AJPERES&CACHEID=e3a45180488553abaff4ff6a6515bb18.
91. Ray, J. 2011, "Young Arabs More Connected in 2010: Cell Phone Access Jumps in Low- and Middle-income Countries", April 11, www.gallup.com/poll/147035/young-arabs-connected–2010.aspx
92. KNOWLEDGE@Wharton 2010, "Opportunities Mixed with Challenges: Creating Technology that Resonates in the Arab World", November 2, at http://knowledge.wharton.upenn.edu/arabic/article.cfm?articleId=2559.

93. *Dubai Chronicle* 2011, "AppsArabia Research Boosts Regions Apps Industry", September 19, at www.dubaichronicle.com/2011/09/20/app sarabia-research-boosts-regions-apps-industry/.
94. *Khaleej Times* 2007, "Saudi Telecom Seeks Increase in Foreign Revenue", May 23, at www.khaleejtimes.com/kt-article-display-1.asp?xfile=data/business/2007/May/business_May746.xml&section=business.
95. *Middle East* 2007, "On the Hoof", 375, pp. 52–54.
96. Dore, L. 2006, "Dubai Has Ambitious Targets for m-Government System", *Khaleej Times*, September 24, at www.khaleejtimes.com/Dis playArticleNew.asp?xfile=data/business/2006/September/business_Sep tember788.xml&section=business.
97. *Middle East* 2007, "On the Hoof", 375, pp. 52–54.
98. Naqvi, S.J., & Al-Shihi, H. 2009, "M-government Services Initiatives in Oman", *Informing Science and Information Technology*, 6, at http://iisit. org/Vol6/IISITv6p817–824Naqvi678.pdf.
99. Alrahbi, T. 2008, "eOman—Transforming Oman, e/m-Government in Arab States:Building Capacity in Knowledge Management through Partnership", United Nations Public Administration Network, November 18–20.
100. *Economist* 1999, "How Women Beat the Rules", October 2, p. 48.

7

ENTREPRENEURSHIP IN AFRICA

Abstract

Africa is arguably the richest continent in terms of minerals and natural resources. Africa has an abundance of entrepreneurs who possess the ability to identify business opportunities and exploit them. However, the continent's entrepreneurial performance has been weak. This chapter reviews various mechanisms by which foreign businesses are exploiting Africa for resources and market, and examines Western response to the low level of entrepreneurial activity in Africa. Finally, this chapter provides case studies of some successful entrepreneurial activities on the continent. The cases indicate that successful businesses do not necessarily need to depend on natural resources.

This chapter's objectives include:

1. To demonstrate an understanding of the natures of entrepreneurial activities in African economies.
2. To analyze the facilitators of and hindrances to entrepreneurship in African economies and compare them with other regions of the world.
3. To evaluate some of the successful as well as unsuccessful activities related to entrepreneurship in African economies.
4. To evaluate the roles of foreign companies in driving entrepreneurship development in Africa and their roles in the local economy.
5. To demonstrate an understanding of the Western response to the low level of entrepreneurial activity in Africa.

7.1. Introduction

Africa is arguably the richest continent in terms of its stock of minerals and natural resources. However, its entrepreneurial performance has been weak. Although entrepreneurial activities arguably existed in Africa before colonization, they have slowed down since the colonial period.[1] Experts argue that Africa's entrepreneurial failure can be attributed to factors such as the lack of sensitivity of raw agricultural products to international prices, poor infrastructure, lack of human and financial capital, and government policies that are not entrepreneurship-friendly.[2] According to a Gallup poll, 59 percent of Nigerians are unhappy with the filing process for registering a business.[3] Productive entrepreneurship in African economies has also been hindered by a lack of quality standards and inappropriate trade policies.

However, there are many successful entrepreneurs in Africa who come from various demographic, cultural and educational backgrounds. Studies have also found the existence of many competitive small businesses in the region. Some successful businesses in the continent have found creative ways to overcome economic, social, political and institutional barriers to entrepreneurship. For instance, the fashion label KEZA was able to overcome various obstacles to enable its business model to work in Rwanda. The company trained manufacturing cooperatives in such areas as design, quality control, product consistency and accounting.[4]

7.2. A Survey of Entrepreneurship in Africa

Most African economies have failed to utilize their natural and human resources productively. A journalist reporting on a conversation among delegates during the World Economic Forum Annual Meeting 2010 in Switzerland, writes: "In Ghana, the unemployment rate can easily be dealt with if most of the available resources are channeled toward entrepreneurship."[5]

According to the United Nations Development Program about 600 million people in Africa live on less than US$3 a day and over 350 million live on less than US$1 a day. Compared to other regions, Africa's progress in fighting poverty in the past three decades has been slower. For instance, while the proportion of East Asia's population living below the poverty line decreased from 80 percent in 1981 to 18 percent in 2009, Africa's poverty level has remained virtually unchanged during this period.[6] According to the UNDP's Human Development Report 2013 (http://hdr.undp.org/hdr4press/press/report/index.html), all of the world's ten economies with the lowest human development indices (HDI) were in SSA. Even South Africa, which is viewed as one of the most successful African economies, ranked 121 in terms of its HDI. The SSA economies' average HDI for 2012 was 0.475, which was slightly higher than the least developed countries' average of 0.449 and significantly lower than the world average of 0.694. Although some African economies are growing fast, because of high-income inequality, the population at the bottom of the economic pyramid has seen virtually no improvement in living standards.

Observers have noted that while entrepreneurial activities existed in Africa before colonization, such activities have slowed down since the colonial period.[7] One problem hindering entrepreneurial efforts in Africa is the large size of the region's informal economy. In Malawi only 50,000 people out of a population of twelve million (0.4 percent of the total population) are estimated to have formal jobs in the private sector.[8] Estimates suggest that 42 percent of the economy in Africa is informal, the highest proportion in the world.[9] A Gallup survey conducted among Nigerians found that 69 percent of potential entrepreneurs would not formally register their businesses and only 19 percent of the respondents said their business would be formally registered in future.[10]

7.2.1. Positive and Encouraging Signs

There are number of positive and encouraging signs in Africa's entrepreneurial landscape. Some African economies have made significant strides in improving their entrepreneurial climate (see "Ghana's entrepreneurial climate", below).

Contrary to the widespread belief that indigenous entrepreneurship is less well represented in Africa, various studies have shown that Africa doesn't lack entrepreneurial talent. The continent has an abundance of entrepreneurs who possess the ability to identify business opportunities and to exploit them, and recent surveys conducted in some African economies have confirmed this view.[11] For instance, a Gallup poll indicated that 67 percent of Nigerians have thought of starting a business. The proportion was among the highest rates in West Africa.[12]

Ghana's Entrepreneurial Climate

Ghana achieved independence from British rule on March 6, 1957. It was the first SSA nation to gain independence. Ghana has an abundance of natural resources including deposits of gold, timber, industrial diamonds, manganese, bauxite, oil, natural gas and hydrocarbon. It also has vast forests and a large amount of arable land. There are rich marine fishing reserves on the coast of the Atlantic Ocean. Ghana is the world's second biggest cocoa producer after the Ivory Coast.[13]

Ghana's major trading partners include Nigeria, China, the US, the UK, Germany, Togo, France, the Netherlands and Spain. In terms of the access to foreign markets, the country's location provides easy access to regional markets of about 250 million people in West Africa.[14]

The Ghanaian government has set a vision to transform Ghana into a prosperous middle-income country by 2020. Five development themes have been identified to achieve the vision: human development, economic growth, rural and urban development, private sector development and enabling the environment.[15] The government has taken measures to facilitate employment creation and is committed to expanding broadband Internet connectivity.[16] The country is described as "a hotbed of technology entrepreneurship".[17] The World Bank's Doing Business report in 2007 ranked Ghana as among the top ten reformers in the ease of doing business, and recognizes Ghana as a top global reformer.[18] Ghana was the winner of the Commonwealth Business Council (CBC) African Business Awards 2008 for the "Best Efforts towards Improving Investment Climate".[19]

There are also some high-profile examples of African businesses with very effective entrepreneurial impacts (see "Ecobank", "Jamii Bora" and "KEZA and Social Entrepreneurship"). South Africa is the largest center of entrepreneurial activities in Africa, and has more than half of the top one hundred companies on the African continent. An example of a South African company, which has been able to build a global brand is South African Breweries Ltd (SAB). SABMiller, which was created by the merger of South African Breweries and the Miller Brewing Company, holds a prominent place in the global beer market. One of its brands, Castle, has been introduced as a premium beer brand across the world.[20] SABMiller has discovered how to tap the local taste for homemade brews, making them with cheap ingredients (instead of barley), while adapting modern technology and promoting local economic development.

In Africa, SABMiller buys local crops such as sorghum instead of importing expensive barley. A SABMiller-commissioned study indicated that for every job in SABMiller's breweries in Uganda, the company supported over one hundred other jobs throughout the country. The company has thus contributed to local economic development by stabilizing the prices of local commodities such as sorghum and increasing farmers' incomes.[21]

While many African economies export oil and a few types of natural resource, some, especially non-resource rich ones such as Kenya, Tanzania and South Africa, have made significant progress in diversifying exports. On average in these countries, seventeen export products of these countries constitute 75 percent of total exports. African countries' progress has been more impressive in diversifying export markets. While developing countries accounted for only about 25 percent of African exports in the early 1990s, their share rose to about 50 percent by 2009.[22]

Ecobank

Ecobank (Ecobank Transnational Inc.) was founded in 1985 and is headquartered in Lome, Togo. As of late 2009, the bank had a customer base of about two million accounts and employed more than 11,000 people. Ecobank is a public company, which had 180,000 shareholders (local and international institutional and individual investors) and US$2.5 billion share capital as of December 2009.[23] Ecobank had a presence in more African countries than any other bank, with over six hundred branches and service offices in twenty-eight African countries and in France.

By January 2010, Ecobank had banking operations in thirty countries in Europe and Africa. Its revenue in 2008 was US$850 million. As of 2009, the bank was listed on three stock exchanges in West Africa—Lagos, Accra and the Bourse Régionale des Valeurs Mobilières (BRVM) in Abidjan.[24]

Ecobank's innovative services include its rapid transfer facility, which allows customers to send and receive funds quickly and its Non-Resident African Account (NRAA) for Africans living and working outside their home countries. The bank has also launched Africa's first multiple currency debit card (Haigh, 2009). Ecobank was the winner of the Commonwealth Business Council (CBC)-African Business Awards 2008 for "Technological Innovation".[25]

Jamii Bora

Jamii Bora, which means "good families" in Swahili, is the largest microfinance institution in Kenya. Jamii Bora had over 150,000 borrowers in 2007[26] which increased to over 300,000 by January 2009.[27] As of September 2009, the institution had about 230,000 members. By May 2009, Jamii Bora's total loan portfolio crossed US$38 million.[28] All members of Jamii Bora were its former clients. Jamii Bora reported that it had made loans to beggars, prostitutes, thieves and gang members and had developed a health insurance program.[29] Kaputei Town, Africa's first eco-friendly town, which was "built by and for the members of" Jamii Bora is its most high-profile project. The town built in 293 acres is located 30 km outside Nairobi. Over 2,500 families from the Kibera slum are planned to be moved to Kaputei.[30]

KEZA and Social Entrepreneurship

The fashion label, KEZA (www.keza.com), which means "beautiful" in Kinyarwanda, was started in Rwanda. KEZA has developed a social entrepreneurship-based business model, which is sustainable and is making a profit. It trains Rwandan women in business development, and has partnered with the women to bring their handmade jewelry to the US. The company started with three major goals: "1. To create locally owned businesses that provided women with an income, and therefore with dignity; 2. To create high-quality products and a preferred brand; 3. To do it all so well that outside vendors are attracted to do more business in Africa."[31]

As of December 2009, KEZA worked with forty-three women who helped build Sisters of Rwanda. These women are provided with a loan of as little as a US$65 to buy the beads and cloth to start embroidery businesses. KEZA's team of international fashion experts helps them in areas such as product design and development. Rwandan women who are KEZA's partners earn US$200–US$300 per month compared to their income of about US$17 per month before they partnered with the company.[32] KEZA has empowered Rwandan women to own their own businesses; they work autonomously.[33]

KEZA focuses on making high-end, high-quality goods, emphasizing the quality of the product instead of "Western pity". KEZA founder Jared Miller put the issue this way: "Pity sells once . . . but quality products sell over and over because people genuinely desire them."[34]

In industrialized countries, the fashion industry is growing and is resilient even in economic recession. Millions of entrepreneurs in the developing world, on the other hand, are actively searching for economic opportunities. KEZA aims to work with existing women's cooperatives in Africa to unite those two worlds.

In some African economies, there is little or no gender gap in entrepreneurship; and men and women are reported to have an equal propensity to become entrepreneurs. A Gallup survey, for instance, indicated that in Nigeria, 67 percent of female respondents and 68 percent of male respondents liked the idea of starting a business.[35] Women's propensity to engage in entrepreneurial activities in Nigeria compares more favorably with many economies in Arab and Asia. In 2006, for instance, the proportion of the adult population (age 18–64) engaged in entrepreneurial activities in India was 18.9 percent for men and 13 percent for women.[36]

More and more entrepreneurial activities in the country are opportunity-based instead of necessity-based. In Nigeria, people with jobs are found to have a higher propensity to start a business than those without a job. Seventy-seven percent of Nigerians who had a job expressed an interest in starting a business compared to only 53 percent of those who were unemployed.[37]

7.2.2. Natural Resources and their Relations to Entrepreneurship

Africa is a source of natural resources, raw materials and commodities; it is considered to be the most mineral rich continent in the world. One estimate suggests that about two-thirds of the world's cobalt is mined in central Africa.[38] Similarly, the Ivory Coast, Ghana, Nigeria and Cameroon are the four major West African cocoa producers. The Ivory Coast alone produces about 43 percent of the world's cocoa. Likewise, Zimbabwe has the second largest reserves of platinum in the world and large quantities of other precious metals such as gold and copper.[39]

African economies carry enormous potential for entrepreneurship in agricultural development because of the continent's abundance in natural resources and labor.[40] Yet it is also apparent that many African countries export agricultural products such as cocoa, coffee, tobacco and cotton, mainly in their raw form.[41] There has been limited success in their attempts to add value to agricultural products through processing and using them to develop other industrial sectors. Moreover, because of the recent global financial crisis (GFC), some African economies are severely affected by declines in global demand and value for these commodities.[42]

The continent holds 8–9 percent of the world's crude oil reserves and provides about 10 percent of global production.[43] This is considerably less compared to the Middle East's 62 percent. However, some industry analysts believe the continent could have much more undiscovered reserves. Indeed, during 2000–2005, 30 percent of the world's newly discovered oil reserves were from the Gulf of Guinea region of Africa's west coast.[44] More importantly, West Africa's oil reserves are of high quality. The low sulphur content of West Africa's oil makes it easier and cheaper to refine.[45] Furthermore, West African reserves are easily accessible to Western Europe and the US by sea.

Natural resources have also transformed some African countries' economic orientation. For instance, after the discovery of oil in 1957, Nigeria began its transformation from an agriculture-based to an oil-dependent economy. Most African countries have made little progress in reforming institutions to promote entrepreneurship. Among the African countries that are Arab League members, there has arguably been shallow institutional reform in Algeria and the region's primary export economies such as Comoros, Djibouti, Mauritania, Sudan and Yemen. Likewise, although Morocco has encouraged economic liberalization, there has also been a convergence of business and government interests in the country.[46]

7.3. Determinants of Entrepreneurship in Africa

7.3.1. Regulatory Framework

Laws, regulations and policy in most African economies have been major barriers to entrepreneurship development (see "The Entrepreneurial Climate in the Democratic Republic of Congo"). The rule of law in many African economies is weak. A survey of twenty-three African countries found that governmental and judicial institutions were "lower than needed for sustained high growth".[47] Factors such as corruption, the quality of the rule of law and the effectiveness of the national legal system in enforcing contracts have acted as barriers to the development of entrepreneurship. According to the African Union, corruption has cost Africa about US$150 billion annually, or a quarter of the region's GDP. The World Bank has estimated the figure to be even higher—US$500 billion to US$1 trillion.[48] Note that these figures are significantly higher than the continent's FDI, which was US$38.8 billion in 2006,[49] and aid inflow into the continent which is estimated at about US$25 billion a year.[50]

The ICRG index, which considers political, economic and financial indicators, is probably the most comprehensive indicator to assess the quality of regulative institutions. SSA has performed poorly in the ICRG index. Likewise, a study comparing the world's geographic regions in terms of market orientation found that Africa performed the worst.[51]

The Entrepreneurial Climate in the Democratic Republic of Congo

The Democratic Republic of Congo (DRC) is located in Central Africa, which has over fifty million people and an area of more than two million square kilometers. Note that the DRC has the third biggest population and is the second largest country in SSA.

The DRC is considered to be the most mineral rich country in Africa. It holds the world's largest deposits of copper, cobalt and cadmium. The DRC has large quantities of gold and diamonds. It also has coltan, a rare metallic ore used in the manufacture of cellular handsets.

However, the DRC has failed to utilize the country's abundant natural resources to improve its citizens' lives. Starting in the mid-1990s, the DRC has experienced several wars in which millions of citizens died and millions were forced to leave their homes. According to a UN report, the wars in the DRC have been the result of various groups competing for access to the country's natural resources. Indeed, the DRC is a perfect example of how a country's natural resources can prove to be a curse rather than a blessing.[52]

According to the World Bank's annual Doing Business 2009 report, which ranked the world's 181 countries on their regulatory climate for businesses, the DRC was the least friendly country for entrepreneurs. The country ranked 181 in 2008 and 2009.

In the 2010 Index of Economic Freedom released by the Heritage Foundation and the *Wall Street Journal*, the DRC ranked 172 out of the 179 economies that were ranked.[53]

To start a business in DRC costs more than four times the country's per capita income. Formal registration of a business takes about 155 days and there is virtually no protection for investors. Very little credit-record information for the country's citizens is maintained.[54] It has been argued that it can be even more difficult for foreigners to start a business in the DRC. Some suggest that for many entrepreneurs in the DRC and other African economies, the cost of operating a business legally is too high and the benefits are too few.[55]

According to Freedom House's Freedom in the World 2013 report, only 22 percent of SSA countries were in the "free category". Thirty-seven percent were in the "partly free" and 41 percent were in the "not free" category. In 2013, Freedom House referred to Africa as the "world's most politically volatile region" in terms of political rights and civil liberties. Commenting on elections and the superficiality of Africa's donor-driven democracy, an article noted: "While donors make regular electoral contests a condition for aid and debt relief, many African regimes have paid little more than lip-service to reforms, aided by the relative weakness of state institutions which enable the subversion of free elections."[56]

Observers have noted that in many African countries with weak institutions, economic policy is dominated by wealth redistribution instead of wealth creation. One reason most African countries have been unable to attract investments concerns the lack of institutions to protect the long-term security of property rights.

Institutional reforms have been initiated in some African economies, for instance in Morocco and Tunisia, which are considered to be ahead of most other economies in the region. In particular, market reforms in Tunisia made the country a model for the IMF. In 1995, Tunisia became the first Arab[57] country to sign a free-trade agreement with the EU. The capital city Tunis houses major multinationals such as Benetton, Danone, Nestle, Peugeot and Citibank.

One way to bring changes in the entrepreneurial climate would be to take measures to bring capable and honest bureaucrats and technocrats into the public sectors. Bureaucrats can help precipitate institutional changes by redirecting attention and providing support and resources.[58] There is growing recognition that internationalist links provide the technocratic and educational expertise necessary for reform. Bureaucrats and technocrats with the above qualities can minimize corruption and make public services more efficient, as well as utilize the continent's enormous endowments of natural resources to generate wealth.

Governments' Involvement in Economies

Most African countries have mixed economies with varying degrees of market economy and state ownership. A number of firms were nationalized in these economies, and private and public firms function side by side. Compared to other regions in the world, in most SSA countries, governments control a significantly higher proportion of national resources and the government is the largest employer.[59] In some African countries, the nationalization process is still going on and large economically central firms are particularly attractive for national takeover. For instance, in 2004, Zimbabwe's President Mugabe announced his government's plan to demand half-ownership of all privately owned mines in the country in order to stay in control of its natural resources.[60]

In Africa, the commercial class and the national elite have a large number of complementary characteristics. As noted above, the African commercial class lacks the financial and managerial ability to run "high markets".[61] The state elite, on the other hand, sees professional and personal rewards in nationalizing such markets.

Capitalism in African Economies

Many African economies are characterized by oligarchic capitalism. Illustrating the existence of oligarchic capitalism and cronyism in Africa, a *Boston Globe* article asserts: "African leaders, their cronies, European traders, foreign heads of state, and American middlemen, among others, have reaped billions from the continent's oil resources over the last four decades."[62] The ruling elite and their family, friends and clients have thus lived a parasitic existence in some African economies. According to creditors and *Publish What You Pay*, in 2004 about US$300 million or about one-third of Congo's oil revenues did not show up in the country's budgets.[63]

Ease of Doing Business

African economies are heterogeneous in their policies to promote entrepreneurship. In this regard, African economies vary widely in terms of costs and time required to start a business (Fig. 7.1). For instance, according to the World Bank, three of the top reformers in 2007–2008 were African economies—Senegal, Burkina Faso and Botswana. Likewise, according to the World Bank's Ease of Doing Business 2013 report, South Africa, Mauritius, Rwanda and Burundi ranked among the world's top fifty countries in the entrepreneurial climate. The report also indicated that Burundi was among the world's top ten economies in making most improvements in business regulations across several areas.

However, the World Bank's study also found that of the ten least business friendly countries, nine were in SSA: Niger, Côte d'Ivoire, Guinea, Guinea-Bissau, the DRC, Eritrea, Congo, Chad and the

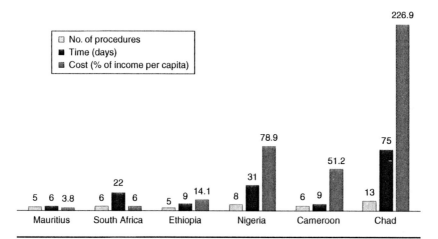

Figure 7.1 Starting a business in some SSA economies
Source: World Bank Group 2010, Doing Business, www.doingbusiness.org/rankings

Central African Republic. Regulatory burden, bureaucracy and lack of political will have severely affected the formal operation of businesses on the continent. In the Central African Republic, which had the world's worst regulatory climate according to the World Bank's Ease of Doing Business 2013, eight procedures must be completed to start a business; they take twenty-two days and cost 173 percent of the country's per capita income. In Sierra Leone, to pay all taxes due, firms need to spend about three times their profit. Likewise, to enforce a contract in Angola, a firm needs to complete forty-seven procedures, which take over 1,000 days.

7.3.2. Values, Culture and Skills

Value and Culture

As noted in Chapter 1, in some societies, family and social obligations act as barriers to productive entrepreneurship. Observers have noted the existence of a culture of "forced mutual help" in Africa.[64] That is, wealthy individuals in many African economies have a social obligation to share their wealth with their relatives and members of the extended family that have less wealth.

Entrepreneurial Skills

Among the biggest roadblocks to entrepreneurial performance in the region are lack of entrepreneurial skills and poor management of human resources. One observer suggests that African private entrepreneurs lack financial and managerial ability to run large and sophisticated businesses.[65] Estimates suggest that about 60 percent of Africa's population is younger than 25.

According to the UNDP's Human Development Report 2013, among the 25 and older population, only 23.7 percent of females and 35.1 percent of males had at least secondary education, which compares with the world average of 52.3 percent and 62.9 percent respectively. Among the students enrolled in secondary education, only 5 percent get vocational training. Moreover, business studies are virtually absent and critics point out that most apprenticeships involve child exploitation.[66]

7.3.3. Access to Finance, Market, R&D and Technology

Access to Finance
Researchers have shown that capital requirements and the availability of financing sources affect entrepreneurial propensity.

Household Saving Savings, credit and insurance have overlapping functions. Savings can partially substitute for credit and insurance, especially when markets for the latter two are imperfect. Analysts have linked the economic under-performance of SSA with a low savings rate. In SSA economies, the median saving rate declined from 14 percent in 1970–1976 to 10 percent in 1980–1986 and then increased to 14 percent in 1987–1994. SSA's saving rate is the lowest across all regions. Estimates that are more recent suggest the average saving rate in Africa is about 10 percent compared to 40 percent in Asia.[67] Saving rates as proportions of disposable incomes in selected African economies are presented in Fig. 7.2. The low savings rate can be attributed to a low-level flow of financing between the informal and

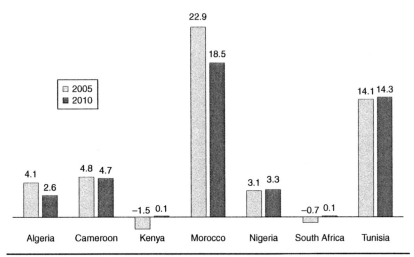

Figure 7.2 Saving as a percentage of disposable income in selected African economies
Source: Euromonitor International's global market information database

formal sectors. Capital flight has worsened the situation. In this regard, household savings are less prone to capital flight.

Remittances   A study by the International Fund for Agricultural Development (IFAD) indicates there are about thirty million African migrant workers living abroad who send home over US$40 billion to the continent annually. In the SSA countries, remittances increased from US$3.1 billion in 1995 to US$18.5 billion in 2007, which were 9–24 percent of GDP and 80–750 percent of official development assistance (ODA).[68]

Although most money sent home by migrants is spent on consumption, remittances also contribute to entrepreneurial activities because they allow even the very poor to save. Although remittance transfer costs have declined significantly in Latin America and in Asia, they are still high in Africa. In Africa, the cost of sending money home can be as high as 25 percent of the sum to be remitted. Moreover, rural areas account for 30–40 percent of remittances to Africa, where the recipients have to travel long distances to get their cash. Africa has the same number of remittance payout locations as Mexico. Note that Mexico has only one-tenth of Africa's population. Restrictive laws and prohibitively high fees have thus hindered the potential of remittance to contribute to poverty reduction and productive entrepreneurship. At the 2009 G8 summit in L'Aquila (Italy), world leaders set a goal of reducing the cost of remittances by 50 percent by 2014 by promoting a competitive environment and removing barriers.

Capital Markets   Capital markets are described as the "lifeblood" of entrepreneurial and economic development. African capital markets are small, lack liquidity and are not properly regulated.[69] In the forty-eight countries of SSA, there were only twelve active stock markets as of 2010. The low level of liquidity has been a concern. At the Uganda Securities Exchange in Kampala, for instance, only nine companies were listed in 2008 and stock trading took place for only eleven days in the month of June 2008.[70] The capitalization of African stock markets increased from 20 percent of GDP in 2005 to 30 percent in 2008.[71] There is also a high degree of intraregional heterogeneity in Africa's capital market development. For instance, in 2010, capitalization of the stock market was 299 percent in South Africa compared to less than 10 percent in Nigeria, Tanzania, Zambia and Uganda. This compares with Brazil's 70 percent in 2008 and 104 percent in 2010.[72] In sum, Africa's nascent and poorly functioning credit markets are linked to the region's underperformance in entrepreneurial development.

Availability and Costs of Bank Financing Availability of bank finances has also been a barrier to entrepreneurial activities. According to a Gallup poll, 73 percent of Nigerians expressed concerns about getting a loan.[73] According to an advisor to the Central Bank of Nigeria (CBN), 60 percent of Nigerians are "under banked".[74]

Studies have found that low interest rates lead to an increase in new business startups. According to Euromonitor International, in 2008, of the world's five countries with the highest annual lending rates (ALR) for the short- and medium-term financing needs of businesses, four were from Africa. In 2008, the ALRs were 28.8 percent in Gambia, 32.4 percent in Sao Tomé e Príncipe, 45 percent in Madagascar and 620.2 percent in Zimbabwe.

R&D and Technology

The growth of new enterprises depends upon the development of the knowledge base through R&D. R&D investment, technology diffusion, patent systems and standards, technological cooperation between firms, broadband access and the university–industry interface affect entrepreneurial performance.

There have been some successful R&D efforts in Africa that are likely to contribute to the continent's entrepreneurial development. For instance, Uganda's Makerere University is engaged in world-class research in various areas relevant to the African context. These include HIV/AIDS, natural resources and food security. The university has partnerships with various Western universities, foundations and development agencies.[75] Likewise, the University of Pretoria, South Africa has been an early adopter of cloud computing, especially its use for next-generation medical research. Students in the university use cloud computing to test the development of drugs that are expected to cure serious illnesses unique to Africa.

Foreign Policy magazine recently conducted a survey with the world's top Internet experts on Internet-related innovations. Seven percent of the experts viewed Africa as "the most innovative place for Internet-related technology". The corresponding proportions for other regions and economies were: Europe, 4 percent; China, 4 percent; India, 7 percent; and Pacific Rim, 5 percent. The experts viewed Africa's Internet-related innovations as: "On-the-ground solutions designed by communities for communities".[76]

Market Access

Domestic markets are small in most African economies. Increased access to foreign markets is therefore important for African entrepreneurs. Some have argued that economic aid tied to regionalization is more likely to be effective in stimulating entrepreneurship in Africa. The Sudanese-British entrepreneur Mo Ibrahim noted: "The World Bank should refuse to fund any project which is not regional. African governments must be pressed to regionalize their economies and stop being 53 little countries, each with their flag, jealously watching each other."[77]

7.4. Foreign Companies' Entrepreneurial Activities in Africa

International entrepreneurship involves exploiting capital, labor and other resources across the globe. Africa's abundance of natural resources makes it an attractive destination for resource-seeking investments for foreign businesses. Note that resource-seeking investments are made to establish access to basic material, input factors and natural resources such as energy, metallic minerals, wood, paper and other raw materials. Most foreign companies have mainly concentrated on accessing the natural resources of the continent. For instance, Western oil companies such as the US's ExxonMobil and Chevron, France's Total and Britain's BP and Shell are planning to invest tens of billions of dollars in SSA.[78]

It is suggested that the US and China are actively competing for access to Africa's oil, gas and other resources. The US imports 15 percent of its oil from Africa and the proportion is expected to reach 25 percent by 2015.[79] It is suggested that by 2017, the US will import more oil from Africa than from the Middle East. Nigeria, Africa's biggest oil exporter and the world's eleventh largest producer, with a capacity of 2.5 million barrels per day, is the fifth largest oil supplier to the US. In 2005, the US imported more oil from the Gulf of Guinea region of Africa's west coast than it did from Saudi Arabia and Kuwait combined.[80]

China's gravitation toward Africa for the acquisition of energy and other natural resources deserves special attention. This is because oil and natural gas production in Asian countries is insufficient to meet the Chinese demand.[81] A large proportion of Middle Eastern exports of oil and gas production goes to the US and Europe. An estimate suggested that Africa accounted for 25 percent of China's oil imports in 2004, which increased to 33 percent in 2006.[82]

Africa is not only a strategic source of raw materials but is also becoming an attractive market. Foreign companies have thus increased market-seeking investments in Africa.[83] Partly because of economic liberalization, there has been greater availability of imported goods. However, it is worth noting that government purchases account for a significant proportion of imports in some African countries. In Ethiopia, government purchases account for 40 percent of total imports, with loans by international financial institutions such as the World Bank and the African Development Bank.[84]

7.4.1. Arbitrage Strategies

Arbitrage strategies entail exploiting opportunities associated with differences across countries. Foreign companies' potential to benefit from utilizing the region's raw materials and natural resources can be described in terms of economic arbitrage, i.e., exploiting specific economic factors. Foreign companies can also benefit from geographic arbitrage, which involves the exploitation of geographic factors such as the region's strategic location.[85] For instance, there is the potential to expand their operations to utilize the continent's labor force to serve international markets, especially European ones. Likewise,

Chinese firms can use Africa's geographical position close to Europe to establish factories on the continent and sell products to the European market. There is also the opportunity to benefit from cultural arbitrage (e.g., language skills of the workforce). For instance, Indian off-shoring companies can utilize the continent's English-, French- and Portuguese-speaking populations to provide call center services to Europeans.

For some multinationals, combining components from the existing institutional environment and reorganizing them strategically has been an important way to operate in Africa. For instance, in Ghana, the British bank Barclays is strategically utilizing Susu collectors, one of the oldest financial groups in Africa (see "Barclays' 'Susu collectors' in Ghana"). This approach can also be described as institutional arbitrage, i.e., exploiting opportunities associated with differences in formal and informal institutions across countries.

Barclays' "Susu Collectors" in Ghana

Susu collectors are among the oldest financial groups in Africa. Mainly based in Ghana, they charge a small fee to provide an informal means of saving and accessing money. They also provide limited access to microfinance credit.[86]

Since 2005, Barclays has worked together with the Ghanaian Susu collectors. Their main function is to collect savings daily from informal traders. Barclays' model in Ghana is considered to a successful business model in the African context; these trades lack other access to banking. In 2006, there were estimated to be about 5,000 Susu collectors in Ghana; in 2008, each Susu collector usually had between 400 and 2,000 clients. Barclays' model allowed the company to capture a US$140-million market that had not been identified by other banks' more traditional model. Barclays subsequently expanded the services to provide special bank accounts. Susu collectors are also provided with training and lending; they can provide credit to their clients.[87] About 70 percent of the Susu collectors have attended Barclays training sessions.[88]

7.4.2. Allegations Regarding the Exploitation of Africa's Resources by Foreign Multinationals

There have been many examples of and complaints about exploitation of African resources by Asian, European and American multinationals at low costs.[89] For instance, global mining companies are making huge profits by extracting gold, diamonds, copper and other metals. Similarly, using fruit, flowers and vegetables from the continent and paying "starvation wages" to African workers, European grocery retailers produce their own-label products.[90]

In recent years, complaints about the exploitation of Africa's minerals and natural resources have been particularly directed at China. Deputy Prime Minister of Zimbabwe Arthur Mutambara notes: "China comes to Africa and extracts raw materials and goes back to China."[91] China's African involvement has also been criticized by some environmentalists. A July 2005 report of the International Rivers Network and Friends of the Earth accused China's Exim Bank of funding environmentally unfriendly projects such as the Merowe Dam in Sudan. Likewise, quoting a primatologist, a *Huffington Post* article stated: "China's thirst for natural resources, including wood and minerals, is leading to massive deforestation in Africa and the destruction of crucial wildlife habitat."[92]

Global multinationals are using their marketing and branding power to make big profits from Africa's natural and labor resources, raw materials and commodities.[93] Giving the example of La Perruche, a brand of cubed sugar sold in New York, a development expert illustrates the problems faced by African companies on the branding front:

> The carton of 1.1 pounds of pure cane sugar pressed into cubes is imported from France. The back of the box states, "Product made of Swaziland or Congo sugar packaged in France." The value of the sugar on the international market is about 12 cents, though the carton, which boasts "since 1837," sells for US$5.99. Africans try to earn a living while selling raw sugar on the international market for 11 cents a pound; the French, with their skills in packaging and marketing, pocket the dollars.[94]

7.4.3. Low Degree of Linkage to the Local Economy

A problem facing the continent is the limited impact on local economies of foreign firms' entrepreneurial activities. For instance, there
are reports that the garment manufacturing industry in many parts of
Africa is shallow, i.e., that this industry has little linkage to domestic
economies. In some African economies such as Namibia and Lesotho,
even skilled direct employees for this industry are foreigners.[95]

7.5. Western Response to the Low Level of Entrepreneurial
Activity in Africa

The member countries of the Group of Eight (G8), which is a forum
for the governments of the world's eight wealthiest countries in the
West, believed that debt relief and increasing aid to Africa would help
promote economic development and entrepreneurship. African economies received US$568 billion in economic aid during 1958–2009.[96]
Donor flow accounts for 30–40 percent of the budget of some of the
poorest African nations such as Guinea-Bissau, Burkina Faso, Togo,
Malawi and Swaziland.[97] In Ethiopia, foreign aid constitutes over 90
percent of the government budget.[98]

A growing number of observers have noted that efforts to relieve
debt and increase aid have been largely unsuccessful in fighting poverty and promoting entrepreneurship in Africa. Some argue that
the US has been a supplier of food aid and contraceptives instead
of development assistance to Africa.[99] Zambian economist Dambisa
Moyo believes that foreign aid in Africa has deepened poverty, led
to economic distortion and fueled corruption and inequality on the
continent. Other analysts have also expressed their disappointment
with the existing system of aid to stimulate economic development
in Africa.

To understand the feelings that accompany the viewpoint of these
critics opposed to the process of increasing aid, consider one detail:
out of every US$1 aid given to Africa, about 16 cents was used to pay
consultants based in donor countries, 26 cents went to emergency aid
and relief operations, and 14 cents into debt servicing. African economies pay about US$20 billion in debt repayments annually.[100] Analysts

suspect that corrupt officials take a large proportion of the remaining, leaving very little to benefit the poor people who really deserve the aid.

An increasing number of observers have advocated the necessity of increasing the private sector's involvement in the economy in order to help develop a market-based system.[101] Analysts have argued that a reorientation of aid to promote private businesses in poor countries would be more effective. Zambian economist Dambisa Moyo has also advocated alternatives such as encouraging trade and foreign direct investment on the continent and developing microfinancing and capital markets. Note that private businesses have been a cornerstone to economic development in fast-growing developing countries. However, promotion of private business has rarely been the principal focus of development aid.

The emphasis on trade and investment rather than aid is echoed by a journalist's observation from the field in Liberia:

> [Liberia] is chock-full of aid groups rushing around in white SUVs doing wonderful work. But it also needs factories to employ people, build skills and pay salaries and taxes. Americans are horrified by sweatshops, but nothing would help Liberia more than if China moved some of its sweatshops there so Liberians could make sandals and T-shirts.[102]

Foreign aids also lack linkages to the local economy. To illustrate this situation, consider US aid. In 2004, the US had provided African economies with US\$1 billion in food aid, 90 percent of which was spent on foods manufactured in the US. Similarly, the plan for AIDS also required use of FDA-approved drugs, which are expensive. Overall, no attention was paid to investing in generic drugs and prevention programs. The poor (the intended beneficiaries), or the NGOs and foundations working with them, receive a small percentage of the total aid and have very little say in how it is used. Aid may benefit the givers and aid administrators as much as or even more than the recipients.[103]

7.6. Concluding Comments

Development of a free enterprise economy in Africa with a strong rule of law and property rights is likely to benefit not only African society but also the global economy. However, Africa's abundant natural and human resources have mainly benefited American, European and Asian multinationals, and the continent's dictators and tiny minorities. There has been a failure to bring economic and developmental advantages for the poor people. There has been a vanishingly small stock of FDI outside the oil industry. Optimism about entrepreneurial development in Africa is thus pretty rare.

A common thread runs through corruption and instability in most countries on the continent—connection to natural resources. In some countries, such as the DRC and Sierra Leone, mineral resources have been blamed for economic, political and social problems such as excessive corruption, political instability and even state collapse.[104] A commonplace observation is that Africa's oil or mineral wealth is a curse rather than a blessing, which has led some countries on the continent to economic and political instability, social conflict and environmental degradation (watch the video "Blood Diamonds—The True Story" at www.youtube.com/watch?v=C7lmjjDlzp0). Faced with examples such as these in many resource-rich African countries, some authors have used the term "resources curse" to describe their economic failure.[105] A journalist has observed: "[B]ecause of wars, dictatorships and thieves, Angola and other oil-rich African nations have failed so far to turn their natural wealth into better lives for their citizens."[106]

An uncomfortable reality is that the development of productive entrepreneurship has been slow in most African economies. As we have said, some argue that Western aid to Africa may have benefited donor countries and aid administrators rather than the intended recipients in Africa.

Some African economies undergoing market and economic reforms have been able to attract foreign investment. Tunisia, which offers a one-stop shop for foreign investors with all services, including courts and customs, in one building, is one example. As of 2000, Tunisia had the third largest FDI stock in the Middle East, which is a phenomenal success considering its small size and a lack of oil.[107] As noted above, democracies and liberalization in some African countries have shifted into reverse gear. However, some countries on the continent have made visible progress toward democracy. According to Freedom in the World 2013, three SSA countries moved from "partly free" to "free": Lesotho, Sierra Leone and Senegal. Likewise, Ethiopia recently moved from a one-party to a multi-party system. Since economic free-dom and political freedom are highly correlated, political freedoms may lead to economic liberalization and boost private entrepreneur-ship. In recent years, Ethiopia has won some of the flower-exporting business away from its neighboring country Kenya.

The above discussion also indicates that African economies need to strengthen the linkage between foreign investments and domestic economies. There is also an urgent need to hasten these efforts to ben-efit from foreign trade and investment.

The preceding examples also point to the fact that many foreign firms' entrepreneurial activities in Africa may have come at the expense of local entrepreneurs. In recent years, thousands of fishermen on Africa's coast have lost their jobs. In this regard, political process in a country has a built-in bias that favors organized groups and industries compared to those that are unorganized.[108] For example, most African countries do not have large and organized local commercial fishing industries to pressure their governments. A lack of domestic entre-preneurs to organize movements can be attributed to such dynamics.

It is also worth mentioning that some African businesses have per-formed well in the international markets. Some businesses such as South African Breweries Ltd and Ecobank have internationalized successfully. Likewise, KEZA helped the Rwandan cooperatives con-nect to an international market for luxury products. However, cases like these are extreme in the present context.

Third-world multinational corporations are familiar with the busi-ness terrains of other developing countries, thanks mainly to economic, cultural and political proximity, and thus experience a lower degree of foreignness associated with dissimilarity or lack of fit in the operating context of these countries. Environment in Africa may thus enable bet-ter arbitrage opportunities for multinationals based in developing econ-omies such as China and India than those in industrialized economies.

Multinational enterprises based in Asia, Europe and North Amer-ica have allegedly exploited natural and human resources in Africa. Foreign governments and multinational enterprises have employed ecological discourse to establish discursive legitimacy and gain access to the continent's natural resources. For instance, EU officials and other beneficiaries of fishing-rights agreements in Africa have argued that unregulated domestic fishermen are the real problem behind the decline in the continent's fisheries stocks. It is argued that most domestic fishermen in Africa tend to fish close to shore, an area which offers a suitable habitat for fish spawning. EU officials have also made the point that most African countries have performed poorly in managing their fish stocks.[109]

African economies have been hard hit by the GFC. Many economies are facing stiff budget cuts because of low foreign aid and declining remittances from the West. Domestic investment is also severely affected by high interest rates and the depreciation of national currencies, in turn affecting the level of entrepreneurship support and resources.

African countries can increase the benefits of foreign trade and investment by creating efficient channels for linkages forward and backward, labor mobility, and stimulation of knowledge and technology transfer to local firms.[110] Income growth among the wider population is likely to produce forward linkages leading to the growth in demand for small businesses' outputs.

7.7. Review Questions

1. Which are some of the best performing economies in Africa? Which are the least performing economies on the continent?
2. Why have complaints regarding exploitation of Africa's minerals and natural resources been directed at China in recent years?
3. Give some examples to illustrate that global multinationals are using their marketing and branding power to make big profits out of Africa's natural and labor resources, raw materials and commodities?
4. What are arbitrage strategies? What are some examples of arbitrage strategies pursued by foreign multinationals in their operations in Africa?

7.8. Critical Discussion Questions

1. How effective are the Western approaches of debt relief and economic aid in promoting economic development and entrepreneurship in Africa?

2. Do you agree with the observation that Africa's oil or mineral wealth is a curse rather than a blessing? Why?

3. Select an African economy that has one of the best entrepreneurial climates in the continent (e.g., Ghana). Select another African economy that has one of the worst entrepreneurial climates in the continent (e.g., the DRC). Research some determinants of entrepreneurship in these countries and compare them. What conclusions can you draw?

7.9. End-of-chapter Case: Entrepreneurship in the African Fisheries Industries

International fishing fleets have been exploiting African coastal waters for low-cost fish. In a testimony to the US Congress, Stephen Hayes, President and CEO of the Corporate Council on Africa, noted: "Africa's fishing reserves are being plundered by the fishing fleets of Europe and Asia."[111]

Overexploitation of Fisheries Stocks

One estimate has suggested that the amount of fish in West African waters has been reduced by 50 percent in the past three decades.[112] In many African economies, there has been over-exploitation of the existing stocks. Studies have suggested that stocks in Uganda are either close to or have exceeded the maximum sustainable yield.[113] Likewise, according to a committee of Mauritanian scientists, the octopus stock in Mauritania in recent years had declined by 31 percent compared to the historical average.[114]

Lack of Infrastructures and Entrepreneurial Skills

A study conducted in Uganda indicated various problems associated with entrepreneurship in the fishery sector of the country. There is a lack of improved catch boats. Uganda also lacks the well-developed support infrastructure necessary for the growth of this industry. Roads are poor and badly maintained. Landing sites lack power for the construction of ice plants and other basic hygienic facilities. Consequently, losses through spoilage are substantial.

Growth and productivity in the fisheries industry in Uganda have been hampered by the lack of development of a commercial aquaculture.[115] The local fishery sector is unaware of the need for quality management of export products. There has been some external investment from the processing industry, but experts point out that this sector is unlikely to attract further investment.[116]

Foreign Fishing Companies in Africa

Foreign fishing companies are increasingly moving into Africa due primarily to the fact that their own fisheries have become overfished. For instance, one estimate has suggested that in EU waters, 88 percent of the fish stock that is commercially used has been overfished.[117]

Over 340 foreign boats were licensed to fish on the coast of Mauritania in 2007.[118] Asian and European countries such as China, Russia and Ukraine have signed fishing deals with Mauritania. In 2007, there were ninety-nine Chinese boats operating in joint ventures with domestic companies. In some instances, these countries paid for fishing rights with military equipment. In 2005, China provided Mauritania with two fighter jets as partial compensation for access to Mauritanian waters.[119]

Estimates suggest that rich countries pay subsidies of US$30 billion a year to their commercial fishermen. The EU and its member countries provide over US$7 billion a year in subsidies. Similarly, China is estimated to provide US$2 billion a year in fuel subsidies. Such policies have increased the global catch, which has led to lower fish prices. Fishermen in poor African nations, on the other hand, get no subsidies from their governments, which makes it difficult for them to compete.[120]

Notes

1. Takyi-Asiedu, S. 1993, "Some Socio-cultural Factors Retarding Entrepreneurial Activity in Sub-Saharan Africa", *Journal of Business Venturing*, 8, pp. 91–98.

2. Robson, P.J.A., & Obeng, B.A. 2008, "The Barriers to Growth in Ghana", *Small Business Economics*, 30(4), pp. 385–403.
3. Rheault, M., & Tortora, B. 2008, "Nigeria: Drivers and Challenges of Entrepreneurship", *Gallup World*, April 9, at www.gallup.com/poll/106345/nigeria-drivers-challenges-entrepreneurship.aspx.
4. Ruxin, J. 2009, "Fashion, Rwanda and the Power of Social Entrepreneurship", *Huffington Post*, December 18, at www.huffingtonpost.com/josh-ruxin/fashion-rwanda-and-the-po_b_397458.html.
5. Salzman, M. 2010, "The Power of One Young World", *Huffington Post*, January 29, at www.huffingtonpost.com/marian-salzman/the-power-of-one-young-wo_b_441695.html.
6. Vassiliou, P. 2010, "A Hand Up, Not a Hand Out", Forbes, January 12, at www.forbes.com/2010/01/12/africa-india-poverty-legatum-tech-opinions-contributors-philip-vassiliou.html.
7. Takyi-Asiedu, S. 1993, "Some Socio-cultural Factors Retarding Entrepreneurial Activity in Sub-Saharan Africa, *Journal of Business Venturing*, 8, pp. 91–98.
8. *Economist* 2006, "Special Report: The Flicker of a Brighter Future—Business in Africa", September 7, at www.economist.com/node/7879918.
9. Ibid.
10. Rheault, M., & Tortora, B. 2008, "Nigeria: Drivers and Challenges of Entrepreneurship", *Gallup World*, April 9, at www.gallup.com/poll/106345/nigeria-drivers-challenges-entrepreneurship.aspx.
11. Elkan, W. 1988, "Entrepreneurs and Entrepreneurship in Africa", *World Bank Research Observer*, 3(2), pp. 171–188.
12. Rheault, M., & Tortora, B. 2008, "Nigeria: Drivers and Challenges of Entrepreneurship", *Gallup World*, April 9, at www.gallup.com/poll/106345/nigeria-drivers-challenges-entrepreneurship.aspx.
13. See "Cocoa", www.spectrumcommodities.com/education/commodity/cc.html.
14. *African Business* 2009, "Welcome to Ghana", 357, pp. 51–52.
15. Ibid.
16. Robson, P.J.A., & Obeng, B.A. 2008, "The Barriers to Growth in Ghana", *Small Business Economics*, 30(4), pp. 385–403.
17. Chafkin, M. 2008, "Meet the Bill Gates of Ghana", *Inc.com*, October 30(10), pp. 106–117, at www.inc.com/magazine/20081001/meet-the-bill-gates-of-ghana.html
18. *African Business* 2009, "Welcome to Ghana", 357, pp. 51–52.
19. africanexecutive.com 2008, "CBC-African Business Awards 2008—Winners Announced", at www.africanexecutive.com/modules/magazine/articles.php?article=3306.
20. Haigh, D. 2009, "Why Africa Must Nurture Home-grown Brands", *Managing Intellectual Property*, 193, pp. 82–84.
21. Kapstein, E.B. 2009, "Africa's Capitalist Revolution", *Foreign Affairs*, 88(4), pp. 119–129.

22. Chuhan-Pole, P., Korman, V., Angwafo. M., & Buitano, M. 2011, Africa's Pulse, April, 3, at http://siteresources.worldbank.org/INTAFRICA/Resources/Africas-Pulse-brochure_Vol3.pdf.
23. See "Ecobank", at http://en.wikipedia.org/wiki/Ecobank.
24. Ecobank Group 2009, *Annual Report 2009*, Togo: Ecobank Transnational Incorporated, Lome.
25. africanexecutive.com 2008, "CBC-African Business Awards 2008—Winners Announced", at www.africanexecutive.com/modules/magazine/articles.php?article=3306.
26. Nicholson, C. 2007, "In Poorer Nations, Cellphones Help Open Up Microfinancing", *New York Times*, July 9, p. C6, at www.nytimes.com/2007/07/09/business/worldbusiness/09micro.html?ref=africa&_r=0.
27. jamiibora.net 2009.
28. Levy, S. 2009, "Microcapital Story: Jamii Bora Trust, Microfinance Institution Based in Kenya, Reaches $38m in Loans; Backers Acquire City Finance Bank", *Microcapital*, at www.microcapital.org/microcapital-story-jamii-bora-trust-microfinance-institution-based-in-kenya-reaches-38m-in-loans-possible-acquisition-by-city-finance-bank/.
29. jamiibora.net 2009, "jamiibora.net: World's 200,000 Most Entrepreneurially Productive Networkers Live in Kenya", at http://jamiibora.net/.
30. socialearth.org 2009, "Kaputei: The Poor Man's Timbuktu", at: www.socialearth.org/kaputei-the-poor-mans-timbuktu.
31. Ruxin, J. 2009, "Fashion, Rwanda and the Power of Social Entrepreneurship", Huffington Post, December 18, at www.huffingtonpost.com/josh-ruxin/fashion-rwanda-and-the-po_b_397458.html.
32. Ibid.
33. ventures-africa.com 2012, "Keza: Fashion Meets Social Entrepreneurship", July 4, at www.ventures-africa.com/2012/07/keza-fashion-meets-social-entrepreneurship/.
34. Moore, T. 2009, "KEZA Fashion Show at Mai", *Nashville Scene*, December 10, at www.nashvillescene.com/2009-12-10/arts/keza-fashion-show-at-mai.
35. Rheault, M., & Tortora, B. 2008, "Nigeria: Drivers and Challenges of Entrepreneurship", *Gallup World*, April 9, at www.gallup.com/poll/106345/nigeria-drivers-challenges-entrepreneurship.aspx.
36. Allen, E., Langowitz, N., & Minniti, M. 2006, *Global Entrepreneurship Monitor: 2006 Report on Women and Entrepreneurship*, Babson Park, MA: Babson College.
37. Rheault, M., & Tortora, B. 2008, "Nigeria: Drivers and Challenges of Entrepreneurship", *Gallup World*, April 9, at www.gallup.com/poll/106345/nigeria-drivers-challenges-entrepreneurship.aspx.
38. See "Future Causes of Conflict", www.ppu.org.uk/war/future_wars.html.
39. Mutasa, H. 2009, "Zimbabwe's 'Special' Relationship", *aljazeera.net*, at www.aljazeera.com/focus/%20chinabuystheworld/2009/08/200981083259504514.html.
40. Stryker, J.D., & Baird, K.E. 1992, "Trends in African Agricultural Trade: Causes and Prognosis", *Policy Studies Journal*, 20(3), pp. 414–430.

41. Sáez, L., & Gallagher, J. 2009, "Authoritarianism and Development in the Third World", *Brown Journal of World Affairs*, 15(2), pp. 87–101.
42. Green, P.L. 2009, "Africa in a Squeeze", *Global Finance*, 23(5), pp. 18–22.
43. Bell, G. 2006, "US, China to Spur Massive Africa Oil Growth", Reuters, March 23, at http://platform.blogs.com/passionofthepresent/2006/03/us_china_to_spu.html.
44. Donnelly, J. 2005, "China Scooping Up Deals in Africa as US Firms Hesitate", *Boston Globe*, December 24, at www.boston.com/news/world/asia/articles/2005/12/24/china_scooping_up_deals_in_africa_as_us_firms_hesitate/; Donelly, J. 2005, "Burdens of Oil Weigh on Nigerians", *Boston Globe*, October 3, at www.boston.com/news/world/africa/articles/2005/10/03/burdens_of_oil_weigh_on_nigerians/.
45. Bajpaee, C. 2005, "The Eagle, the Dragon and African Oil", *Asia Times*, October 12, at www.atimes.com/atimes/ China_Business/GJ12Cb01.html.
46. Schlumberger, O. 2000, "Arab Political Economy and the European Union's Mediterranean Policy: What Prospects for Development?" *New Political Economy*, 5(2), pp. 247–268.
47. Sievers, S.E. 2001, "Competitiveness and Foreign Direct Investment in Africa", in Nsouli, S.M. (ed.), *Policies to Promote Competitiveness in Manufacturing in Sub-Saharan Africa*, Paris: OECD.
48. Global Witness 2006, "Breaking the Links between the Exploitation of Natural Resources, Conflict and Corruption", UNCTAD Expert Meeting on FDI in natural resources, at www.globalwitness.org/sites/default/files/pdfs/gw_report.pdf.
49. Turner, M. 2007, "Scramble for Africa", *Guardian*, May 2, at www.theguardian.com/environment/2007/may/02/society.conservationandendangeredspecies1.
50. Global Witness 2006, "Breaking the Links between the Exploitation of Natural Resources, Conflict and Corruption", UNCTAD Expert Meeting on FDI in natural resources, at www.globalwitness.org/sites/default/files/pdfs/gw_report.pdf.
51. Business Monitor International 2006, *Egypt Business Forecast Report 2006*, chap. 3, "Special Report", 4th quarter, pp. 26–38
52. Warren, D. 2009, "Natural Resources: Africa VP Calls for 'Creative Dissatisfaction' Campaign", blogs.worldbank.org, October 5, at http://blogs.worldbank.org/meetings/natural-resources-africa-vp-calls-for-creative-dissatisfaction-campaign.
53. Miller, T. 2010, "The U.S. Isn't as Free as it Used to Be: Canada Now Boasts North America's Freest Economy", *Wall Street Journal*, January 19, at http://online.wsj.com/news/articles/SB10001424052748704541004575011684172064228.
54. Cowley, S. 2008, "10 Worst Countries for Startups", *CNNMoney*, September 11, at http://money.cnn.com/galleries/2008/smallbusiness/0809/gallery.20_worst_countries_for_smallbiz.smb/index.html.
55. *Economist* 2006, "Special Report: The Flicker of a Brighter Future—Business in Africa", September 7, at www.economist.com/node/7879918.

56. Sáez, L., & Gallagher, J. 2009, "Authoritarianism and Development in the Third World", *Brown Journal of World Affairs*, 15(2), pp. 87–101.
57. The Arab world consists of the twenty-two Arabic-speaking member countries of the League of Arab States (LAS). Some African economies are also members of the LAS.
58. Duerst-Lahti, G. 2002, "Governing Institutions, Ideologies, and Gender: Toward the Possibility of Equal Political Representation", *Sex Roles*, 47(7/8), pp. 371–388.
59. Mvunganyi, J. 2010, "African Youth Bear Brunt of Global Economic Crisis", *Voice of America*, January 24, at www1.voanews.com/english/news/africa/African-Youth-Bear-Brunt-of-Global-Economic-Crisis-82601422.html.
60. *African Times* 2004, "Zimbabwe", September 15–September 30, 17(10), p. 1.
61. Wilson, E.J. 1990, "Strategies of State Control of the Economy: Nationalization and Indigenization in Black Africa", *Comparative Politics*, 22(4), pp. 401–419.
62. Donnelly, J. 2005, "In Oil-rich Nation, Charges of Skimming", *Boston Globe*, November 25, at www.boston.com/news/world/africa/articles/2005/11/25/in_oil_rich_nation_charges_of_skimming/.
63. Ibid.
64. Raymond, F. 1951, *Elements of Social Organization*, Boston: Beacon Press.
65. Wilson, E.J. 1990, "Strategies of State Control of the Economy: Nationalization and Indigenization in Black Africa", *Comparative Politics*, 22(4), pp. 401–419.
66. Smith, A.D. 2009, "Is Trade, Not Aid, the Answer for Africa?", *Guardian*, May 25, p. 27, at www.theguardian.com/business/2009/may/25/africa-entrepreneurs-charity.
67. AllAfrica.com 2007, "Uganda: Alexander Forbes Launches Retirement Fund", at http://allafrica.com/stories/200708140497.html.
68. Mbaye, S. 2010, "Unlock Africa's Migrant Fortune", *Guardian*, at www.theguardian.com/commentisfree/2010/jan/30/africa-migrant-workers-banking.
69. Alagidede, P. 2008, "How Integrated are Africa's Stock Markets with the Rest of the World?" African Development Bank Group, African Economic Conference, Addis Ababa, Ethiopia, November 12, 2008, at www.afdb.org/fileadmin/uploads/afdb/Documents/Knowledge/30754264-EN-2.1.4-ALAGIDEDE-AEC-PAPER.PDF.
70. Christy, J.H. 2008, "Africa: The Last Investment Frontier", *Forbes*, July 7, at www.forbes.com/2008/07/05/economies-stocks-investment-pf-summit08-cx_jhc_0707africa.html.
71. Ibid.
72. Ernst & Young 2012, *Moving Towards the Mainstream: Stock Market Development and Performance in the Rapid-growth Markets*, at www.ey.com/UK/en/Issues/Driving-growth/Skolkovo-Stock-Market-report—Overview.
73. Rheault, M., & Tortora, B. 2008, "Nigeria: Drivers and Challenges of Entrepreneurship", *Gallup World*, April 9, at www.gallup.com/poll/106345/nigeria-drivers-challenges-entrepreneurship.aspx.

74. Awhotu, E. 2010, "60 Percent of Nigerians Don't Have Access to Bank", *CBN Adviser*, at http://mobilemoneyafrica.com/details.php?post_id=717.
75. Lindow, M, 2009, "Innovation Flowers in a Crowded, Crumbling African University", *Chronicle of Higher Education*, 56(3), pp. A23–A24.
76. *Foreign Policy* 2011, "The FP Survey: The Internet", September/October(188), pp. 1–9.
77. Smith, A.D. 2009, "Is Trade, Not Aid, the Answer for Africa?", *Guardian*, May 25, p. 27, at www.theguardian.com/business/2009/may/25/africa-entrepreneurs-charity.
78. Thompson, C. 2007, "The Scramble for Africa's Oil", *New Statesman*, at www.globalpolicy.org/ component/content/article/154/25931.html.
79. Donnelly, J. 2005, "China Scooping Up Deals in Africa as US Firms Hesitate", *Boston Globe*, December 24, at www.boston.com/news/world/asia/articles/2005/12/24/china_scooping_up_deals_in_africa_as_us_firms_hesitate/
80. Thompson, C. 2007, "The Scramble for Africa's Oil", *New Statesman*, at www.globalpolicy.org/ component/content/article/154/25931.html.
81. Brookes, P, & Shin, J.H. 2006, "China's Influence in Africa: Implications for the United States", February 22, Heritage Foundation, at www.heritage.org/Research/AsiaandthePacific/bg1916.cfm.
82. Alessi, C., & Hanson, S. 2008, "China, Africa, and Oil", Council on Foreign Relations, February 8, at www.cfr.org/publication/9557.
83. Pritchard, C. 1997, "Into Africa", *Marketing Magazine*, 102(38), p. 12.
84. US Department of State 2010, *Doing Business in Ethiopia: 2010 Country Commercial Guide for US Companies*, Washington, DC: US Department of State.
85. Ghemawat, P. 2003, "The Forgotten Strategy", *Harvard Business Review*, 81(11), pp. 76–84.
86. See "Susu Account", http://en.wikipedia.org/wiki/Susu_account.
87. *Economist* 2006, "Special Report: The Flicker of a Brighter Future—Business in Africa", September 7, at www.economist.com/node/ 7879918.
88. See "Increasing Access", http://group.barclays.com/Sustainability/Inclusive-banking/Broadening-our-reach/Working-with-others/Promoting-access-through-partners.
89. Haigh, D. 2009, "Why Africa Must Nurture Home-grown Brands", *Managing Intellectual Property*, 193, pp. 82–84.
90. Ibid.
91. Newstime Africa 2009, "Mutambara Attacks China's Exploitation of Africa", at www.newstimeafrica.com/archives/2242.
92. huffingtonpost.com 2009, "Jane Goodall: China Plundering African Natural Resources", at www.huffingtonpost.com/2009/03/11/jane-goodall-china-plunde_n_173803.html.
93. Haigh, D. 2009, "Why Africa Must Nurture Home-grown Brands", *Managing Intellectual Property*, 193, pp. 82–84.
94. Colburn, F.D. 2006, "Good-bye to the 'Third World'", *Dissent*, 53(2), pp. 38–41.

95. Rasiah, R., & Ofreneo, R.E. 2009, "Introduction: The Dynamics of Textile and Garment Manufacturing in Asia", *Journal of Contemporary Asia*, 39(4), pp. 501–511.

96. Vassiliou, P. 2010, "A Hand Up, Not a Hand Out", Forbes, January 12, at www.forbes.com/2010/01/12/africa-india-poverty-legatum-tech-opinions-contributors-philip-vassiliou.html.

97. Green, P.L. 2009, "Africa in a Squeeze", *Global Finance*, 23(5), pp. 18–22.

98. Moyo, D. 2009, "Why Foreign Aid is Hurting Africa", *Wall Street Journal* (Eastern edn), March 21, p. W1.

99. Awori, A. 2009, "An African Perspective on Environment and Development", *Voices from Africa*, Number 5, Sustainable Development, Part 1, at www.un-ngls.org/orf/documents/publications.en/voices.africa/number5/vfa5.04.htm.

100. Moyo, D. 2009, "Why Foreign Aid is Hurting Africa", *Wall Street Journal* (Eastern edn), March 21, p. W1.

101. Prahalad, C.K. 2005, "Aid Is Not the Answer", *Wall Street Journal* (Eastern edn), August 31, p. A8, at http://online.wsj.com/news/articles/SB112544438457127227.

102. Kristof, N.D. 2009, "How Can We Help the World's Poor?" *New York Times Book Review*, November 20, p. 27, at www.nytimes.com/2009/11/22/books/review/Kristof-t.html?_r=0.

103. Prahalad, C.K. 2005, "Aid Is Not the Answer", *Wall Street Journal* (Eastern edn), August 31, p. A8, at http://online.wsj.com/news/articles/SB112544438457127227.

104. Sáez, L., & Gallagher, J. 2009, "Authoritarianism and Development in the Third World", *Brown Journal of World Affairs*, 15(2), pp. 87–101.

105. Auty, R. 1998, *Resource Abundance and Economic Development*, Helsinki: World Institute for Development Economics Research.

106. Donnelly, J. 2005, "Oil Wealth Helping Few of Angola's Poor: Vast Reserves Cannot Undo Legacy of War, Corruption", *Boston Globe*, December 11, at www.boston.com/news/world/africa/articles/ 2005/ 12/11/ oil_wealth_helping_few_of_angolas_poor/.

107. Foroohar, R. 2003, "A Country that Works; Smart Policies and Soft Dictatorship Make Tunisia Something Unique: A Successful Arab Economy", *Newsweek*, May 26, 32.

108. Mitra, D. 1999, "Endogenous Lobby Formation and Endogenous Protection: A Long-run Model of Trade Policy Determination", *American Economic Review*, 89(5), pp. 1116–1134.

109. Miller, J.W. 2007, "Global Fishing Trade Depletes African Waters", *Wall Street Journal*, July 18, at http://online.wsj.com/news/articles/SB118470420636969282.

110. Markusen, J.R., & Venables, A.J. 1999, "Foreign Direct Investment as a Catalyst for Industrial Development", *European Economic Review*, 43(2), pp. 335–356.

111. Hayes, S. 2009, "US–Africa Trade Relations: Creating a Platform for Economic Growth". Testimony to the US Congress, June 24, at www.gpo.gov/fdsys/pkg/CHRG-111hhrg66816/html/CHRG-111hhrg66816.htm.
112. Miller, J.W. 2007, "Global Fishing Trade Depletes African Waters", *Wall Street Journal*, July 18, at http://online.wsj.com/news/articles/SB11847 0420636969282.
113. Kaelin, A.J., & Cowx, I.G. 2002, "Outline of the Path Forward in Uganda's Fisheries Sector", prepared for the Presidential Conference on Export Competitiveness, at www.finance.go.ug/docs/Fish.pdf (accessed February 12, 2002).
114. Miller, J.W. 2007, "Global Fishing Trade Depletes African Waters", *Wall Street Journal*, July 18, at http://online.wsj.com/news/articles/SB11847 0420636969282.
115. Kaelin, A.J., & Cowx, I.G. 2002, "Outline of the Path Forward in Uganda's Fisheries Sector", prepared for the Presidential Conference on Export Competitiveness, at www.finance.go.ug/docs/Fish.pdf (accessed February 12, 2002).
116. Ibid.
117. Stop Illegal Fishing, 2011, "Empty Nets, Empty Future", September 28, www.stopillegalfishing.com/news_article.php?ID=460.
118. Miller, J.W. 2007, "Global Fishing Trade Depletes African Waters", *Wall Street Journal*, July 18, at http://online.wsj.com/news/articles/SB1184704 20636969282.
119. Ibid.
120. Miller, J.W. 2007, "Global Fishing Trade Depletes African Waters", *Wall Street Journal*, July 18, at http://online.wsj.com/news/articles/SB11847 0420636969282.

8

ENTREPRENEURSHIP IN CHINA

Abstract

The Chinese entrepreneurship landscape has undergone a significant transformation in the past few decades. Institutions influencing entrepreneurship have changed dramatically. During the Mao era, private entrepreneurship was virtually eradicated and was a political taboo. As reflected in macro-level economic data, there has been an evolution of entrepreneur-friendly institutions in the country. A constellation of factors linked to China's global integration is pushing through fundamental changes in institutions related to Chinese entrepreneurship. The logics or governance structures and organizing principles related to entrepreneurship are rapidly changing.

This chapter's objectives include:

1. To demonstrate an understanding of the nature of transformation taking place in entrepreneurship in China.
2. To analyze the drivers of entrepreneurship in China.
3. To assess the nature of institutional change related to entrepreneurship in China.
4. To evaluate some of the barriers to institutional change related to entrepreneurship in China.
5. To demonstrate an understanding of the impacts of entrepreneurship in China.

8.1. Introduction

Entrepreneurship is undergoing a significant transformation in China. During the Mao era, private entrepreneurship was virtually eradicated and a political taboo. Entrepreneurs were shunned and disgraced in the country as late as the 1980s, and entrepreneurship was often considered an occupation for individuals, such as those with criminal records, who were not able to find other jobs.[1] The idea of entrepreneurship in China was therefore an oxymoron and a paradox before the country began its political and economic reforms in 1978.

In recent years, China has earned a reputation as one of the world's most entrepreneur-friendly countries. In a telephone poll conducted among Americans by Zogby International and 463 Communications, 49 percent of the respondents said that China or Japan provide the "creative and entrepreneurial milieu required to form the world's next technological innovator".[2] Only 21 percent said that the next Bill Gates would come from the US. Likewise, according to the 2009 GEM report, China has a higher rate of nascent entrepreneurship than the US. China also outperforms the US in both the rate of ownership of new businesses and the rate of ownership of established businesses.[3] Moreover, China performs better than many countries, including the US, in the rates of new business growth. According to the 2009 GEM Report, China has the world's highest rate of high-expectation entrepreneurship. Over 4 percent of China's working-age population was engaged in high-growth-expectation entrepreneurship during 2004–2009 compared to less than 1.5 percent in the US.[4]

The leaders of the Chinese Communist Party (CCP) have publicly acknowledged the benefit that entrepreneurs and capitalists can bring to the economy. They have especially encouraged the growth of high-technology entrepreneurship. The CCP has welcomed entrepreneurs into the inner circle and upper echelons of the party. There has been a transformation of SOEs and inward FDI has provided learning opportunities for Chinese firms. Whereas China's so-called "red hat entrepreneurs" were a form of political entrepreneur, the new entrepreneurs increasingly resemble market entrepreneurs and are moving away from dependence on political connections.[5]

Entrepreneurs are increasing their dominance in the Chinese political arena and are gaining more respect in society. A recent survey conducted among Chinese found that 70 percent of respondents thought entrepreneurship was a good career choice.[6] Chinese society has embraced the idea of entrepreneurship rapidly. Entrepreneurial role models in China encourage people to start their own businesses, and networks of family members and relatives support entrepreneurs.

8.2. A Survey of Entrepreneurship in China

While internal security is the number-one concern for Chinese political leaders, they have also set economic growth as a top priority. The shift in the base of regime legitimacy from Marxist Leninism to economic growth, coupled with the entrepreneurial spirit of the Chinese, has helped transform the Chinese economy.

Analysts disagree as to the role of the government in shaping the Chinese entrepreneurship landscape. Some scholars have argued that close state control has led to the failure of apparently abundant Chinese entrepreneurship. Others maintain that Chinese politics was arguably the most liberal in the 1980s. The 1989 Tiananmen events, which ended in a bloody military crackdown, impeded China's entrepreneurial progress. It is also noted that, in the 1990s, China reversed the gradualist political reforms begun in 1978. Others argue that China has "inbuilt" and "government-fostered" mechanisms[7] that have helped unleash the entrepreneurial spirit of the Chinese. Comparing the Chinese entrepreneurial environment with that of the US, forecaster Gerald Celente recently put the issue this way: "China is invigorated with a sense of entrepreneurship that is supported by its government, while in the USA, such a spirit is on the decline."[8]

8.2.1. Some Macro-economic Indicators

Entrepreneurialism is booming in China. The evolution of entrepreneur-friendly institutions and China's quantum leap on the entrepreneurship front are reflected in macro-level economic data and Chinese companies' global performance, outreach and expansion. According to China Macro Finance, during 2000–2009, the number of registered private businesses in China grew by over 30 percent annually. One estimate suggested that there were 43 million companies in China in 2010, of which 93 percent were private companies, which employed 92 percent of the country's workers.[9] SMEs account for 99.8 percent of the total number of enterprises, 60 percent of total industrial output value and 57 percent of total sales revenues.[10]

According to the OECD, China's rate of self-employment was 51.2 percent in 2009, compared to 7.2 percent in the US. Moreover, the China–US gap in self-employment has not changed significantly since 2001, when the data first became available.[11] According to the 2009 GEM study, only 7 percent of the US population in the 18–64 age group that did not have a business intended to start one in the future. In China, the proportion was 23 percent.[12] Nationwide, SMEs account for 75 percent of new jobs.[13]

8.2.2. Emergence of World-class entrepreneurial Firms and Global Brands

China is home to many world-class entrepreneurial firms that have championed technology and innovation, and performed at high levels of productivity and quality. Two Chinese companies made it to Fast Company's 2013 list of "The World's 50 Most Innovative Companies": Tencent (no. 16) and Landwasher (no. 38) (www.fastcompany.com/most-innovative-companies/2013/full-list). In 2011, Tencent, China's most innovative company according to Fast Company's 2013 list, launched WeChat (or Weixin), a suite of social networking plug-ins that is less expensive, clearer and faster than calling on the phone. WeChat had over 300 million users in less than two years after its launch. Due to its popularity among a large number of Chinese expatriates in the US, WeChat was also a top twenty free social networking app in Apple's Store in the US.

Likewise, in 2013, 136 Chinese companies were included in Forbes' Global 2000 list of the world's biggest companies, ninety-one in 2009.[14] Indeed, the two biggest companies in Forbes' Global 2000 list of 2013 were from China: Industrial and Commercial Bank of China Limited (ICBC) and China Construction Bank.

8.2.3. Inequalities in Income and Wealth

Inequalities in income and wealth in China have accelerated at a phenomenally unprecedented pace. According to an ADB study of twenty-two Asian developing countries, China was the region's second most unequal country, behind Nepal. In the early 1990s to the early 2000s, China's increase in inequality was also the second highest, again only behind Nepal.[15] It is also worth noting that over 90 percent of China's richest 20,000 people are related to senior government officials or senior members of the CCP.[16]

8.2.4. The Informal Economy

As noted in Chapter 1, one way to measure the impact of entrepreneurship is to look at the informal economy. There is no systematic data on the size of the Chinese informal economy. The number of workers employed outside the formal sector was estimated to increase from 15,000 in 1978 to 168 million (59.4 percent of the total number of workers) in 2006.[17]

One estimate has suggested that formal salary and wage employment as a proportion of total compensation is 15 percent in China compared to 40 percent in Indonesia, the Philippines and Thailand, and 90 percent in G-7 nations.[18] Other estimates suggest that the size of the shadow economy as a proportion of official GDP increased from 10.2 percent in 1994/1995 to 13.4 percent in 2000/2001.[19]

8.2.5. Motivation of Chinese Entrepreneurs

According to the 2009 GEM report, proportionately more Chinese entrepreneurs than those in the US are motivated by the desire to make money. The GEM study found that fewer than 40 percent of Chinese entrepreneurs started businesses to have more independence, and more than 60 percent of them did so to increase their income. On the contrary, in the US, only about 40 percent of entrepreneurs started businesses to increase income, while almost 60 percent did so to gain more independence.[20] Keming Yang, author of the book *Entrepreneurship in China*, notes: "The Chinese people have a very strong desire, perhaps the strongest among all nations in the world, to lead an enviable material life. It is a life-long struggle as they constantly compare their standard of material life with that of others around them."[21]

8.3. Institutional Changes and Entrepreneurship

From the perspective of entrepreneurship, formal institutions such as legal frameworks and rules, macro-economic policies and political regimes, as well as informal institutions such as cultures, social norms, customs, practices, conventions and traditions have changed dramatically in the past fifty years. These changes, which have facilitated entrepreneurship in China, deserve a closer look. Table 8.1 gives some examples.

Three institutional change mechanisms include: institution formation, deinstitutionalization and reinstitutionalization.[22] Institution formation entails the birth of a new logic or governance structure. In the Chinese entrepreneurship terrain, for instance, Deng Xiaoping's famous statement provides a new logic for entrepreneurship: "To be rich is to be glorious." Similarly, entrepreneurs' entry into the CCP's inner circle and upper echelons, and new laws to protect private property and IPR are changing institutions related to entrepreneurship by providing a new governance structure.

In deinstitutionalization, an existing logic or governance structure is dissolved. Deinstitutionalization is related to delegitimation. For instance, the widespread view that only people with criminal records become entrepreneurs has been dissolved in recent years.

Finally, reinstitutionalization involves an existing logic or governance structure being replaced by a new logic or governance structure. The old logic among CCP leaders was that private entrepreneurship was associated with a rising income gap and social unrest, which would lead to a negative image of the party. In recent years, there has been growing recognition among CCP leaders that a richer economy increases respect for the party.

8.3.1. Changes in Formal Institutions

China's poor performance in transparency, official accountability, and the rule of law is widely recognized. Corruption in the courts has been an issue of great concern. The CCP's Political-Legal Committee, local

Table 8.1 Understanding institutional changes influencing entrepreneurship in China

INSTITUTIONAL COMPONENT	INSTITUTIONS IN THE PAST	INSTITUTIONS TODAY
Formal	Entrepreneurial ventures perceived as potential threats to the CCP regime.	Marriage between entrepreneurship and party membership.
	Weak laws related to private property and entrepreneurship and poor enforcement mechanisms.	China has enacted many new laws and enforcement mechanisms have been strengthened.
Informal	Chinese societies had a highly negative perception of entrepreneurs. Entrepreneurs were sensitive to the communist regime and society, which resist ownership of private property.	Entrepreneurs are gaining more respect in society. Society's attitude toward business increasingly favoring entrepreneurship, especially related to high technologies.
	Entrepreneurs had to fulfill social obligations.	Social obligations are not expected.
	Culture of complacency, conformity and risk aversion. VC funds were related to the Chinese government, which cannot accept the Western level of risk taking.	Overseas Chinese with education and entrepreneurship experience in the industrialized world are more similar to managers from the Western world. Inflow of foreign VC thanks to dense networks of overseas Chinese.
	Entrepreneurship as an occupation was often considered for individuals not able to find other jobs (e.g., those with criminal records).	Attitude towards entrepreneurship is rapidly shifting.

party committees and local governments control personnel and funding in the courts.[23]

Formal institutions, which previously obstructed the growth of entrepreneurship in China, are undergoing fundamental and extraordinary shifts. This has been true for attitudes of rule-making bodies such as the CCP as well as laws and rules influencing entrepreneurship. Richard L. King, a venture partner at GRP Venture Partners, observes: "Despite the flaws of the Chinese system, the Chinese people are not unhappy with it. They may be unhappy with corrupted officials, and corruption remains a major problem."[24] He further explains how prospective leaders in China are "groomed" and have many years to prove their capability and competence. Thomas Friedman of the *New York Times* echoes King: "One-party autocracy certainly has its drawbacks. But when it is led by a reasonably enlightened group of people, as China is today, it can also have great advantages."[25]

The CCP's Orientation Toward Entrepreneurship

The conservative faction in the CCP considers entrepreneurial ventures to be potential threats to the party's dominance, ideology, administrative authority and moral standards. Leaders of this faction perceive improved legal institutions to be challenges to the CCP's legitimacy, and have used the rising income gap and social unrest to justify measures against entrepreneurship.[26] Some analysts have argued that the delay in granting full rights to entrepreneurs was due to institutional inertia.

Chinese legal institutions related to entrepreneurship had been victims of political ideology. Following the 1989 Tiananmen events, the conservative faction's actions severely impacted entrepreneurship. Estimates suggest that the number of private enterprises was reduced by 50 percent that year.[27]

While Russia and Eastern Europe followed Western prescriptions, China has successfully blended nationalism with Marxism. The CCP expects that a richer economy might help burnish China's image worldwide and increase respect for it. For that reason, the Chinese government encourages entrepreneurship. In general, China has failed to reform its political institutions but has been successful in constructing the economic and market institutions needed to encourage innovation and entrepreneurship.[28]

Institutional actors bringing regressive changes in Chinese entrepreneurship are likely to weaken over time. Why might this be? First, as noted above, although some Chinese policy makers consider China's integration with the global market to be associated with significant socioeconomic costs, they cannot openly reject global integration.[29] To gain legitimacy from international institutions such as the WTO, China is required to respect private entrepreneurship and ownership of private property.

Second, entrepreneurs are being openly accepted into the CCP's inner circle. The CCP's policies and formal legal institutions encourage entrepreneurship. In 2002, the CCP changed its bylaws to allow entrepreneurs to become members. In a 2001 speech during celebrations of the party's eightieth anniversary, then President Jiang Zemin acknowledged the benefit that capitalists bring to the economy. He also handed party membership to a capitalist and founder of one of China's most respected private companies, the first private company to list on a foreign stock exchange. In another instance, in January 2003, the CCP appointed one of China's wealthiest private entrepreneurs as deputy chairman of an advisory body to the government of Chongqing municipality. He was the first private businessman in China to be awarded such a high position. Although some analysts argue that this seemingly impressive position carried "no real power", optimists suggest that these entrepreneurs will give the private sector a more powerful voice in policy making. These activities have undoubtedly bolstered the legitimacy of entrepreneurs.

The CCP's legitimacy-seeking process (logic) and governance structure are thus changing significantly from the standpoint of entrepreneurship. First, the old logic that entrepreneurial ventures threaten the CCP's dominance, ideology, administrative authority and moral standards is losing ground in relation to competing institutions. The new logic is that a richer economy helps burnish the CCP's image worldwide. There has therefore been reinstitutionalization. Second, as entrepreneurs exert a strong grip on the CCP, one can expect the formation of new institutions through a new governance structure. The legitimacy-seeking process requires the appeasement of multiple institutions that are conflicting and inconsistent. The Chinese government, for instance, has to take measures to satisfy both the conservative faction in the CCP and entrepreneurs. As entrepreneurs strengthen their positions in the CCP, Chinese policy makers are expected to take substantive measures to appease them.

Strong Rules of Law and Enforcement Mechanisms
There has been a rapid shift in formal institutions related to entrepreneurship. Following the 1978 economic and political reforms, China enacted thousands of new laws to protect private property and IP; and abolished or amended many laws in these areas to comply with the

WTO obligations. The formation of new institutions and governance structures is thus likely to promote entrepreneurship.

Under new laws, buyers of pirated goods can be fined five to ten times the value of the goods, and manufacturers face jail time and equipment confiscation.[30] The government has given significant power to regulatory agencies involved in IPR issues, for example the State Administration of Industry and Commerce, the State Administration of Press and Publications, the Intellectual Property Rights Office and the State Pharmaceutical Administration.[31] Similarly, China announced its plans to open special centers in fifty cities by 2006 to handle IPR infringement complaints as well as to provide consulting services.[32]

Entrepreneurs as Institutional Change Agents

In China's context, researchers have identified four approaches institutional entrepreneurs employ to create market-oriented institutions by breaking regulative barriers: open advocacy, private persuasion, making a case for exceptions, and ex ante investment with ex post justification.[33] First, open advocacy works only if the government is "tolerant enough for opinions that may criticize existing policies, regulations or laws" and the advocated changes are perceived to be beneficial to the general public. Second, entrepreneurs may persuade policy makers privately. Third, an entrepreneur may argue for a special case that is an exception to the existing laws and regulations. Finally, if a business formed or expanded by breaking existing laws generates jobs, tax revenues and other forms of social benefits, the entrepreneur reports to the government and persuades policy makers to bring changes in existing laws and regulations.

In addition to entrepreneurs' roles in bringing changes in existing rules and laws, entrepreneurs may also engage in strengthening enforcement mechanisms. Consider China's IPR laws. With the increase in local firms' IP creation, the firms are forcing the government to take substantive measures to strengthen the country's IP regime. According to the Chinese Supreme Court, in 2005, over 16,000 civil cases and 3,500 criminal cases related to IPR violations were handled by Chinese courts, and more than 2,900 people were jailed.[34] The number of cases involving IPR protection including patents, trade secrets and counterfeit goods increased by 21 percent in 2005.[35] It is also important to note that in 2005, 95 percent of China's IPR cases were brought by Chinese companies.[36]

The Chinese nanotechnology industry provides another visible example of how local entrepreneurs are taking more aggressive action in trying to alter the trajectories of institutions related to entrepreneurship. The Nanometer Technology Center established in Beijing is actively involved in protecting IPR.

Shift from Double Entrepreneurship to Legal Entrepreneurship

Institutional boundaries for economic activities are not well defined in China. Exploitation of the regulative uncertainty and the weak rule of law has arguably become an important form of entrepreneurship in China. This phenomenon is also known as double entrepreneurship; it entails maximizing economic rewards and minimizing sociopolitical risks. Entrepreneurs find attractive economic niches from outside the current institutional boundaries. For instance, they may depend on their relationship with government bureaucrats to obtain a business license. At the same time, because of ineffective enforcement of property rights, they have to acquire political and administrative protection or depend on informal norms.

In many developing countries, starting a business entails overcoming a significant amount of red tape. In China, one way to overcome bureaucratic red tape has been to be close to the CCP to gain advantage and preferential treatment. Membership of the CCP gives an entrepreneur easier access to loans and official protection and discourages the entry of new players. Entrepreneurs also spend time and energy in forming *guanxi* and cultivating ties with officials. In sum, whereas entrepreneurship in the West is about identifying profitable opportunities, in China, an alliance with those who control financial, physical or human resources is critical to success.[37]

Improvement in market-supporting institutions or transformation of a socialist economy into a market economy can thus be an important force in converting double entrepreneurship into legal entrepreneurship.[38] In recent years, the Chinese regulative landscape has undergone significant improvement in rule-setting and monitoring activities.

Consequently, the institutional actors' values are entrepreneurship-friendly and progressive.

8.3.2. Changes in Informal Institutions

Societal Perception of Entrepreneurs

The historical perception of entrepreneurship in China has been drastically different from that in market economies. Mao arguably developed a fierce critique of capitalism, private property, income and wealth inequality and material interest. During the Mao era, private entrepreneurship was virtually non-existent and was a political and social taboo.[39] Entrepreneurship was shunned even in the 1980s. Thanks to mindsets that were reminiscent of the Chinese Communist Public Goods Regime, as late as the 1990s, Chinese societies had highly negative perception of those trying to build their own company.

Faced with such societal perception, some Chinese entrepreneurs are still sensitive to social and party views that resist ideas related to the ownership of private property. Accumulating a huge amount of wealth is thus a delicate subject. Some people in China still consider entrepreneurs to be selfish people who think and act only in regard to their own interests.[40]

That is not to say that the institutional environment has not changed. Indeed, attitudes toward businesses and private entrepreneurship are becoming more positive. Chinese leaders have also provided societal validity to entrepreneurship. With the new institutional logic associated with Deng Xiaoping's statement "To be rich is to be glorious", entrepreneurs are gaining more respect in the society.

Society's Expectation of Entrepreneurs

Some still consider entrepreneurs to be members of the working class striving for China's development. Some entrepreneurs are seen as "cadres" and judged by their ability to provide socialist benefits. From the social standpoint, the road to entrepreneurship is beginning to look a little smoother. In particular, educated entrepreneurs running high-tech businesses are considered to be highly respected businesspeople. There has thus been deinstitutionalization of the logic that entrepreneurs need to fulfill social obligations.

Chinese Culture and Entrepreneurship

Overseas Chinese with education and entrepreneurship experience in the industrialized world are likely to possess the knowledge and ability to adapt to the Chinese context. "Social remittances" associated with immigrants (i.e., ideas, behaviors and identities) play a critical role in promoting entrepreneurship.[41]

Chinese returnees from overseas are influencing institutions related to the Chinese entrepreneurship landscape in a number of ways. For instance, overseas Chinese control assets worth trillions of dollars and have developed complex and dense social organizations and institutions. In recent years, Chinese returnees have developed similar institutions in China, which promoted innovation and risk taking and stimulated interaction among various ingredients of entrepreneurship. This trend is especially evident in the country's industrial and high-tech parks. Overseas Chinese have also contributed by producing synergies and thickening existing institutions.[42] Successful entrepreneurial spin-offs from Chinese returnees have promoted risk-taking behavior among Chinese.

Cognitive Assessment of Entrepreneurship as an Occupation

While working lifelong for big enterprises is viewed as an ideal job in Japan, employment in big state-owned enterprises used to be the most desired career for the Chinese. One observation is that people who spent most of their lives in such careers dislike entrepreneurship.

Traditionally, entrepreneurship has not been considered the most desirable occupation for China's best and brightest and has been considered to be for people with criminal records who have found it difficult to find other jobs. The situation is changing. A recent survey conducted among Chinese found that 70 percent of the respondents thought entrepreneurship was a good career choice and 32 percent expected to start a business in the next three years.[43]

8.4. Determinants of Entrepreneurship in China

8.4.1. Regulatory Framework

We noted above that there has been a rapid shift in formal institutions related to entrepreneurship. Traditionally, regulative institutions such as the insecurity of property rights and close state control hindered entrepreneurship. Private entrepreneurs lacked legal protection. However, the situation is changing. China is making a shift from top-down, state-directed policies to flexible and market-oriented approaches.

There are many examples to illustrate this trend. The story related to state-run China Telecom's complaint against two entrepreneurs offering callback services in Fujian deserves mention.[44] Their business challenged China Telecom's monopoly and high charges. The courts weren't convinced the brothers had violated any laws and ruled against China Telecom. To take another example, Pfizer successfully opposed a major Chinese ministry-level government agency to defend its Viagra patent. In these two examples we see evidence of deinstitutionalization or diluting the control and power of state-owned monopolies and government agencies.

Despite these advances, China has a long way to go in the pursuit of its entrepreneurship-related goals. Starting a business involves time-consuming and lengthy steps. According to the World Bank's Ease of Doing Business 2013 assessment (www.doingbusiness.org/reports/global-reports/doing-business-2013), China ranked 91 out of the 185 economies considered in terms of regulatory climate. To start a business, thirteen procedures are needed to be completed which take thirty-three days and cost 2.1 percent of the country's per capita income.

8.4.2. Values, Culture and Skills

Entrepreneurial Culture

While some argue that Chinese culture is entrepreneurship-friendly, others suggest that the Chinese, in general, tend to lack characteristics needed to be a successful entrepreneur, for example independent thinking, risk taking, innovation and self-determination. It is also sometimes suggested that entrepreneurship as discovery and exploitation of market opportunities is incompatible with China's culture of complacency, conformity and adherence to standard rules and procedures.[45] That said, it would be erroneous to claim the existence of a generic Chinese culture. As discussed earlier, there is a major difference between the social organization and risk-taking behavior of Chinese living in China and overseas Chinese.

Finally, there is the view that the fatalistic orientation of Chinese people works against entrepreneurship. Compared to people in the West, the Chinese arguably believe more in fate and thus tend to rely on opportunism over long-term entrepreneurial strategy.[46]

Entrepreneurial Skills and Capabilities

Intel ex-CEO Craig Barrett argued that the Chinese are "capable of doing any engineering, any software job, any managerial job that people in the United States are capable of".[47] Indeed, more scientists and engineers are staying in or returning to China with graduate degrees from foreign countries to perform R&D work for foreign affiliates or local firms or to start their own businesses. By 2005, 170,000 Chinese with graduate degrees overseas had returned to China. According to the Chinese Ministry of Education, in 2009 and 2010, 108,300 and 134,800 Chinese respectively returned to the country after completing their studies in foreign countries. MNCs are capitalizing on the huge and growing Chinese research pool to launch products that will help them compete globally.

Following the post-1978 reforms, Chinese firms gradually started importing Western management techniques. Traditionally, the import was concentrated on the tangible and quantitative approach. Soft management concepts, such as marketing and consumer behavior, are relatively less integrated into the Chinese way of thinking, as they were perceived by the CCP to be a threat to communist ideology. Chinese entrepreneurial firms are taking measures to overcome these weaknesses. Some Chinese firms are seeking to overcome weaknesses in the areas of branding, sales, marketing, and technology through M&A.

In a process known as "brain circulation", Chinese engineers and entrepreneurs with work experience in Silicon Valley are contributing to entrepreneurial development in their home countries.[48] They initially enjoyed home-country advantage by tapping the low-cost skill base and subsequently moved into a higher gear and engaged in the localized processes.

8.4.3. Access to Finance, Market, R&D and Technology

R&D and Innovations

Overall China lags behind the West in terms of the state of technology, organizational and managerial ability. That said, it is also the case that Chinese companies, thanks to their accelerated pace of technological and scientific advances have developed strong prowess to compete globally in certain technology sectors. Some visible examples of such technologies include nanotechnology, open-source software, cloning technology and cellular telecommunications.

China's increasing R&D and innovations profile is reflected in the emergence of globally competitive Chinese technology firms. A communications satellite project with the Nigerian government is probably China's highest profile project in the developing world. A Chinese-made communications satellite was put into orbit for Nigeria in 2007. The package included satellite, launch vehicle and launch service. "Nigcomsat-1" was launched successfully on the "Long March 3B" carrier rocket. It was developed by the China Research Institute of Space Technology.

China spent US$141.4 billion on R&D in 2010, which is expected to increase to US$153.7 billion in 2011, overtaking Japan.[49] Patents are an important proxy for innovations. In 2009, China increased its patent filing under World Intellectual Property Organization (WIPO) Patent Cooperation Treaty (PCT) by 29.7 percent. It overtook France to become the fifth largest patent filer to the PCT that year. In 2010, China ranked fourth among the PCT-filing countries, only behind the US, Japan and Germany. In 2010, China filed 12,337 patents under the PCT compared to 7,900 in 2009. Among companies, China's Huawei Technologies had the second highest number of patents (only behind Japan's Panasonic) in 2009. In 2008, Huawei had the world's highest number of patents.

In 2009, China's SIPO was the third largest patent office in the world. According to WIPO's World Intellectual Property Indicators 2012, SIPO became the world's largest patent office in 2011 by overtaking the US Patent and Trademark Office (USPTO). It overtook the Japan Patent Office (JPO) in 2010 in terms of the number of patents registered. A comparison of five major patent offices' patent volumes during 2004–2008 indicated that patent filing in China had been growing at the fastest rate.[50] Clean technology (CT) patents are among the leading category of patent filing with the SIPO. They come from both domestic and international companies.

Market Conditions

The huge domestic market has helped Chinese entrepreneurial firms compete successfully in foreign markets. Among prominent examples are dam projects undertaken by Chinese companies in developing countries. Chinese hydropower companies gained international experience on smaller dams in small developing countries such as Albania, Algeria, Burma and Nepal. For instance, in early 2010, Chinese companies were building about 40 percent of the thirty-four planned hydropower projects in Laos and all twenty plants in Burma.

The economies of scale in the home country and their ability to adapt Western technology to the needs of developing countries at a low cost helped these companies move into a higher gear. In power projects, Chinese companies' per kilowatt costs are in the US$700–800 range, while developed world-based firms tend to price at about US$1,000.

Physical Infrastructure

The development of modern highways, ports and telecommunications infrastructure has provided the foundation for entrepreneurial development. A comparison with India is helpful to understand the development of physical infrastructures in China. It is important to note that every year following the 1978 political and economic reform, China built more modern highways than India had done in the whole period since it achieved independence in 1947.[51]

As of early 2013, China had 93,000 km of railway track.[52] Investment and infrastructure spending on the rail network has been a key factor in China's economic recovery. In December 2009, China launched the world's fastest long-distance passenger train, overtaking Western countries and its Asian neighbors. The Harmony express raced 1,100 km in less than three hours, traveling from Guangzhou to Wuhan. The journey used to take over eleven hours. The Harmony express reached a top speed of 394 km/hour in pre-launch trials and averaged 350 km/hour on its debut. This compared with a maximum service speed of 300 km/hour for Japan's Shinkansen bullet trains and France's TGV service. In the US, Amtrak's Acela "Express" service takes 3.5 hours to travel between Boston and New York, a distance of 300 km. The Chinese government spent US$17 billion on the Harmony express line's construction over 4.5 years. The country has used the recent GFC as an opportunity to modernize its economy.

Access to Finance

Domestic savings have been an important source of investment. Household saving rates are showing increasing trends. The household saving rate as a proportion of GDP was 17 percent in 1995, which increased to 38 percent in 2010.[53] In 2008, household saving accounted for 28 percent of disposable income in urban households.

One argument is that, as in the case of other Asian economies, the high savings rates in China can be attributed to income insecurity associated mostly with informal jobs. The high saving rates therefore may not automatically translate to higher investment rates. The size of the informal capital market in China, however, indicates that the high domestic saving rate is playing an important role in promoting entrepreneurial activities in the country. According to the 2009 GEM report, about 6 percent of the Chinese in the 18–64 age group made an informal investment in the past three years, compared with less than 4 percent in the US. Informal investment was 11.3 percent of China's GDP in 2009, compared with only 1.5 percent in the US.[54]

To finance their ventures, many entrepreneurs depend on the informal banking systems, which are formed by pooling household savings and charging annual interest rates of as high as 70 percent. Estimates suggest that China's informal banking system was a US$630-billion industry in 2011.[55] Due to the GFC-led credit crunch, inflation and rise in the price of raw materials, an increasing number of entrepreneurs are on the verge of bankruptcy. It was reported that in Wenzhou city many private entrepreneurs went into hiding, fled to foreign countries or committed suicide.

The Chinese venture capital landscape is also changing rapidly. China represents one of the fastest-growing markets for VC investment in the world (Fig. 8.1). By 2008, US$9.3 billion in VC was invested in Chinese startup companies.[56] Local firms accounted for US$1.4 billion in 2008, compared to US$402 million in 2007.[57]

It is also important to note that a significant proportion of VC funds is linked to the government and can be considered to be a loan.[58] Enterprises that are able to obtain VC funds feel an obligation not to lose the resources. Moreover, an incubator losing the government-owned money also becomes a target of official criticism. Chinese government VC funds thus cannot accept a Western level of risk taking. Chinese returnees may also change other components of Chinese institutions such as the Chinese VC landscape.

Bank lending is widely available. Many Chinese entrepreneurial firms have benefited tremendously from the government's cheap credit and soft loans. In the first half of 2009, new loans issued by Chinese banks amounted to US$1.1 trillion.[59] The real irony, however, is the government's failure to introduce policies that favor the population at the bottom of the economic pyramid. For instance, lending is disproportionately oriented toward powerful economic and political interests such as state-controlled companies in China. SMEs account for 70 percent of GDP but have access to only 20 percent of the country's

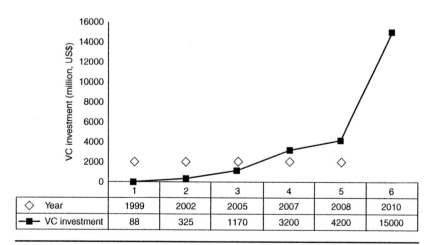

◇ Year	1	2	3	4	5	6
	1999	2002	2005	2007	2008	2010
■ VC investment	88	325	1170	3200	4200	15000

Figure 8.1 VC investments in China
Source: For 1999, UNDP;[60] for 2002 and 2005, Balfour 2006;[61] for 2007 and 2008: Boudreau 2009;[62] for 2010, China Venture Capital Research Institute (CVCRI)

financial resources.[63] The effects of crisis-led spending are clearly skewed towards the big enterprises.

8.5. Concluding Comments

A constellation of factors linked to China's global integration is pushing through fundamental changes in institutions related to Chinese entrepreneurship. China's successful blend of capitalism, nationalism and Marxism has provided the impetus to entrepreneurship and investment. Most CCP leaders have realized that entrepreneurs' contribution to the ambitious economic agenda outweigh the costs related to challenges to the CCP's legitimacy. For this reason, they are wholeheartedly promoting and facilitating entrepreneurial thinking and practices. The preceding examples also point to an emerging trend in thickened entrepreneurial institutions.

Changing Profiles of Entrepreneurs

The institutional changes discussed above are likely to result in altering the profiles of successful entrepreneurs. In the Chinese entrepreneurship landscape, there are a few commonly accepted rules and norms to govern relationships. This results in greater institutional and social uncertainties, a situation in which personal relationships are important resources. The institutional entrepreneurs who depend on government officials for their success face risks in a market economy. Strengthened rule of law and a higher level of regulative certainty are likely to encourage legal entrepreneurship instead of double entrepreneurship.

Western Influence on Chinese Entrepreneurship Patterns

We have discussed a number of mechanisms associated with Western influence on Chinese entrepreneurship culture. For instance, the arrival of an increasing number of overseas Chinese, some with significant entrepreneurial experience, is set to transform the Chinese entrepreneurship landscape. These returnees are likely to be more like Western entrepreneurs in terms of habits of thought and behavior related to entrepreneurship. Successful entrepreneurial spin-offs from Chinese returnees may further promote risk-taking behavior among Chinese. Likewise, inflow of VC from the Western world is rapidly growing in China. Recall that Western VC differs drastically from most domestic VC funds that are linked to the government. With China's growing global integration, the further influence of Western entrepreneurship culture can be observed.

The Weakest Link in the Chinese Entrepreneurial Landscape

The adoption rate of values promoting entrepreneurship has been very slow among some critical institutional actors such as incubators, state-owned banks, local cadres, tax officers and government officials. After decades of socialism, the idea of respecting the constitutional rights of entrepreneurs has been slow to diffuse among some institutional actors. Chinese incubators, for instance, lack the proper cognitive mindset to assist entrepreneurs. Private enterprises often complain about the difficulties of dealing with state-owned banks and other agencies, as well as harassment and extortion from local cadres, tax officers and government officials.[64] These actors have been the weakest link in China's entrepreneurship landscape. Measures are needed to accelerate the diffusion of progressive, entrepreneurship-related change among these actors.

8.6. Review Questions

1. Compare China and the US in terms of the various indicators related to entrepreneurship. What are some of the indicators that would suggest that China's entrepreneurial progress may be faster than in the US?
2. Give some examples of China-originated world-class entrepreneurial firms and global brands.
3. Has entrepreneurship helped to narrow inequalities in income and wealth in China?
4. Have the institutional changes taking place in China promoted entrepreneurship?

8.7. Critical Discussion Questions

1. Thomas Friedman noted: "One-party autocracy certainly has its drawbacks. But when it is led by a reasonably enlightened group of people, as China is today, it can also have great advantages." Do you agree with Friedman? Elaborate your response.

2. How should industrialized countries such as the US respond to China's entrepreneurial progress?

3. Intel ex-CEO Craig Barrett argues that the Chinese are "capable of doing any engineering, any software job, any managerial job that people in the United States are capable of". Do you agree or disagree? Why?

8.8. End-of-chapter Case: Entrepreneurship in the Chinese Clean Technology Industry

The clean technology (CT) market in China has gone from "niche" to "mainstream". According to Tsing Capital, a Chinese VC firm, the Chinese CT market is growing 20 percent annually. Entrepreneurial activities in the CT sector are also reflected in job creation. The CT industry is a big employment generator in China. China's renewable energy industries add 100,000 jobs each year.[65]

Export of CT

Some Chinese companies are gearing up to respond to the global trend toward CT policy and rapidly entering foreign markets. In September 2009, CLP Holdings Limited entered into an agreement with Vestas Wind Technology India Private Limited to develop a 99 MW Theni project in the Indian state of Tamil Nadu. It was CLP's sixth Indian wind farm.

The Chinese auto- and battery maker, BYD, announced the possibility of selling rechargeable electric cars in the US as early as in 2010. Chinese companies are also planning to export wind turbines. China exported wind turbines worth US$1.5 billion to the US in 2010.[66] Likewise, GCL-Poly and China Guangdong Nuclear Wind Power have announced that they will be entering the US market soon.

A Wall Street Journal article reported that Duke Energy was talking with China's biggest electricity distributor, State Grid, about a joint venture on power transmission lines in the US.

Emergence of Entrepreneurial Firms in the Chinese CT Sector

Many promising entrepreneurial firms have evolved in the Chinese CT industry. China's Yingli Green Energy Holdings and Suntech Power Holdings are two of the world's largest solar panel makers. In 2009, GCL-Poly Energy Holdings became the world's third-largest poly-silicon maker following its US$3.4-billion acquisition of solar assets.[67]

Until 2004, China had virtually no wind turbine production. By 2009, China had 70 turbine manufacturing companies and was the largest wind turbine producer in the world.[68] According to the International Energy Agency, China's Sinovel and Goldwind are the world's top ten turbine makers. Note that Sinovel did not make wind turbines until 2005.

In recent years, there has also been some consolidation in this industry. During 2007–2009, due to falling prices, over three hundred solar panel manufacturers, or about 10 percent of Chinese solar companies, went out of business.[69]

Availability of CT-related Natural Resources, Skills and Labor Resources

China has the advantage of being well endowed with the natural resources needed for the success of the CT industry. One estimate suggests that China produces 97 percent of the world's rare earth elements (REEs). The country has tightened the export of REEs since 2003.[70]

Thanks to China's cheap labor, the distinguishing mark of Chinese CT players is their cost competitiveness. Chinese companies are in a position to undercut their foreign competitors' costs, and to price more aggressively than foreign CT manufacturers. Consider, for instance, polysilicon, which is a critical raw material for solar panels that convert sunlight to electricity. Chinese solar panel makers procure poly-silicon at cheap prices from manufacturers that have lower electricity and labor costs. In 2010, Chinese companies sold solar panel modules at about US$1.50 per watt compared to US$2.50 charged by European manufacturers. Likewise, GCL-Poly Energy Holdings expects to sell the solar raw material at US$45 per kg in 2011 compared to

US$50 per kg in 2010. Outside China, manufacturers sell polysilicon at US$60 per kg.[71]

Domestic economies of scale and a low-cost workforce will continue to make Chinese exports cheaper than those of Western companies. China is also attempting to develop higher levels skills. China has increased funding for ten universities, the aim of which is to produce specialists in diverse areas of science and technology. China was reported to be providing training in CT products for 30,000 salespeople in 2010.[72]

The Government's Role in Stimulating Entrepreneurship in the CT Industry

In recent years, there has been a focused priority in the development of this sector. One of the environmental goals of China's Eleventh Five-year Plan was to reduce sulfur dioxide emissions by 10 percent during 2005–2010. At the 2009 Copenhagen climate conference, China's ex Prime Minister Wen Jiabao announced that by 2020, his country would reduce greenhouse gas intensity by 45 percent compared to the 2005 levels.

About 40 percent of the Chinese economic stimulus package of US$586 billion announced in 2008 went on environmental and energy-efficient projects.[73] The country's stimulus package allocated to the CT industry as a percentage of 2008 GDP was the world's highest. China's massive subsides have encouraged consumers to adopt solar energy, driving down costs for companies. China provides a US$3-a-watt subsidy for solar projects or about half the capital cost, which is arguably "the most generous subsidy in the world".[74]

China's strategic regulation has resulted in the cost competitiveness of Chinese CT firms. While CT firms face public resistance in Western countries, China lacks cumbersome regulations, which allows businesses to deliver CT projects in the shortest time. Moreover, state loans are available at cheap rates.

Strategic Regulations

The Chinese government has introduced a number of CT-related strategic regulations. For instance, in 2007, China raised national drinking water standards and established teams to examine and monitor water quality. The country's Health Ministry added seventy-one bench-marks to the existing thirty-five. The trade service division of the Ministry of Commerce has announced a plan to build 10,000 green hotels by 2012, which are required to install the latest water treatment technology.[75] Similarly, in September 2009, the Ministry of Industry and Information Technology was considering additional restrictions on the production and export of REEs as well as other industrial raw materials.

China has encouraged the growth of CT industries within its bor-ders by reducing the export of crucial raw materials. In addition, China has also given foreign CT companies incentives to set up operations in the country so as to secure access to supplies. Some of China's CT-related strategic regulations have created frameworks and processes to meet various challenges associated with the development of the local CT industry and have paid off brilliantly. In 2003, China restricted imports, requiring its wind farms to source 70 percent of their parts from the domestic market. The restriction was lifted in 2009. By that time, home production had come to dominate the business.

Investment in the CT Sector

Entrepreneurial activities in the Chinese CT sector are associated with and facilitated by increasing investment. During 2000–2008, US$41 billion in private capital was invested in the Chinese CT industry. China's share of global CT investment is increasing rapidly. In 2008, China surpassed the US in private capital investment for renewable energy.[76] It may well be that China's generous incentives and the low-risk investor environment have helped to attract private investment in this sector.

During 2010–2020, China is expected to invest US$440–660 bil-lion in the CT industry.[77] In 2009, there were thirty-two IPOs in the CT sector which raised US$4.7 billion worldwide. China accounted for about 50 percent of the IPOs and 75 percent of total global IPO capital.[78] The Chinese wind power company Longyuan Electric Power Group raised US$2.2 billion on the Hong Kong exchange, which was the biggest renewable energy IPO in 2009.[79] In 2009, China gained its global VC share in the CT industry.

David Sandalow, a US assistant secretary of energy for policy and international affairs—a CT expert—recently put the issue this way: "China's investment in clean energy is extraordinary. Unless the US makes investments, we are not competitive in the CT sector in the years and decades to come."[80]

Innovations in the Chinese CT Industry

China is behind the US and other industrialized countries in CT innovations.[81] According to Chatham House, no Chinese company is among the top CT patent holders. For instance, there is no Chinese company among the top twenty holders of patents for clean-coal technology.[82] Most Chinese players are concentrated at the low end of the CT industry. For instance, while China has a large number of players in the solar devices sector, most focus on low-tech rooftop water-heaters or cheap, low-efficiency photovoltaic panels. Likewise, the quality levels of China's wind-turbine manufacturers lag far behind those of General Electric, Vestas and Siemens.[83]

Notes

1. Nair, S.R. 1996, "Doing Business in China: It's Far from Easy", *USA Today*, 124(2608), pp. 27–29.
2. America 2007, "The Next Bill Gates", January 15, 196(2), p. 4.
3. Bosma, N., & Levie, J. 2009, Global Entrepreneurship Monitor: 2009 Global Report, Babson Park: Babson College.
4. Shane, S., & Venkataraman, S. 2000, "The Promise of Entrepreneurship as a Field of Research", *Academy of Management Review*, 25(1), pp. 217–226.
5. Richter, F. 2000, "China's Entry into the WTO and the Impact on Western Firms", *China Economic Review*, 11(4), pp. 423–427.
6. Gangemi, J. 2007, "Study: U.S. Startup Activity Down Slightly in '06", *Bloomberg Business Week*, January 11, at www.businessweek.com/stories/2007–01–10/study-u-dot-s-dot-startup-activity-down-slightly-in-06busi nessweek-business-news-stock-market-and-financial-advice.
7. Monro, A. 2007, "Mysteries of the East", *New Statesman*, 136(4826), pp. 58–59.
8. Manning, A. 2006, "What's in the Cards for 2007?", *USA Today*, December 25, at http://usatoday30.usatoday.com/news/nation/2006–12–25-trends_x.htm.

9. *Economist* 2011, "Let a Million Flowers Bloom", March 10, www.econo mist.com/node/18330120.

10. China Knowledge 2010, "China's SMEs Need Efficient Financing Channels", February 19, www.chinaknowledge.com/Newswires/News_Detail. aspx?type=1&NewsID=31452.

11. OECD 2009, "Stabilisation and Renewed Growth: Key Challenges", in *OECD Economic Surveys: Russian Federation* 2009, 6, pp. 19–51.

12. Shane, S. 2010, "If You Want to See Entrepreneurs, Go to China", *Business Week*, March 12, at www.businessweek.com/smallbiz/content/mar2010/ sb20100311_996919.htm.

13. Loyalka, M.D.A. 2006, "A Chinese Welcome for Entrepreneurs", *Business Week*, January 6, at www.businessweek.com/stories/2006–01–05/a-chinese-welcome-for-entrepreneurs.

14. DeCarlo, S. 2013, "The World's Biggest Companies", April 17, at www. forbes.com/sites/scottdecarlo/2013/04/17/the-worlds-biggest-compa nies-2/.

15. Asian Development Bank 2007, *Inequality in Asia, Key Indicators 2007, Special Chapter Highlights*, Manila: Asian Development Bank.

16. Kwong, K.K., Yau, O.H.M., Lee, J.S.Y., Sin, L.Y.M., & Tse, A.C.B. 2003, "The Effects of Attitudinal and Demographic Factors on Intention to Buy Pirated CDs: The Case of Chinese Consumers", *Journal of Business Ethics*, 47(3), pp. 223–235.

17. Huang, P.C.C. 2009, "China's Neglected Informal Economy", *Modern China*, 35(4), pp. 405–438.

18. Klein, B.P., & Cukier, K.N. 2009, "Tamed Tigers, Distressed Dragon", *Foreign Affairs*, 88(4), pp. 8–16.

19. Bajada, C., & Schneider, F. 2005, "The Shadow Economies of The Asia-Pacific", *Pacific Economic Review*, 10(3), pp. 79–401.

20. Bosma, N., Jones, K., Autio, E., & Levie, J. 2008, *Global Entrepreneurship Monitor 2007 Executive Report*, London: Global Entrepreneurship Research Association.

21. Shane, S. 2010, "If You Want to See Entrepreneurs, Go to China", *Business Week*, March 12, at www.businessweek.com/smallbiz/content/mar2010/ sb20100311_996919.htm.

22. Scott, B.R. 2001, "The Great Divide in the Global Village", *Foreign Affairs*, 80(1), pp. 160–177.

23. Liu, D. 2006, "The Transplant Effect of the Chinese Patent Law", *Chinese Journal of International Law*, 5(3), pp. 533–572.

24. King, R. 2010, "A Journey Home", *Chinese American Forum*, 25(3), pp. 22–25.

25. Mufson, S. 2009, "Asian Nations Could Outpace U.S. in Developing Clean Energy", *Washington Post* (Suburban edn), July 16, p. A14.

26. Kahn, J. 2006, "A Sharp Debate Erupts in China over Ideologies", *New York Times*, March 12, p. 1.

27. Ling, Z. 1998, *Chenfu: 1989–1997 Zhongguo Jingji Gaige Beiwanglu* [Ups and downs: Memorandum of China's economic reform during 1989–1997], Shanghai: Tongfang Chuban Zhongxin.
28. Nee, V. 1992, "Organizational Dynamics of Market Transition: Hybrid Forms, Property Rights, and Mixed Economy in China", *Administrative Science Quarterly*, 37(1), pp. 1–27.
29. Heer, P. 2000, "A House Divided", *Foreign Affairs*, 79, pp. 18–24.
30. Kanellos, M. 2002, "Software Comes of Age: Piracy Crackdown Pays Off", CNET News.com, at http://news.com.com/2009–1001–940335. html (retrieved July 11, 2009).
31. Yang, D.M. 2002, "Can the Chinese State Meet its WTO Obligations? Government Reforms, Regulatory Capacity, and WTO Membership", *American Asian Review*, 20(2), pp. 191–121.
32. MacLeod, C. 2006, "China Grows More Aggressive in Thwarting Counterfeiters", *USA Today*, April 21, p. 4B.
33. Li, D.D., Feng, J., & Jiang, H. 2006, "Institutional Entrepreneurs", *American Economic Review*, 96(2), pp. 358–362.
34. Culpan, T. 2006, "Industry Awaits IP Court in China", *Billboard*, 118(16), p. 14.
35. AFX News Limited 2006, "Louis Vuitton Sues Carrefour in China—Report", AFX.COM, April 20.
36. Culpan, T. 2006, "Industry Awaits IP Court in China", *Billboard*, 118(16), p. 14.
37. Krug, B. 2004, *China's Rational Entrepreneurs: The Development of the New Private Business Sector*, London: RoutledgeCurzon.
38. Yang, K. 2002, "Double Entrepreneurship in China's Economic Reform: An Analytical Framework", *Journal of Political and Military Sociology*, 30(1), pp. 134–148.
39. Peng, Y. 2004, "Kinship Networks and Entrepreneurs in China's Transitional Economy", *American Journal of Sociology*, 109(5), pp. 1045–1074.
40. Hsu, C. 2006, "Cadres, Getihu, and Good Businesspeople: Making Sense of Entrepreneurs in Early Post-Socialist China", *Urban Anthropology & Studies of Cultural Systems & World Economic Development*, 35(1), pp. 1–38.
41. Levitt, P. 1998, "Social Remittances: Migration Driven Local-level Forms of Cultural Diffusion", *International Migration Review*, 32(4), pp. 926–948.
42. Amin, A., & Thrift, N. 1995, "Globalisation, Institutional Thickness and the Local Economy", in Healey, P., Cameron, S., Davoui, Gram, S., & Madani-Pour, A. (eds), *Managing Cities: The New Urban Context*, Chichester: Wiley, pp. 91–108.
43. Gangemi, J. 2007, "Study: U.S. Startup Activity Down Slightly in '06", *Bloomberg Business Week*, January 11, at www.businessweek.com/stories/2007–01–10/study-u-dot-s-dot-startup-activity-down-slightly-in-06businessweek-business-news-stock-market-and-financial-advice.
44. Sender, H. 2000, "China's future: Entrepreneurs", *Far Eastern Economic Review*, January 27, p. 73.

45. Mourdoukoutas, P. 2004, "China's Challenge", *Barron's*, 84(7), p. 37.
46. Liao, D., & Sohmen, P. 2001, "The Development of Modern Entrepreneurship in China", *Stanford Journal of East Asian Affairs*, 1, pp. 27–33.
47. Segal, A. 2004, "Is America Losing Its Edge?", *Foreign Affairs*, 83(6), p. 2.
48. Saxenian A. 2005, "From Brain Drain to Brain Circulation: Transnational Communities and Regio", p. 35.
49. Naik, G. 2010, "China Surpasses Japan in R&D as Powers Shift", *Wall Street Journal*, December 13, http://online.wsj.com/article/SB100014240 52748703734204576019713917682354.html
50. Kachan, D. 2009, "Latest U.S. Cleantech Weapon: Patent Acceleration", at http://cleantech.com/news/5392/latest-us-cleantech-weapon-patent-a (retrieved March 15, 2010).
51. Overholt, W.H. 2009/2010, "China in the Global Financial Crisis: Rising Influence, Rising Challenges", *Washington Quarterly*, 33(1), pp. 21–34.
52. Rabinovitch, S. 2013, "Rail Helps China Back on Track", January 16, at www.ft.com/cms/s/0/3a2c7c86–5fc1–11e2–8d8d-00144feab49a.html# axzz2mzkbFSpec.
53. Power, C. 2010, "Savers and Spenders: How Household Savings Stack Up in Asia, the West, and Latin America", June 10, www.businessweek.com/ magazine/content/10_25/b4183010451928.htm.
54. Shane, S. 2010, "If You Want to See Entrepreneurs, Go to China", *Business Week*, March 12, at www.businessweek.com/smallbiz/content/mar2010/ sb20100311_996919.htm.
55. Barboza, D. 2011, "China Rattled as Business Owners Flee", *International Herald Tribune*, October 12.
56. Fannin, R. 2010, "India: The Gap Is Narrowing", *Forbes*, March 10, at www. forbes.com/2010/03/09/google-twitter-facebook-intelligent-technology-india.html.
57. Boudreau, J. 2009, "Venture Capital Investments in China Remain Strong", *Mercury News*, January 23, at www.mercurynews.com/business/ ci_11538914.
58. Harwit, E. 2002, "High-technology Incubators: Fuel for China's New Entrepreneurship?", *China Business Review*, 29(4), pp. 26–29.
59. Schwartz, N.D. 2009, "Asia's Recovery Highlights China's Ascendance", *New York Times*, August 23, at www.nytimes.com/2009/08/24/business/ global/24global.html.
60. UNDP 2001, *Human Development Report*, New York: UNDP.
61. Balfour, F. 2006, "Venture Capital's New Promised Land", *Business Week*, January 15, p. 44, at www.businessweek.com/stories/2006–01–15/venture-capitals-new-promised-land
62. Boudreau, J. 2009, "Venture Capital Investments in China Remain Strong", *Mercury News*, January 23, at www.mercurynews.com/business/ ci_11538914.
63. Klein, B.P., & Cukier, K.N. 2009, "Tamed Tigers, Distressed Dragon", *Foreign Affairs*, 88(4), pp. 8–16.

64. *Economist* 2002, "Not in the Club; China's Private Sector", October 12, p. 12; Yang, D.M. 2002, "Can the Chinese State Meet its WTO Obligations? Government Reforms, Regulatory Capacity, and WTO Membership", *American Asian Review*, 20(2), pp. 191–121.
65. sustainablebusiness.com 2010, "Can the US Compete with China in Cleantech?", February 1, www.sustainablebusiness.com/index.cfm/go/news.display/id/19668.
66. finfacts.ie 2009, "Asia's rising 'CT tigers'—China, Japan, and South Korea—to Overtake United States", November 20, at www.finfacts.ie/irishfinancenews/article_1018490.shtml.
67. Walet, L. 2010, "China's Green Tech Revolution", January 29, at www.reuters.com/article/2010/01/29/us-davos-green-china-idUSTRE60S3HA20100129.
68. Martin, C., & Efstathiou, J. 2010, "China's Labor Edge Overpowers Obama's 'Green' Jobs Initiatives", February 4, at www.businessweek.com/news/2010-02-04/china-s-labor-edge-overpowers-obama-s-green-jobs-initiatives.html; Parker, N., & Youngman, R. 2009, "Green Minds: Where is the Worldwide Market for Sustainable Technologies Heading?", *Financial Times Deutschland*, December 14.
69. *Asiamoney* 2003, "Chinamoney Entrepreneurs Summit", November (Supplement), pp. 39–41.
70. cleantech.com 2010, "New Report: A Cleantech Resource Crisis?", January, at www.tremcenter.org/index.php?option=com_attachments&task=download&id=2.
71. Walet, L. 2010, "China's Green Tech Revolution", January 29, at www.reuters.com/article/2010/01/29/us-davos-green-china-idUSTRE60S3HA20100129.
72. Wadhwa, V. 2010, "Will China Eat America's Lunch in Cleantech?", Techcrunch, January 30, at http://techcrunch.com/2010/01/30/will-china-eat-americas-lunch-in-cleantech/.
73. Brenhouse, H. 2009, "China's Water Needs Create Opportunities", *New York Times*, October 28, at www.nytimes.com/2009/10/27/business/energy-environment/27iht-rbobcan.html?pagewanted=all.
74. Mufson, S. 2009, "Asian Nations Could Outpace U.S. in Developing Clean Energy", *Washington Post* (Suburban edn), July 16, p. A14.
75. Brenhouse, H. 2009, "China's Water Needs Create Opportunities", *New York Times*, October 28, at www.nytimes.com/2009/10/27/business/energy-environment/27iht-rbobcan.html?pagewanted=all.
76. Atkinson, R. 2010, "America Risks Missing Out in CT: Asia's 'Clean-Tech Tigers' Are Out-investing the U.S. in Renewable Power and Energy Efficiency", *Business Week*, February 3, www.businessweek.com/innovate/content/jan2010/id20100122_369263.htm.
77. Harrison, S. 2010, "Cleantech Investment in Asia", *Financier Worldwide*, February 15, at www.financierworldwide.com/article.php?id=11233.

78. Coppa, B. 2010, "Cleantech Investing Status amidst Stock Market Declines", examiner.com, February 4, at www.examiner.com/article/clean tech-investing-status-amidst-stock-market-declines.

79. Gold, R. 2010, "Investment Dollars Flow to Green Energy Start-Ups", *Wall Street Journal*, February 3, at http://online.wsj.com/article/SB100014 2405274870365760457500508316062631.html.

80. Lean, G. 2010, "Did China Block Copenhagen Progress to Pave Way for its Own Dominance in Cleantech?", grist, http://grist.org/article/2010–01–22-did-china-block-copenhagen-to-pave-way-for-dominance-in-cleantech/.

81. Wadhwa, V. 2010, "Will China Eat America's Lunch in Cleantech?", Tech-crunch, January 30, at http://techcrunch.com/2010/01/30/will-china-eat-americas-lunch-in-cleantech/.

82. Stokes, B. 2009, "Giving Away Green Technologies", *National Journal*, November 21, 1, p. 1.

83. Mufson, S., & Pomfret, J. 2010, "There's a New Red Scare. But is China Really so Scary?", February 28, at www.washingtonpost.com/wp-dyn/con tent/article/2010/02/26/AR2010022602601.html.

9

ENTREPRENEURSHIP IN INDIA

Abstract

India is touted as a new entrepreneurship powerhouse and the next Asian miracle. There have been some successful and many unsuccessful attempts to promote entrepreneurship in India. There are also some well-founded rationales as well as a number of misinformed and ill-guided viewpoints about the friendliness of the country's environment to entrepreneurship. This chapter examines various indicators related to entrepreneurship in India and analyzes factors affecting India's entrepreneurial performance. Specifically, we provide a detailed assessment of the Indian environment for entrepreneurship in terms of various dimensions of the OECD framework. The dimensions include the regulatory framework, market conditions, access to finance, R&D- and technology-related factors, physical infrastructure, entrepreneurial capabilities and entrepreneurial culture. We provide a detailed treatment of various forms of financing from the standpoint of small business development such as bank loans, the IPO market, venture capital, microfinance, remittance inflow, domestic savings and informal investments. This chapter also compares India with its neighboring country China and major global economies in terms of many of these dimensions. We also analyze how the lack of trickledown effect and the emergence of oligarchic capitalism have affected entrepreneurship and small business development.

This chapter's objectives include:

1. To demonstrate an understanding of the changes taking place in the Indian entrepreneurship landscape.
2. To analyze the facilitators and inhibitors of entrepreneurship in India.

3. To assess the nature of entrepreneurial activities in the Indian ICT and offshoring sectors and their impacts on the Indian economy.
4. To evaluate the impacts of entrepreneurial activities in India on poverty reduction.
5. To demonstrate an understanding of the nature and availability of various forms of entrepreneurial finance in India.

9.1. Introduction

Because of India's improving entrepreneurial performance, some analysts consider the country to be the next Asian miracle.[1] The state's domination of the economy is gradually declining and there are some signs that the country is moving toward a market-oriented system. India has also set an explicit policy objective to become a leading business-friendly economy.[2] In a number of important areas, institutional reform has gained a greater momentum in India than in China. India also outperforms China in many of the World Bank's governance indicators such as rule of law and voice and accountability. Some observers have noted that India is shedding its legacy of entrepreneur-unfriendly rules and regulations and that Indian politics is becoming open and accountable.

Despite this progress, however, red tape, bureaucracy and corruption, at both national and state levels, lead to longer time, higher costs, and reduced speed and flexibility for entrepreneurs.[3] While some influential entrepreneurs are in a position to take advantage of institutional holes, SMEs tend to be more adversely affected by dysfunctional institutions. Some observe that reform inertia has been an obstacle to India outperforming China. Observers also often note that most Indian multinational companies are at a primitive or an embryonic stage.[4]

India suffers from a lack of basic infrastructures and services required for carrying out entrepreneurial activities. According to the Country's Planning Commission, inefficient power supplies have hindered entrepreneurial activities, employment creation and poverty reduction.[5] As of 2008, about half of India's population lacked access to electricity.

9.2. A Survey of Entrepreneurship in India

We begin this section by considering India's economic reform initiatives. India started relaxing industrial regulation in the early 1970s. Trade liberalization began in the late 1970s and the pace of reform picked up significantly in the mid-1980s. Indian entrepreneurship, however, got a big boost following the 1991 economic liberalization, which transformed India's entrepreneurial landscape. Many large and inefficient firms could not survive the competition created by the 1991 liberalization. For instance, of the largest twenty private firms listed on the Indian stock market in 1990, only five were in the top twenty list in 2011.[6]

Various indicators point to the improved entrepreneurial performance of India. In 2009, forty-seven Indian companies were included in Forbes' Global 2000 list of the world's biggest companies.[7] The country has also achieved positive societal changes. For instance, Indian divisions of some leading financial institutions such as HSBC, JPMorgan Chase, Royal Bank of Scotland, UBS and Fidelity International were headed by women. Women also accounted for about half of the deputy governors at the Reserve Bank of India.[8]

9.2.1. Entrepreneurship in the Indian ICT and Offshoring Sector

The story of India's entrepreneurial performance is incomplete without a reference to its offshoring sector. India has been a global capital of offshore ICT and the business process (BP) of offshore outsourcing. According to a study, six of the world's ten leading cities for offshoring are in India.[9]

India's offshoring industry started from back office works, moved to BP and is gradually shifting toward high-end functions such as R&D. To illustrate this point one may think of the drug industry. Many US-based drug companies are outsourcing drug development processes to India. One estimate suggested that developing a drug in India costs on average about US$100 million compared with over US$1 billion in the US.[10]

India's business and technology services companies' revenues increased from US$4 billion in 1998 to US$108 billion in 2102. This sector accounted for 1.2 percent of national GDP in 1998, which increased to 6.4 percent in 2012.[11] India's entrepreneurial ICT firms are heavily export-oriented. The industry exports US$3.75 for every dollar earned in India. For the leading ICT company, Infosys, the domestic market accounts for only 1.2 percent of revenue.[12] According to NASSCOM, the export portion of the sector in 2011 was 26 percent of India's exports and 11 percent of services revenue.[13]

The unprecedented growth of this sector has generated opportunities for employment for millions of Indians and vastly improved their living standards. Direct employment created by this industry was estimated at 2.2. million in 2012.[14] The offshoring industry's indirect job creation was estimated to be eight million in 2009.[15]

In addition to making an economic impact, entrepreneurial activities in the offshoring sector have brought some positive societal changes. For instance, women have entered into new status hierarchies. In the offshoring industry, women account for 65 percent of the workforce, and 85 percent of those women work on night shifts. Call centers are breaking the societal taboos as men and women work together at night to meet the daylight needs of Westerners. In the state of Rajasthan, the law forbidding women to work after sunset was changed at the request of the outsourcing company, Genpact.[16]

9.2.2. Low Overall Entrepreneurial Performance

Despite all the hype surrounding entrepreneurship in India's ICT and offshoring sector, a closer look at the overall economy paints a different picture. The country falls behind many other developing economies on important indicators related to entrepreneurial activity. For instance, in terms of high-expectation business launchers per capita, India underperforms Brazil.[17] On the World Economic Forum's competitiveness index, India ranked forty-ninth in 2009.

The informal economy is substantial and increasing. The size of the informal and shadow economy as a proportion of official GDP was estimated to increase from 18.1 percent in 1988/1989 to 22.8 percent in 2000/2001.[18] Likewise, about 70 percent of the non-agricultural workforce is informally employed. If agricultural employment is included, this proportion rises to over 90 percent. Informality thus remains a pervasive characteristic of the Indian labor market.

Consider another indicator related to the impact of entrepreneurship—poverty reduction. According to the UNDP's Human

Development Report 2013, during 2002–2011, 32.7 percent of the population in the country lived on less than US$1.25 a day. The traditional economic sectors are disadvantaged and there has thus been very little progress in poverty reduction. While the Indian offshoring sector has been a vibrant and prosperous economy with a rapidly rising income driven by highly skilled human resources fostering high productivity and innovation, the rest of the economy mainly consists of poverty-stricken, unemployed and deprived masses of people.

9.2.3. Lack of Trickledown Effect and Signs of Oligarchic Capitalism

The benefits of economic growth are highly concentrated and disproportionately distributed to the wealthiest individuals—a handful of large companies—and have failed to trickle down to the poor.[19] About ten families are estimated to control more than 80 percent of the stock in the country's largest corporations.[20] According to the ADB, large Indian companies win most of the lucrative government contracts, hold power over the country's natural resources and have "privileged access to land". In a 2007 government survey of about 200,000 services firms in the formal and informal sectors, the top 0.2 percent accounted for about 40 percent of output.[21] Likewise, in 2011, the Bombay Stock Exchange (BSE) 100 index of the largest firms accounted for about 70 percent of Indian stock market value.[22]

The geographic concentration of entrepreneurial activity also deserves mention. The 2007 government survey noted above found that companies in two states—Maharashtra and Karnataka—accounted for about 50 percent of output.[23]

India obviously has some elements of a market economy and some elements of political democracy. However, the country lacks a true democratic market system. A report from the ADB suggested that the Indian economy has many characteristics of oligarchic capitalism and there is a possibility that this form of capitalism would consolidate further, the effect of which would be to slow long-term development.[24] As is characteristic of oligarchic capitalism, India has shown signs of adverse impact on incentives required for structural change as well as the state's reduced autonomy.[25]

Most Indian billionaires have built their wealth by using their economic power to secure favorable policies. One commentator noted: "While many Indian publicists and economists hail the 'Indian miracle' and classify India as an 'emerging world power' because of the high growth rates of the past five years, what really has transpired is the conversion of India into a billionaire's paradise."[26]

9.3. Determinants of Entrepreneurship

9.3.1. Regulatory Framework

Entrepreneurial firms are likely to thrive and act in socially responsible ways if there are strong and well-enforced legislation and regulations in place to ensure such behavior. In this regard, notwithstanding the existence of some essential elements of a democracy, the Indian political system has become inherently "unaccountable, corrupt, and unhinged from the normal bench marks voters use to assess their leaders". One scholar noted: "Corrupted as they are by the party system, India's institutions are incapable of enforcing accountability. India's elites tolerate a level of poor governance and abuse of power that has led to the collapse of democracy elsewhere."[27]

Beyond all that, in India, there are groups with the disposition to support traditional values, norms and institutions, which hamper entrepreneurial practices. Notwithstanding their support of modern values, the Indian government and court system have to settle for compromise, which means slower progress than they would like to see.

Indian court systems are overburdened and are characterized by procedural delays and red tape. The Bureau of Democracy, Human Rights and Labor's report, "Supporting Human Rights and Democracy: The US Record 2004–2005" noted: "poor enforcement of laws, especially at the local level, and the severely overburdened court system weaken the delivery of justice". According to the South Asia Human Rights Documentation Center, there was a backlog of 23.5 million cases in 2002. The court system is decentralized and is largely administered by states. National labor laws are administered at the state level.[28] Due to budget problems, the states have failed to comply with federal directives to upgrade legal infrastructure and court facilities.

Moving to the specific context of entrepreneurship, weak laws and inappropriate regulatory processes hinder efficient entrepreneurial behaviors. For instance, it is argued that corruption is likely to make state subsidies to entrepreneurship, such as the Israeli government's incentive to provide 80 percent of the first $500,000 for every idea identified, highly ineffective in India. It is speculated that such a model "will lead to favoritism, cronyism and corruption" in the country.[29]

According to the World Bank's Ease of Doing Business 2013 Report (www.doingbusiness.org/reports/global-reports/doing-business-2013), India ranked 132 out of the 185 economies considered in terms of the regulatory climate for entrepreneurship. To start a business, twelve procedures need to be completed which take twenty-seven days and cost 50 percent of the country's per capita income. According to the World Bank, it takes seven years to close a business in India compared to the OECD average of 1.7 years. Likewise, the average time to register property in South Asia is 106 days compared to the OECD average of twenty-five days. Moreover, companies with over a hundred employees require government permission to dismiss workers.[30]

Entrepreneurial and marketing activities are hindered by complex regulations. In the retail sector, for instance, there are barriers such as anti-hoarding laws and signboard licenses. Competition laws have not yet been introduced in some sectors of the Indian economy. For instance, in the Indian retail sector, the existing laws work against retailers and favor small mom and pop stores.[31]

9.3.2. Values, Culture and Skills

Entrepreneurial Culture

Societal norms that "permit variability in the choice of paths of life" are likely to promote entrepreneurial behavior.[32] A society's religions strongly dictate such a possibility. According to the 2001 census, Hinduism accounted for 80.5 percent of the Indian population. Islam is the second largest religion, practiced by 13.4 percent of the population. Hinduism and Islam have many similarities from the standpoint of entrepreneurship. Both promote fatalism and orientation toward the present or the past rather than the future.

The distinguishing mark of Hinduism, the most popular religion in India, is that it is centered around dharma (duty) and karma (a Sanskrit word that means "actions" or "deeds"). Furthermore, each individual's dharma and moral codes are specific to his/her caste of birth, which frequently lead to conflicting, confusing, misleading and often contradictory social and ethical values.[33] More importantly, many beliefs and values run counter to capitalism and entrepreneurship.[34]

Accepting one's destiny rather than trying to control life can be viewed as a central core of traditional cultural values in India. Reincarnation is an essential tenet of Hinduism, which maintains that if nothing wrong is done in this life, there are prospects for a better life next time.[35]

A distinguishing feature of Hinduism is its social structure based on the caste system, which has acted as a major barrier to entrepreneurship.[36] The studies of many researchers over the past few decades have indicated that various obligations associated with the Indian caste system make it more compelling and convenient to follow the family occupation rather than to launch a new venture. The caste system has thus hindered class mobility. Unsurprisingly, the Vaishya (the caste of merchants) and non-Hindu communities (such as Jains and Parsis) have historically dominated the Indian businesses community.

Entrepreneurship thrives in a society that places a high value on work and innovation. It is argued that work in itself is not valued in India. Observers also suggest that people work primarily because of emotional attachment to the workplace or as a favor to the supervisor or the employer.

Indian culture also places relatively less value on innovation and gradual improvements. For example, a belief among many people in India is that for the inner soul and mind, being passive and satisfied with the status quo is healthier than trying to improve the situation.[37] Moreover, Hinduism considers work as the performance of duty instead of the ambition to innovate or improve.[38]

Women entrepreneurs in India face additional obstacles. Some communities think that a respectable girl should not expose herself to outside influences. In traditional sectors, it is a taboo and probably hard to imagine young women working at night. During 1993–2001, 53 percent of adult Chinese worked, compared to 37.7 percent of Indians.[39]

This difference is largely due to lower female participation in work in India. Traditionally, women have not been allowed to work after sunset.

It is also argued that Hinduism has contributed to the promotion of corruption and hindered the country's anti-corruption efforts. First, it is suggested that Hinduism has a forgiving tendency and that Hindus are too lenient toward offenders. Second, the fatalistic orientation of Hindus is associated with the belief that the status quo cannot be changed, which is an obstacle to the fight against corruption.

Some argue that Indian society has a negative attitude toward entrepreneurship in general and especially toward failure as an entrepreneur. An executive of Google India noted:

> And don't even think about what will happen if you fail as an entrepreneur. Socially, you will have lost your eligibility for marriage until you get a job. Financially, you'll be saddled with loads of debt, and politically, good luck on somebody acknowledging your entrepreneurial endeavor as real work experience. With all these challenges, one wonders why anyone bothers trying to become an entrepreneur in India?[40]

Entrepreneurial Capabilities

Human development in the country has been slow. According to the UNDP's Human Development Report 2013 (http://hdr.undp.org/hdr4press/press/report/index.html), among the 25 and older population, only 26.6 percent of females and 50.4 percent of males had at least a secondary education. India's rank was 136th in the Human Development Index. The labor force participation rate was only 29 percent for women compared to 80.7 percent for men.

Although English is an official language in India, only a small proportion of graduates meet the standard required to interact with foreigners. This goes contrary to the widely held belief that India's huge English-speaking population will give it an edge over China and other rising nations in doing business with Western corporations.[41] Customers' complaints about difficulties understanding the operators forced some companies to relocate call centers from India to the Philippines.[42]

While India has some professionally run global companies such as Wipro, Infosys and TCS, these are exceptions rather than the norm. Overall, the country's management style is highly traditional.

Characteristics such as willingness to follow logical processes and attention to detail are virtually absent in the Indian work culture.[43] In the same vein, whereas Western countries have a time-is-money culture, Indians have a more flexible approach to deadlines.[44] Experts argue that the country needs to go far before a culture of modern and professional management emerges. Similarly, most businesses in the country perform poorly in terms of product quality, reliability and on-time delivery. Addressing this challenge may be no small feat.

That said, some Indian firms have made significant progress in adopting the culture of modern management. This is especially noticeable in the offshoring sector. In an attempt to address their clients' fear that customer data will be stolen and even sold to criminals, firms have enhanced security mechanisms. For instance, call center employees have to undergo security checks, although these checks are considered to be "undignified".[45] Firms have established biometric authentication controls for workers, and have banned cell phones, pens, paper and Internet/e-mail access for employees. Similarly, computer terminals at most offshoring firms lack hard drives, e-mail, CD-ROM drives, or other ways to store, copy or forward data. In general, Indian outsourcing firms monitor and analyze employee logs extensively.[46]

Finally, there have been some measures taken to develop entrepreneurial capabilities. In 2010, it was reported that India had around forty incubators, which mentored between four and twenty startups each.[47] One of these, Villgro was reported to have mentored sixty-four startups and invested US$740,000.[48]

9.3.3. Access to Finance, Market, R&D and Technology

Market Conditions
As noted above, the Indian economy has many characteristics of oligarchic capitalism, which have hindered SMEs' market access. Research has indicated that the 1991 reforms have had little or no effect in promoting SMEs and their development. A small number of well-connected industrialists have dominated the Indian economy and protected themselves from outside competition.[49]

It is also the case that various regulations hinder access to the domestic market in India. For instance, there are taxes for bringing goods into a state, for taking them out of a state as well as for moving them within a state.[50]

Perhaps the greatest advantage offered by India's big domestic market is that it has helped some Indian entrepreneurial firms to compete successfully in other developing markets. Indian companies are in a position to reconfigure their resources and adapt the business models used in the domestic market to operate successfully in other developing economies.[51] It is argued that Indian firms' capacity to deliver value for money in the domestic market has been an important source of competitive advantage to operating in Africa or other developing countries.

Physical Infrastructure   A lack of well-developed physical infrastructure has been a barrier to market access. Most roads are narrow. In 2007, there were only 1,500 trucks and one-third of perishable products were reported to have rotted before reaching their customers.[52] The GFC further hindered the development of India's infrastructure. In late 2008, reports indicated that about half of India's planned highway improvement projects, which were valued at over US$6 billion, could be delayed by two years.

Access to Finance

Access to finance has been a major barrier facing many potential entrepreneurs in India. An executive of Google India notes:

> A bank loan or angel investment is not impossible to get but extremely unlikely. Getting funding is even harder if, like most aspiring entrepreneurs, you are not from a top-tier university and don't have a family with deep-pockets. There are countless "micro-entrepreneurs" in Indian society who finance their own small businesses as a means to survival but don't have access to the capital necessary to grow them.[53]

Below we describe the situation regarding the common forms of entrepreneurial financing.

Bank Loans   India's state banks, which account for 70 percent of bank assets in the country, are a major source of financing for entrepreneurial firms.[54] The SBI is the country's largest lender. According to the July 2009 issue of the *Banker*, a *Financial Times* publication, SBI was the world's sixty-fourth largest bank. As of March 2009, SBI had 12,100 offices worldwide, over 150 million customers, a capital reserve of more than US$12 billion and a total business of US$273.6 billion.

That said, SBI is only about one-tenth of the size of China's biggest bank in terms of profits.[55] The state banks have done little to promote productive entrepreneurship in India. A complaint often heard is that business merits play a small role in loan disbursements.[56] Lending is disproportionately oriented toward powerful economic and political interests such as influential family-owned groups.

The Indian Stock and IPO Markets   In 2007, India ranked as having the world's ninth largest IPO market. India captured 3 percent of the global IPO market share in 2007.[57] In 2007, the total wealth of all companies listed on the Bombay Stock Exchange, measured in terms of cumulative market capitalization, was over US$1.7 trillion.[58]

According to Ernst & Young's Global IPO Trends 2012 report, there were forty IPO deals in the country in 2011, which raised US$1.2 billion and accounted for 3.3 percent of the global IPO. In recent years, poor returns have made IPO relatively unattractive for many Indian companies. One study indicated that stocks of 70 percent of companies that launched IPOs in 2010 were trading below their price in June 2011.[59]

Institutional investors such as pension funds and life insurance companies, which pool huge large sums of money and invest those in securities, property and other assets, account for about one-eighth of Indian stock market profits compared to over half in Western economies. State-backed firms are estimated to account for 40 percent of stock market profits in the country.[60]

VC Investments   The Indian VC industry is at a nascent stage of development. For one thing, VC culture is not well developed in India. Observers have noted that Indian entrepreneurs often fail to understand the reality that not all VC-funded companies are likely to achieve an IPO. While there is a greater likelihood of a VC-funded company exiting through an M&A than an IPO in the US, Indian entrepreneurs are less prepared for the M&A option.[61]

In recent years, India has become an increasingly attractive destination for VC investments. In a survey conducted by Deloitte in 2009, 12 percent of US-based VC investors considered India to be the most attractive market. The country ranked only behind China (42 percent) and the US (24 percent).[62] By 2008, US$8.5 billion in VC was invested in Indian startup companies, which compares with China's US$9.3 billion by that time.[63]

The Microfinance Industry The flourishing microfinance industry is perhaps the most notable feature of the Indian capital market. By early 2007, fifty million households had benefited from microfinance. By the end of 2009, SKS Microfinance, India's largest MFI, had 1,675 branches, which lent US$600 million to seven million customers. Private-equity firms and other investors have invested billions of dollars in microfinancing.

At the same time, some negative experiences related to microcredit have been reported. As of early 2010, over fifteen million borrowers in India owed microfinance debts of US$2.3 billion.[64] The average Indian household's debt to microfinance banks increased fivefold during 2005–2010. It was also reported that some borrowers used loans intended for business purposes to buy luxury items such as TVs and refrigerators.

In Chapter 3, we discussed the abusive behavior of micro-lenders and their engagement in activities that violated borrowers' human rights. In 2010, the government of Andhra Pradesh state made the accusation that the microfinance industry's aggressive collection tactics forced many borrowers to commit suicide. The government issued new rules for the functioning of the microfinance industry and almost all issued loans in the state were written off. This led to the strong decline of the microfinance industry. In recent years, the industry has been reported to be gradually reviving. It is estimated that the microfinance industry's outstanding loans in early 2013 were US$2–3 billion, which was significantly lower than the peak value of around $5 billion a few years before.[65]

Remittance Inflow   India receives more remittances than any other country. Remittances have led to the establishment of new businesses and social service organizations such as nursing homes and educational institutions. In January 2010, the Chief Minister of the state of Gujarat noted that the state's economy was growing despite the GFC due to "record-breaking investments made by the Indian diasporas".[66]

Domestic Savings and Informal Investments   Finally, domestic savings have also been an important source of investment. Household saving rates are showing increasing trends, comprising 34.7 percent of GDP in 2010.[67] As is the case in China and other Asian economies, the high savings rates in India can be attributed to income insecurity associated mostly with informal jobs. The high savings rate may therefore not automatically translate to a higher investment rate.

R&D- and Technology-related Factors
India's ICT adoption and usage rates have been relatively low compared to most countries. For instance, India's subscription rates of cellular and fixed phones, PC, the Internet and high speed broadband are well below China (Fig. 9.1). According to a study released by Google India in mid-2011, only two million of the country's thirty-five million SMEs were online.[68]

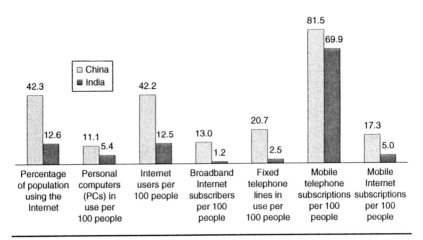

Figure 9.1 Comparing India's ICT usage indicators with China's (2012)
Source: Euromonitor International

Nonetheless, there have been some highly visible instances of ICT usage in promoting entrepreneurial activities. As a high-profile example, in October 2010, Intel announced an agreement with an alliance of seventy companies, including the BSE and CtrlS, to develop hardware and software for an open and interoperable cloud. The Open Data Center Alliance (ODCA) works to address security, energy efficiency and interoperability. The BSE expects that the new trading platforms supported by mobile telephony and clouds will broaden participation by allowing real-time, seamless access to data across phones, laptops and other devices. This approach would also deepen and widen traded asset classes. The new platforms will increase the participation of younger Indians in pension funds, insurance and mutual and other funds. The popularity of mobile-based cloud applications, in particular, is promising. Only eighty million Indians were online in early 2011, but more than 670 million used cell phones.

India's overall innovation and R&D profile is weak. Few of the businesses in India carry out the core R&D needed for cutting-edge products. As indicated in Fig. 9.2, India lags behind industrialized countries and its neighbor China in terms of the various indicators

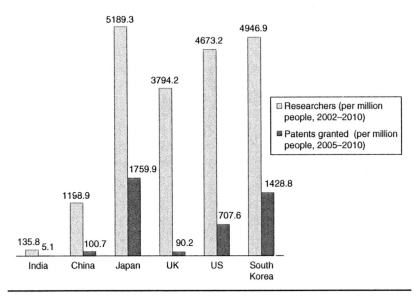

Figure 9.2 R&D and innovations profiles: comparing India with some major economies

Source: UNDP 2013 Human Development Report, http://www.undp.org/content/undp/en/home/librarypage/hdr/human-development-report-2013/

related to R&D and innovations. Due to India's poor R&D and innovation performance, some say entrepreneurial activities in the Indian
ICT and offshoring industry have a "hollow ring". An *Economist* article notes: "India makes drugs, but copies almost all of the compounds;
it writes software, but rarely owns the result . . . [it has] flourished, but
mostly on the back of other countries' technology."[69]

9.4. Concluding Comments

The 1991 economic reform facilitated and stimulated entrepreneurship in India. Its impact on the broad economy, however, has been
barely noticeable. While billionaires, oligarchs and state-owned
companies are benefiting from privileges, the playing field is not
level for SMEs and new venture startups, which face a host of barriers. Inappropriate regulatory elements and legal bottlenecks have
severely hampered productive entrepreneurial activities. Severe,
widespread poverty persists in the country while there is a great,
rising affluence among people working in the outsourcing sector.
In sum, we cannot really take the existence of a few entrepreneurial
firms in the Indian ICT sector as proof positive that India provides a
conducive environment for entrepreneurship. In fact, it is possible to
draw the opposite conclusion on the basis of the fact that very little
entrepreneurial impact is felt by the mass of the population. Moreover, many Indian entrepreneurs still struggle with a culture that
looks down on capitalism and is indifferent to hard work, improvement and innovation.

To some extent, the structural inertia of the Indian economy has
acted as a barrier to fostering modern entrepreneurship. India's heavy
reliance on agriculture, for instance, has resulted in constraints in
resources for entrepreneurial development. For instance, industry and
agriculture compete in the allocation of water between states, which
has created inter-state rivalries and tensions.[70]

9.5. Review Questions

1. What is the current state of the Indian microfinance industry?
   What are some of the negative effects of this industry?

2. Comment on the ADB observation that the Indian economy has many characteristics of oligarchic capitalism.
3. Why do some observers argue that the Israeli model of government funding for startups (note that 80 percent of the first US$500,000 for every idea identified is funded by the government in Israel) would be ineffective in India?
4. How would you rate India's R&D and innovations profile?

9.6. Critical Discussion Questions

1. Compare China and India in terms of various indicators related to entrepreneurship. Which country is better prepared to embrace the global movement towards entrepreneurship? Why?
2. Compare and contrast Hinduism and Islam (see Chapter 6) from the standpoint of entrepreneurship development.

9.7. End-of-chapter Case: The Entrepreneurial Chief Minister and Andhra Pradesh State's Emergence as a Global ICT Hub

Thanks to initiatives taken by Chief Minister Chandrababu Naidu, in a short period of time, the state of Andhra Pradesh has become Asia's major ICT hub as well as a significant producer, consumer and exporter of ICT products. HITEC city at Hyderabad, the capital of AP, is Asia's largest software technology complex; it houses Microsoft's development facility and the operations of global companies such as Infosys, Oracle, Dell, GE Capital, IBM, Motorola, Ericsson, Citicorp, Baan/Invensys and HSBC.

AP's entrepreneurial initiatives were perceived as successful when Naidu gained popularity abroad and at home. The impacts were shared across India and the world. Many teams from other Indian states and developing countries visited Hyderabad to learn how they could adapt AP's development model to their economies.

Formal and Regulative Institutions Behind AP's Entrepreneurial Success

AP Government's Efficiency
The AP government led by Naidu was well known for efficiency. When Microsoft wanted to open a software development center at

Hyderabad, it was reported that the AP government responded to some of Microsoft's demands within a single day, even though that day was a holiday. This led to Microsoft's decision to open such a center in 1998. In the same year, Microsoft launched its Indian Development Center (IDC) at Hyderabad for the development of core technologies such as Windows NT and Microsoft Back office.

To attract investments, the AP government also started two mega-projects: Cyber City and HITEC City. Cyber City consisted of 10 acres for industrialists, where the government provided minimum infrastructure. By 1997, companies such as SQL Star, Infotech, Info-systems and Intelli Group Asia were allotted land. The AP Industrial Infrastructure Development Corporation (APIIDC) and Larsen and Tubro jointly developed HITEC City adjacent to Cyber City. The US$850 million, ten-story building became the largest of its kind in India.

Naidu also appropriately combined marketing, networking and promotion to locate and attract ideal partners. On the home front, for instance, in 2000 he set up an IT Steering Committee to advise AP on e-governance and persuaded India's three leading IT entrepreneurs—Azim Premji of Wipro, N.R. Narayana Murthy of Infosys and Rama-linga Raju of Satyam Computers—to come on board. In September 1998, he visited the US and met the World Bank President, the governor of New Jersey and high-ranking officials of IBM, Microsoft, GE, HP, Sun Microsystems, Cisco, Teledesic, Oracle, Morgan Stanley, DII of San Francisco, Oxbridge, Invensye Technologies, Cybertech International, Stevedoring Services of America and AMOCO. Naidu also visited Japan and China in 2000 and focused on attracting investments in the hardware sector.

Bureaucrats' Responses
ICT threatened bureaucrats' jobs and were perceived as incompatible with their daily routines including extracting bribes. They vigorously opposed Naidu's IT plans and protested against computerization by threatening an indefinite strike in 1999. Naidu, however, motivated the bureaucrats to champion IT usage in their departments. The resistive force from the bureaucrats not only disappeared but transformed

into one of the strongest drivers of AP's IT development process. This was because of compensatory rewards such as strong support and recognition from the chief minister and likely approbation from the public.

Naidu gave publicity to people associated with IT projects and achieved results through them. Many bureaucrats were labeled as ex-officio IT secretaries. They shared common platforms of views on IT issues and spoke the same language in public forums.[71] Such parallelism had reinforcing and cementing effects on the different groups of stakeholders.

Eliminating Structural Sources of Inefficiency
Unlike his predecessors, Naidu did not like to draw crowds or generate emotional appeal. He also took decisions that went against the value system of Indian politicians. To take one example, in February 1999, the AP government decided that the Indian Institute of Information Technology (IIIT) would not reserve places for the Backward and Scheduled classes and would strictly adhere to admissions based on merit.

Environmental Conditions for AP's Entrepreneurial Success

Ingredients of Entrepreneurship Development
After a detailed assessment of several countries as locations for its new product development center, Microsoft chose India. In a comparison of seven Indian cities on twenty factors, Hyderabad scored the highest. With 7 percent of India's population, AP accounted for 23 percent of software professionals in India[72] and more than 39 percent of Indian software professionals working in the US.[73]

New problems in India's major ICT hub Bangalore, including congested roads, increasing rents and power outages, started becoming more commonplace. Companies that had not established a presence in India started looking elsewhere to set up operations. They viewed Hyderabad as a viable alternative. By 1997, global companies such as Baan Info Systems, Citicorp, D.E. Shaw and Freesoft had operations in AP.

STP Units Established

In software technology park (STP) units, 100 percent of export-oriented firms get tax-free status for five years of their first eight years of operation, and can import hardware duty free. The scheme became operational in 1988 and three STP units were established in 1990 in Bangalore, Bhubaneshwar and Pune. At the time AP lacked strong leadership and the benefits of the IT-friendly policies of central government accrued to other Indian states.

The Effect of the 1991 Liberalization

In 1991, India issued a new industrial policy statement which welcomed FDI in industrial development. It abolished import licensing and brought in measures to lower tariff and non-tariff barriers. The highest tariff rate came down to 45 percent and the average to less than 25 percent. The policy reforms of the mid-1980s mainly facilitated body shopping on-site (Indian programmers working at the client site). The shift to offshore production, allowing the programmers to work at facilities in India, was possible following the 1991 reforms, particularly with the removal of the need for licenses on imports of industrial equipment and with the establishment of STPs.[74]

In the "quasi-federation" Indian political structure, central government has exceptional powers but state governments have a high degree of independence on state-level policies. Before the 1991 liberalization, virtually all important decisions were centralized. For instance, it was reported that to get a business license, some entrepreneurs had to make thirty or forty trips to Delhi over a period of two years. The 1991 reform also led to the significant decentralization of power. Licenses were no longer needed to import most products and a company could get a license in half a day in the same city.

Attracting Foreign Multinationals

During the visit of Microsoft's then CEO Bill Gates to India in March 1997, Naidu talked to Gates about his vision of the role of ICT in government, and his dream of Hyderabad as a global ICT hub. In October 1997, Gates offered to provide the help of a Microsoft senior manager to help AP firm up its IT programs. Gates wrote: "I am personally excited about your Information Technology Vision Group for Andhra Pradesh. As a software technology leader, I believe we can contribute to this group. If you agree, I would be happy to nominate one of my senior managers to participate in this group."

In November 1997, the AP government signed an agreement with Microsoft to establish the Microsoft School for Software Technology (MSST) as part of the IIIT. MSST is South Asia's first competency center for software, systems and application engineering skills. The AP government agreed to provide the necessary infrastructure for Microsoft through IIIT. Microsoft installed state-of-the-art requisite systems and provided highly skilled and qualified trainers for the school. Microsoft planned to train 1,500 people at the MSST in three years.

The software development center at Hyderabad developed rapidly. In April 2000, Microsoft's IDC Hyderabad launched its Microsoft Windows Services for UNIX 2.0 (SFU2.0). It was completely designed and developed in IDC Hyderabad for the global market.[75] IDC Hyderabad also developed Microsoft Windows SFU 3.0.

During his visit to AP in September 2000, Gates announced a US$50-million investment in IDC Hyderabad. He also committed US$1 million per year for five years to promote India's rural IT education program. Gates again visited India in November 2002 and announced a US$400-million investment in India, with US$100 million of that to go to IDC Hyderabad.

Microsoft's entry strengthened AP's importance in the global IT map and triggered a chain reaction. Shortly after Microsoft's decision, Oracle decided to invest in HITEC City. In June 1998, Oracle announced its decision to invest US$10 million in AP. In October 2002, Oracle announced its plan to invest US$20 million over five years. The fully developed facility was expected to house 3,000 professionals, primarily involved in e-business application development for the company's global customer base.[76] The Oracle School of Advanced Technology was a part of the company's technical education initiative.

In February 1999, the AP government and London-based WorldTel entered into an MoU to develop Internet community centers in AP, aimed at providing information to common citizens at affordable rates. Motorola started a new software center for designing the next generation wireless solutions with emphasis on cellular handsets, 3G systems and network management solutions for satellite communication, with sixty professionals. It invested US$5 million in the first year of operation. The Hyderabad software center became one of ten Motorola software centers around the world.[77]

In 1999, the AP Industrial Infrastructure Corporation Ltd (APIIC) and GE capital signed an MoU to provide 30 acres of land to establish an ICT-enabled services facility. In the same year, Ericsson commissioned its new software design center in Hyderabad to design and develop software for its new generation of Internet and networking products. By 2000, IBM, Lumley Technology, Toshiba, Metamor, Baan, D.E. Shaw and Ericsson had operations in Hyderabad. HSBC set up its software development center and disaster management and customer services center there.

Development Activities Excluded the Rural Part of the State

While the capital city of Hyderabad was home to over 95 percent of the IT units, the rest of the state—which had the majority of voters—did not see too many percolating benefits. They voted Naidu out. The economic success and IT agglomeration that Naidu had created, however, had a momentum of their own, and AP continues to grow as a major IT hub.

The majority of the population that depended on agriculture for their livelihood opposed Naidu's plans. Naidu's neglect of agriculture development and his focus on the ICT industry cost him the election in 2004. A rural woman who voted against Naidu said: "He did nothing for us, only for those in the cities. We're happy that he's gone."[78] Y. S. Rajashekha Reddy, who replaced Naidu, said: "We stand committed to their [the peoples'] development, to mitigate their sufferings. Mr. Naidu only made five percent of the population richer. We raised the farmers' issue in the assembly, and Naidu ignored it."[79]

Conclusion

A SWOT analysis conducted by Baan in the mid-1990s had indicated that it was important for Hyderabad to overcome its poor image in order to attract foreign investors. A Baan executive said: "Hyderabad can achieve a quantum leap only if a leader like IBM comes here. Then one will see the multiplier effect."[80] In this case study we have discussed a number of measures on the part of the AP government that led to the improved image of Hyderabad and AP state.

The AP story provides a classic example of the dynamics possible in the entrepreneurship landscape of an emerging economy that has a capable and entrepreneurial government. This case also highlights a number of barriers to entrepreneurship in a developing economy and provides insight into how some of them may be overcome. To acquire the critically missing component—capital—the government employed marketing, networking and promotion and expedited decision-making processes. The government was also able to invent hidden resources, such as AP's strategic location, and sell them to potential investors.

Notes

1. Huang, Y. 2008, "The Next Asian Miracle" *Foreign Policy*, (167), pp. 32–40.
2. World Bank 2008, *Doing Business 2008: India, Bhutan, and Sri Lanka Lead South Asia's Jump in Reform*, Geneva: World Bank.
3. Majumdar, S.K. 2004, "The Hidden Hand and the License Raj to an Evaluation of the Relationship between Age and the Growth of Firms in India", *Journal of Business Venturing*, 19, pp. 107–125.
4. Kumar, N., Mohapatra, P.K., & Chandrasekhar, S. 2009, "Challenges for Indian Multinationals—The Global Future", HBS Press chapter, October 26, at http://harvardbusinessonline.hbsp.harvard.edu/b02/en/common/item_detail.jhtml;jsessionid=D5WRHOBIDCOVMAKRGWDR5VQBKE0YIISW?id=6745BC&_requestid=50809.
5. UNDP 2008, *Human Development Report 2007/2008: Fighting Climate Change: Human Solidarity in a Divided World*, New York: UNDP, at http://hdr.undp.org/en/media/HDR_20072008_EN_Complete.pdf (retrieved March 15, 2010).
6. Foulis, P. 2011, "Adventures in Capitalism: Indian Businesses are Rewriting the Rules of Capitalism in a Distinctive and Unexpected Way", October 22, *Economist*, www.economist.com/node/21532448.

7. DeCarlo, S. 2013, "The World's Biggest Companies", April 17, at www. forbes.com/sites/scottdecarlo/2013/04/17/the-worlds-biggest-compa nies-2/.

8. Wadhwa, V. 2010, "Addressing the Dearth of Female Entrepreneurs", *BloombergBusiness Week*, February 4, at www.businessweek.com/technol ogy/content/feb2010/tc2010023_986637.htm.

9. economist.com 2013, "On the Turn", January 19, at www.economist. com/news/special-report/21569571-india-no-longer-automatic-choice- it-services-and-back-office-work-turn.

10. Yusuf, S., & Nabeshima, K. 2006, *Post-Industrial East Asian Cities: Innovation for Growth*, Stanford, CA: Stanford University Press.

11. washingtonpost.com 2013, "US Immigration Bill's New Visa Rules Could Slow Indian Outsourcing Juggernaut", April 23.

12. *Economist* 2009, "Reforming through the Tough Times", September 12, p. 71.

13. Hindu Business Line 2011, "India's Low-cost BPO Tag Helps Draw Global Investors: E&Y", June 6, www.thehindubusinessline.com/indus try-and-economy/info-tech/article2082418.ece?homepage=true.

14. washingtonpost.com 2013, "US Immigration Bill's New Visa Rules Could Slow Indian Outsourcing Juggernaut", April 23, www.washingtonpost. com/business/us-immigration-bills-new-visa-rules-could-slow-indian- outsourcing-juggernaut/2013/04/23/d5a76360-abf7-11e2-9493- 2ff3bf26c4b4_story.html (retrieved April 23, 2013).

15. NASSCOM 2009, *Nasscom Strategic Review 2009: Executive Summary*, November 25, at www.nasscom.in/sites/default/files/upload/60452/Exec utive_summary.pdf.

16. Wadhwa, V. 2009, "Lessons from a New Industry Cluster in India", *Bloomberg Business Week*, December 30, at www.businessweek.com/small biz/content/dec2009/sb20091230_959975.htm.

17. Lewis, G. 2007, "Who in the World is Entrepreneurial?", *FSB: Fortune Small Business*, 17(5), p. 14.

18. Bajada, C., & Schneider, F. 2005, "The Shadow Economies of the Asia- Pacific", *Pacific Economic Review*, 10(3), pp. 379–401.

19. UNDP 2008, *Human Development Report 2007/2008: Fighting Climate Change: Human Solidarity in a Divided World*, New York: UNDP, at http:// hdr.undp.org/en/media/HDR_20072008_EN_Complete.pdf (retrieved March 15, 2010).

20. Malhotra, H.B. 2009, "Oligarchic Capitalism May Take Hold in India", *Epoch Times*, September 22, at www.theepochtimes.com/n2/content/ view/22829/.

21. Foulis, P. 2011, "Adventures in Capitalism: Indian Businesses are Rewriting the Rules of Capitalism in a Distinctive and Unexpected Way", October 22, *Economist*, www.economist.com/node/21532448.

22. Ibid.

23. Ibid.

24. Malhotra, H.B. 2009, "Oligarchic Capitalism May Take Hold in India", *Epoch Times*, September 22, at www.theepochtimes.com/n2/content/view/22829/.
25. EMF 2009, *India 2039: An Affluent Society in One Generation*, at www.emergingmarketsforum.org/papers/pdf/2009-EMF-India-Report_Overview.pdf.
26. Petras, J. 2008, "Global Ruling Class: Billionaires and How they 'Make It'", *Journal of Contemporary Asia*, 38(2), pp. 319–329.
27. Yester, K. 2010, "India Plays Catch-up", *Foreign Policy*, July 26, at www.foreignpolicy.com/articles/2008/08/12/india_plays_catch_up#sthash.LdLmj6mI.dpbs.
28. Deloitte 2006, *China and India: The Reality Beyond the Hype*, Deloitte Development LLC.
29. Shah, H.J. 2010, "Valuate the India Opportunity through Incubators, Demographics and PEG", *India Chief Mentor*, March 9, at http://blogs.wsj.com/india-chief-mentor/2010/03/09/valuate-the-india-opportunity-through-incubators-demographics-and-peg/.
30. Deloitte 2006, *China and India: The Reality Beyond the Hype*, Deloitte Development LLC.
31. *Economist* 2008, "Business: Unshackling the Chain Stores", 387(8582), p. 80.
32. Hoselitz, B.F. 1960, *Sociological Aspects of Economic Growth*, New York: Free Press.
33. Elliot, J. 1998, "Held Back by Hindu Gods?" *New Statesman*, 127(414), p. 28.
34. Dana, L.P. 2000, "Creating Entrepreneurs in India", *Journal of Small Business Management*, 38(1), pp. 86–91.
35. Elliot, J. 1998, "Held Back by Hindu Gods?" *New Statesman*, 127(414), p. 28.
36. Dana, L.P. 2000, "Creating Entrepreneurs in India", *Journal of Small Business Management*, 38(1), pp. 86–91.
37. Ibid.
38. Elliot, J. 1998, "Held Back by Hindu Gods?" *New Statesman*, 127(414), p. 28.
39. Deloitte 2006, *China and India: The Reality Beyond the Hype*, Deloitte Development LLC.
40. Gandhi, G. 2010, "Indian Entrepreneurs Need a Hug: Google's Gandhi", February 16, at http://blogs.wsj.com/india-chief-mentor/2010/02/16/indian-entrepreneurs-need-a-hug-google percentE2 percent80 percent99s-gandhi/.
41. Mehta, S.N. 2005, "India on the March", *Fortune*, 152(2), pp. 191–193.
42. Fairell, D., Kaka, N., & Stürze, S. 2005, "Ensuring India's Offshoring Future", *McKinsey Quarterly* (Special Edition), pp. 74–85.
43. Piramal, G. 2004, "In Depth Offshoring: In My Opinion", *European Business Forum*, 19, pp. 40–41.
44. Slater, J. 2003, "India's Nifty Number-crunchers", *Far Eastern Economic Review*, October 2, p. 7.
45. *Economist* 2005, "Business: Busy Signals; Indian Call Centers", September 10, 376(8443), p. 66.

46. Fest, G. 2005, "Offshoring: Feds Take Fresh Look at India BPOs", *Bank Technology News*, 18(9), p. 1.
47. Chaudhary, D. 2010, "Start-ups in Fund Trouble, even as Incubators Hike Early-stage Funding", *Live Mint*, January 25, at www.livemint.com/Money/miteX1LHbGb8RP0gRaBknO/Startups-in-fund-trouble-even-as-incubators-hike-earlysta.html.
48. economist.com 2013, "Contacts and Commitment", April 1, www.economist.com/blogs/schumpeter/2013/04/start-up-incubators-india.
49. Weitzman, H. & Fontanella-Khan, J. 2011, "US and India: The Squeeze on Small Business", May 31, at www.ft.com/cms/s/0/33de9812–8b8f–11e0–8c09–00144feab49a.html#axzz2mzkbFSpe.
50. *Economist* 2008, "Business: Unshackling the Chain Stores", 387(8582), p. 80.
51. *Harvard Business Review* 2009, "The New Frontiers", 87(7), pp. 130–137.
52. Hamm, S., & Lakshman, N. 2007, "Widening Aisles for Indian Shoppers", *Business Week*, April 30, p. 44.
53. Gandhi, G. 2010, "Indian Entrepreneurs Need a Hug: Google's Gandhi", *Wall Street Journal*, February 16, 2010, at http://blogs.wsj.com/india-chief-mentor/2010/02/16/indian-entrepreneurs-need-a-hug-google%E2%80%99s-gandhi/.
54. *Economist* 2009, "Reforming through the Tough Times", September 12, p. 71.
55. Foulis, P. 2011, "Adventures in Capitalism: Indian Businesses are Rewriting the Rules of Capitalism in a Distinctive and Unexpected Way", October 22, *Economist*, www.economist.com/node/21532448.
56. Bikchandani, S. 2010, "Israel Model Will Not Work in India", March 10, at http://blogs.wsj.com/india-chief-mentor/2010/03/10/israel-model-will-not-work-in-india/.
57. businessstandard.com 2007, "India Ranks 9th in Global IPOs", *Business Standard*, November 2.
58. economictimes.com 2007, "India's Market Cap Crosses Rs 70 Trillion Mark", December 30, at http://economictimes.indiatimes.com/news/economy/indicators/Indias-market-cap-crosses-Rs–70-trillion-mark/articleshow/2662275.cms.
59. Kohli, D. 2011, "Some Investors Keeping away from IPOs in Indian Market", June 20, at www.channelnewsasia.com/stories/marketnews/view/1136181/1/.html (retrieved 20 June 2007).
60. economist.com 2011, "Building India Inc: A Weak State Has Given Rise to a New Kind of Economy", October 22, at www.economist.com/node/21533396www.economist.com/node/21533396.
61. Tagare, P. 2011, "India's Entrepreneurs Need to See Beyond IPOs", *Wall Street Journal*, June 7, http://online.wsj.com/article/SB10001424052702304432304576370803985701380.html?mod=googlenews_wsj.
62. Deloitte 2009, *Global Trends in Venture Capital: 2009 Global Report*, Deloitte Touche Tohmatsu.
63. Fannin, R. 2010, "India: The Gap Is Narrowing", *Forbes*, March 10, at www.forbes.com/2010/03/09/google-twitter-facebook-intelligent-technology-india.html?boxes=Homepagechannels.

64. Kalesh, B. 2010, "SKS Microfinance Gets Venture Capitalists as Promoters for IPO", March 10, at www.livemint.com/2010/03/10205245/SKS-Microfinance-gets-venture.html.

65. economist.com 2013, "Road to Redemption", Jan 12, at www.economist.com/news/finance-and-economics/21569447-industry-starting-revive-road-redemption.

66. mangalorean.com 2010, "Gujarat Gained from Investments by Indian Diaspora", January 9, http://mangalorean.com/news.php?newstype=broadcast&broadcastid=163822.

67. Power, C. 2010. "Savers and Spenders: How Household Savings Stack Up in Asia, the West, and Latin America", June 10, www.businessweek.com/magazine/content/10_25/b4183010451928.htm

68. Narasimhan, T.E. 2011, "57% of SMEs Use Internet as Sales Channel, Finds Survey", June 21, www.business-standard.com/india/news/57smes-use-internet-as-sales-channel-finds-survey/439821/.

69. *Economist* 2007, "Imitate or Die; Technology in China and India", 385(8554), p. 9.

70. UNDP 2008, *Human Development Report* 2007/2008: Fighting Climate Change: Human Solidarity in a Divided World, New York: UNDP, at http://hdr.undp.org/en/media/HDR_20072008_EN_Complete.pdf (retrieved March 15, 2010).

71. Bhatnagar, S. 1999, "What Can We Learn from Andhra Pradesh?", *Information Technology in Developing Countries*, 9(3).

72. Ramachandraiah, C., & Bawa, V.K. 2000, "Hyderabad in the Changing Political Economy", *Journal of Contemporary Asia*, 30(4), pp. 562–574.

73. Prasanna, S. 2001, "Hardware Sector to be a Growth Engine", *Express Computer Online*, at www.expresscomputeronline.com/20010827/andhra_1.html (retrieved August 2001).

74. Saxenian, A. 2000, "Bangalore: The Silicon Valley of Asia?", Conference on Indian Economic Prospects: Advancing Policy Reform, Center for Research on Economic Development and Policy Reform, Stanford, CA, at www.stanford.edu/group/siepr/cgi-bin/siepr/?q=system/files/shared/pubs/papers/pdf/credpr91.pdf.

75. rediff.com 2002, "Microsoft to Invest $50 Million in Hyderabad Center", January 3.

76. Reddy, C.P. 2002, "Oracle Buys 8 Acres in Hitec City", *Hindu Business Line*, October 23, at www.thehindubusinessline.com/bline/2002/10/24/stories/2002102401330700.htm.

77. *Computer Today* 1999, "Motorola, Microsoft Set Up SW Centers in Hyderabad", March 16, at www.india-today.com/ctoday/16031999/buzz.html (retrieved March 16, 1999).

78. Adiga, A. 2004, "The Face of Reform", *Time*, May 31, www.time.com/time/asia/magazine/article/0,13673,501040531–641208,00.html.

79. *India Travel Times*, "YSR Elected CLP Leader, To Take Over As Andhra CM, May 15", May 12, at www.indiatraveltimes.com/news/news2004/may04/may1204_poll.html.

80. *Business India* 1997, "Hyderabad Goes Hi-tech", March.

Appendix 1

Integrative Cases (ICs)

IC1: Entrepreneurship in the Brazilian Offshoring and Outsourcing Industry

Brazil has made it clear that it wants to compete with India in the development of the offshoring and outsourcing industry. Some recent indicators suggest that the country's offshoring industry has made significant progress. In a survey of US-based firms conducted by the Aberdeen Group, Brazil ranked third, only behind China and India, in terms of its attractiveness as a global outsourcing destination.[1]

The indicators presented in Table A1.1 relate to the development of the offshoring industry, which compare the four BRIC economies. Brazil's outsourcing industry is relatively small compared to other BRIC economies but is growing rapidly. Brazil exported about US$400 million in software and IT services in 2004, which is increased to US$5 billion in 2010.[2] According to IDC, Brazilian call center revenues grew by 16.7 percent in 2009 to US$7.8 billion.[3] In 2010, call center revenues increased by an estimated 11 percent and the call center workforce by 13.3 percent.[4]

Brazilian firms have secured such clients as Whirlpool, Gap and GE for business process outsourcing (BPO) and information technology outsourcing (ITO). Brazil represents 50 percent of BT's Latin American business.[5] In particular, US companies are combining call and IT centers in Brazil with those in India and other locations. For instance, in 2004, IBM revealed plans to send a large number of highly skilled programming jobs to Brazil. In June 2010, IBM opened an R&D center in Brazil, its first in Latin America. Similarly, Lilly is expanding clinical trials on human patients in Brazil.[6] Other firms with a significant presence in Brazil include Affiliated Computer Services (ACS), Sakonnet and Fidelity National Information Services.

A Review of the Brazilian Offshoring and Outsourcing Industry

As of mid-2010, Brazil had an estimated 4,000 indigenous IT companies.[7] Multinationals such as IBM, Accenture, HP, Electronic Data Systems, Intel, Microsoft, Cisco, HSBC, BT, Motorola, Dell, Siemens, Unisys, Exxon Mobil, and Johnson & Johnson have operations there.

The software and IT services industry in Brazil generated over US$29.4 billion (software sector: US$3.2 billion, services: US$10 billion, and hardware: US$16.2 billion) in 2008, making the country eighth largest in the world. In comparison with the Latin American market, which is estimated at US$61 billion, Brazil had a 48 percent share in 2008.[8] In 2008, the country's domestic IT-BPO market generated US$59.1 billion and the total IT market was US$139.1 billion.[9]

The Brazilian call center industry has made heavy investments in infrastructure as well as skill. It is observed: "After years of investment Brazil is better poised than China or India to address the full spectrum of IT outsourcing needs."[10]

In terms of size distribution, Brazil's fourteen large companies and nine subsidiaries of multinationals account for 88 percent and thirty companies account for 90 percent of software exports.[11] Brazil's structural composition in terms of size is similar to that of Russia[12] and China. That is, most Brazilian companies are much smaller than their Indian counterparts, thus limiting their capability to handle large outsourcing projects. For instance, in 2009, Brazil's biggest IT provider, Politec had just over 7,000 employees, fifteen technology centers and fifteen branch offices[13] compared to the Indian company Tata Consultancy Services' (TCS) employment size of over 160,000 in March 2010.

A study conducted by McKinsey Global Institute showed that multinationals' executives value a stronger infrastructure such as ports, roads and reliable telecommunications and network services rather than government incentives. In this regard, Brazil's well-developed infrastructure was a major factor for a North American airline's move toward a vendor in the country. As of 2010, Brazil had eighteen fully operational technology parks and an additional twelve were in the final stages of implementation.[14]

Determinants of Entrepreneurship in the Brazilian Offshoring and Outsourcing Industry

Table A1.1 compares the BRIC economies on major determinants of entrepreneurship in the offshoring and outsourcing. In this section, we discuss them in terms of the framework developed in Chapter 1.

Regulatory Framework

Brazil's judicial system is arguably comparable to that of the US. Brazil has the highest Regulatory Quality index of the four economies and its Rule of Law index is second only to India. The lowest FDI Restrictive Index scores indicates that Brazil is the most open economy for FDI among the four BRIC economies. Brazil also has the highest overall Economic Freedom index among the four BRIC economies.

The Brazilian federal government's Productive Development Policy (PDP) launched in May 2008 considered the software and IT services industry to be strategic. There are various financial incentives to encourage the development of the offshoring sector. Companies established in technology parks do not need to pay property taxes and receive discounts on service taxes. In addition to the 50 percent reduction in excise tax to purchase R&D equipment and the 100 percent deduction to import software development materials, spending on staff training and R&D are eligible for an income tax deduction of 200 percent.[15]

Among the negative aspects of Brazil's regulatory environment are the labor laws. Employment costs in Brazil tend to be high because of regulations such as constraints on firing workers. Moreover, restrictions on hiring temporary workers prevent businesses from adjusting their workforces to account for fluctuations in demand.

Values, Culture and Skills

Cultural Compatibility with Major Clients   One of Brazil's strengths is its culture. Latin America's culture is closer to that of the US compared to India's. Speaking of cultural similarity between the US and Brazil, Carlos Diaz, vice president of Pan-America, global accounts officer for Meta4 and an expert on HR issues in Latin America noted: "The countries share many cultural references—music, movies, television shows, etc. . . . You wouldn't have to explain who Mickey Mouse is to a Brazilian, but that may not necessarily the case when it comes to somebody from India."[16]

Cultural compatibility is important because even those with a good command of English may not understand the cultural contexts and business practices of a client firm. Brazil's potential as an outsourcing venue is connected with a culture that is similar to that of the West in terms of race, religion and family lifestyle. In addition, Brazilian companies emphasize teamwork in software development projects. Brazilians arguably also understand Western business rules and environments better than the citizens of other BRIC economies. Experts say that a greater understanding of the business context is especially important for higher-value outsourcing jobs that require interaction with clients.

Brazilians can provide services in English, Spanish, German, Italian and even Japanese, as a result of twentieth-century migrations to the country. Brazil has the second-largest number of English speakers (10.2 million) behind India.[17] While Russians and Chinese use alphabets different from those used in most Western languages, Brazilians share their alphabet with the West. In light of the growing Hispanic market in the US, Brazilian contact centers can also serve Spanish-speaking US regions.

Skills Needed for the Industry Brazil has an IT expertise pool of about 1.7 million people. The country's 1,714 IT-related technical and graduate courses produce 100,000 graduates annually.[18] In 2008, its universities produced more than 220,000 graduates.[19] A *Time* magazine article asserted that Brazil's 123 national institutes of science and 400 incubators are key components of the entrepreneurial ecosystem.[20] Moreover, the trade association, BRASSCOM is providing IT-specific English proficiency courses to sector professionals. Big cities such as São Paulo have an abundant supply of young people with engineering and business skills and English-language proficiency. They possess skills required for a wide range of activities outsourced by US companies, such as programming for banking software, developing video games and analyzing mortgage defaults. Brazil also has more Java programmers than any other country and the world's second largest number of mainframe COBOL programmers.[21] Note that COBOL programmers are still in demand in banks. Finally, Brazil's local IT staff turnover is estimated at 20 percent compared to India's 40 percent.[22]

While some observe that Indians perform better in the "academic understanding of products",[23] Brazilian firms' have the advantages in some industries. In aerospace, for instance, Brazilian firms' expertise far exceeds that of other developing economies. The Brazilian firm Embraer is the world's largest maker of regional jets and has become a serious challenger to the low-end Boeing 737 and Airbus A318 aircraft models. Brazilian firms are also ahead of Indian firms in delivering product quality.

Access to Finance, Market, R&D and Technology

The Domestic Market While India has developed a strong export-oriented software sector, the Brazilian software sector, like China's, grew primarily to meet the needs of domestic firms. Brazilian IT firms have focused on serving a well-developed, sophisticated domestic market for over fifty years.

IT accounts for about 7 percent of Brazil's GDP. Of the four BRIC economies, Brazil has the greatest per capita domestic spending in application and personal software. Experts note that "local companies are the ace card for Brazil".[24]

Brazil's banks are arguably among the world's most automated. Brazilian technology vendors are experienced in providing sophisticated IT solutions to local financial institutions. In the early 1990s, Brazilian banks developed sophisticated, efficient, and reliable fund-management software to deal with hyperinflation.[25]

In the early 2000s, the country switched to electronic voting machines in all elections and became one of the world's first to adopt electronic voting.[26] Similarly, tens of millions of Brazilians file their tax returns online.[27] In addition, manufacturing firms in chemicals, pharmaceuticals and cosmetics, plastics, paper and textiles are also driving substantial IT spending growth.

A final source of externality concerns knowledge about quality and the value perceptions of consumers. A study found that Brazil has caught up with, or surpassed, Italy in "reliable product quality", "speed of response", "punctual delivery" and "flexibility in coping with changes in large orders".[28] As service quality is important in outsourcing, Brazil's experience and expertise in delivering high-quality products can produce potentially important externalities.

Access to Foreign Markets
The export orientation of Brazilian firms is a key contribution to Brazil's success in the growth of the offshoring and outsourcing industry. Like China, Brazil has emerged as a manufacturing hub for consumer durables such as televisions, cars and computers. These products are exported to the US, Japan, and Europe. Brazilian companies are thus relatively well versed in the export business. Brazilian firms in the offshoring and outsourcing industry are taking measures to improve export orientation and global brand performance. A group of Brazilian companies created Brazil IT, a brand name for the US market. Among other things, these companies have sponsored trade shows in the US. In 2005, another group of companies created BRASSCOM, which hired McKinsey/AT Kearney Consulting to devise international strategies. Softex, a group of over a hundred companies, has launched an ambitious three-year global marketing program.

One observation, however, is that Brazilian IT companies are less aggressive on export orientation than their Russian counterparts. For instance, every third Russian company has sales/representative offices in North America and over one-third of software developers have sales offices in Western Europe.[29]

Physical Proximity to Major Markets and the Nearshoring Trend   While Brazil performs poorly on cost dimension, the country is likely to benefit from the trend for nearshore outsourcing, especially for projects that require physical supervision. Note that the world's major offshoring clients are located in North America. For instance, North American companies are the primary engineering outsourcers, accounting for 70 percent of the business.[30] Arguably, for North American outsourcers, when the costs of travel and training and the "soft" cost of managing people have been taken into consideration, the costs of hiring tend to be lower for Brazil compared to India. One study found that the cost of employing one call center agent in 2005 was US$13.05 in Brazil compared to US$15.00 in India.[31]

Brazil's transportation links with major clients, which are associated with transport costs and travel time, also favor the country. In 2010, there were 150 direct flights a week from the US to Brazilian cities.[32] Brazil is practically in the same time zone as the US so offshore outsourcing teams can operate as remote members of the same project group, which facilitates active and continuous collaboration.

R&D and Technology

In comparison with the other BRIC economies, Brazil lacks the manpower to perform highly sophisticated technical work (see Table A1.1 for indicators related to IT and human capital). For instance, Russia's competitive advantage lies in its ability to perform sophisticated technical works at relatively low cost.[33] In Brazil, multinationals are mostly undertaking adaptive R&D projects aimed at local markets, in contrast to a number of globally oriented innovative R&D works taking place in India and China.[34] The number of researchers in R&D per million people in Brazil is higher than in India but Brazil underperforms Russia and China on this indicator (see Table A1.1).

Access to Finance

In Chapter 3, we discussed the role of Brazil's development bank, the Banco Nacional de Desenvolvimento Econômico e Social (BNDES) in providing low-interest loans for longer periods. The BNDES also has special credit lines for technology projects.[35]

Case Conclusion

Notwithstanding some challenges, such as language problems, the perception of macroeconomic stability (e.g., unstable currency) and a high crime rate, Brazil has become an increasingly attractive outsourcing destination. While some analysts had previously been concerned about

Table A1.1 A comparison of BRIC economies on outsourcing-related indicators

	BRAZIL	CHINA	INDIA	RUSSIA
Exports IT and BP services (2008)[36]	US$800 million	US$5 billion	US$40 billion	US$3.7 billion
Population (million, 2007)	190.1	1329.1	1,164.7	141.9
GDP per capita (current US$, 2011)[37]	12,594	5,445	1,509	12,995
Annual growth rate in GDP (%, 2011)[38]	2.7	9.3	6.3	4.3
ICT goods exports (% of total goods exports, 2011)[1]	0.7	26.8	2.2	0.3
R&D expenditure (1997–2002, % of GDP)[39]	1.0	1.2	0.8	1.2
Patents granted to residents per million people (2002)[40]	4	5	0	105
Researchers in R&D per million people (1990–2003)[41]	324	633	120	3415
Percentage of Individuals using the Internet (2012)[42]	49.9	42.3	12.6	53.3
Fixed (wired)-broadband subscriptions per 100 inhabitants (2012)[43]	9.2	13.0	1.1	14.5
Mobile-cellular telephone subscriptions per 100 inhabitants (2012)[44]	125.2	81.3	68.7	183.5
Overall economic freedom (2013)[45]	57.7	51.9	55.2	51.1
The World Bank's ease of doing business rank (2013)[46]	130	91	132	112

[1] The World Bank, http://data.worldbank.org/indicator/NY.GDP.MKTP.KD.ZG

the lack of political stability and relative lack of performance in over-all education levels, these concerns have been adequately addressed in recent years.

The country's advanced telecommunication and financial net-works, well-developed domestic IT market, manufacturing prowess and export orientation have generated inter-organizational as well as intra-organizational externalities or spillover for the offshoring sec-tor. Such externalities take such forms as knowledge spillover, learning curves, brand loyalty, the availability of tools and resources, knowledge about quality, and value perceptions of consumers as well as production externalities. Foreign IT firms have also generated externalities in the form of indirect economic impact on local organizations.

Case questions

1. Examine the Brazilian offshoring sector in terms of the deter-minants of entrepreneurial performance discussed in Chapter 1: access to capital, access to R&D and technology, capabilities, market conditions, regulatory framework and culture.
2. What are the natures of externalities and linkages in the Bra-zilian offshoring sector?
3. Compare various ingredients of the entrepreneurial ecosystem in the Brazilian offshoring industry with those of the other BRIC economies.
4. For entrepreneurship in the offshoring sector, in what aspect is Brazil most similar to a) China, b) India, and c) Russia?

IC2: Mobile Payments and Entrepreneurship in Developing Economies

Mobile payments—payment services conducted via a mobile device—have been a key driver of entrepreneurship and socioeconomic development in emerging markets. Factors such as advancements in technology, socioeconomic conditions, and the high penetration rate of mobile devices are driving m-payment development in certain emerging markets. As Tom Standage notes, it is "easier to use your mobile phone to pay for a taxi in Nairobi [Kenya's capital] than in New York".[47]

Due to m-payments, potential entrepreneurs in developing economies have been able to gain access to entrepreneurial finance. M-payments have also facilitated Internet entrepreneurship. For instance, the popularity of m-payment solutions has allowed many entrepreneurs in Kenya to set up online businesses to market and sell their products. Intrepid Data Systems' real-time online payment service called iPay incorporates m-payment systems to enable buying and selling products online.[48]

A well-developed m-payment ecosystem has evolved in Kenya that, as of February 2012, had over eighteen million m-payment users.[49] In the Asia Pacific region, m-payment is expected to grow by 15 percent annually, reaching US\$3.8 billion by 2015.[50] Likewise, the mobile money market in Africa was worth over US\$61 billion in 2012, bigger than the combined mobile money markets in Europe and North America.[51] Table A1.2 presents some examples of m-payment systems in the emerging economies of Africa, Asia, and Latin America.

M-payments can support a variety of services—in particular, person-to-person transfers (P2PT). P2PT is significant for emerging economies, because it offers financial services to potential entrepreneurs and other unbanked users (those without bank accounts). M-payments have also helped facilitate emergency response and disaster recovery. For example, following the 2010 earthquake in Haiti, Voila teamed up with Mercy to distribute virtual vouchers. An inexpensive phone loaded with \$40 T-Cash (provided using an e-wallet service from Indonesia's largest cellular operator, PT Telkomsel) was provided to each victim. Subsequent aid distributions involved just sending a text message.

Most m-payment systems are primarily domestic in scope. Some operators have, however, launched international money transfer services that are primarily targeted at diasporas. In May 2012, MTN Rwanda and MFS Africa launched mobile remittances services for Rwanda and Ivory Coast. Thanks to these services, customers with mobile money accounts in these countries can receive money from abroad.[52]

M-payment Ecosystem: Driving Factors

Several different factors are driving m-payment growth in emerging markets.

Table A1.2 Some examples of m-payment systems

SYSTEM	COVERAGE	MAIN USES
Safaricom's M-PESA	Kenya, Tanzania, South Africa, and Afghanistan (and there are plans to expand to India)	– Make Person-to-person transfers (P2PTs) – Receive mobile phone credits – Pay school fees – Pay electricity bills – Save money
Easypaisa	Pakistan	– Pay utility bills – Make P2PTs (domestic and international) – Use as a mobile wallet – Increase airtime credits
Voilà's T-Cash	Haiti	– Receive salary – Make P2PTs – Pay bills
Airtel Money	India and sixteen African countries, including Kenya, Tanzania, and Uganda	– Make P2PTs – Make purchases
MTN MobileMoney	Africa, including Uganda, Ghana, Cameroon, Cote D'Ivoire, Rwanda, and Benin	– Make P2PTs – Pay for goods and services – Check balances – Buy airtime – Pay utility bills, school fees, or tuition

Socioeconomic Conditions

Most people in developing economies lack alternatives to cash, such as credit cards or checking accounts. In Africa, only 20 percent of families have bank accounts—10 percent in Kenya, 5 percent in Tanzania and 15 percent in Liberia.[53] In Pakistan, less than 15 percent of the population has access to formal savings or credit products. In Haiti, there were only two banks for every 100,000 people, and individuals seeking to cash paychecks and pay bills had to stand in line at a bank for hours. In some economies (such as in Zimbabwe), people prefer to use m-banking to reduce the risk of someone robbing them of their money.[54]

Formal safety nets and social protection instruments, such as unemployment benefits and health insurance, aren't available, so when unfavorable financial circumstances occur (owing to a poor harvest or an illness, for example), people rely on informal risk-sharing arrangements involving networks of friends and family.[55] In some cases, informal methods are also used to transfer money, which presents several risks. Poorly developed transportation systems and expensive money-transfer services also help make m-payments more appealing.

Rapid Diffusion of Mobile Phones
According to the International Telecommunication Union, mobile phone penetration reached 89 percent in the developing world in early 2013.[56] As shown in Fig. A1.1, the gap between developing and developed countries is lower in mobile phone than in Internet penetration. By 2015, in SSA, more people will have mobile phones than access to electricity.[57] Emerging markets thus have a huge population of unbanked mobile subscribers. For example, there were ninety million mobile subscribers and only twenty-five million bank accounts among the 167 million people living in Nigeria in early 2012.[58]

Increased Efficiency and Lower Costs
In developing economies, most transactions are small. The average mobile transaction conducted via M-PESA is about a hundredth of the

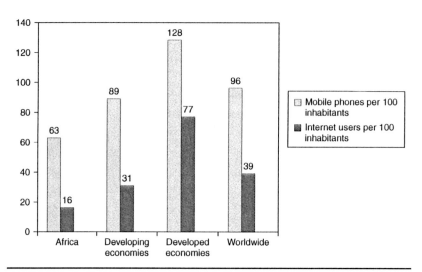

Figure A1.1 A comparison of mobile phone and Internet penetration in various economies[59]

average check transaction and half of the average ATM transaction.[60] For small transactions, a typical m-payments transfer costs around 1 percent of the transferred amount. In South Africa, for example, before the availability of m-payment, individuals paid US$30–50 to couriers to deliver cash to relatives. M-payment services offered by MTN and Wizzit cost only US$0.50.[61]

Branchless banking, which involves a distribution channel to deliver financial services without relying on bank branches, is appropriate for the emerging markets. A study indicated that, for a transaction involving US$23, branchless banks cost 38 percent less than commercial banks and 54 percent less than informal money transfer channels.[62] Opening bank branches requires a huge investment in infrastructure, equipment, human resources and security. Branchless banking services, on the other hand, leverage local resources, infrastructure, skills and equipment (such as agent shops and mobile phones). M-payment is thus likely to benefit the bottom-of-the-pyramid households.

Convenience

M-payment is much more convenient for consumers in the developing world, where financial and banking services aren't easily accessible. As of mid-2013, there were over 40,000 retailers who were M-PESA agents in Kenya compared to fewer than 900 bank branches.[63] Families in Africa's rural areas must travel far from home to pick up remittances, which adds significant travel costs and time to the already high transfer fees.

Local M-payment Innovations

Some African economies have been sources of micro-payment and mobile banking innovations. Some consider M-PESA to be among the most disruptive innovations in Africa. The fact that with a text message, M-PESA customers can pay off or collect on their loans makes this innovation ideal for Africa, given the rarity of bank accounts and the increasing pervasiveness of mobile phones.

New Initiatives

Initiatives of non-governmental and international organizations have facilitated the diffusion of m-payments. The Department for International Development, which manages UK aid to developing countries, helped to develop the M-PESA system. Similarly, the GSMA Development Fund and Gates Foundation started the Mobile Money for the Unbanked program, which targets people living on less than US$2 a day. The Easypaisa system (see Table A1.2) secured a US$6.5 million grant from the Gates Foundation.

Constraints
Despite the success of m-payment systems, certain factors have constrained further growth.

An Underdeveloped M-payment Ecosystem M-payment transactions currently occur in largely underdeveloped ecosystems. In many cases, underdeveloped infrastructure, immature standards, mobile phones with very primitive features, overloading and network congestion, as well as outages have hindered the diffusion of m-payment services. There are also interoperability issues. In Haiti, for example, two companies—Voila and Digicel—offer mobile money programs, but the two can't interact.

Users and providers of m-payment services have also realized the need for special types of intermediary. For example, the m-payment system in Kenya is facing an "e-float" problem, because most transactions are deposits made in cities and withdrawals made in villages. For the system to run efficiently, M-PESA relies on intermediaries who help manage the liquidity by converting mobile money to cash. For example, PEP Intermedius (http://pepintermedius.com), which is a network of cash merchants, works as an intermediary between M-PESA agents and banks. The M-PESA system has thus created a lot of job opportunities. Some retailers reportedly earn commissions of up to US$1,000 a month.

Restrictive and Vague Regulations M-payment-related regulatory systems are evolving more slowly compared to technological developments. For example, when M-PESA was launched in 2007, there were no clear regulatory guidelines for m-payments. M-PESA exploited the loophole and operated without a banking license. Kenya's retail banking sector viewed M-PESA as a threat and called it a Ponzi Scheme. A lobby of Kenyan banks led to an investigation of SafariCom and M-PESA by Kenya's Central Bank. The audit, however, indicated that M-PESA offered "bank-grade security and controls".[64]

Central banks in other countries, however, have regulations supporting the role of the retail banks as central players in the m-payment chain. The retail banking sector in other African economies has established its influence, authority, and dominance over m-payment. Similarly, in Bangladesh, the mobile e-marketplace CellBazaar has stimulated entrepreneurship by facilitating information exchanges between sellers and buyers, but the lack of a clear policy orientation and poor support for mobile operators to provide m-payment services has hindered its further growth.[65]

Lack of Collaboration   In some cases, the lack of collaboration among key players in the value chain of m-payment has created a roadblock to m-payment diffusion. For example, deposits initiated by M-PESA users take a long time to be credited to customers' accounts in financial institutions. Customers have also found it difficult to use the M-PESA channel to withdraw money from bank accounts.[66] One problem is that traditional banks lack the proper tools to deal with m-payments.

Security Issues   Cybercriminals have targeted unsuspecting m-payment users. This problem is especially critical in emerging markets, where cybercrime-related legal frameworks and enforcement mechanisms are poorly developed. There have been instances of phishing attacks targeting mobile money users. For example, according to reports Kenyan job seekers were being victimized by phishers: cybercriminals had created imitation websites resembling East African Breweries Limited and had posted vacancies for accountants, brew masters, technicians and drivers. The job applicants had to pay a "refundable" application fee of approximately US$70 via Safaricom's M-PESA system.[67]

More serious effects are likely to be felt in the future as cybercriminals find ways to monetize mobile malware and increase its revenue-per-infection ratio. Despite the fact that some mobile innovations are coming from emerging markets, they are more likely to be victims of mobile malware because their antivirus industry is less developed and their antivirus products are less affordable.

Concluding Comments

The rapid growth of m-payment in emerging markets is mainly driven by domestic rather than international remittances. To understand the socioeconomic impact of m-payments, it is important to note that domestic and international remittances correspond to different population segments. Evidence from Thailand and the Philippines indicates that most overseas workers are from urban areas with lower poverty rates. Most international remittances are sent to urban areas in developing countries, while most of the P2PTs to rural areas are domestic transfers from urban areas. This means that domestic remittances, which are facilitated by m-payment, are more relevant than international remittances to bottom-of-the-pyramid households.[68] In this regard, P2PT has been an important source of socioeconomic development and change among the poorest of the poor.

Payment models that rely on advanced technology aren't appropriate for the developing world. In this regard, what differentiates M-PESA from other providers is a simple, low-tech mechanism for providing money transfers. To improve the m-payments ecosystem, service providers, including banks and mobile operators, must increase their collaboration and partnership with key value-chain partners, such as solution vendors, app developers, retailers, merchants, handset and device vendors, and consumer associations. Even more importantly, the diffusion of m-payment hinges on measures taken to increase consumers' awareness and willingness to adopt such services.

IC3: The Diaspora Effect on Entrepreneurship in Sub-Saharan Africa

Diaspora networks associated with economies in SSA constitute the single biggest source of financial inflows to Africa. For instance, according to the International Organization for Migration (IOM), African diasporas sent US$60 billion to their homeland in 2012.[69] According to the World Bank, Nigeria is the fifth biggest recipient of diaspora remittances. A report of the World Bank and African Development Bank indicated that remittances from Ugandan diasporas account for 20 percent of the total investment in Uganda in recent years.

While substantial diaspora remittances provide a clear economic benefit to the SSA economies, it is apparent that non-economic benefits associated with the diaspora networks could be even more significant. The concept of remittances has been broadened from an exclusively economic term to include social, political and cultural contributions such as transfers of entrepreneurial skills, experience, ideas, technology and knowledge as well as cultural and civic awareness. The former UN Secretary-General Kofi Annan noted that the African diaspora has transferred skills and brought innovation to Africa. Some SSA economies such as Rwanda, Ethiopia and Kenya have created "diaspora bonds" to encourage the involvement of their diasporas in development projects.[70] For instance, Diaspora Policy has been a key component of Rwanda's long-term development plan. Likewise, Nigeria has pursued a policy of encouraging diaspora investment in the country's emerging industries.

Businesses and Business Connections Established by
the Diaspora in the Homeland

Diaspora networks associated with SSA economies are involved in the establishment of businesses as well as the creation of business connections in the homeland. In this way alliances with homeland classmates, friends, families and social networks are built. For many potential entrepreneurs in SSA economies, diaspora networks are becoming a reliable channel to facilitate access to information, funding, talent, technology and contacts. For instance, some diaspora associations related to SSA economies provide information on investment opportunities and sourcing in their homeland, and facilitate contacts between traders in their host and origin countries.[71] Similarly, immigrant entrepreneurs from SSA economies share information, develop contacts and establish trust in Africa as well as in the US.[72] Diaspora communities thus identify underutilized entrepreneurial ingredients such as skill, talent and knowledge in their homeland and link them into global networks.

In recent years, some international agencies have also been encouraging members of diasporas to establish innovative businesses in SSA economies. One such example is the African Diaspora Marketplace (ADM). The chief innovation officer and director of the office of innovation and development alliances at USAID stated that it is ADM's mission to encourage "African diaspora entrepreneurs who are looking to create innovative, sustainable businesses in their country of origins".[73]

Some Effective Diaspora Policy Responses in SSA: The Case of Rwanda

Following the Rwandan genocide of 1994, Rwanda initially focused mainly on rebuilding its economic infrastructure and at first diaspora engagement was not a high priority. As noted in Chapter 2, Rwanda's Vision 2020 plan aimed at transforming its coffee- and tea-growing economy into a middle-income, service-based economy by 2020. In the early 2000s, Rwanda started to recognize the key role of its diaspora in achieving high economic growth. A country of five provinces, Rwanda refers to its diaspora community as the sixth province.

In 2001 the Rwanda government launched the Rwanda Global Diaspora Network (RGDN), which was an independent association led by members of the Rwandan diaspora. In the same year, the government established a department on diaspora engagement in the Ministry of External Relations and Internal Cooperation (MINAF-FET). In 2008, the government established the Diaspora General Directorate (DGD) (www.rwandandiaspora.gov.rw/), which focuses on and serves Rwandan diaspora networks. The DGD's mission and vision include mobilizing the Rwandan diaspora for the "national development of their motherland". In 2009, MINAFFET published the Rwanda Diaspora Policy, which considered the diaspora to be a key component of the Vision 2020. The government of Rwanda also works closely with a number of international organizations such as the IOM, Voluntary Service Overseas (VSO), and the UNDP as well as NGOs to utilize its diaspora networks effectively for the country's economic and social development.[74]

The total amount of remittances received from Rwandan diaspora networks increased from US$43 million in 2005 to US$100 million in

2010, making up more than 1.5 percent of the country's GDP.[75] The increasing focus on the part of the government and private sector organizations on attracting Rwandan diaspora networks to work in the country indicates how much emphasis is being placed on the role of social remittance. Among other things, Rwanda's DGD provides information on job vacancies, especially in public institutions.[76] In December 2011, the Ministry of Foreign Affairs and International Cooperation, Job in Rwanda Ltd and Wakening Abilities for the Future (WAF) organized the first Career Day for the Rwandan diaspora networks. Its theme was "Inspiring Careers in Rwanda". The idea is to provide Rwandan diaspora members with the opportunity to meet with organizations to discuss the possibility of collaborating with them as consultants, and to promote their organization and market their products and services.[77] These initiatives have produced clear positive effects that have resulted in the receipt of significant social remittances. The Return of the Diaspora—Rwanda (www.julieddl.be/index.php?/project/the-return-of-the-diaspora—rwanda/) reports on Rwandan diaspora members, detailing their experiences as entrepreneurs, engineers, journalists, managers, and artists, as well as specialists in areas such as marketing, finance, insurance and international relations. Having gained their experience in the West and other African countries they have returned to Rwanda to contribute to their homeland's development.

Concluding Comments

Networks created by diaspora communities are likely to be more effective in helping diffuse high-quality entrepreneurial ideas than both those created by domestic networks and multinationals associated with non-diaspora sources. A common culture, shared values and familiarity with social norms promote mutual understanding and trust. In both national and international policy circles interested in developing entrepreneurial activities in SSA economies, it is important to develop a comprehensive diaspora strategy designed for large-scale impact on the broader community.

Finally, all diaspora networks are not equal. Diaspora networks that possess skills and experience are likely to stimulate and facilitate productive entrepreneurship and help bring positive changes to institutions in the homeland. The SSA economies must exploit the opportunities afforded by diaspora networks while minimizing the risks associated with undesirable migrant networks such as those involved in human trafficking and illegal migration. The emphasis should be on diaspora networks that promote productive rather than destructive entrepreneurship.

Notes

1. *Journal of Commerce* 2005, "Eastern Europe's Low Costs Attract Multinationals", August 1, p. 7.
2. Mari, A. 2010, "Brazil IT Struts the World Stage", *Computer Weekly*, June 17, at www.computerweekly.com/Articles/2010/06/17/241637/Brazil-IT-struts-the-world-stage.htm.
3. Tomás, J.P. 2010, "Revenues from Call Center Market Expected to Grow 11% this Year", July 1, Bnamericas, at www.bnamericas.com/news/telecommunications/Revenues_from_call_center_market_expected_to_grow_11*_this_year.
4. Ibid.
5. Mari, A. 2010, "Brazil IT Struts the World Stage", *Computer Weekly*, June 17, at www.computerweekly.com/Articles/2010/06/17/241637/Brazil-IT-struts-the-world-stage.htm.
6. Engardio, P., Arndt, M., & Foust, D. 2006, "The Future of Outsourcing", *Business Week*, January 30, 3969, pp. 50–58.
7. Mari, A. 2010, "Brazil IT Struts the World Stage", *Computer Weekly*, June 17, at www.computerweekly.com/Articles/2010/06/17/241637/Brazil-IT-struts-the-world-stage.htm.
8. brazilcham.com 2010, "The Brazilian New Brand Strengthens the Global IT Industry", at http://brazilcham.com/articles/the-brazilian-new-brand-strengthens-the-global-it-industry.
9. Gil, A., & Sowinski, L.L. 2010, "Building Brazil's IT Infrastructure", *World Trade*, 23(2), pp. 41–42.
10. Ibid.
11. Brasil, A. 2005, "Software Exports from Brazil Tripled in Three Years", October 28, at www.anba.com.br/ingles/noticia.php?id=9045.
12. In Russia, most local companies have less than 20 people and export-oriented firms with more than a hundred people are rare; Cusumano, M. 2006, "Where Does Russia Fit into the Global Software Industry?" *Communications of the ACM*, 49(2), pp. 31–35.
13. *Foreign Affairs* 2009, "A Giant Awakens Brazil", 88(1), pp. E1–E2.
14. Gil, A., & Sowinski, L.L. 2010, "Building Brazil's IT Infrastructure", *World Trade*, 23(2), pp. 41–42.

15. Ibid.
16. Ruiz, G. 2007, "Brazil Seeks Outsourcing Dominance", *Workforce*, November 30, at www.workforce.com/articles/brazil-seeks-outsourcing-domi nance.
17. Gil, A., & Sowinski, L.L. 2010, "Building Brazil's IT Infrastructure", *World Trade*, 23(2), pp. 41–42.
18. Mari, A. 2010, "Brazil IT Struts the World Stage", *Computer Weekly*, June 17, at www.computerweekly.com/Articles/2010/06/17/241637/Brazil-IT-struts-the-world-stage.htm; Gil, A., & Sowinski, L.L. 2010, "Building Brazil's IT Infrastructure", *World Trade*, 23(2), pp. 41–42.
19. Gil, A., & Sowinski, L.L. 2010, "Building Brazil's IT Infrastructure", *World Trade*, 23(2), pp. 41–42.
20. Ioannou, L. 2010, "Brazil's Start-Up Generation", *Time*, August 23, at www.time.com/time/magazine/article/0,9171,2010076,00.html.
21. Helyar, J. 2012, "Outsourcing: A Passage out of India", *Business Week*, March 15, at www.businessweek.com/articles/2012–03–15/out sourcing-a-passage-out-of-india.
22. Mari, A. 2010, "Brazil IT Struts the World Stage", *Computer Weekly*, June 17, at www.computerweekly.com/Articles/2010/06/17/241637/Brazil-IT-struts-the-world-stage.htm.
23. Fielding, M. 2006, "Stay Close to Home", *Marketing News*, April 15, 40(7), pp. 29–30.
24. Kobayashi-Hillary, M. 2010, "Could Outsourcing Put Brazil on the Map?", June 23, at www.techrepublic.com/blog/cio-insights/could-outsourcing-put-brazil-on-the-map/.
25. Benson, T. 2005, "Brazil Aims to be Outsourcing Giant", *New York Times*, May 8, at www.nytimes.com/2005/05/17/technology/17iht-outsource.html?_r=0.
26. Mari, A. 2010, "Brazil IT Struts the World Stage", *Computer Weekly*, June 17, at www.computerweekly.com/Articles/2010/06/17/241637/Brazil-IT-struts-the-world-stage.htm.
27. Benson, T. 2005, "Brazil Aims to be Outsourcing Giant", *New York Times*, May 8, at www.nytimes.com/2005/05/17/technology/17iht-outsource.html?_r=0.
28. Schmitz, H., & Knorringa, P. 2000, "Learning from Global Buyers", *Journal of Development Studies*, 37(2), p. 177.
29. Dranitsyna, Y. 2006, "Software Developers Making Global Impact", *St. Petersburg Times*, February 14, at www.sptimesrussia.com/index.php?action_id=2&story_id=16812.
30. Sehgal, V., Sachan, S., & Kyslinger, R. 2010, "The Elusive Right Path to Engineering Offshoring", *Strategy and Business*, January 11, at www.strategy-business.com/article/00016?pg=0.
31. Fielding, M. 2006, "Stay Close to Home", *Marketing News*, April 15, 40(7), pp. 29–30.

32. Gil, A., & Sowinski, L.L. 2010, "Building Brazil's IT Infrastructure", *World Trade*, 23(2), pp. 41–42.
33. Cusumano, M. 2006, "Where Does Russia Fit into the Global Software Industry?" *Communications of the ACM*, 49(2), pp. 31–35.
34. UNDP 2005, "Human Development Indicators", *Human Development Report*, New York: UNDP, at http://hdr.undp.org/en/media/HDR05_complete.pdf.
35. Gil, A., & Sowinski, L.L. 2010, "Building Brazil's IT Infrastructure", *World Trade*, 23(2), pp. 41–42.
36. levi9.com 2009.
37. The World Bank, http://data.worldbank.org/indicator/NY.GDP.MKTP.KD.ZG.
38. Ibid.
39. UNDP 2005, "Human Development Indicators", *Human Development Report*, New York: UNDP, at http://hdr.undp.org/en/media/HDR05_complete.pdf.
40. Ibid.
41. Ibid.
42. ITU, The World of ICTs, at www.itu.int/en/ITU-D/Statistics/Pages/stat/default.aspx.
43. Ibid.
44. Ibid.
45. heritage.org, Index of Economic Freedom, at www.heritage.org/index/ranking.
46. www.doingbusiness.org/rankings.
47. Standage, T. 2011, "Virgin Territory", *Economist*, November 17, at www.economist.com/node/21537920.
48. *East African* n.d., "iPay becomes second service to offer mobile online shopping in Kenya", at www.theeastafrican.co.ke/business/-/2560/ 870454/-/view/printVersion/-/vucs3m/-/index.html/
49. Gakure-Mwangi, P. 2012, "Seizing the Mobile Money Retail Opportunity in Kenya", *thinkM-PESA.com*, February 24, at www.thinkm-pesa.com/2012/02/seizing-mobile-money-retail-opportunity.html.
50. D. Oketola, 2010, "$200bn M-Payment Market: Slow Penetration in Nigeria Worries Experts", *Punch*, October 10, at http://archive.punchontheweb.com/Articl.aspx?theartic=Art201010101275826 (retrieved October 10, 2010).
51. *Bloomberg Business Week* 2013, "A Mobile Banking Revolution", at http://images.businessweek.com/slideshows/2013–05–03/digital-innovation-is-booming-in-africa.html#slide2.
52. techrwanda 2012, "Rwanda: MTN Mobile Money Now Extends to Rwandan Diasporas", June 1, at www.techrwanda.com/investment/538/rwanda-mtn-mobile-money-extends-rwandan-diasporas/.
53. Dovi, E. 2011, "Boosting Domestic Savings in Africa", *Africa Renewal*, 22(3), p. 12, at www.un.org/africarenewal/magazine/october-2008/boosting-domestic-savings-africa.

54. Nyakazeya, P. 2010, "Punitive Bank Charges Discourage Savings", *Zimbabwe Independent*, August 25, at www.theindependent.co.zw/2010/08/26/punitive-bank-charges-discourage-savings/.
55. *Mobile Payment Magazine*, 2011, "In Rural Kenya, M-Pesa Used as Savings Account Too", March 3, http://mobilepaymentmagazine.com/m-pesa-kenya-savings-transfe.
56. ITU 2013, "The World in 2013: Facts and Figures", Geneva: ITU.
57. Mutua, W. 2011, "The Significance of Mobile Web in Africa and its Future", blog, October 3, at www.wfs.org/content/significance-mobile-web-africa-and-its-future.
58. *Business Day* 2012, "Nigeria to Become Dominant in Africa's Mobile Payment Market", January 3, at www.businessdayonline.com/NG/index.php/news/76-hot-topic/31507—nigeria-to-become-dominant-in-africas-mobile-payment-market.
59. ITU 2013, "The World in 2013: Facts and Figures", Geneva: ITU.
60. Jack, W., & Suri, T. 2010, "The Economics of M-PESA", August, www.mit.edu/~tavneet/M-PESA.pdf.
61. Kiman, M. 2008, "A Bank in Every African Pocket?", Africa Renewal, 21(4), p. 3, at www.un.org/africarenewal/magazine/january-2008/bank-every-african-pocket.
62. McKay, C., & Pickens, M. 2010, " Branchless Banking Pricing Analysis", Consultative Group to Assist the Poor, at www.ifc.org/wps/wcm/connect/7dd2ed8049586089a332b719583b6d16/Tool+5.6.+CGAP+ Report+-+Pricing+Analysis.pdf?MOD=AJPERES.
63. safari.com n.d., "M-PESA Agents", at www.safaricom.co.ke/personal/m-pesa/m-pesa-agents.
64. Collins, G. 2011, "How Over-Regulation Has Stifled the Pace of Mobile Money Adoption in Africa", Memeburn.com, September 5, at memeburn.com/2011/09/how-over-regulation-has-stifled-the-pace-of-mobile-money-adoption-in-africa.
65. Zainudeen, A., Samarajiva, R., & Sivapragasam, N. 2011, "CellBazaar: Enabling M-Commerce in Bangladesh", *Information Technologies & International Development*, 7(3), pp. 61–76.
66. Mugweru, G., Murithi, J., et al. 2011, "Riding the M-PESA Rails: Advantages & Disadvantages", Microfinance Gateway, November 6, at www.microfinancegateway.org/p/site/m/template.rc/1.9.51349/.
67. Wafula, P. 2011, "Kenya: Cyber Criminals Hit Harder with Identical Websites of Top Firms", *Business Daily*, January 13.
68. Bala, G., & Alampay, E. 2013, "Mobile 2.0: M-money for the BoP in the Philippines", *Information Technologies & International Development*, 6(4), pp. 77–92.
69. Nzeshi, O. 2013, "Africa: Diaspora Remittances to Africa Hits US$60 Billion", February 5, at http://allafrica.com/stories/201302050877.html.
70. Provost, C. 2012, "Rwanda Seeks Diaspora Investment to Cut Reliance on Foreign Aid", October 11, at www.guardian.co.uk/global-development/2012/oct/11/rwanda-diaspora-investment-foreign-aid.

71. Ratha, D., Sanket M., Caglar Ö., et al. 2011, "Leveraging Migration for Africa: Remittances, Skills, and Investments", at http://siteresources.world bank.org/EXTDECPROSPECTS/Resources/476882–1157133580628/ AfricaStudyEntireBook.pdf.

72. Portes, A. 1996, *The New Second Generation*, New York: Russell Sage Foundation.

73. Kriss, J. 2012, "Pioneering African Entrepreneurship on Display at Diaspora Marketplace", July 23, http://blog.usaid.gov/2012/07/pioneering-african-entrepreneurship-on-display-at-diaspora-marketplace/.

74. Fransen, S., & Siegel, M. 2011, "The Development of Diaspora Engagement Policies in Burundi and Rwanda", UNU-MERIT Working Papers ISSN 1871–9872, Maastricht: Economic and Social Research Institute on Innovation and Technology, UNU-MERIT #2011–038, http://ideas. repec.org/p/dgr/unumer/2011038.html.

75. Provost, C. 2012, "Rwanda Seeks Diaspora Investment to Cut Reliance on Foreign Aid", October 11, at www.guardian.co.uk/global-development/ 2012/oct/11/rwanda-diaspora-investment-foreign-aid.

76. Rwanda Ministry of Foreign Affairs and Cooperation 2010, Diaspora General Directorate, www.minaffet.gov.rw/index.php?id=890.

77. igihe.com 2011, "Rwandan Diaspora Urged to Work in Rwanda", December 7, http://en.igihe.com/diaspora/rwandan-diaspora-urged-to-work-in-rwanda.html.

Appendix 2

Online Sources of Global Entrepreneurship-related Data and Statistics

The sources below provide data and statistics on a variety of indicators, mainly at the macro level, related to determinants, performance indicators and the impacts of entrepreneurship.

The Global Entrepreneurship Monitor

The Global Entrepreneurship Monitor (GEM) (www.gemconsortium.org/) is a not-for-profit academic research consortium. It has stated its goal as "making high quality information on global entrepreneurial activity readily available to as wide an audience as possible". GEM is arguably the "largest single study of entrepreneurial activity in the world". GEM started studying worldwide entrepreneurship in 1999 with ten countries. By 2009, it covered fifty-four countries.

Data on entrepreneurial activities covered in GEM studies can be accessed by clicking the link to the "Data" tab at the top of the GEM homepage (www.gemconsortium.org/).

GEM's policy is to make the full datasets publicly available only three years after the yearly data collection cycle. As of August 2010, GEM data for 1999–2009 were publicly available. One needs SPSS statistics software to open GEM datasets. GEM requires a researcher to provide some information to download the datasets.

The World Bank Group

The World Bank Group has created rich datasets and databases for various macro-level indicators mainly related to worldwide development. The Data Catalog (http://data.worldbank.org/data-catalog) has a list of World Bank datasets and databases, and provides access to over 2,000 indicators from various sources.

The World Development Indicators (WDI)

The World Development Indicators (WDI) (http://data.worldbank. org/data-catalog/world-development-indicators) is the World Bank's premier compilation of development-related macro-level data. The WDI provides a comprehensive selection of economic, social and environmental indicators as far back as 1960. These indicators are based on data from the World Bank as well as over thirty partner agencies. Most of the WDI-related statistics are from the national statistical agencies of the respective countries. As of August 2010, the WDI covered over nine hundred indicators for 210 economies.

Doing Business Survey

Of special importance is the Doing Business Survey (www.doing business.org/), which provides the most comprehensive comparative survey on the regulatory aspects of entrepreneurship affecting the ease of getting a business up and running. This survey provides objective measures and comparisons of regulations and their enforcement affecting businesses and is especially relevant for SMEs. The 2013 Ease of Doing Business index ranked the world's 185 economies (from 1 to 185). The index of economy was the simple average of its percentile rankings on the following ten indicators: (1) starting a business; (2) dealing with construction permits; (3) employing workers; (4) registering property; (5) getting credit; (6) protecting investors; (7) paying taxes; (8) trading across borders; (9) enforcing contracts; and (10) closing a business.[1]

The Central Intelligence Agency (CIA) World Factbook

The World Factbook (www.cia.gov/library/publications/the-world-factbook/) is probably the most highly used online reference source for country-level economic, political, legal, geographic, military, demographic and social indicators. The CIA World Factbook is constantly updated and contains the latest data on indicators such as population size, terrain and per capita GNP.

The first unclassified version of the Factbook was published in 1971 and the 1975 edition was the first that was made available to the public by the US Government. The CIA has been providing online editions of the Factbook ever since. According to the CIA, "Hard copy editions for earlier years are available from libraries."[2] One limitation of the Factbook is that since it is updated on a regular basis, new changes overwrite the previous versions of the report. Researchers thus need to refer to the hard copy editions if past data about some indicators are needed.

The Organization for Economic Cooperation and Development (OECD)

The OECD statistics portal (www.oecd-ilibrary.org/statistics) is a useful data source for various macro-level indicators, mainly for members of the OECD. Some datasets are available for free download while others require subscription. The OECD collects data related to a wide range of public policy areas. They include agriculture, education, environment, taxation, trade, science, technology, industry and innovation.[3]

The Statistics Portal provides links to two key tables: Country Statistical Profiles and the OECD Factbook:

Country statistical profiles (www.oecd-ilibrary.org/economics/country-statistical-profiles-key-tables-from-oecd_20752288) contains data selected from over forty statistical databases from the OECD's online library, SourceOECD. This statistical profile is updated annually. Links to data sources are provided; here one can also find up-to-date and time series data.

The OECD has been publishing the OECD Factbook (www.oecd-ilibrary.org/economics/oecd-factbook_18147364) annually since 2005. In 2013, the OECD Factbook was in its ninth edition and cost US$70. The OECD Factbook 2013 provides statistics on over a hundred indicators. Areas covered include population, economic production, foreign trade and investment, energy, labor force, information and communications technologies, public finances, innovation, environment, foreign aid, agriculture, taxation, education, health and quality of life.

The OECD Factbook 2013 also contains a special chapter on gender equality.

The International Telecommunication Union (ITU)

The ITU is a UN agency for ICT issues. The ITU makes available a wide range of indicators for the ICT sector. By clicking the "Statistics" tab at the top of the ITU homepage (www.itu.int/en/pages/default. aspx), one can access various ICT-related statistics (www.itu.int/ ITU-D/ict/index.html). The ITU also publishes the World Telecommunication/ICT Indicators Database. The seventeenth edition of the World Telecommunication/ICT Indicators Database was published in December 2013. CD-Rom as well as online versions of this publication are available for purchase at www.itu.int/en/ITU-D/Statistics/ Pages/publications/wtid.aspx.

Human Development Report (HDR)

The UNDP has been publishing the HDR (http://hdr.undp.org/en/ reports/) annually since 1990. It presents a wealth of statistical information on various aspects of human development. HDRs contain national-level data on indicators that are the causes of and associated with three components of human development—life expectancy, education and GDP. The data are freely available for download on UNDP's website (http://hdr.undp.org/en/statistics/data/). The UNDP also publishes regional, national and sub-national HDRs.

The Heritage Foundation

The Heritage Foundation (www.heritage.org/) publishes data on economic freedom of economies every year. The Foundation measures ten components of economic freedom. Each country is assigned a score in each component (on a 0 to 100 scale, 100 representing the maximum freedom). The overall economic freedom for an economy is the average of the scores for the ten components. The ten components are: business freedom, trade freedom, fiscal freedom, government spending, monetary freedom, investment freedom, financial freedom, property rights, freedom from corruption and labor freedom.[4]

The Political Risk Services (PRS)

The PRS (www.prsgroup.com/) publishes the International Country Risk Guide (ICRG) and other publications, which rate 161 countries on political, economic, financial and other risks related to international businesses. Since 1980, the ICRG has been published on a monthly basis. The PRS makes the ICRG available to subscribers online, in print and on CD-ROM. However, free samples of some data and reports are also available.

Euromonitor

Euromonitor (www.euromonitor.com/) is a private-sector research firm, which publishes various market research reports and global business and market intelligence. Some content, such as summaries of reports and articles on the Euromonitor website, are free, while most need to be purchased.

Euromonitor covers many industry sectors such as those related to consumer goods, health care and travel services. In-depth reports, analyst comments, statistics and external sources are included in each category. There are multiple search options available and results can be integrated across categories.[5] Data and information on Industries, Countries & Consumers and Companies can be searched by country or region. Under Industries, indicators such as market share and trends as well as country-specific industry reports are available. In Countries & Consumers, country-specific statistics and reports on consumer behavior and lifestyles are available. Under Companies, there are data and information on company profiles, market analysis and key trends. To ensure comparability, Euromonitor also provides standardized international definitions for variables.

There are five major constraints related to the use of international secondary data: accuracy, age, reliability, lumping and comparability.[6] Euromonitor largely addresses these constraints and its data are considered to be of high quality.[7]

Notes

1. doingbusiness.org 2013, "Doing Business", www.doingbusiness.org/econo myrankings/.
2. Buneman, P., Müller, H., & Rusbridge, C. 2009, "Curating the CIA World Factbook", *International Journal of Digital Curation*, 4(3), at www.ijdc.net/ index.php/ijdc/article/viewFile/132/171.

3. oecd.org 2010, "OECD Work on Statistics", at www.oecd.org/std/oecd workonstatistics.htm.
4. heritage.org 2010, "How Do You Measure Economic Freedom?", at www. heritage.org/index/.
5. Bentley University Library 2010, "Database of the Month: Euromonitor", July 10, at http://blogs.bentley.edu/intheknow/2010/07/10/database-of-the-month-euromonitor/.
6. Kotabe, M., & Helsen, K. 2001, *Global Marketing Management*, New York: Wiley.
7. Kotabe, M. 2002, "Using Euromonitor Database in International Marketing Research", *Academy of Marketing Science Journal*, 30(2), pp. 172–175.

Appendix 3

Preparing an International Business Plan (IBP)

A business plan is a written document prepared by an entrepreneurial firm based on a current and future state analysis of the firm (e.g., management team, product or services) and the environment facing it. It defines short-term and long-term goals and how they will be accomplished.[1] The most common readers of a business plan include potential funders, who make their funding decision based on the company's business plan.

An international business plan (IBP) describes internal and external elements associated with internationalizing a business. An IBP thus demonstrates the feasibility of internationalization and helps organize associated activities. As is the case for any business plan, a good IBP is based on sound international market research (see Appendix 2 for various information sources) and accurate financial projections.

Elements of an IBP

Executive Summary

The most important component of an IBP is probably the executive summary. The executive summary must be clear, concise, convincing, appealing and effective so that it is able to capture the reader's interest. At a time of intense funding competition, potential investors often dismiss an IBP after reading the executive summary. An effective executive summary tells the reader, inter alia, what the business is about and helps understand the main points the entrepreneur is making. Whereas there may be some disagreement as to the length of an executive summary, a single page is probably the best.

The first part of the executive summary normally includes the name and location of the business, the product or service being sold and the purpose of the IBP. Other important elements to be included in the IBP are:

a. Business description: Nature and unique features of products or services, how they will fit in the foreign market and whether they are going to change in the future.

b. Strategic direction and strategy formulation: Appraisal of the current status of the company, direction and goals of the company for the next five to ten years and how they will be achieved.

c. Description of the foreign market: Profile of the market segment in the foreign country that the company is targeting, the channels through which they are reached and the value proposition to the target groups of the company's products or services.

d. Management team: Professional background, responsibilities and potential contributions to the company of the founders and top management.

e. Financial aspect: Expected revenue and net earnings for the next five years and contributions of the foreign operations, capital needed and how it will be used, expected returns to investors and how and when they will get their money (e.g., IPO or sale of the company through an acquisition).

The rest of the business plan consists of information about the following:

I. History and Overview of the Company

a. History of the company: History of the company's products and services and evolution to the current stage.

b. Background information: Background and experience (including international experience) of the owners, number of years in business, number of employees, why and by whom the organization was formed, whether the organization's mission has changed since it was formed, strategic fit of the company's international business activities with the existing resources.

c. Current status of the company: Definition, scope, nature and importance of the business (the company's product or services, where and how they will be used, number of countries in which the company is doing business, profile of the customer), technical specification, features and design (for technologically complex products).

d. The business concept: Key factors that determine success in the industry (e.g., low price, high quality, technological/

marketing capability), how the company's products meet these requirements, unique selling propositions of the products or services, evidence and reasons as to why buyers in the foreign market are likely to prefer the company's products over its domestic and international competition.[2]

e. Objectives: Overall objective, specific objectives for sales, profitability, market share, product, innovation, branding, management development, employee morale, social responsibility.

II. Foreign Market Entry and Expansion

The elements to be included in this section include:

a. Whether the company has received inquiries from foreign markets for its products or services.

b. Availability of the financial resources to perform market research and promote the product in the foreign market.

c. Whether the company has the personnel export skills, customer service and networking skills required for the operation in the foreign market.

d. Whether a new position will be created in the company to develop international markets.

e. The level of control the company wants to maintain in the foreign country over sales, customer service and customer credits. Choosing a market entry method (e.g., licensing, joint venture or investment as possible options).

III. Industry and Market Analysis

The following are described in this section:

a. Overall market: Description of present and project markets in terms of locations, sales, growth rate, profitability and trends.

b. Projected industry sales: Over the next three to five years and the company's market share, and whether they will be different in the foreign market.

c. Specific market segment: Description of present and future market segments and major competitors in each segment.

Expected strategic changes about market segments, detailed information about major customers and prospects.

Competitor analysis: Expected effects on sales due to existing competitors, potential competitors, buyers' substitute products, detailed information about the leading competitors (e.g., sales volume, market share, profitability), whether the company's domestic competitors are exporting similar or closely related products or services, whether foreign competitors in the industry are active in the home country.

IV. Macro-economic Factors

Some important indicators related to macro-economic features include:

a. GDP growth.
b. Inflation rate.
c. Effects of disruptive economic events such as the GFC and whether such events have differential effects in the foreign country.
d. Infrastructural situation.
e. Credit rating of the country.
f. Currency fluctuation issues and how they will affect customers' ability and willingness to buy the company's product.

V. Development, Production and Logistics

It is important to explain the following in detail with necessary diagrams:

a. Stages involved in the development and production process and budget and time for each stage.
b. A comparison of production vs subcontracting.
c. Whether the factory will be located in the target country, the home country or a third country.
d. A description of the engineering and operations department.
e. Production requirements (raw materials, supplies, labor).
f. Details of plant facilities, machinery and equipment required.
g. The most appropriate form of transportation.
h. Shipping and associated costs.
i. The degree and location of R&D activities.

j. How quality assurance will be undertaken.

k. Whether the product requires special storage and if the foreign country has such facilities.

l. The current status of the company's production capacity (operating at full capacity, running under capacity) and difficulty involved in increasing the capacity to meet international demand.

m. Whether there is a minimum order requirement and if this requirement is different for international sales.

n. Whether the company uses a freight forwarder for export shipments.

o. Packaging and labeling needed for the product to reach the foreign country.

p. Documentation needed to meet the government regulations in the home country and the foreign country.

q. The bank to be used for international transactions.

r. Acceptable payment methods in the foreign market.

VI. Political and Legal Forces that are Likely to Shape the Industry and the Business
It would be important to explain the following in detail:

a. Whether there are special policies favoring the industry.

b. Whether subsidies are available for the industry.

c. Special economic zone benefit (e.g., Kaspersky Lab in Tianjin, China, benefited from the Chinese government's special economic zone for startups; see Chapter 5).

d. Tax breaks and import tariff reductions.

e. Political stability condition.

f. The legal system and rule of law status.

g. Whether the foreign country has a special trade relation with the home country and if so how it would affect the company's business.

h. Laws and enforcement mechanisms to protect from the infringement of copyright and related rights (for products with copyright issues).

i. Whether there are certain business ownership restrictions for foreigners.
j. Whether accreditation from agencies such as professional associations is needed.
k. Whether the product can be manufactured in a cost-effective way to meet the overseas regulatory requirements or standards.

VII. Social Forces that are Likely to Shape the Industry
The potential readers of an IBP would be interested to know about the following:

a. Demographic profile of the customer: age, gender, income, occupation, etc.
b. Predicted shift in the demographic make-up of the foreign country's population and how it will affect the company's business.
c. The public's perception of the industry.
d. Whether there are some cultural aspects that influence the product's acceptance in the foreign market (e.g., religious beliefs, taste preferences, habits and lifestyles).
e. Crime rates including organized crimes and cybercrimes and how they will affect the company's business in the foreign country.

VIII. Technical Forces that are Likely to Shape the Industry
It would be necessary to discuss the following in detail:

a. Penetration rates of various technologies in the foreign market and their effect on the company's business.
b. The foreign country's position in the adoption of emerging technologies and the effect this may have on the success of the business.
c. The level of the product's technology (simple, advanced, state of the art).

d. Degree of fit of the technology in the foreign market.
e. Potential profitability of the industry in the foreign market.
f. Important trends in the industry in the foreign market.

IX. SWOT Analysis
An analysis of a firm's strengths, weaknesses, opportunities and threats (SWOT) entails the process of analyzing the firm and its environment, and is commonly used to assist in identifying strategic direction.

X. Organizational Overview
The typical contents of this section are:

a. Organizational structure.
b. Human resource strategies.
c. Key personnel and other personnel.
d. International staffing requirements and degree of fit with the available resource skills in the organization.

XI. Financial Overview
The primary components of this section are:

a. Business financing issues.
b. Selected financial ratios (e.g., return on assets, net sales to net worth ratio and net income to net sales ratio, earnings per share).
c. Projected profit and loss statement.
d. Projected balance sheet.
e. Capital needed and how it will be spent: working capital, marketing, R&D, export budget, international overhead expenses, startup costs.
f. Break-even analysis.
g. Seasonal effect on financial performance.
h. Receivables and payable management.

XII. Marketing Strategy

The major components of this section are:

a. Results of international market research.

b. Segmentation: Selection of market segments and rationales; environmental analysis of various market segments.

c. Products: Description of products and services and comparison with major competitors, selection of possible products and services to be exported; importance of the protection of proprietary methods, trademarks and intellectual property rights for the product; product adaptations (e.g., technical, design, content, functionality and cosmetic changes) needed to meet regulative, cultural, economic and technical conditions in the foreign country; modifications needed in product packaging, instructions, manuals and translations involved; whether there are technical terms that might be difficult to translate in the language of the foreign country; differences in geography- or climate-related factors (e.g., humidity, heat, cold, rain, wind, sand, dust, terrain) that may affect product functions in the foreign country; buyer preferences in the foreign country with respect to various product features (e.g., size, packaging, color); warranty and servicing standards in the foreign market and whether the company needs to include this in pricing; stage of the product life cycle (introduction, growth, maturity and decline) and whether the stage is different in the foreign market; whether and how after-sales services will be provided in the foreign country.

d. Pricing: Pricing strategy, whether the company prefers to have the ability to change price; terms and conditions; profit margin in the company's domestic price; relative price sensitivity of the foreign market and its effect on profit margin; whether the company's price is competitive after adding export-related costs and tariffs to the product's price; direct materials and labor costs involved in the production for export.

e. Distribution: Standard distribution practice in the foreign market; how the company's domestic competitors sell in the foreign market; distribution channels to be employed by the company in the foreign country; selection of distribution partners; types of discount (trade, cash and quantity) or allowances (advertising, trade-off) commonly given to a member of the distribution channel for similar products in the foreign market; agent and distributor markups in the foreign country.

f. Promotions: Advertising tactics and other promotional measures; whether different benefits of the product will be emphasized in the foreign country; activities related to branding, packaging and labeling.

g. Sales forecast for the next five years.

XIII. Strategic Gap Analysis
The elements of this section constitute:

a. Company's current position.
b. An alternative strategy better suited to the current context (due to change in objectives, decision makers or performance levels).
c. Ideal outcome corresponding to the alternative strategy.
d. Changes needed to achieve the ideal outcome.

XIV. Ownership
Key elements of this section should include the following:

a. Legal form of ownership (e.g., sole proprietorship, partnership, corporation).
b. Whether there has been a change in ownership in recent years.
c. Investment made by the business founders.
d. Debt and equity funding needed.
e. Condition for doing business if it is established as a partnership.
f. List of owners (e.g., individuals, corporations, trusts) if the business is established as a corporation.
g. Proportion of stocks owned by the employees.
h. The company's share price.
i. The number of shares owned and investment by each director.

XV. References

XVI. Appendices and Supporting Information

Notes

1. Schilit, W.K. 1987, "How to Write a Winning Business Plan", *Business Horizons*, 30(5), pp. 13–22.
2. Murphy, P. 2004, *International Business Plan Workbook*, Boston: Massachusetts Export Center, at www.msbdc.org/publications/intlbizplan/intl_busplan.pdf.

Index